Blitzkrieg Unleashed:

The German Invasion
of Poland 1939

Blitzkrieg Unleashed:

The German Invasion of Poland 1939

Richard Hargreaves

Pen & Sword
MILITARY

First published in Great Britain in 2008 by
Pen & Sword Military
An imprint of
Pen & Sword Books Ltd
47 Church Street
Barnsley
South Yorkshire
S70 2AS

ISBN 978 1 84415 778

A CIP catalogue record for this book is
available from the British Library

Printed and bound in the UK
By Biddles

Pen & Sword Books Ltd incorporates the Imprints of Pen & Sword Aviation,
Pen & Sword Maritime, Pen & Sword Military, Wharncliffe Local History,
Pen & Sword Select, Pen & Sword Military Classics, Leo Cooper, Remember
When, Seaforth Publishing and Frontline Publishing

For a complete list of Pen & Sword titles please contact
PEN & SWORD BOOKS LIMITED
47 Church Street, Barnsley, South Yorkshire, S70 2AS, England
E-mail: enquiries@pen-and-sword.co.uk
Website: www.pen-and-sword.co.uk

Contents

And we have seen – and experienced – tragic scenes: German soldiers burning, torching, plundering, without giving it a second thought. Mature men, who are not in the slightest bit aware that what they are doing contravenes laws and conventions and offends the honour of the German soldier.

– *Oberstleutnant* Heinrich von Nordheim, Warsaw, October 12 1939

Regarding the course of the Polish campaign all that needs saying is that it demonstrated the tremendous potency of Germany's young Wehrmacht on such a scale that the whole world sat up and took notice.

– *Generaloberst* Alfred Jodl, Munich, November 7 1943

It is a characteristic of man that he gladly forgets bad times and recalls those much dearer happy times – every detail of which he can still recall years later. Perhaps it is good for our health that time locks away so many brutal blows of fate sent our way and with the help of subsequent happier times, even allows us to overlook the scars which have been left behind. But there are also periods in our lives which we should never forget – first of all to protect us from the same again and, secondly, so that we may enjoy happier times having survived such misery.

– German *Major*

Abbreviations Used in References

AOK	*Armeeoberkommando* – staff of an army in the field
BA-MA	*Bundesarchiv-Militär Archiv* – Bundesarchiv Military Archive, Freiburg
CSDIC	Combined Services Detailed Interrogation Centre
DBFP	*Documents on British Foreign Policy*
DGFP	*Documents on German Foreign Policy*
Div	Division
FRUS	*Foreign Relations of the United States*
HGr	*Heeresgruppe* – Army Group
IWM	Imperial War Museum, London
Kdo	Kommando – command
KTB	Kriegstagebuch – war diary
NA	National Archives, Kew
NCA	*Nazi Conspiracy and Aggression*
NHB	Naval Historical Branch, Portsmouth
NO/NOKW	Documents prepared for the Nuremberg Trials
OKH	*Oberkommando des Heeres* – German Army High Command
OKW	*Oberkommando der Wehrmacht* – German Armed Forces High Command
Pz	Panzer
TB	*Tagebuch* – diary
VfZ	*Vierteljahrshefte für Zeitgeschichte*

Author's note

German ranks throughout, with the exception of Generalfeldmarschall (field marshal), have been left in their original language. An explanation of the comparative ranks can be found in the appendix. Except for places commonly known in English, towns and villages are referred to by both their German and Polish names. Polish Army units are italicised to avoid confusion with German formations.

Acknowledgements

No historian can contemplate tackling the Polish campaign without two ground-breaking works: Stephen Zaloga's and Victor Madej's *September Campaign* and William Russ' *Fall Weiss*; the latter is worth the asking price for its maps alone. Bill was also kind enough to provide me with XIX Panzer Corps' war diary for September 1939, read various chapters drafts, and answer numerous questions. Jan-Hendrik Wendler too deserves special mention for providing extracts from the histories of 29th Infantry Division and 7th Panzer Regiment and sparing me numerous pitfalls and *faux pas*. All images are taken from contemporary Nazi publications, except where stated. Elsewhere, Frau Brabant of the Bundesarchiv in Freiburg guided me through Germany's daunting military archives. Also worthy of my gratitude are Stephen Walton and his colleagues in the Department of Documents at the Imperial War Museum, London; Public Record Office, Kew; Capt Christopher Page of the Naval Historical Branch, Portsmouth; the staff of the following libraries: University of Nottingham, University of Manchester, University of Sussex, University of Portsmouth, University of Warwick, and Lancashire, Portsmouth, and Nottinghamshire; New York Public Libraries; British Newspaper Library; Jason Pipes and his colleagues at www.feldgrau.net; Jason Mark for help with tracking down details on obscure German units and officers; Michael Miller for filling in the blanks in Albert Forster's career; Howard Davies for his inestimable knowledge of the German language; Andy Brady for the maps; Tom Houlihan, Yan Mann, Andreas Biermann, Darren Beck, Helen Craven and Allison Tupper for proofreading, advice, and occasional moral support. The book which follows is all the richer for their input. For its shortcomings, I alone bear responsibility.

Introduction

The history of Poland is a chain of tragedies of which the current one is the greatest.

– UDO VON ALVENSLEBEN

WILLI Reibig stood in the turret of his panzer, a radio headset over his Schutzmütze – a padded helmet covered by the distinctive black beret of the Reich's new armoured force. In the half-light, the outline of his Panzerkampfwagen – literally armoured fighting vehicle, but to Germans and the world, simply 'panzer' – Mark III was barely visible. The column drove in darkness, in silence apart from the constant reassuring deep growl of a Maybach engine. The only light came from the tail light of the vehicle in front, bouncing up and down as it rolled through the Silesian lanes. Reibig watched the sun climb in the east. 'It promises to be a beautiful day,' he thought. 'A good sign for us.'

At 4.45am that Friday, 1 September 1939, the guns of 103rd Artillery Regiment barked 'sending their iron greetings' towards the hills around the small town of Krzepice, twenty or so miles northwest of Czestochowa – Tschentochau to Germans. Overhead the Luftwaffe roared eastwards. Far below, the panzer crews waved and shouted. The barrage ceased. The panzers jerked forward. German customs officers cheered the armour on as it rolled across the Polish frontier. 'It's a strange feeling knowing that we have left Germany and are now on Polish soil,' thought Reibig.

Within an hour the panzers were across a small brook, the Pankovka. Within two they had driven through Krzepice. This was ideal tank country, Willi Reibig observed, and ideal anti-tank country. But there was no sign of the enemy. The panzers kicked up huge clouds of dust as they raced across a potato field. They passed through nondescript settlements of small cottages with straw-covered roofs. They crashed into the Lisswarthe, a small tributary of the Warthe. The waters of the Lisswarthe smacked against the side of the tanks, foaming, spewing through the driver's slit hatch. The panzers climbed the opposite bank and into Opatow, eight miles inside Polish territory. Onwards went the armour, avoiding the copses which littered the valley of the Lisswarthe. Only now were the first signs of war were apparent: a blown-up railway bridge, a dead Pole. There was the distant thunder of cannon and the rattle of machine-gun fire, barely audible above the throb of the Panzer Mk III's engine. Reibig glanced at his map. Up ahead was the village of Mokra III – there were three Mokras, barely a mile apart, here in the Lisswarthe valley. The name meant nothing to Willi Reibig.

A few hundred yards east of Mokra ran the railway line to Czestochowa and on to the heart of Silesia. Drawn up behind it were Polish troops with anti-tank guns, anti-tank rifles and small tanks – tankettes – and *Armoured Train No.53, Smialy*. *Smialy* (The Bold) was a strange-looking beast, a relic of the Polish-Soviet war with 75mm guns in turrets atop its wagons. Around one hundred panzers and armoured vehicles were bearing down on them. The guns barked once more, but this time Polish guns. Several panzers were knocked out, the rest fell back.

From the high ground west of Opatow, Georg-Hans Reinhardt watched his panzers falter. This was supposed to be the 'crowning glory' of his career. 'To be a divisional commander on the field of battle is probably the most wonderful, the greatest position of command, where the personal influence and link still exists between the leader and those led,' he enthused. And now, at the first sign of enemy resistance, his men had been repulsed.

With his narrow, inquisitive eyes peering through round pince-nez, the balding Reinhardt looked more professor than warrior. But looks could be deceptive. Georg-Hans Reinhardt – *der lange Reinhardt*, the tall Reinhardt – was a born warrior. He had marched to the Marne with his infantry regiment a generation before. He had commanded infantry companies, cavalry squadrons, infantry battalions, rifle brigades, and now, since the autumn of 1938, the armour of Würzburg's 4th Panzer Division. The 52-year-old *Generalleutnant* had faith in his Führer – 'a genius,' he gushed to his wife Eva. He convinced himself, like most Germans, that the Polish crisis would be solved 'bloodlessly'. But the Führer's genius had failed him, failed Germany. And so 4th Panzer Division would have to drive on Warsaw, a task Georg-Hans Reinhardt approached 'not enthusiastically, not lusting for war, but seriously and dutifully'. In his ten months in command of 4th Panzer, Reinhardt had sought 'to instil the spirit of attack' in his men and 'banish bunker psychosis'. Evidently, he had failed. He ordered his armour to regroup and attack Mokra again.

Attacking was also on the mind of Major Stanislaw Glinski, commander of *21st Armoured Battalion*. Glinski's tankettes had orders to hold Mokra and drive the enemy back. They would be joined in their attack by a squadron of horsemen from the *Wolynian Cavalry Brigade*.

Willi Reibig's Panzer Mk III bogged down in the marshy, ditch-strewn terrain west of Mokra. He ordered his platoon to continue the attack on the village without him. And then, out of the mist and smoke, an unforgettable sight: Polish cavalry, sabres drawn, lances fixed, thundering towards the advancing panzers. 'Surely they don't want to attack us – that would be madness and merely bring about their destruction', Reibig thought to himself. But they *were* attacking. Five hundred metres away. Then four hundred. Three hundred. Reibig adjusted his sights slightly and aimed at the horses' bodies. At two hundred metres, his finger pressed the trigger. 'The bursts from the machine-gun act like a scythe in a ripe corn field,' the panzer commander wrote. 'In a few minutes it's all over. Only a few succeed in escaping to the protection of the forest.'[1]

This remains the enduring image of the Polish campaign. And it is a myth. The charge of the *Wolynian Cavalry Brigade* at Mokra was never a charge; the riders ran into the German armour by accident. The handful of deliberate charges Polish horsemen unleashed in the early autumn of 1939 were against enemy infantry, not panzers. They carried carbines not lances. They invariably fought dismounted, not on horseback. But it suited German propaganda – and heroic Polish mythology – to perpetuate the legend, a legend often accepted by historians and generals alike.[2]

There are enduring sounds of the Polish campaign, too, notably the 'trumpets of Jericho', the siren fixed beneath the nose of the Junkers 87 which wailed as the *Sturzkampfflugzeug* – dive-bomber, usually abbreviated to 'Stuka' – hurtled groundwards, preparing to unleash its 250kg bomb.

The combination of panzer and *Stuka* created a powerful image, an image of a new form of warfare: an American journalist dubbed it *Blitzkrieg* – lightning war.[3] He described its effects:

> Even with no opposition, armies had never moved so fast before. Theorists had always said that only infantry could take and hold positions. But these armies had not waited for the infantry. Swift columns of tanks and armoured trucks had plunged through Poland while bombs raining from the sky heralded their coming. They had sawed off communications, destroyed stores, scattered civilians, spread terror.[4]

Such was Blitzkrieg unleashed. And yet Blitzkrieg unleashed was never as omnipotent and infallible as the popular image suggests. The panzers raced to the gates of Warsaw, but could not take the city. They raced to the citadel of Brest, but could not subdue the great fortress. The Stukas pounded the Polish depot on the Westerplatte opposite Danzig for a week, yet made little headway. They pounded the fortress of Brest, too, but it did not capitulate. The panzer-Luftwaffe combination did not defeat Poland in September 1939 – the much-heralded 'campaign of eighteen days' which actually lasted twice as long – but they did pave the way for victory. The burden of the Polish campaign was borne, as it was a generation early, by the Germany infantry, the ordinary *Schütze* (rifleman) or the mountain infantryman, *Gebirgsjäger*, who relied chiefly, though not entirely, on the horse for transportation. The war of 1939 was closer to the war of 1914 than the German propaganda machine would have the world believe.

And yet there *was* something new about this way of war. Few people, save the German military, expected such a rapid defeat of Poland – certainly not the Poles themselves. Set to a soundtrack of bombs exploding, artillery and naval guns pounding, machine-guns clattering, bombastic Germanic music, the inflammatory speeches of Hitler and Goebbels, the triumphalist commentary of the newsreel reporters, Blitzkrieg mesmerised friend and foe alike.

As the trigger for the 20th Century's second terrible conflagration, the German invasion of Poland has largely been ignored by English and, to some extent, German historians.[5] The occupation of Poland, rightly, has received a great deal of attention from scholars. No nation suffered greater losses between 1939 and 1945 than Poland: more than one in every eight Poles was killed, over six million people in all, half of them Jews. But the 'campaign of eighteen days' which cleared the way for such bloodletting is dismissed in a couple of paragraphs in general histories, or a chapter in a memoir.

Precisely why is difficult to fathom. The English-speaking world has an insatiable appetite for books on the Eastern Front. Perhaps, I reasoned as I tentatively embarked on this project, disinterest in the Polish campaign could be attributed to a shortage of source material. Sadly, my linguistic shortcomings have prevented me tapping the vast Polish-language literature on the September campaign. German material is equally bountiful, however, if not more so. The records of many, though not all, of the Army units which fought in Poland survive. So, too, do *Erlebnisberichte* – experience reports – memories of the campaign compiled in the autumn of 1939 by hundreds of soldiers. Some reports were filed away, others were published in regimental or divisional 'memorial books'. And other literature abounds. To justify an unpopular war to its people, the Nazi propaganda machine produced countless books of varying quality.

Relying on contemporary publications poses problems, however. Accounts of the war in Poland published between 1939 and 1941 are laden with National Socialist propaganda, either deliberately or subconsciously. They are a paean to Nazi ideology, the heroic Teutonic warrior smiting invidious Poles. But the German Army's role in the Polish campaign was far from heroic. It blooded its hands in the villages and towns of Poland. German soldiers rounded up Polish civilians, men, women, children. They executed them. They beat or killed Jews. They shot prisoners of war, evicted Poles from their homes, burned villages to the ground. These atrocities – and many more – are also documented in the contemporary accounts, in letters home, in diaries. You will find little mention of them in propaganda books or post-war memoirs.

Atrocities in the summer and autumn of 1939 were not solely the domain of Germans, however. Polish memoirs, like their German counterparts, are invariably silent on the subject. But before and during the September campaign, Poland's ethnic German population – *Volksdeutsche* – were persecuted: beaten, attacked, evicted, force-marched, murdered. The oppression was never as organised, never as systematic, never as wholesale as that committed by the invaders, but that was slim consolation for the victims.

Terror, persecution, brutality, these were as much a part of Blitzkrieg unleashed as the panzers and Stukas. 'War will be waged with all means,' the theorists of the German High Command predicted eighteen months before war engulfed Europe. 'It will be directed against the enemy's armed forces, against the sources of his material strength, against the moral strength of his people. The watchword of its leadership must be: necessity knows no rules.'[6]

The story which follows is a human one – and an inhuman one. It is the story of men and women, not of armies and corps. It is the story of centuries of burning hatred, of ruthless politicians, of soldiers and airmen, of sailors and marines, of police and paramilitary, all of which conspired to bring war to Europe for the second time in a generation on one fateful Friday in September 1939.

Gosport, January 2008

Notes

1. Based upon Reibig, pp. 14–16, Hürter, *Hitlers Heerführer*, pp. 136, 158, 161, 162 and Neumann, *Die 4 Panzer Division*, i, pp. 2–4, 29–30.

2. See, for example, the official history of 3rd Panzer Division which described a Polish counter-attack on 1 September: 'The squadrons ride with their sabres drawn. It's like a scene from the beginning of the First World War. Unfortunately, the Polish cavalrymen don't want to believe, or cannot believe, that German panzers are made of steel, not wood or cardboard. Machine-gun fire has a devastating effect on the enemy's lines of cavalry. But still they don't give up – they ride back, re-group and attack again.' *3 Panzer Division*, p. 17. More than half a century after the war, former panzer grenadier and Polish campaign veteran Bruno Fichte told author Carl Schüddekopf: 'The Poles believed their own propaganda that our panzers were made of cardboard. Their cavalry sometimes rode with lances against the panzers. They were extremely courageous, but they had no chance.' See Schüddekopf, Carl, *Krieg: Erzählungen aus dem Schweigen*, p. 31.

3. The phrase was probably coined by German journals in the mid-1930s, but it was rarely, if ever, used in contemporary official documents.

4. Anon, 'Blitzkrieger', *Time*, 25/9/39.

5. The chief English-language exceptions are William Russ' *Fall Weiss* and Stephen Zaloga and Victor Madej's *September Campaign*.

6. Denkschrift des Chefs des Oberkommandos der Wehrmacht, 'Die Kriegführung als Problem der Organisation', 19/4/38, Anhang 'Was ist der Krieg der Zukunft?' cited in Hürter, p. 115.

Prologue: The Polish Danger is Greater than Ever

The Poles are still half-savages. Poor, dirty, incapable, stupid and vulgar, depraved and treacherous.

– HAUPTMANN HEINZ GUDERIAN

FOUR grey limousines pulled off the Boulevard de la Reine moving slowly up the driveway towards the gleaming white façade of the hotel, built less than a decade earlier. The forget-me-nots in full bloom in the hotel grounds vied with the blue uniforms of the French *poilus* standing guard. The cars came to a halt in front of the steps. Ropes held the surging crowd back as they strained to see ten bowler-hatted men dressed in black step out of the limousines and begin to ascend the steps. At their head, a tall, pale, gaunt figure, his hair neatly parted in the centre, his short dark moustache neatly trimmed, Ulrich Graf von Brockdorff-Rantzau. As he passed, swinging his walking stick, some British and French officers saluted, others turned their backs. Entering the Trianon Palace Hotel, the aristocrat removed his cap and was led by a French Foreign Office official, dressed in black and silver in mourning for his son. The Frenchman threw open the doors to the conference room with vigour and declared: '*Messieurs, les délégués allemands!*' Brockdorff-Rantzau removed his gloves and bowed. To a man, the 200 people in the chamber rose, returned the bow, then sat down again. To Allied eyes, the count and his colleagues strode into the hall arrogantly, almost as victors, 'cold and unrepentant' before taking their seats.

Now Georges Clemenceau took centre stage. Two years shy of his eightieth birthday, the 'Tiger' cut a strange figure, a smallish man with a distinctive bushy white moustache. For his age, he was remarkably fit – he fenced daily, read for four hours each day and worked for a good dozen more. He was also remarkably stubborn and prickly. And he possessed a lifelong hatred of Germany. Now the moment of reckoning had arrived.

'The hour has come for a weighty settlement of our account,' he told the German delegation. 'You asked for peace. We are prepared to grant it you. We will, however, take the necessary precautions and guarantees so that with this second peace of Versailles, which brings such a terrible war to an end, no more follow.'

As Clemenceau spoke, the heavy volumes of the Versailles Treaty, hurriedly translated into German, were presented to the delegates. The terms were onerous: the Reich and her allies would bear sole responsibility for the war – and pay reparations of 270 million Marks; the once mighty Imperial Army would be scythed to just 100,000 men; the Navy would be limited to a handful of obsolete ships; the Luftwaffe was banned outright; ten per cent of Germany's land and one in nine citizens would be subjected to foreign rule. She would suffer most in the East, at the expense of the renascent Poland. A corridor would be driven through West Prussia to give the Poles access to the sea; in doing so the historic cities of Bromberg and Thorn would become Bydgoszcz and Torun; the great Hanseatic port of Danzig would become a free city; and East Prussia would be cut off from the German heartland.

'Does anyone wish to speak?' the French premier asked.

Brockdorff-Rantzau raised his hand. He did not stand but remained seated. Rantzau was a career diplomat, not an orator. His voice was harsh, rasping, monotonous. His style, his manner, was not of a beaten man, nor a beaten nation. 'We are not under any illusions about the scale of our defeat, nor the degree of our powerlessness,' he admitted. 'We know that the might of German arms is broken. We know how great the hatred we encounter is and we have heard the passionate demand that as the vanquished we will be made to pay.' The pitch of Rantzau's voice grew louder, the tone sharper. 'It is expected of us that we admit that we alone are guilty; such a confession from my mouth would be a lie.'

As Rantzau droned, his colleague Walter Simons glanced out of the window. There stood a cherry tree in full bloom, an uplifting sight. 'This cherry tree and its kind will still be blooming when the states whose representatives gathered here exist no longer,' Simons mused.

Germany's foreign minister continued his monotonous tirade. His country, he admitted, was responsible for 'injustices' – not least in Belgium. But Germany 'was not alone in making mistakes in the way she waged war'. The Allies had strangled the Reich; they continued to strangle her with a naval blockade. The count pointed the finger. 'The hundreds of thousands of non-combatants who have died since 11 November because of the blockade were killed by the cold calculations of our enemies after they'd achieved and secured victory,' he rasped: 'Think of that when you talk about blame and atonement.'

It went on like this for another ten or so minutes, each clear, precise, bitter word from the German delegate's mouth translated into French and English. British premier David Lloyd-George played with his pince-nez; a beguiling smile was etched on Clemenceau's face; President Woodrow Wilson scribbled furiously, occasionally placing his hands in his pockets and leaning back in his chair.

The count was almost done. 'A peace which cannot be defended before the world in the name of justice will always provoke fresh opposition. No-one could sign it with a clear conscience because it cannot be realised.'

His speech over, Rantzau removed his glasses and placed his hands upon the table. The murmuring in the hall ceased. The 'Tiger' stood up. 'Has anyone any further observations to make? No-one wishes to speak? No, then the session is over.'

Ulrich von Brockdorff-Rantzau stood up and left, followed by the rest of the German delegation. The session had lasted less than fifty minutes. Outside the hotel, he stood on the steps, leaning against his ebony stick. He raised his hand and lit a cigarette, which wavered in his mouth. His lips were still trembling. The forty-nine-year-old diplomat was seething. 'That thick volume was utterly unnecessary,' he fumed. 'It would have been easier if they had declared: *L'Allemagne renonce à son existence* – Germany renounces her existence.'[1]

News of the terms of the treaty began to filter to Berlin late that afternoon; it arrived in earnest the following day, courtesy of the nation's newspapers. Everywhere, the reaction of the German people and their press was no less indignant than their foreign minister. The socialist newspaper *Vorwärts* branded 7 May, 1919 'The hour of surrender'; the Treaty was, said the *Deutsche Allgemeine Zeitung* – the semi-official organ of the government – 'a document of hatred and blindness'; our enemies, proclaimed the *Frankfurter Zeitung* 'have shown themselves to be the most exquisite masters of strangulation.' Picking up the newspapers that Thursday morning, Berlin industrialist Oskar Münsterberg felt compelled to write in his diary. 'Today is the blackest day of the war.' Münsterberg steeled himself. 'This cannot be the end,' the businessman assured himself. 'No, this cannot be the end of a military state which is unbeaten on the field of battle.'

The politicians vented their anger in the Great Hall of the University of Berlin, temporarily the home of the parliament of this uncertain German Republic. Opposition to the Treaty was led by the nation's chancellor, Philipp Scheidemann. Six months earlier, the fifty-three-year-old had proclaimed the Republic from a balcony in the *Reichstag*, the traditional home of Germany's parliament. Now this pooterish figure, a journalist-turned-socialist politician, held the second highest office in the land. Brandishing a copy of the treaty, he seized his moment on his nation's most important stage. 'We are flesh and blood, and whoever tries to separate us, slices the living body of the German *Volk* with a murderous knife!' Thunderous applause rippled around the hall. 'Today it seems as if the bloody battlefield from the North Sea to the Swiss border has come alive once more in Versailles, as if ghosts are fighting one last battle of hatred and despair on top of the heaps of corpses.' The peace proposed by the Allied nations was 'unacceptable'. For a minute, Philipp Scheidemann soaked up the applause and cries of bravo reverberating inside the hall. 'I ask you: What honest man – I will not say German – what honest, loyal man would accept such conditions? What hand would not wither rather than bind us in these chains?' For five hours the parliament condemned – the session wasn't so much a debate as an outpouring of hatred – the peace terms, then rose to a man. The strains of *Deutschland über Alles* filled the hall.[2]

Nowhere was opposition to the Versailles Treaty, the Versailles *Diktat* – a settlement imposed on Germany against its will – as it would become known, greater than in the German East. Roaming around Danzig and the historic lands of West Prussia, a newspaper reporter found widespread disbelief – and bitterness. The inhabitants had expected to lose *some* land to the re-born Poland. 'No-one wanted to believe that almost all of West Prussia would be swallowed up by the new Polish empire.' Surrendering land was a bitter blow, but to Poles, to Slavs, to 'sub humans', to a nation, a people *kulturlos* – without culture –

that was the bitterest blow of all. 'Whatever culture exists in West Prussia, it is the work of its German inhabitants and the welfare of the Prussian state,' the nationalist politician Graf zu Dohna fumed. 'To deliver this land with more than one million German inhabitants to the Poles is an unreasonable demand of such monstrous audacity.'[3]

Hauptmann Heinz Guderian seethed. The thirty-one-year-old officer had survived the dash to the Marne, the mincing machine of Verdun, the mud of Flanders, and finally the collapse of the Austrian armies in Italy – although he never actually led men into battle. Now his birthplace would be surrendered, surrendered 'to the barbarians'. For most of its 850-year history Kulm had been known as Chelmno, a town ruled and inhabited chiefly by Poles. Since 1772 it had been ruled by Prussia which, a century later, had renamed it Kulm in an attempt to Germanise it – even though two out of three of its 20,000 inhabitants were Poles. It was there, in June 1888 that Clara Guderian gave birth to a son, Heinz, on the family estate of Gross Klonia. And now, barely three decades later, Kulm would become Chelmno once more; one of the towns of West Prussia which would be swallowed up by the 'Polish Corridor' which would give re-born Poland access to the sea. Heinz Guderian feared for his estate. 'The Poles are still half-savages,' he wrote angrily to his wife Gretel. 'Poor, dirty, incapable, stupid and vulgar, depraved and treacherous.' But what could Germany do about it? 'If we accept this peace we are finished – and if we don't, we're probably finished anyway.' For the sake of honour, Heinz Guderian was in favour of rejecting the Versailles *Diktat* and continuing the struggle, even if the once great Imperial Army had crumbled to dust. Let the Allies come, Heinz Guderian challenged. 'They can do no more than destroy us.'[4]

'I suffer from an unprecedented inner conflict,' divisional commander *Oberst* Albrecht von Thaer recorded in his diary as he pondered the fate of Germany. Thaer was a man of honour, a holder of *Pour le Mérite* – the Blue Max – Germany's highest military honour, a gifted staff officer and now the commander of troops in the important industrial town of Schneidemühl. Like many towns in the Posen region, Schneidemühl had been ruled by both Poles and Germans in its 500-year existence. Today it was undeniably Prussian, under German rule for a century, an important hub for the railway network, and home to a garrison. And it was also now a front-line town. The Allied politicians in Paris had drawn the border of the resurgent Poland barely half a dozen miles to the south of the town. Schneidemühl would remain German, but other towns and villages around Posen – included Posen itself – would be ceded to the Poles. Albrecht von Thaer found it difficult to accept. He had witnessed the collapse of Imperial Germany from the very heart of government. On the staff of the German High Command he had witnessed the physical and moral breakdown of his idol, Erich Ludendorff, Germany's military leader, indeed *de facto* leader, as the Allied armies swept relentlessly eastwards in France and Belgium. Now in the summer of 1919 he was shaken to his core once again. 'Should we here simply quietly give in to the Poles?' he asked himself. 'Should I myself still lead the troops back, troops I have educated solely with the thought: do not give up one foot of ground?' Wearily, Thaer toured the towns and villages his men were to abandon to the Poles. The German populace cried, appealed for help. The divisional commander could do nothing about such heartbreaking scenes. 'The troops still want to fight,' the *Oberst* observed. 'Let them advance.'[5]

Like Albrecht von Thaer, General Kurt Gotthilf Kreuzwendedich von dem Borne held Germany's highest military decoration. He also commanded troops, but on an even greater scale, protecting the disputed territories of Silesia. Unlike Thaer, von dem Borne was not a man to accept the *Diktat*. 'The Officer Corps in particular feels that agreeing to the "shame paragraphs" is the bitterest insult to our honour,' he told his men. Signing the treaty would humiliate Germany and her Army.[6]

Such feelings permeated the Officer Corps from the youngest *Leutnant* to a Field Marshal, Paul Ludwig Hans Anton von Beneckendorff und von Hindenburg, who as Chief of the General Staff was its physical, spiritual and moral head. No man enjoyed greater public support during or after the war than this imposing figure, a gruff, tall general – at 6ft 5in he towered over most men – with short cropped hair, a distinctive thick moustache and a permanent scowl etched across his face. But the legend of Hindenburg, the myth of Hindenburg, was greater than the reality of Hindenburg. He was a man of courageous words but rarely courageous decisions. Not so his deputy, *Generalleutnant* Wilhelm Groener. Groener was a realist, not a fantasist, a Württemberger, not a Prussian. He was almost alone among Germany's generals, a man who put his nation before the arrogant pride of the Officer Corps. 'Oath to the colours?' he had hissed at Kaiser Wilhelm six months earlier. 'These are only words, an idea.' As his master sat silently, Wilhelm Groener had told the emperor what none of his entourage dared say, not even his trusted Field Marshal: 'Sire, you no longer have an Army.' The Kaiser abdicated.

And now, in the late spring of 1919, Wilhelm Groener found his Field Marshal immovable once again, bound by notions of honour in a world which was passing him by. The hour had come, the elderly Hindenburg suggested, for the Officer Corps and a few thousand loyal subjects to 'sacrifice themselves for our national honour'.

Groener shook his head. The majority of Germans would fail to understand such a gesture. 'There would be talk of an officers' rebellion, counter-revolution, militarism.' The Allies would invade the Fatherland, showing no mercy. 'Germany's name would be stricken from the ranks of the great nations.' The Officer Corps would forever be tainted for threatening the peace of Europe. 'There might be moments in the life of a nation when self-sacrifice for the sake of honour is not allowed, when self-preservation becomes the most important historic requirement.'

Paul von Hindenburg could not agree. 'I cannot and will not abandon the views which have been binding for me all my life,' he retorted.

And so when the German government sought the views of its General Staff – should it sign the Versailles Treaty or resist? – the advice given in Paul von Hindenburg's name was ambiguous. If Germany took up the sword again she could re-take province of Posen and keep the Poles at bay; but in the West, the Allies would sweep through the Fatherland. Still the Field Marshal could not bring himself to tell the politicians to sign the treaty. 'As a soldier I would prefer death with honour to a shameful peace.'[7]

The politicians, too, were torn. Their Field Marshal was telling them that he could not resist an Allied onslaught, but that for honour's sake he preferred to sacrifice his Fatherland in one last, futile Wagnernian battle. Most of Germany's Cabinet concurred. There were few voices of reason. One was defence minister Gustav Noske, a man of contradictions: a socialist journalist who had calmed a socialist mutiny among the Fleet in Kiel, put down a socialist uprising in Berlin, and who enjoyed the respect of most of the Officer Corps. But Noske, like Wilhelm Groener, was a realist. 'It's all very fine for us fifteen heroes to sit here and refuse to sign,' he sighed as the politicians argued incessantly. 'But behind us there is a nation which is down and out. What is the use of heroics in that situation?'[8] Heroics prevailed. The Cabinet was split. The chancellor and his foreign minister resigned. And the hours ticked away towards the deadline imposed by the Allies.

There was, perhaps, a solution. Might Germany sign the treaty, *but* not accept the sections which irked her so – the *Schmachparagraphen*, the 'paragraphs of shame' which demanded the Kaiser and other 'war criminals' be brought to book before Allied tribunals and, above all, that Germany bear responsibility for the war. Of that, the politicians were marginally in favour. They would agree to the Allied terms, but not Germany's sole guilt for four years of war. The telegraph wires between Paris and Berlin buzzed. The response from Paris was swift, devastating. The Allies were not for turning. Sign unconditionally, they demanded. Once again the politicians conferred. Once again they turned to their Field Marshal for advice.

The telephone in Paul von Hindenburg's headquarters at Kolberg, a picturesque small seaside town on the Pomeranian coast beloved by holidaymakers and the wealthy looking to recuperate, rang shortly after lunch on 23 June. On the line was Friedrich Ebert, a former saddler and journalist, now first president of the German Republic, a small, rotund figure with a thick comb-like beard. Ebert was usually a jovial character; today he was torn between duty and honour. Honour told him to reject the Versailles Treaty; duty suggested his country had suffered enough. If the Army could resist the invader in the West, then he would reject the treaty. He gave Hindenburg the afternoon to ponder. With Ebert about to call Kolberg again, Wilhelm Groener pressed his master for an answer. 'You know as well as I do that armed resistance is impossible,' the marshal sighed. But Hindenburg could not bring himself to tell the politicians this. He left the room, leaving Groener to impart the news to the president. 'Resuming the fight is hopeless,' the general told Ebert forlornly. 'We must make peace under the conditions laid down by the enemy.' Wilhelm Groener sat down, thoroughly dispirited. Upon his words, Germany would decide to sign the despised second Treaty of Versailles. When Hindenburg drifted back into the room somewhat later, he found his subordinate disconsolate. The Field Marshal placed his hand on Groener's shoulder. 'You have taken a heavy burden upon yourself,' he said. Groener raised his head. 'I know how to bear it.'[9]

And so on the evening of Monday, 23 June 1919 the telegraph wires between Berlin and Versailles hummed once more. Germany would sign. But she would do so under duress. 'Yielding to overwhelming might, the Government of the German Republic declares that it is prepared to accept and sign the peace treaty imposed on it by the Allied and associated governments. In doing so, in no way does it forsake its belief that these peace terms are an injustice without parallel.'

As the note was handed to the Allied leaders in Paris, the sub-editors of the right-wing *Tägliche Rundschau* were making up the pages of the following day's edition. The editorial pages would come later, now it was time for the classifieds, the adverts: the private detective, the painters and decorators, carpets, antiques, jewellery, diamonds, the volunteers for the front. *Freikorps Peitsch*, a makeshift band of militia who had taken up arms to protect East Prussia, invoked the name of Hindenburg. 'The Polish danger is greater than ever,' the *Freikorps* (corps of volunteers) warned. It urged veterans of the war just passed to join battle once more – infantrymen, engineers, machine-gunners, medics, telephonists. It urged them to head for the idyllic historic city of Lyck, on the banks of a lake, one of scores in Masuria, surrounded by forests. Just a few miles to the south lay Poland. 'We will defend our honour, our homes and our future against internal and external threats and will fight – if necessary – to the last drop of blood.'

The 61st Infantry Regiment needed men, too. It needed them to report to the Schneider Guest House in the attractive small town of Culmsee in West Prussia. In a few months' time, under the terms of the Versailles Treaty, Culmsee would become Chelmza. A few miles to the west, the industrial and trading centre of Bromberg would be renamed Bydgoszcz, to the south Thorn – one-time bastion of the Teutonic Knights – would be known as Torun. 'Our enemies want to cede German land in East and West Prussia to Poland,' the regiment declared. 'Do you want to allow that? Do you want millions of Germans forced to become Polish?' it asked. 'Everyone help to form well-disciplined, good units so that we are not raped by Poland.'[10]

Poland would be re-born despite such calls to arms; she would drive a corridor through West Prussia to the sea at Danzig, and for all this – and more – Germany would despise her.

Notes

1. *New York Times*, 10/5/19, *Tägliche Rundschau*, 8/5/19, Luckau, p. 68, Ulrich Graf von Brockdorff-Rantzau, *Dokumente*, pp. 113–15, and Rabenau, p. 169.
2. *Vorwärts*, 7/5/19, *Deutsche Allgemeine Zeitung*, 9/5/19, *Frankfurter Zeitung*, 8/5/19 and *Berliner Morgenpost*, 13/5/19.
3. *Deutsche Allgemeine Zeitung*, 9/5/19 and *Berliner Morgenpost*, 13/5/19.
4. Guderian's letters to his wife, 14/5/19, 24/5/19, 12/7/19 in Bradley, Dermot, *Generaloberst Heinz Guderian und die Entstehungsgeschichte des modernen Blitzkrieges*, pp. 117, 121, 125–6.
5. KTB Thaer, 25/6/19, 28/6/19 in Thaer, pp. 317, 319.
6. BA-MA N97/6.
7. Volkmann, pp. 278–82 and Baumont, pp. 96, 112.
8. Nowak, p. 267
9. Volkmann, p. 303; Wheeler-Bennett, *Hindenburg: The Wooden Titan*, p. 220.
10. *Tägliche Rundschau*, 24/6/19.

CHAPTER ONE

A Certain Foreboding

We will inevitably have a war with Germany.

– JOZEF PILSUDSKI

IN GENEVA'S great Salle de la Réformation, the clang of Paul Hymans' bell silenced the chatter of forty-one nations. It was ten minutes before mid-day on Monday, 15 November, 1920. It was time to call the first session of the new court of world opinion, the League of Nations, to order. Britain's delegates had spent the morning in the church of the Holy Trinity praying for the future of the new assembly. The Swiss had marched through the city's streets bearing the flags of every nation – save the three defeated Central Powers. Expectations and hopes were high. The world looked to these men in Geneva to shape a better world. Hymans, the Belgian president of this new council, was more cautious. 'We are far from believing that we are going to change the world with the wave of a wand. The world changes slowly – and men change most slowly of all.'

Some 800 miles to the northeast, British Army officer Lieutenant-Colonel Edward Lisle Strutt prepared to hand the great Baltic city of Danzig into the care of the League. He too had high hopes. 'May Danzig and Poland serve as an example for Eastern Europe,' he pleaded. 'May both nations live happily and contentedly, grow and prosper through mutual support, trust and friendship.'[1] Such hopes would be shattered. German and Polish hatred was too deeply rooted to allow the nations to live amicably side-by-side.

Danzig was born in the dying years of the first millennium. It was the Poles, not the Germans, who gave birth to Gyddanyzc as a fortress at the point where the Vistula met the Baltic. As the port grew as a centre of trade, so Germans came to Kdansk, Gdanzc, Dantzk, Dantzig, Dantzigk, Dantzike, as it was known variously. German influence turned to German rule in 1308 under the Teutonic Knights, whose control over Danzig lasted for 150 years. When Danzigers rebelled against the knights, they sought the protection of the Polish kingdom. For more than three centuries the city flourished as a semi-independent state under the Poles. The tongue of Danzigers was German, but most of their business was with the Poles as the port became a great outlet for Poland's wares and a great inlet for its imports. But with the partition of Poland at the end of the 18th Century, Danzig became German once more, first under Prussian rule, then under the united German Empire. From then until the outbreak of the Great War, Danzig boomed. Its population doubled as it became one of the centres of German shipbuilding while the port handled thousands of tons of coal, iron, coffee and fish. But that success as a port made Danzig the obvious choice for the new Polish state to gain 'access to the sea' as the Allied leaders re-drew the map of Europe in Paris. Danzigers were horrified. 'Our historic Hanseatic city of Danzig was born and has grown as a result of German culture, it is German to the core,' fumed the city's mayor, Dr Bail. 'We want to remain German forever.'[2] Poles, however, regarded the port as 'indispensable'. The reborn nation needed 'its window on the sea', its negotiator in Paris pleaded. The Allied leaders decided neither for Warsaw nor Berlin. They decided that Danzig should be a free city. It suited neither Pole nor German.

The Free City of Danzig actually encompassed more than just the port itself. Its coast stretched for more than thirty miles from the spa resort of Zoppot to the Frisches Haff lagoon. To the south, it almost reached as far as Dirschau where rail and road spanned the Vistula. In all 760 square miles of land, home to more than 350,000 people – forty-nine in every fifty of them Germans – inhabiting 300 towns, villages and hamlets. The city enjoyed its own currency, its own flag, its own stamps, its own anthem – *Für Danzig*, For Danzig. Poles and Danzigers shared control of the railways, the port, the customs offices.

Losing Danzig alone gnawed at the nerves of German nationalism. But 'access to the sea' demanded more than just a port. It demanded a strip of land linking the coast with the hinterland, a 'corridor' – a corridor which would separate the heart of the Reich from the province of East Prussia. Germany seethed again. But unlike Danzig, the towns of the Polish Corridor, as it would come to be known, were Polish, not German. In none did Germans outnumbered Poles. In fact, in most towns in the corridor, Germans constituted barely a quarter of the populace. Percentages mattered little to the average German, however. The loss of 'German' soil, the amputation of East Prussia, the fact that more than one million fellow Germans were living under Polish rule – all were seen as a potential time bomb. Danzig and the corridor would plunge the world into another conflagration one day, warned novelist H G Wells in his prophetic *The Shape of Things to Come*. 'That corridor fretted it as nothing else in the peace settlement had fretted it. There were many other bitter memories and grievances, but this was so intimate, so close to Berlin, that it obsessed all German life.'

Danzig and the Corridor were powder kegs for the future. The industrial region of Upper Silesia was already a flashpoint. Part of Prussia and subsequently the Second Reich, like the Corridor it had stubbornly refused to be 'Germanised'. The Polish tongue was still more prevalent than the German in the first years of the 20th Century. That was hardly surprising: two out of every three inhabitants of Upper Silesia were Poles. They did the work the Germans would not. They worked in the steel mills, in the mines, they toiled in Silesia's factories. They ensured the Upper Silesian basin became one of the powerhouses of Germany. And for that reason Germany was determined to hold on to Upper Silesia: it was responsible for a quarter of all its coal, eighty per cent of its zinc, one third of its lead. When the Allies threatened to hand the region to the Poles, so vehement were German protests that they procrastinated and proposed a plebiscite instead.

Upper Silesia's Polish population were not prepared to wait that long. In August 1919, a general strike turned into a widespread uprising. It lasted only a week. More than 20,000 German soldiers were dispatched to put it down – which they did, brutally. As many as 2,500 Poles were executed in the aftermath of the revolt. Exactly a year later, a German-language newspaper celebrated Warsaw's capture by the Red Army as war raged between Poland and the Soviet Union. Silesia's Germans celebrated: Poland's rebirth would be short-lived. But the report was false. The Poles revolted once again. It took a month before the insurrection was quelled – this time by Allied troops acting as peacekeepers.

Such unrest made a vote on Upper Silesia's future impossible. Only in March 1921 were Silesians able to go to the polls. Nearly 1.2 million people cast their votes. Fewer than 500,000 of them voted to secede from Germany; over 700,000 wanted to remain in the Reich – a mandate bolstered thanks to 190,000 Silesian-born Germans who had moved away from the region who were enticed to return by a very effective propaganda campaign. After six weeks of tension, Upper Silesia exploded again. The third uprising was the largest, longest and most brutal. Some 70,000 Polish 'volunteers' seized eastern Upper Silesia. And in response some 25,000 *Freikorps* 'volunteers' marched against the Poles. In pitched battles, notably on the dominating heights of Annaberg 1,000ft above the right bank of the Oder forty miles northwest of Katowice, the *Freikorps* prevailed. The Allies intervened before the German troops could press home their advantage, finally forcing an uneasy peace upon Upper Silesia in the summer of 1921. The League of Nations ruled on the region's fate that autumn. Their decision pleased neither German nor Pole. Most of the land fell to the Germans as did most of the populace. But most of the industry and most of the raw materials, including three out of every four coal mines, became part of the new Polish republic. The Germans of Upper Silesia were livid at the loss of their industrial base. The Poles of Upper Silesia still living under German rule would smoulder for two decades. In time, Adolf Hitler would exploit their simmering hatred to justify his war.

By the time the borders of Silesia were fixed, the frontiers of the new Polish republic were beginning to solidify. It was a nation born into a world of enemies. 'From the first moments of its existence, envious hands were stretched towards the new Poland,' observed the country's leader Jozef Pilsudski. Carved out of lands previously occupied by the empires of Russia, Austria-Hungary and Germany, Poland was surrounded by nations old and new which were at best cool, at worst downright hostile towards the republic, save for Romania and Latvia. In the East, there were eighteen months of battle with the Red Army, crowned by a decisive victory in front of Warsaw, before the eastern frontier with Russia was settled.[3]

Moscow was no more satisfied with its new border with Poland than Berlin was. Hans von Seeckt knew it. To Germans and Russians, Poland's existence, the monocled head of Germany's armed forces wrote, was 'intolerable'. One day, Seeckt predicted, Russia and Germany would join hands to crush Poland. That was a day Hans von Seeckt yearned for. His armed forces, the *Reichswehr*, were just 100,000 men strong in the wake of Versailles. They possessed no aircraft. No tanks. No battleships. No U-boats. The German Army of the early 1920s could achieve nothing. In war, its seven divisions would exhaust their ammunition in barely an hour. But the wily von Seeckt was thinking not of today, but of tomorrow. 'History has shown us that in the lives of nations one must be the hammer or the anvil, that the strong always destroy the weak, and that every nation reaches for the sword when the most important and last assets are at stake,' he told an audience in Hamburg in February 1920. 'New, bloody conflicts, perhaps on an even greater scale, are already looming on the horizon, and this so-called peace treaty holds fresh disasters – like Pandora's box – which can only be dealt with by blood and iron.'[4]

Hans von Seeckt's Germany not only lacked the means for war, it lacked the will for war. But one day – and that day was coming – 'the foolish cry: "No more war!"' would be drowned out. The German *Volk*, Seeckt's senior operations officer Joachim von Stülpnagel told fellow officers in February 1924, realised 'that a nation without its own weapons in this age of sabre rattling is merely a pawn of another nation, but also that the *Diktat* of Versailles was merely the end of one phase of the war which will be followed by a new phase of the war waged with the utmost ferocity, whose objective is the end of Germany, the destruction of its independent political, economic and cultural identity.' Stülpnagel continued:

We see Germany, our Fatherland, with its fruitful plains and wooded mountains, the silvery ribbons of its rivers, Germany, the country of poets and thinkers, the country with a varied, yet still proud history. Today this land is occupied by the enemy, vast areas are plundered by him.

Amid a whole host of thoughts and questions, confusing and depressing, the historical responsibility of liberation of our land looms in front of us, something which we have to prepare for and, God willing, will be called to carry out.

1924 was not the year for that liberation. Neither people nor army were ready. But they would be. 'It was no different for the men of the Wars of Independence,' the *Oberstleutnant* added. 'I cannot conclude any better than with the words of Gneisenau from 1808: "A certain foreboding tells me that the day of the revenge will come – and that all our efforts should be directed to the possibility of this day arising." It is the greatest thing we can achieve: the freedom of the German people.'[5]

Seeckt and Stülpnagel were surrounded by like-minded men. 'We must see to it that the shameful peace is not enforced, that our proud Army does not vanish, than an attempt is at least made to save its honour,' *Hauptmann* Heinz Guderian wrote to his wife. 'You know the *Wacht am Rhein* and the old *Prussian March*: "As long as a drop of blood still flows, a fist will brandish the sword..."'[6] He did not know it yet, but Heinz Guderian would re-fashion that sword.

The clouds hung low over the Masurian Lakes which peppered East Prussia. Only a forest of flags added colour to the occasion – black banners adorned with the skull and cross bones, the Imperial battle ensign, a few standards of the growing National Socialist movement, carried by men dressed in *feldgrau* jackets. Towering above them was a vast castle-like structure, its twenty-foot-high red brick ramparts linking eight imposing square turrets. Here, on the edge of the small provincial town of Hohenstein on a gloomy late summer Sunday in 1927, 80,000 Germans commemorated their greatest victory of the Great War. Here, three years in the making, was the Tannenberg *Denkmal*, the Tannenberg memorial, built half a dozen miles from Tannenberg itself.

But then Tannenberg was a battle named not for its location but for its historical resonance – to erase five centuries of German shame. Tannenberg was 'a word pregnant with painful recollections for German chivalry, a Slav cry of triumph'. For here, in 1410, the Teutonic Knights, the crusaders who carried German colonialists, German customs, and German rules into the lands of the Poles and Lithuanians, were crushed by an army of Slavs. Twice the Teutonic Knights had erected memorials on this battlefield. Twice the Slavs had destroyed them. Tannenberg cast a shadow upon the German soul for the next 504 years until the dying days of August 1914. Once again an army from the east and an army from the west collided in the forests of East Prussia. And when it was over, this time the army from the west was triumphant: 30,000 Russian dead or wounded littered the battlefield; another 90,000 marched into captivity. As the victorious German generals composed their report for their Kaiser, they sought a name for the battle they had just won. They chose the name of the village where they headquarters were: Frögenau. A junior staff officer interjected. Poring over the maps of East Prussia, he spied the name of Tannenberg. It was, he suggested, 'an historic name'. His masters agreed.

Now, thirteen years after the battle, its victor Field Marshal Paul von Hindenburg led veterans in an act of commemoration as the memorial was dedicated. The strains of the soldiers' hymn *Ich hatt' einen Kameraden* drifted across the fields in front of the monument. Two hundred and forty trombones sounded a fanfare in unison as the elderly Field Marshal entered the sprawling inner courtyard of the monument, where a makeshift altar had been erected. Generals and veterans laid wreaths and then the men filed past Hindenburg for almost two hours. Tannenberg had made Hindenburg rather more than Hindenburg had made Tannenberg; his staff and his front-line commanders had largely determined the course of the battle. But Paul von Hindenburg, a few days shy of his eightieth birthday, understood the *power* of Tannenberg. 'A *Volk* who won a Tannenberg cannot go under as long as it knows how to safeguard the spirit which imbued its ranks that day,' he declared. The war of 1914 was not the fault of Germany. 'Not envy, hatred or lust for conquest thrust weapons into our hands. Rather, war was our last resort, a way of asserting ourselves against a world of enemies which demanded the gravest sacrifices. We set off in defence of our Fatherland with pure hearts, and the German *Volk* wielded the sword with clean hands.' Hindenburg hoped that this monument would unite his fellow Germans. 'May it be a place which all hands reach out for, which imbues love for the Fatherland, and where German honour surpasses everything!'

Each year 50,000 Germans made the pilgrimage each to demonstrate their love for the Fatherland. But the Tannenberg memorial was more than just a monument to Germany's war dead. Even at its dedication, guests were welcomed to a land 'surrounded by Slavs'. And so the *Denkmal* served as a rallying point for the nationalist cause. It inextricably bound the battles of 1410 and 1914 as one, Erich Maschke, an expert on the German East at the University of Jena, explained. They shared a common battlefield, yes. But, crucially, they shared a common foe. 'Both revolved around the struggle for the freedom of German soil against a numerically superior enemy, against a threat from a world whose blood and customs were alien and hostile; across five centuries the defence of German soil as well as safeguarding Europe from the forces of the steppe were united.' *Vergeßt den Deutschen Osten nicht* – Do not forget the German East – cried souvenir postcards featuring the monument. And how could they forget the German East? Anyone from the Reich visiting the memorial had to cross the Corridor to reach it. Each August veterans groups and the German Right gathered at the monument. They commemorated the dead, but they celebrated a victory over Germany's traditional foe. 'Without Tannenberg,' they proclaimed, 'Germany's border markers in the East would probably stand on the Oder.'[7]

Poland too had a great monument to its warriors. Like the German memorial it did not lie on the battlefield. Unlike the German monument it celebrated the victory of 1410 and bore the name not of Tannenberg, but another village a stone's throw away: Grunwald. To Poles, Grunwald was not something historic but something tangible, an hour when the Pole was mightier than the German. And in the opening years of the 20th Century it was a beacon, a symbol – particularly in German-occupied Poland. For a generation, the Germans had sought to destroy the Polish identity. The Poles, Germany's leaders declared, were *Reichsfeinde* – enemies of the Reich. Towns with Polish names were Germanised. Chelmno on the Vistula became Kulm, Leszno north of Breslau became Lissa, Pila in West Prussia would be known henceforth as Schneidemühl. The German tongue replaced Polish in schools. Polish language textbooks for children were banned. Even teaching Polish as a second language was forbidden. When children in the town of Wrznesia, near Poznan – Posen to Germans –, refused to give up their mother tongue, they were whipped and beaten by their German teachers. Such actions fuelled rather than capped Polish nationalism. The closing years of the 19th Century and the opening years of the 20th saw an upsurge in the Polish national identity. From the pen of the greatest novelist of the age, Henryk Sienkiewicz, came *Krzyzacy*, (*The Teutonic Knights*), a rousing yarn which celebrated the Polish struggle against the Germanic hordes, and above all trumpeted the victory at Grunwald. 'There were many battles and encounters back then, but no man alive could recall such a crushing defeat,' Sienkiewicz wrote of the aftermath. 'Before the feet of the great king lay shattered not only the Teutonic Order, but all of Germany, for the flower of its knights were at the forefront of the Teutonic Order which gnawed ever deeper into the Slavic body.'

Within a decade of Sienkiewicz's novel appearing there was an even more striking reminder of Grunwald, a 60ft statue of the battle's victor, King Jagiello, unveiled in the heart of Krakow on the 500th anniversary of the battle. More than 150,000 Poles attended three days of quincentenary celebrations which reached their climax on Friday, 15 July, 1910, as the renowned pianist – and Polish nationalist – Ignacy Paderewski revealed the great monument he had donated to his countryfolk. Like Hindenburg, Paderewski hoped his memorial would appeal to man's most noble qualities. It was born not of hatred but of 'a deep love for the motherland'. It would serve 'to raise hearts with a visible symbol of the sacred past'. As the pianist's words faded, a huge choir whose members were drawn from across Poland, sang an anthem composed specially for the occasion – *Grunwald* – inspired by the nationalist poet Maia Konopnicka. Whatever Ignacy Paderewski's hopes, the words of the anthem, which Poles would come to know as *Rota* (*The Oath*), better captured the feelings of his compatriots:

No enemy can drive us from our home soil,
Never can he force us to give up our language,
We are the nation of Poles,
Never will the enemy turn us into Germans,
Fight to the last drop of blood for our soul
Until the Teutons fades into powder and dust
The German will not spit in our faces
Nor turn our children into Germans
Our phalanx will rise up in arms
The spirit will lead us
When the golden horn sounds, we advance!

In time, *Rota* would become Poland's unofficial anthem. But it was not the sole rallying cry for Poles to take up arms against the Germans. *Silesjanka* by Augustyn Swider, sung to the tune of *Marseillaise*, called Silesian Poles to battle:

Hear how the Teutonic hordes
Smash the strings of our souls,
They do not want to allow us to live any more,
Instead they sow treason and murder all around!
To battle all of Silesia!
Free men, rally behind them!
To battle, to battle,
Because the cruel Teutonic serpent
Is spilling blood![8]

Other Poles predicted that the 'Teutonic serpent', embittered by the defeat of 1918 and its dismemberment in the East, would rise again. The Germans, warned historian Kazimierz Kierski, 'think about the suppression of others and fresh plunder. An obsession of revenge and hatred for all those who dared to stand in their way flourishes.' No nation could 'carry on as usual, indifferent to its losses,' Stanislaw Sopicki wrote in his treatise on Germans and Poles in 1931. 'Germany's losses in the East are also humbling because the occupiers of former German soil created a nation which many Germans consider to be weak, lacking culture, inferior, a nation which is to be despised and mocked.' The popular press saw only one solution: Germany had to be dealt a crushing blow. 'The struggle between Poland and Germany is inevitable,' one Warsaw newspaper declared in October 1930. It continued:

We must prepare ourselves for it systematically. Our goal is a new Grunwald – but this time a Grunwald in the suburbs of Berlin. In the war with Germany there will be no prisoners; there's no room for humane or cultural feelings. The world will be shaken by this war. We must bring a superhuman sense of sacrifice to the ranks of our soldiers and a spirit of merciless revenge and cruelty. From today we will dedicate every edition of this newspaper to the coming Grunwald in Berlin.[9]

Whipping up patriotic fervour was not solely the preserve of Polish newspapers or Polish politicians. The nationalists were equally vocal in the Reich. 'In the depths of our soul we remember the carved-up lands on the Vistula, the unhealed wound on our eastern flank,' Gottfried Treviranus, the Minister for the Occupied Territories, declared on the steps of the *Reichstag* during a rally of East and West Prussians in August 1930. Dressed in the uniform of a Great War torpedo boat commander, Treviranus demanded Germany's eastern frontier re-drawn. 'An unjust border cannot withstand international law and the national will to live. Down with talk of catastrophe. Rally round with courage to banish all troubles. The day will come when the fight for right will free Germany and Europe.'

Gottfried Treviranus was, of course, not alone in voicing such views. Demanding the return of Danzig and the Corridor were common themes in the policies of Nationalist parties – none more so than the National Socialists. For the first half dozen years of their existence in Danzig, however, the Nazis had made little headway; they enjoyed a solitary seat in the city's parliament at the end of 1927. A 'fanatical leader' was needed to turn about the Party's fortunes in the Free City. That fanatical leader was a former bank clerk from southern Germany, Albert Forster, 'one of the men,' a hagiographer gushed, 'around whom the heavens and earth could collapse, but who would never abandon their absolute loyalty to their leader'. Forster galvanised the Danzig Nazis. Within a month of his arrival in the Baltic port, the National Socialists were the second largest political party. Yet for the most part, Albert Forster found Danzigers almost apathetic to their situation. In 1930, they seemed more interested in the collision of the schooner *Flottbek* and the trawler *Heisternest* in the harbour canal, causing the fishing vessel to sink, than politics. Cityfolk mulled over Danzig's waste problem: 1.35 million barrels of rubbish had to be dealt with each year, enough, the *Danziger Neueste Nachrichten* reckoned, to fill the city's principal shopping street up to the third storey along its entire length. Work started on the Ufa Palast cinema, large enough to hold a 1,500-strong audience. A fire raged through the Deo Gloria warehouses, smouldering for more than two months. And the airship *Graf Zeppelin* cast its shadow over Danzig in the high summer of 1930.[10]

There was another, more ominous shadow being cast increasingly over the free city. It was losing trade to a rival upstart less than a dozen miles away, Gdynia. For the first 650 years of its life, Gdynia had been a gentle fishing village barely ten miles north of Danzig, home to no more than 1,200 people. But in 1921, the Polish authorities began a decade-long construction programme believing their republic could not rely on trade passing through its near neighbour. In 1925, just 50,000 tons of goods passed through Gdynia. Even in 1930, Danzigers comforted themselves that their port handled more than twice the trade of its Polish challenger. But Danzig's days of supremacy in the western Baltic were numbered. The Poles offered tax breaks and other incentives to entice trade to Gdynia. By 1933 it was the busier of the two ports. Polish newspapers celebrated the 'Sword of Gdynia', but there were other daggers thrust into Danzigers' sides. Poles boycotted the city's wares – margarine, paper, cheese, paint, coffee, even Dr Oetker's famous puddings. In the space of two years, nearly sixty businesses went bankrupt. As the 1930s opened, one in five Danzig workers was unemployed.

To Danzigers, it seemed everything the Poles did was designed to antagonise them. They forbade direct trains to the city from Germany; passengers had to change in Marienburg, two dozen miles to the southeast, and buy tickets with Polish currency from railway officials who refused to converse in German. They despatched a destroyer to visit the port in the summer of 1932, the *Wicher*, but deliberately did not request permission; her captain had specific orders to snub Danzig's leaders. The Grudziaz newspaper *Stragnica Baltycka* called on fellow Poles to take advantage of Germany's momentary weakness to strike at Danzig just fifty miles away. 'Soldiers! It is your duty to conquer this small piece of Polish land which is waiting impatiently for you. Raise yourselves up for this deed!'[11] Poland's foreign minister brashly declared that 'only a Polish Army could solve the Danzig question'. And, in the late winter of 1933, the Poles flouted international laws by bolstering their garrison on the Westerplatte.

Jutting into the Bay of Danzig, the Westerplatte was a sandy peninsula, no more than twenty-five feet high, little more than a mile long and at most 600 yards wide. Flanked on the one side by a tributary of the Vistula which had been widened into a canal and by the expanse of the Baltic on the other, the spit had been fortified in times gone by but the ravaging of the ages and technological progress had nullified their importance. By the early 1920s, the fine sandy shore had become popular with Danzigers. Bathing huts went up; there was a spa and a hotel.

But the Poles saw a less peaceful use for the headland. They wanted to turn the Westerplatte into a depot and ammunition store. They got their way. A garrison four-score strong moved in with the permission of the League of Nations and the bathers were gradually displaced. For the next eight years, the small garrison lived peacefully, if uncomfortably, side-by-side with Danzig's German populace who detested its presence. But at dawn on 6 March 1933, a steamer appeared off the peninsula and quickly disgorged 120 troops to bolster the garrison. It was a flagrant disregard for the League of Nations. But Warsaw's move was meant to test not the League, but the new German Chancellor. Would Adolf Hitler react? He did not. There was widespread public condemnation in Germany. There was condemnation too in Geneva, home to the League. Warsaw backed down. The additional troops were pulled out.

Adolf Hitler did not react because he was in no position to react. But he *wanted* to react. And one day he *would* react, he candidly told Germany's military leaders just four days after seizing power. After dark on Friday, 3 February 1933, the senior generals and admirals gathered in the Berlin flat of *Freiherr* (Baron) Kurt von Hammerstein-Equord, the head of the German Army. Hammerstein, more politician than general, had no time for the National Socialists, their methods or their aims. 'The Army will never allow them to come to power,' he promised the politicians. And now, on a bitingly cold winter's evening, the general introduced his National Socialist dinner guest: *Herr Reich Chancellor*. Hitler bowed awkwardly in front of the array of leading officers. He sat nervously through dinner. Then, when the small talk faded away, he stood up and outlined his plans for Germany. The problems facing his new government were perhaps almost insurmountable – internal unrest, unemployment, a global depression. His goals were clear: to re-assert Germany's political and military strength. At home, he would wage war on his opponents. The Bolsheviks wanted 'to return highly-cultured people to the dark ages'. They had to be 'eradicated hook, line and sinker'. Just four days after being appointed chancellor, Adolf Hitler told Germany's generals he was prepared to destroy the political apparatus which had made him the country's leader. 'Democracy is a utopia, it is impossible, the most disastrous thing there is,' he explained. National Socialism would become the new state religion. Its tentacles would reach every corner of German society. 'The people must learn to think as a nation and be welded together,' the fledgling chancellor explained. 'This cannot be done by persuasion alone, only by force.' Once the German people were willing, were ready to take up arms once more, he would re-introduce compulsory military service. 'The hour will come one day when we can raise a great army.' For a great army would be crucial if Germany was to achieve her goals. And what goals were they? Firstly, the nation had to fight against the Versailles Treaty. And then? 'Perhaps conquering new *Lebensraum* (living space) in the East.' Such conquered living space would face ruthless *Germanisierung* – German colonisation. Only the National Socialists could achieve all these goals, and only Adolf Hitler could lead Germany. He explained:

> There can be only one man giving the orders. I have worked to this end since 1918 and when I think that my movement, which has grown from seven people into one 12-million strong, has raised me, a simple soldier, to the Reich Chancellor of the German Reich, then this shows that there's still a majority of the people to be won over to this idea…
>
> The Fatherland has been given a miracle in my movement. This miracle only comes once, therefore we must make use of it.

Thus did Adolf Hitler light the long fuse on the European powder keg.[12]

Jozef Pilsudski suspected as much. 'We will inevitably have a war with Germany,' the Polish president predicted. 'It will be necessary to prepare for it. We always beat the Russians as soon as they leave their native soil and we will beat them in every instance. With the Germans, it's a different matter.' In the spring of 1933 it seemed such a war was looming – but on Polish terms. The country's armament factories had stepped up production, men born between 1913 and 1915 had been called up, the garrison on the Westerplatte had been strengthened, newspapers warned of the danger of war, and there were rumours of an imminent invasion of East Prussia. Such rumours soon reached the ears of the German Ambassador in Warsaw, Hans Adolf von Moltke, who believed there was sufficient weight behind them to alert Berlin. The Polish people were perturbed by the Nazis and Germany's new-found nationalism, the diplomat warned. There seemed little doubt the two nations would come to blows one day. Many Poles asked: Why wait until Germany was strong once again? Nevertheless, the ambassador remained to be convinced. 'It is hard to tell how much of this is genuine and how much merely serves as bluff,' he told his masters. They were rumours and only that, Polish Foreign Minister Jozef Beck assured all who would listen, and there was no truth in them. Why, Beck argued, the rumourmongers might just as well accuse Poland 'of throwing itself into the arms of Germany.' Within a year, Poland would do just that.[13]

In fact, it suited both Poland and Germany to strike a deal. Warsaw felt threatened after Germany stormed out of the League of Nations. Berlin felt threatened by its powerful mortal foe along its eastern border. In the dying months of 1933, Jozef Lipski, Poland's chubby-faced ambassador in Berlin, noticed a distinct thaw in German attitudes to his country. The thaw emanated from Germany's leader, as Lipski learned in an audience with Hitler in January 1934. Poles and Germans should abandon the idea that the two nations were mortal enemies, the German Chancellor told him. The German people had to accept that the Polish state was a reality. 'It is impossible to exterminate the Polish nation,' Hitler assured the Pole. 'Both nations have to live side-by-side.'[14] The next day Lipski signed a ten-year non-aggression pact between the two nations. Henceforth, Poland and Germany would settle any differences amicably.

Having safeguarded Germany's eastern frontier, Adolf Hitler looked to assert the Reich's position in central Europe. Four days after assuming power he had promised his generals he would bring back conscription. On Sunday 17 March, 1935, *Heldengedenktag* (Heroes' Memorial Day) when Germany paid homage to its fallen sons, Hitler made good on that promise. Today, however, the self-styled Führer (leader) of the German people sat in the former royal box of the National Opera House on Berlin's Unter den Linden and let his defence minister, *Generaloberst* Werner von Blomberg, declare the Reich's freedom to bear arms (*Wehrfreiheit*). On a stage adorned with the banners of eighty regiments, Blomberg waited for the orchestra to finish Beethoven's funeral march from *Eroica*, then he addressed his audience – a mass of uniformed men, some in their pre-war *Pickelhaube* spiked helmets. Compulsory military service, the general told them, would lay 'the foundation for the security of the Reich'. It was time for Germany to 'take the place she deserves among nations'. That did not mean that the Reich's newly-declared legions would march across the continent. 'Europe has become too small for the battlefield of a second world war; its cultural treasures are too valuable to expose them to the destructive effects of modern arms,' Werner von Blomberg assured his listeners. 'We Germans need no revenge because in four years, the Great War harvested glory enough for the next 100 years.'[15]

It was a message echoed by the Führer two months later in an address to the *Reichstag*, branded his 'peace' speech. 'From the depths of its ideological convictions National Socialist Germany wants peace,' Hitler stressed. 'Germany needs peace and it wants peace!' Conflict would not solve Europe's problems, he explained, it would add to them. 'Whoever lights the torch of war in Europe can hope for nothing but chaos. We, however, live firmly convinced that our age will see not the end of the West but its re-birth. It is our proud hope and unshakeable belief that Germany may make an everlasting contribution to this great aim.'

Instead, the Reich lit the torch of war. Hitler marched his troops across the Rhine, demilitarised since 1918. He sent aircraft and soldiers to Spain to support Franco's forces. He browbeat Austria into *Anschluss* (union). And, in the summer of 1938, he threatened to plunge Europe into its second conflagration in a generation, demanding Czechoslovakia cede the Sudetenland and its ethnic Germans. With Prague tottering under the threat of a German onslaught, Warsaw also pounced, determined to settle its long-standing differences. A Polish army 200,000 strong was poised on the Czech border as Jozef Beck demanded Prague relinquish Teschen, 300 square miles of disputed territory nestling amid the Carpathians southwest of Katowice. Teschen was home to coal mines, steel mills, the Jablunka Pass carrying the main railway line from Warsaw to Vienna, and 260,000 people, two thirds of them Poles. Prague gave way. On the afternoon of 2 October, Polish soldiers marched into Teschen, their standards unfurled, their uniforms adorned with flowers. Loudspeakers trumpeted Polish nationalist tunes, military marches, speeches. Poles lined the banks of the Olza which separated Teschen from their mother country, cheering the soldiers and showering them with flowers as they crossed the rover. The Czech general surrendering the region failed to share the widespread euphoria. The Poles, he prophesised, would soon be surrendering the region themselves – to Hitler.[16]

The Poles were satiated by the seizure of Teschen. But the occupation of the Sudetenland merely gave Adolf Hitler a hunger for more. Within three weeks of the Munich agreement, he was ordering his armed forces to prepare for 'the liquidation of the remainder of the Czech state should it pursue an anti-German policy'. But it was also time, Hitler decided, to resolve all issues between Germany and Poland for good. Resolving *all* issues, of course, eventually boiled down to just *one* issue: Danzig and the Polish Corridor. For almost five years, relations between Warsaw and Berlin had been relatively cordial – but the fate of the Free City was a constant thorn. Danzig *was* German, *always* had been German and *always* would be German, German Foreign Minister Joachim von Ribbentrop stressed to Polish Ambassador Jozef Lipski over three hours at Hitler's alpine retreat in late October. Therefore it should be incorporated back into the Reich, while an extra-territorial Autobahn and railway line would be driven through the Corridor to the city and to East Prussia, Ribbentrop suggested. Lipski baulked at Ribbentrop's suggestions. Danzig was not quite as German as Joachim von Ribbentrop liked to think it was, the Pole countered. For centuries the Vistula and the great port at its mouth had been 'the outlet to the sea' for Poland. The city was 'almost a symbol' to Poles. Nevertheless, Lipski did not give a formal response to the German proposals and nor did Ribbentrop expect one. Lipski headed headed to Warsaw for instructions from his master, Jozef Beck. A month later, the Polish Ambassador gave Ribbentrop his answer, this time in Berlin. The meeting between the two was a near carbon copy of the encounter in Berchtesgaden. Danzig was a German-Polish wound which should not be opened, Lipski pleaded. Ribbentrop urged the Pole to reconsider. He was offering to forge 'something permanent here and bring about real stability'. [17]

While Ribbentrop and Lipski were deadlocked in talks, Adolf Hitler was closeted with 400 of Germany's newspaper editors and senior journalists in Munich. This was not a speech for public consumption – the bland official account in German newspapers talked only of an overview of political events provided by the Führer and the need to carry out important tasks in the future. But over forty-five minutes at the Führerbau, the Party headquarters, Hitler revealed that his talk of peace all these years had been just that – talk. Now it was time to tell the German people 'that there were things which had to be resolved with force if they could not be solved peacefully'. As 1938 drew to a close, he explained, Germany stood not at the end of an historic epoch, rather on the eve of one. Once Germany possessed the greatest empire. It would do so again. 'I know all too well that we stand at the dawn of a German life and with it a German future,' he continued.

Meine Herren, I believe in such a future for the German *Volk*. The history of the world is made by men. It was made by men in the past and it is made today by men. The quality of these men is vital as is, in addition, the number of such men. The quality of the German people is without equal. I have never believed that any other nation possesses more quality!'[18]

To Propaganda Minister Joseph Goebbels, 1938 had been 'a magnificent year, a year without equal'. And like his master, he too believed Germany and her *Volk* stood at the dawn of a great future. 'Never before have we looked forward with as much confidence and courage to a new year as we do to 1939,' he proclaimed to the German people on the cusp of 1939. 'May it be filled with success and victory! May it bring our land and its *Volk* blessings and good fortune!'[19]

In Danzig, League of Nations High Commissioner Carl Burckhardt did not foresee blessings and good fortune in the year to come. 'People rearmed – we heard it officially: in Germany, in Poland, even in the free city,' the Swiss historian and diplomat observed. 'Almost daily paramilitary formations marched endlessly past our house, the *Hitlerjugend* wearily marching in step, dragging their feet to their terrible songs: *Today Germany belongs to us and tomorrow the whole world...*'[20]

Notes

1. Proclamation of the Free City by the Deputy Military Commander Lieutenant-Colonel Edward Strutt, 15/11/20. Ruhnau, p. 21.
2. Ruhnau, p. 9.
3. Davies, *White Eagle, Red Star*, p. 238 and Watt, *Bitter Glory*, pp. 172–3.
4. Schuddekopf, pp. 163–5 and Seeckt Rede in Hamburg, 20/2/20 in Rabenau, p. 184.
5. Nachlass Stülpnagel, BA-MA, N 5/10, cited in Dirks, pp. 193–209.
6. Letter to his wife from Mitau, 12/7/19 in Bradley, Dermot, *Generaloberst Heinz Guderian und die Entstehungsgeschichte des modernen Blitzkrieges*, pp. 125–6.
7. Hindenburg, *Out of My Life*, p. 92, Pfundtner, pp. 183, 210–12 and Tietz, pp. 51–3.
8. Golczewski, p. 312.
9. Golczewski, pp. 69, 236 and *Münchener Neuesten Nachrichten*, 3/10/30. Cited in Lindenblatt and Bäcker, *Bromberger Blutsonntag*, pp. 45–6.
10. Schenk, *Hitlers Mann in Danzig*, pp. 30, 33.
11. Ruhnau, p. 59.
12. IFZ Munich, Zs 105 in Dirks, pp. 232–6 and Vogelsang, Thilo (ed), 'Neue Dokumentation zur Geschichte der Reichswehr 1930–1933', VfZ, Band 2, Heft 4, 1954, pp. 434–435. The following Monday in the Reich Chancellery, Hitler addressed the members of the Cabinet in a similar vein: for the next four or five years, the watchword of the German economy had to be 'everything for the Armed Forces'. Germany's standing in the world would grow as her Army grew. See DGFP, C, i, Doc.16.
13. Riekhoff, p. 361, DGFP, C, i, Doc.180 and Adamthwaite, p. 122.
14. Lipski, pp. 124–5.
15. *New York Times*, 18/3/35.
16. *New York Times* 2/10/39–3/10/39 and Roos, p. 156.
17. DGFP, D, iv, Docs.81, 101, 104.
18. W Treue (ed), 'Rede Hitlers vor dem deutschen Presse, 10 November 1938', VfZ, Band 6, 1958, pp. 175–91.
19. *Völkischer Beobachter*, 1/1/39.
20. Burckhardt, p. 236.apers.

CHAPTER TWO

One Hundred Powder Kegs

I will go down as the greatest German in history.

– ADOLF HITLER

We Poles do not understand the concept of 'peace at any price'. There is one thing in the life of men, nations and states which is priceless – honour.

– JOZEF BECK

IN THE affluent Danzig suburb of Langfuhr, people were readying themselves for bed on the eve of a new working week. 1939, a year in which Adolf Hitler promised the German people their nation would 'contribute to peace across the world', was just twenty-two days old. It had been an uneventful Sunday in the free city. Then, over the fine villas, over the broad avenues of Langfuhr, a 'bright gleaming sun' appeared this bitter Baltic night. For a few seconds the bedrooms and parlours of Langfuhr were lit up 'as bright as day'. A meteor streaked across the sky, heading south. It tumbled across the Bay of Danzig. The white gleam faded, turned a shade of red then vanished as the spinning rock vaporised thousands of feet above the port. It was an omen for the year to come, Danzigers told themselves. But was it good or evil?[1]

On the inter-continental express snaking its way from Monte Carlo across the Alps towards Bavaria, Jozef Beck also pondered the fate of the free city. In an age when old men, or at least *older* men, dominated politics, forty-four-year-old Jozef Beck was relatively youthful. He enjoyed the trappings of politics, the official functions, the opportunity to improve his country's standing in Europe and the world. But *enjoying* being foreign minister and *being* foreign minister were entirely different. Jozef Beck might have been the dominant figure in Polish politics in the late 1930s, but his policies had almost entirely failed. Beck had tried to ally the powers of central and eastern Europe – Italy, Poland, Yugoslavia, Hungary and Romania – to create a united bloc to stand up to Germany and the Soviet Union. Poland was not the great power her leaders thought she was. Italy and Hungary chose to align themselves with Berlin, not Warsaw, and Jozef Beck's great 'Third Europe' plan disintegrated. Still the former colonel was unbowed. He had a new policy: to maintain favourable relations with Nazi Germany.

How difficult achieving such a goal would be Beck learned over three gruelling hours at Hitler's alpine retreat, the Berghof, in the presence of the Führer and his ingratiating foreign minister. Joachim von Ribbentrop was an arrogant, overbearing, former wine importer and trader who had bought his aristocratic 'von' from a distant relative and weaselled his way to the top of the Nazi Party after engineering a naval agreement between Britain and the Reich. But in everything else as a diplomat, Joachim von Ribbentrop had been a disaster. As ambassador in London he had committed *faux pas* upon *faux pas* such that Britons branded him 'von Brickendrop'. No senior figure in the Nazi Party could abide him – and Ribbentrop in turn loathed them. But Adolf Hitler had no more faithful a lapdog who avidly supported every one of his master's political moves.

Today, on this first Thursday of 1939, it was the master who did most of the talking. 'Danzig is German, will always remain German, and will sooner or later become part of Germany,' the Führer told the Pole bluntly. He did, however, concede that Poland too needed Danzig – she needed an 'outlet to the sea'; he did not want Poland to be 'bottled up', for then she would be a loaded gun likely to go off at any moment. It was as vital to give Poland access to the sea, the Führer continued, as it was for the Reich to be connected with East Prussia once more; for that Germany needed a railway and Autobahn driven through the heart of the Corridor. In return for such concessions, the Reich would be prepared to guarantee Poland's existing borders. Jozef Beck did not bite. In all his seven years in office, Beck said, he had never listened to 'coffee house' gossip, but when it came to Danzig it would be impossible to ignore public opinion. He did not, however, dismiss Hitler's proposals outright. Before giving his final answer, he told his German hosts, he wanted 'to sleep on the matter'.[2]

The Pole slept on the matter for three weeks. He gave his uncompromising answer when his German counterpart visited Warsaw to mark the fifth anniversary of the non-aggression treaty between the two nations. Outwardly, relations were cordial: swastika flags flew uncomfortably alongside the Polish white eagle in Warsaw's central station; the platform was lined with top-hatted Polish diplomats and officials, led by Beck, and uniformed German diplomats and functionaries, led by Hans Adolf von Moltke, the Reich's Ambassador to Warsaw. A guard of honour, composed of Polish police officers in steel helmets, greeted Ribbentrop, his wife Annelies, and their entourage of fifty journalists, secretaries and Foreign Ministry staff, while a police band struck up the *Deutschlandlied* and Poland's *Mazurek*. In the square in front of the station, a police cordon swayed as it struggled to hold back a crowd several hundred strong. The masses were to be disappointed. They caught no glimpse of the German visitors; Ribbentrop was whisked through side streets. That evening in the Polish Foreign Ministry a dinner celebrated five years of friendship between the erstwhile enemies. The 1934 pact had laid the foundation for firm bonds between Germany and Poland, the German minister proclaimed. 'All problems arising between our two countries in the future will be solved in the same friendly manner,' Joachim von Ribbentrop toasted his hosts.

Behind closed doors the exchanges between the two diplomats were far icier, however. The German repeated the demands his master had made three weeks before. Every German regarded the loss of Danzig and the Corridor 'as a great injustice', Ribbentrop warned. Driving a railway and Autobahn across the Corridor to East Prussia and bringing Danzig under German rule once more were 'extremely moderate' demands. After all, Ribbentrop continued, ask 100

English or Frenchmen what should happen to Danzig, and ninety-nine would say it should return to the Reich. Jozef Beck shook his head. Ask 100 Poles and they would refuse to allow Danzig to be swallowed up by Germany again. No, the minister told the German envoi, the Polish people could not consent to the Reich asserting her sovereignty over the free city. Nor would they allow railway lines and roads to be bludgeoned through the Corridor to East Prussia. And nor would they align themselves with Germany, Italy and Japan in some great anti-Bolshevik alliance. A line had been drawn in the sand.[3]

Publicly the Reich's leader maintained the façade of friendship. Hitler celebrated the anniversary of the Nazi seizure of power on the penultimate evening of January as he always did with a rambling speech in the *Krolloper*, an eighty-seven-year-old opera house which had served as home to the *Reichstag* since fire damaged it in 1933. He railed against Bolshevism, against Jews – promising their annihilation if *they* plunged the world into another conflagration – and proclaimed himself a man of peace who had forged a great German empire 'without spilling a drop of blood'. Where might Germany, indeed all of Europe, be had the Reich and Poland not struck a deal five years before. The pact had been 'a great relief' for both nations. And it would continue to be, the Führer assured his audience. 'German-Polish friendship has become something reassuring in a Europe dogged by political strife'.[4]

Within a fortnight, Adolf Hitler returned to the *Krolloper*, but this time his words were not for a wide audience. Gathered before him was every officer who commanded a regiment or larger, plus their naval and Luftwaffe counterparts. For six years, Hitler told them, Germany had been blessed by 'one stroke of good fortune after the next. In fact, in these six years, we have achieved miracles.' She had, but she would not stop there. 'I have taken it upon myself to resolve the German question.' The German question, he explained, was 'Germany's problem of space'. He continued: 'Take it from me that as long as I live this single thought will dominate my existence. And take it from me, too, that I will never step back from the brink because I am convinced that this question must be resolved one way or another.' There could be no delay, no leaving this 'problem' to future generations to solve. No, it was the duty of today's Germans to act. And if the Reich had to wield the sword, she would do so with untold brutality, for the ensuing conflagration would be 'an out-and-out war of ideologies, a racial war, a war of nations.' In the past, the German officer had led his men in battle 'with the sword and Bible'; today, Adolf Hitler expected the Bible to be replaced by ideology. 'That is what whips the men up, what carries them forward. It is ideology which will also sustain a nation through a long war.' But war, the Führer explained, was not his objective. His goal was to achieve all the Reich's 'irrefutable' demands for space, for raw materials 'using all the means at my disposal.' That could mean politics. It could also mean brandishing the sword. 'Be assured that I have always thoroughly weighed up these problems beforehand, that I've looked at them from every angle, and that once I declare my decision to do this or that, then this decision is irrevocable and I will carry it out whatever the odds.'[5] He would reveal his next irrevocable decision in barely a month.

Little more than three weeks after the Munich accord, Germany's Armed Forces had received explicit instructions from their Supreme Commander: draw up plans 'to smash the remainder of the Czech state at any time'. Throughout the autumn and winter of 1938, nebulous Nazi agencies stoked the flames of Slovak independence in an attempt to destroy the rump of Czechoslovakia from within. When Czech troops marched into Bratislava to stamp their authority on these insidious pro-German Slovaks, Adolf Hitler was presented with an opportunity to act. By mid-day on Tuesday, 14 March 1939, the Wehrmacht was ready to march across the Czech frontier. Hitler summoned the Czech president Emil Hacha to Berlin to discuss the 'crisis'. As Hacha's train steamed for the Anhalter Bahnhof – Berlin's imposing 'gateway to the south' – the Führer dined then retired to the drawing room of his sprawling new Reich Chancellery with his guests to watch a romantic comedy, *Ein hoffnungsloser Fall* (*A Hopeless Case*). The film was still running when Ribbentrop reported Hacha's arrival at the station. Let him wait for a couple of hours, Hitler, instructed; the Czech was a 'very fragile old gentleman' who should be allowed time to recover from the exertions of his journey before coming to the chancellery. It was midnight before the aged former lawyer was called to the Wilhemstrasse, and gone 1am on the fifteenth when he was finally ushered into Hitler's study. In five hours, the Führer told Hacha, German troops would march into his country 'from all sides'. The Czechs stood on the threshold of 'a great turning-point in history'. If Czechoslovakia resisted, her army, Hitler assured the Czech leader, 'would cease to exist in two days'. If she chose not to resist, she would enjoy the 'protection' of the Reich – but this was 'the last good turn' he would offer the Czech people. Hacha tottered, at one point fainted – or possibly even suffered a heart attack – and was treated by Hitler's personal physician. Once revived, Emil Hacha buckled under the German pressure. He had faced 'the most difficult task of his life', but he realised that resistance was folly. He agreed to sign his country over to the protection of Germany, convinced 'that the destiny of Czechoslovakia lay in the Führer's hands' and that destiny would be safe in those hands. Perhaps in fifty years' time people would regard his decision 'as a blessing'.

It was almost 4.30am when the huge doors were opened and a delighted Hitler walked past the two SS *Leibstandarte* soldiers who formed the guard of honour outside the study. Beaming, he stood in the middle of the 480ft marble gallery which dominated the new chancellery, urging his secretaries to peck him on both cheeks. 'This is the most wonderful day in my life,' he told them. 'I've succeeded in doing something which we've striven for in vain for centuries – union between the Czechs and the Reich has been achieved by me. I will go down as the greatest German in history.'[6] By 9am, German troops had entered Prague. Within an hour of nightfall that Wednesday, Adolf Hitler had driven up to the Hradcany, once the seat of power of the Czech kings, to claim his new prize.

The Reich's conquests that March did not end with Czechoslovakia. The ink had hardly dried on the agreement between Hitler and Hacha than the Reich's ravenous eyes focused upon the former Teutonic fortress of Memel. Immortalised in Germany's national anthem as the easternmost extremity of the Reich, Memel – like Danzig – had been stripped from Germany by Versailles.

Unlike Danzig, however, it had been swallowed whole by its neighbouring state, Lithuania. Now, in a repeat of the bully-boy tactics which crushed Emil Hacha, the Lithuanian Foreign Minister Juozas Urbsys was ordered to Berlin. This time it was Joachim von Ribbentrop who turned the screw. Memel wanted to be part of the Reich once again, he told Urbsys. And it would be part of the Reich again, the foreign minister continued. There were two possibilities. 'One would be a friendly settlement,' Ribbentrop explained. But if, on the other hand, there was unrest, shootings, 'Germany could not idly look on. The Führer will act with lightning speed – the situation would slip from the hands of the politicians and be decided by the military.'

Shortly after 3pm the following day, Urbsys bowed to the German pressure. By dawn on 23 March, the Lithuanians had pulled out of Memel. Mustered off the port was a formidable German naval force: three pocket battleships, three light cruisers, destroyers, flotillas of torpedo boats and ancillary vessels. All morning German soldiers marched into the city and environs while the Luftwaffe droned overhead. At 2pm, the Führer stepped ashore from a torpedo boat having spent the night in the pocket battleship *Deutschland*. After reviewing a guard of sailors and police, he drove to the centre of Memel to address the crowds from the balcony of a theatre. 'You know a mighty Reich, a great united nation, stands behind you,' he told them. 'You shall now partake in the surge of our national life, our work, our faith, our hopes and – should it become necessary – our sacrifices.'[7]

Prague and Memel told Jozef Beck quite bluntly: there could be no deal with the Reich, no solving the Danzig question amicably. The day after Adolf Hitler stood on the theatre balcony in Memel, the Polish Foreign Minister gathered his senior diplomats. 'The Germans are marching all across Europe with nine divisions'. Poland, however, Beck told his diplomats, would not 'join that category of eastern states that allow rules to be dictated to them'. It was time to stand up to Hitler. 'The mighty have been humble to him, the weak have capitulated to him even at the cost of honour.' The Poles would not be humble. They would not sacrifice their honour. No, Beck declared, 'We will fight.'[8]

Adolf Hitler had come to realise that too. There could be no deal with Warsaw. The Poles would fight. Emboldened by his crushing blows to Prague and Vilnius, he ordered the Army to drawn up plans which would leave Poland 'beaten down' for decades to come. *Fall Weiss* – Case White – as it came to be known would be unleashed upon the Polish nation on any day from 1 September. It was time, the Führer ruled, to contemplate a 'final settlement' with Poland. Danzig would be annexed to the Reich. The rest of the country would fall prey to the Wehrmacht. And how. The language of the directive was unambiguous, uncompromising: annihilate, destroy, eliminate. Poland's armed forces would be crushed, driven from the skies, chased and harried on the ground, the nation's lifelines strangled at sea.

It was a mission the Wehrmacht relished. 'I believe I am addressing many of you from my heart when I say there is a weight off our minds with the end of "friendly relations" with Poland,' the Chief of the Army General Staff Franz Halder told his officers. After all, the general pointed out, neither Pole nor German was really committed to friendship. Now the German Army would 'fall upon the Poles with a devastating blow'. German armour and German aircraft would hound the enemy relentlessly – 'march the Polish Army to death'. Nevertheless, the German Army had never underestimated a foe, and it would not do so now, Halder explained. Poland possessed the fifth largest army in Europe. She could raise seventy divisions. But – and this was an important 'but' – those seventy divisions were filled with badly-trained men. The Polish soldier, Halder confidently told his staff, was the 'most stupid' in Europe – save perhaps for the Romanian. Stupidity was made worse by backwardness. Polish tanks were dismissed as toys. The air force was 'backward'. The army relied on cavalry 'trained for battle with shiny weapons'. These were the tactics not of 1939 but of 1870–71. The Pole, of course, would defend himself desperately – but he was no match for the most modern army of the age. 'We know, when the hour comes, who is facing us,' the Chief of the General Staff impressed upon his fellow officers: 'No serious opponent.' His audience drew a sharp intake of breath. '*Meine Herren*, I know that what I'm telling you now sounds impossible. But it must be made possible,' the Chief-of-Staff urged. '*We must be finished with Poland in three weeks at the most, fourteen days if at all possible.*'[9]

In Warsaw, Lieutenant Colonel Edward Roland Sword had reached a similar conclusion to Franz Halder: the Poles' position was as good as hopeless. Britain's military attaché to Poland, Sword – known by all as 'Roly' – had toured the land extensively, visited armament factories, watched air raid precautions. The Polish spirit impressed him. The men of 1939 were 'tough and courageous. The Polish soldier of today would probably live up to the high standard of endurance set by his forebears.' Courage alone was not enough. Face-to-face, one Polish division was no match for one German division. The arms factories were working around the clock but it was too late. It would be spring 1940 at the earliest before the Polish Army could offer any form of effective battle against the Wehrmacht. Germany would not wait that long. She held all the cards. Poland was all but encircled. The Corridor was 'virtually indefensible', the vital Silesian industrial region was ripe for plucking by German troops advancing from the Reich and what was Czechoslovakia. In short, 'Roly' Sword concluded bleakly, Poland could do little more than offer token resistance to the Germans.[10]

Time and again, however, Poland's military and civilian leaders dismissed the Wehrmacht as a gigantic bluff. An article from the military journal *Polska Zbrojna* 'We are ready' was widely reproduced. It captured the spirit of the nation and its Army perfectly, brushing aside the numerical strength of any foreign aggressor. The Polish soldier's equipment and zeal would guarantee victory for an army fighting under the white eagle.[11] Adolf Hitler would now demonstrate that his armed forces were no bluff.

Berlin in the middle of April 1939 was in a festive mood. Huge swastika banners hung beneath the arches on the Brandenburg Gate, swinging in the breeze. Beyond Berlin's great triumphal arch, stretching across Pariser Platz and along Unter den Linden, the capital's finest boulevard, were four rows of tall gleaming white columns, crowned with golden eagles clutching a swastika medallion. The swastika fluttered everywhere: from the façades of apartments, hotels, government buildings, every few metres, and more personal banners:

Führer, wir danken dir – Führer, we thank you. 'The name "Adolf Hitler" is today a political slogan for the entire world,' Propaganda Minister Joseph Goebbels declared on state radio. 'It travels around the globe almost like a legend.' He continued: 'The pinnacle of achievement for someone on this earth is to give his name to an historical era and to leave his indelible mark on his age. That's something one can most certainly say about the Führer. It's impossible to imagine today's world without him.'[12]

After dark on the eve of his fiftieth birthday, Adolf Hitler and his chief architect Albert Speer drove the short distance from Hitler's new chancellery to the Brandenburg Gate which, like the white columns stretching into the distance behind it, basked in the glow of spotlights. A large crowd of Berliners strained at the rope cordon to see their Führer, while others scrambled up lamp posts in the hope of a glimpse. Candles flickered on the balconies of apartments. Brass bands struck up military marches. Hitler and his friend spent perhaps no more than five minutes in the shadow of the great arch as the newsreel cameras whirred, before climbing back into the black Mercedes for a drive along the newly-widened Charlottenburger Chaussee which dissected the Tiergarten, the finest of Berlin's parks. The broad avenue, now renamed the East-West Axis, was just one strand of the Führer's grand plan for the re-design of Berlin and tonight it was lined with Berliners as the motorcade moved down it, accompanied by a soundtrack of cheers and applause. Back in the New Reich Chancellery Speer had built him, the Führer dined with his entourage while representatives from every *Gau* – district – of the Reich marched down Wilhelmstrasse by torchlight. So too veterans of Hitler's failed attempt to seize power in Munich in 1923. And so too ordinary soldiers in their *feldgrau* uniforms and steel helmets. A choir from Hitler's personal bodyguard, the SS *Leibstandarte*, serenaded their Führer in the chancellery's *Ehrenhof* – Courtyard of Honour. And then, shortly after midnight on Thursday, 20 April, 1939, after receiving platitudes from his personal staff, Hitler stepped out on to the balcony to the appreciation of the crowds still milling around below, before retiring to the smoking room where his deputy Rudolf Hess and Danzig's leader Albert Forster were waiting to offer their congratulations. The conversation with these two old Party cronies lasted long into the night. 'It is a pity that I did not come to power ten years earlier,' Hitler mused. 'Now I am already fifty. I can no longer delay my plans.' He looked forward to the coming day: a military parade the likes of which the world had never seen – six divisions, more than 600 panzers, a procession moving through the heart of Berlin for four hours. 'At the parade tomorrow I shall prove to the entire world that I fear no war.'[13]

Adolf Hitler rose early the next day – early for Adolf Hitler at any rate. At 8am the band of the *Leibstandarte* struck up in the Chancellery garden, before the entire bodyguard regiment lined up for their Führer, dressed in his brown Party uniform, a gold-embroidered cap and a gold belt in place of his traditional Sam Browne to signify he was Supreme Commander of the Wehrmacht. There was a flurry of visitors to the Voss Strasse: the crestfallen Emil Hacha, the Slovakian leader Tiso, senior officers, *Gauleiters* (party leaders), SS chief Heinrich Himmler. There were gifts by the hundreds to admire: a silver model of the House of

German Art in Munich, from the people of Saaz in the Sudetenland a basket of Easter eggs and a jar of hops salad, paintings – even 'a wonderful Titian' – porcelain figures, books, vases, drawings, carpets, handicrafts, globes, radios, clocks, pies, sweets, fruit juices, liqueurs, a sailing vessel made entirely of flowers, from his deputy Rudolf Hess a collection of fifty letters by Frederick the Great. But what delighted the Führer most were military models – a miniature West Wall fort which lit up, aircraft, ships, panzers. 'He's just like a young lad with them,' observed secretary Christa Schroeder.

From miniatures, Adolf Hitler moved on to the full-sized versions. At 11am his Mercedes move slowly down the East-West Axis, past the throng kept in check by thousands of brown shirts, past the troops preparing to march, eventually drawing up opposite the Technical High School in Charlottenburg where a white dais had been erected, overlooked by terraced seats for Party grandees, senior officers, foreign dignitaries and attachés. The heads of the Navy, Erich Raeder, Army, Walther von Brauchitsch, and Luftwaffe, Hermann Göring took their place alongside their Führer in the centre of the tribune, joined by other senior commanders: the Luftwaffe's Albert Kesselring, head of air forces in and around Berlin; Otto Schniewind, the Navy's Chief-of-Staff; and the panzer commanders, Heinz Guderian, Gustav Wietersheim, Hermann Hoth, Erich Hoepner.

On came the standard-bearers with gold, green and red banners flying from poles topped by silver eagles, lining up opposite the tribune. The band in front of the bearers struck up the national anthem, the Nazi Party anthem the *Horst Wessellied* and the *Badenweiler March*, one of Hitler's favourites. For the next four hours the procession of military might was endless: 40,000 men drawn from four divisions, training regiments, specialist pioneers, smoke detachments, cavalry, Luftwaffe regiments, *Fallschirmjäger* – paratroopers, on public display for the first time – motorised infantry, motorised artillery, panzers; end to end, the phalanx would have stretched more than sixty miles. 'What an army,' the correspondent of the French newspaper *Le Journal* wrote with uneasy admiration. 'What might. Never has Germany possessed a mightier army.'[14]

To the world, the German tank, the vaunted panzer, was at the heart of this mighty army. No nation, it seemed, possessed a more mechanised army. That she did could be attributed largely to one man: Heinz Guderian, 'the father of the panzer division'. Guderian was a Prussian, a West Prussian, born in the Vistula town of Kulm in the summer of 1888. There was only one career for the young Heinz. His father was an infantry officer. His predecessors had fought with Frederick the Great and, later, against Napoleon at Waterloo. And so, aged eighteen, the young Heinz joined the battalion his father commanded, the light infantry of the 10th Hanoverian *Jäger*. But the junior officer's time with the infantry was brief. His father encouraged him to learn the new art of wireless telegraphy instead of taking a course on the machine gun, a weapon, Guderian senior suggested, which did not have 'much of a future'. The young officer's education did not end there. He became fluent in English and French. And, at the age of 25, he was selected for the three-year course which would allow him to wear the coveted red stripe of the *Grosser Generalstab* – Great General

Staff. Fate intervened before Guderian could complete his training. When war engulfed Europe, the *Leutnant*'s signal expertise was in demand. He was sent west with the Army bearing down on Paris. It was, he believed, his sacred duty. 'What matters now is our standing in the world and the existence of our nation – an existence which the other nations found uncomfortable,' he wrote to his wife Gretel. He marched to the Marne, witnessed the first battle around the historic Belgian town of Ypres and the crystallisation of the Western Front. By Christmas 1914, the optimism of the first days of war had evaporated. 'It's probably rare that the future hanging over the Fatherland and over the individual has been so dark, so uncertain,' he wrote to his wife from Belgium. 'May 1915 be the milestone in German history, the beginning of it in full bloom. That is my ardent wish. May all our bloody sacrifices not be in vain so that we should not be ashamed of our dead.' 1915 was not the milestone year in Germany's history, nor 1916 – which Guderian spent as an intelligence officer first at Verdun, then back in Flanders – nor 1917. 1918 promised victory, but delivered defeat, a defeat the newly-qualified General Staff officer found difficult to bear. 'Our fine German Reich is no more, Bismarck's work lies in ruins!' he wrote passing through Munich three days after the Armistice. 'Every concept of law and order, duty and honour seems to have been destroyed.' Heinz Guderian considered dispensing with the uniform he had worn proudly for a dozen years, but the Fatherland needed him. He fought against the Bolsheviks in the Baltic with the *Freikorps* through the winter and spring of 1919 before serving as a General Staff officer and infantry company commander in the rump of an army permitted by Versailles.

Guderian's career to date had been solid yet unspectacular. But in January 1922 he was posted to Munich with the Inspectorate of Transport Troops to study the possibilities of motorised warfare – something the now *Hauptmann* freely conceded he knew nothing about. But he threw himself into his new assignment. He studied what little German material there was relating to the army's limited use of armour in the Great War. He studied French and English books on armoured warfare. He spent a month in Sweden observing German-built tanks. He observed German Army war games – dummy tanks moving across exercise areas, sometimes in conjunction with infantry, sometimes in conjunction with aircraft, sometimes moving in groups as a tank platoon, tank company, even a tank battalion. By the end of the 1920s Heinz Guderian was convinced that the *Panzerkampfwagen* – armoured fighting vehicle, commonly shortened to panzer – combined in unified divisions, fighting on their own, not tied to the infantry, was the way of the future. His superiors remained to be convinced. When he asked one *Oberst* to convert supply trucks into combat vehicles, he was told bluntly. 'To hell with the front-line troops! These trucks should carry grain!' Otto von Stülpnagel, the Inspector of Transport Troops at the turn of the decade, watched the 1929 exercises where a theoretical panzer division performed admirably, then dismissed the idea of such divisions as 'a Utopian dream'. When Stülpnagel left office in 1931, his parting words to the panzer advocate were discouraging. 'You're too impetuous. Believe me, neither of us will ever see German panzers in action.' Stülpnagel's successor did not share such reticence. Oswald Lutz believed war would sweep across Europe once more and when it came, Germany could not wage it as she had waged the last war: she would surely lose. No, wrote Lutz, a future war had to be waged 'as a war of movement with the most modern weapons which the motor engine permitted'. To Oswald Lutz, like Guderian, the motorised vehicle was 'not a means of transportation, but a weapon' – a weapon which should not be placed in the hands of the infantry, but which should rove over the battlefield on its own 'as a principal weapon of war'.[15]

All the studies, all the theories, all the enthusiasm of Guderian and Lutz were, of course, academic. Germany did not possess any panzers. But in 1932, the Army placed an order for a *landwirtschaftlicher Schlepper* ('agricultural tractor'); history would know it as the *Panzerkampfwagen I*. It was sluggish, under-armed, under-powered, poorly armoured – but it would serve as the kernel of Germany's new *Panzerwaffe* (panzer force) for the next decade.

When the first panzers were delivered at the end of 1933, the Reich had a new master. Like many of his fellow officers, Guderian's attitude to Hitler and his National Socialists was ambivalent. 'Tomorrow we will swear the oath to Hitler,' he wrote to his wife in August 1934. 'A momentous oath! May God see to it that both sides remain true to it for the good of Germany. The Army is used to keeping its oath. May it be able to keep it again with honour.' But, like many of his fellow officers, Heinz Guderian was seduced by what the new regime promised. 'For years the entirely inadequate armament of the Reich had weighed on the Officer Corps like a nightmare,' he wrote later. 'No wonder that the initiation of a rearmament programme won them over to the man who promised to put new life into the Wehrmacht after fifteen years of stagnation.'[16]

If Heinz Guderian was seduced by the Nazis, so Adolf Hitler was seduced by the weapon the officer was developing. When the Führer visited the Army's exercise area at Kummersdorf, fifteen miles south of Berlin, Guderian demonstrated what platoons of motorcyclists, panzers and motorised infantry could achieve. Hitler was enthralled. 'That's what I need! That's what I want!'[17]

Adolf Hitler may have been won over, but the General Staff were not. Guderian clashed furiously with Ludwig Beck, Chief of the General Staff in the mid-30s, over the need for massed armoured units, panzer *divisions*. 'How many of these divisions do you want?' Beck asked during one heated exchange. 'Two to begin with, later twenty.' And how would these twenty panzer divisions be led, the head of the General Staff inquired. 'From the front – by wireless.' Beck shook his head. 'Nonsense! A divisional commander sits back with maps and a telephone. Anything else is Utopian!' Guderian was not the sole advocate of armoured warfare – he was surrounded by 'a number of outstanding and enthusiastic "old warriors"' – but he was, one junior officer recalled, 'the engine which never stopped'. Colleagues referred to him as *Schnell Heinz* ('Quick Heinz') not merely because of his passion for armoured warfare. He acted swiftly in everything he did, sometimes rashly. He quarrelled with senior officers frequently. '*Klotzen, nicht kleckern*' he repeatedly told his staff: 'Smash 'em, don't scatter 'em' or, more liberally, don't do things by halves. And yet inwardly, Heinz Guderian was often racked by doubt. 'I am a strange chap,' he wrote once. 'Sometimes

I feel fine and believe that everything I do will succeed and nothing bad can happen. Such illusions do not last long.' Outwardly, however, he impressed the coterie of junior officers who would eventually rise to become practitioners of mobile warfare. Guderian, his admiring deputy Walter Nehring observed, struggled 'almost alone against a world of naysayers'. Nehring was struck by his master's 'unshakable tenacity and persistence, his courage, his persuasive power, his firm belief in what he advocated'.[18] The persistence paid off – Beck was never the opponent of the panzer Guderian painted him as. On 15 October, 1935, Germany announced to the world it would form three armoured divisions: 1st Panzer in Weimar, 3rd Panzer in the capital of the Reich, and, in Würzburg, 2nd Panzer under one *Oberst* Heinz Guderian. By 1939, there would be seven such formations and four hybrid armoured-infantry divisions, *Leichte* (light) divisions. As for the weapons which were these formations' backbone, the Panzer I was followed by the Panzer II, no faster than its predecessor, but better armed, with a more potent engine and a 20mm cannon, the Panzer III with an even more powerful engine and 37mm cannon, and finally, the Panzer IV heavier and better armed still. But the Panzer III and IV were tanks of the future, not the present. In the summer of 1939 they were outnumbered ten to one by their older forebears.

Still, Heinz Guderian had his panzer and his panzer divisions. Now he developed his theories on how best to use them. They should have a single role: 'to smash enemy resistance quickly and decisively'. It was not enough to temporarily paralyse the foe or unnerve him, the panzer had to destroy the enemy on the battlefield. 'The panzer attack must be led with the greatest speed, taking advantage of the element of surprise, thrusting deep into enemy territory to prevent his reserves from intervening and to turn tactical success into operational success.'[19] Still there were those who believed otherwise. Over the winter of 1936–1937, Guderian worked on a manuscript at the urging of Oswald Lutz to convince the public as much as the army of the need for the tank. *Achtung! Panzer! – Look out! Panzers!* – was the bible for panzer crews and commanders, but there was little new in its pages; it merely summarised fifteen years of research by Guderian and fellow advocates of mobile warfare. It was, however, required reading for foreign attachés and military intelligence sections and from its title to its final paragraphs, it was a clarion call for the panzer – and for decisive action. 'Only time will tell who is right,' Guderian concluded. He continued:

It is incontrovertible that as a general rule new weapons call for new ways of fighting. You should not pour new wine into old vessels.

Actions speak louder than words. In the days to come, the Goddess of Victory will bestow her laurels only on those who are prepared to act with daring.[20]

The German Air Force possessed no Heinz Guderian. It possessed no singular man of vision. It did, however, possess Hermann Göring, the second man in the Third Reich, as its Commander-in-Chief. For better and worse, the German Air

Force, the Luftwaffe – literally 'air weapon' – owed its rebirth to the Great War fighter pilot turned politician. Göring had set out in life as an infantry officer before qualifying as a fighter pilot. He had scored 22 'kills' in the skies, rising to command the legendary *Jagdgeschwader 1* – 1st Fighter Squadron – the squadron of the Red Baron, in the final four months of the war. In peacetime he tried flying for civilian companies, before joining the Nazi Party in 1922 and taking part in Hitler's failed *Putsch* in Munich the following year. Göring was shot during the ensuing melee and fled the country, eventually ending up in a Swedish asylum for treatment for his addiction to morphine. He railed against the Jews – they even wanted to cut his heart out, he told doctors. He tried to take his own life. He suffered visions, heard voices, showed signs of self-contempt. He possessed, his doctors, noted, 'inflated self-esteem' and 'hysterical tendencies', was 'egocentric' and lacked 'fundamental moral courage'.[21] Yet when Hermann Göring returned to Germany from his self-imposed exile, he quickly re-established his position as a leading figure in the Nazi Party. In 1928 he was elected to the *Reichstag*. Three years later he was named its president. And, in 1933, when the Nazis seized power, he was named Prussian Minister of the Interior – in charge of the police. He would lay the foundations for the state police, the Gestapo, and a wiretapping and intelligence agency. In years to come, he would acquire new titles – and responsibilities: *Reichsforst- und Jägermeister* (Reich forestry and hunting master) and head of the Four Year Plan, the economic strategy to prepare the nation for war. And from March 1933, he would be in charge of the new Air Ministry, ostensibly to develop civil and commercial aviation; in reality, the aim was to create a new German Air Force.

Hermann Göring could only provide the impetus; he possessed neither the application nor aptitude to create an air force, for the Reich possessed none – it was forbidden under the Versailles Treaty. Germany barely even possessed an aviation industry. More than half the 4,000 people employed in it worked for the Junkers company, but each year the firm could produce no more than eighteen of its new three-engine Ju52s which would become the mainstay of the air force's transport fleet – and only then if it abandoned all other production. It would take an organiser of supreme ability to galvanise this industry. Hermann Göring found him in the shape of Lufthansa director Erhard Milch, a fellow Great War flier – but an observer rather than a pilot. In seven years, Milch had turned Lufthansa from nothing into an airline of national and international standing. Now, as Göring's deputy, he would be expected to do the same for a military force. 'Money,' Göring told him, 'is no object.' And perhaps it wasn't. Between 1934 and 1938, more than thirteen billion Reichsmarks were ploughed into the Luftwaffe – more than one third of Germany's defence budget. Investment in the air force reached its peak in 1937; for every ten Reichsmarks spent on the Wehrmacht, four went to the Luftwaffe. And Erhard Milch spent it – every penny. Between the Nazis' seizure of power and the outbreak of war, German industry produced more than 15,000 aircraft for the Luftwaffe. But Milch did not merely organise the Reich's aero industry, ruthlessly at times, he also laid the foundations for a truly modern air force – 20,000 strong in 1935, 400,000 strong in 1939 – with new airfields, a first-rate ground organisation, navigational aids, and he saw to it that crews were trained to fly in any weather, at all times of day. Milch was 'a very able man, very efficient and energetic,' Göring's adjutant Karl Bodenschatz recalled, but fellow Luftwaffe officers sneered at him – 'they considered him a businessman and administrator'. He was also 'pathologically ambitious'. He craved rank, he craved a front-line command, he clashed with Göring frequently – and Hermann Göring, the self-styled '*Der Eiserne*' ('The Iron One'), in turn felt threatened by Milch's ability.[22]

And there was no denying Erhard Milch's ability. But he was not a thinker, not a strategist, not a tactician. More than 200 of the most able General Staff officers transferred from the army to the clandestine air force to grapple with such issues. The undoubted star was Walther Wever, regarded by his contemporaries as the finest military brain in the army. Wever was an infantry officer. He knew little of air power, but threw himself into his new role as the Chief of the Luftwaffe General Staff. He learned to fly. He mulled over the potential wars of the future – and the weapons the Reich would need to wage them: fighters, ground-support aircraft to assist the soldier on the battlefield, long-range bombers to strike at the enemy's heartland. And like many aerial enthusiasts of the age, he saw great possibilities in the skies. 'The realms of the air are not restricted to the fronts of the Army; they are above and behind the Army, over the coasts and seas, over the whole nation, and over the whole of the enemy's territories.' Armies could be halted by obstacles, natural or man-made, they could bleed to death 'in the mud of shell craters and trenches. In the air forces we have a weapon which knows no such boundaries.'[23] Walther Wever would never realise his dreams; he died in an air crash in the summer of 1936.

With and without Walther Wever, the Luftwaffe mushroomed. But none of his successors possessed his ability to work with both Göring *and* Milch – nor his breadth of vision. Before 1936 was out, plans for a four-engine bomber, at the heart of Wever's strategy, were cancelled; Germany lacked the engines to power them and the raw materials to build them. Instead, the punch of the Luftwaffe would be provided by two medium-range twin-engine bombers, Dornier's Do17 – developed as a fast 'air mail' aircraft – and Heinkel's He111. Dornier's 'flying pencil', named for its slender fuselage, could carry a payload of just 2,200lbs; the more sturdy Heinkel could deliver 5,500lbs of bombs. Yet neither the Do17 nor the He111 could drop their bombs with pinpoint accuracy – much of their effect, actual and moral, was scattered. Not so the aircraft which came to symbolise the Luftwaffe, the Junkers Ju87 *Sturzkampfflugzeug* – dive-bomber, commonly abbreviated to *Stuka*.

The Ju87 was born not on German soil but in the United States where Great War 'ace' Ernst Udet had watched Curtiss Hawk dive-bombers performing and had even been permitted to pilot one. At the end of 1933, Udet brought two Hawks back from the USA and demonstrated them at the Luftwaffe's test airfield in Rechlin, sixty miles outside Berlin, climbing to more than 13,000ft before plunging the Hawk earthwards, pulling the aircraft up just a few hundred feet from the ground. Within two months, Hermann Göring decided his air force needed the dive-bomber.

There were other *Stukas* before the Ju87, but none so numerous nor so effective. The first prototype appeared in 1936 and immediately proved popular with pilots and senior Luftwaffe officers alike. There would be no more powerful image of 'Blitzkrieg' in the Reich and beyond than the Ju87 hurtling towards the ground, the sirens on its landing gear – *Jericho Trompete* (trumpets of Jericho) – wailing, terrifying the enemy below. Not only did the Ju87 sound distinctive, it looked distinctive with its angled wings and its fixed undercarriage. That fixed undercarriage and the Ju87's single engine limited its top speed to under 200mph (although improved models reaching the front line from 1938 could manage 235mph). In the dive, pilots were prone to passing out as they threw the aircraft groundwards, at speeds of more than 350mph. They often failed to pull up in time and plunged their aircraft into the earth. Brakes which slowed the Ju87 in its dive ensured the bomber was vulnerable to anti-aircraft guns – especially as it pulled up having released its bombs. Yet for all these failings, the Ju87 had one winning attribute: 'It promised the greatest success with a minimum expenditure of material and manpower,' observed future Luftwaffe general Adolf Galland. A skilled Ju87 pilot could deliver his 1,100lb payload to within thirty yards of its target – even an average pilot scored a twenty-five per cent success rate; the finest He111 and Do17 pilots, on the other hand, were fortunate if one in fifty of their bombs hit their mark. Senior Luftwaffe officers came to regard the dive-bomber as the ultimate panacea. What can only be called *Stuka* mania swept through the High Command. 'Single precision attacks on pin-pointed targets instead of mass attacks on large areas became the motto of German bomber strategy,' Galland recalled.[24] Bombers already under development now had to be able to dive as well as drop their bombs horizontally. The finest medium bomber of the age, the Ju88, might have been ready for operations over Poland; instead its development was dogged as engineers tried to make it capable of diving.

Whether it possessed *Stukas*, medium, or even heavy bombers, the Luftwaffe relished its independence. It was to attack the enemy's air force, support the army and navy, strike at the enemy's 'sources of strength' and the 'flow of that strength to the front' – enemy columns on the move, troop concentrations, rail lines and roads, airfields, bridges.[25] It did not, as Walther Wever had set out, wish to be 'restricted to the fronts of the Army'. But neither Wever nor his successors ruled out the possibility of German aircraft intervening directly on the battlefield. It was not a mission the Luftwaffe relished, but it was one it would increasingly be called upon to perform – providing direct support for ground troops as 'flying artillery'. It was a role the fledgling Luftwaffe performed admirably in Spain under the banner of the *Legion Condor*, the 'volunteers' dispatched to support Franco. The world, however, would remember the Spanish 'volunteers' for a singular act on the afternoon of Monday, 26 April, 1937. The *Legion Condor*'s bombers were unleashed upon the historic Basque town of Guernica, ostensibly to halt the retreat of enemy forces, but the aim in part was also to terrorise its inhabitants. The German bombers succeeded on both counts.

The bombing of Guernica was immortalised on canvas by Picasso and in newsprint by *Times* correspondent George Steer, who visited the town the following day and found it 'flaming from end to end. The reflection of the flames could be seen in the clouds of smoke above the mountains from ten miles away.' All through the night the timber-framed houses of Guernica toppled into the streets. The town, Steer declared, was not a military objective. No, he continued, 'the object of the bombardment was seemingly the demoralisation of the civil population and the destruction of the cradle of the Basque race.' The world's media, recalled staff officer Erwin Jaenecke, 'outdid itself in condemning the German Hun and their work of destruction'. Newspapers talked of 'mountains of corpses of the innocent' and 'waves of Hitler bombers which darkened the skies'.[26]

Guernica may have blackened Germany's name but Adolf Hitler was not troubled. He wanted the world to fear his air force. Numbers. Numbers were what mattered, Hermann Göring explained to his staff, 'to impress Hitler and enable Hitler, in turn, to impress the world'. By the summer of 1939, the Luftwaffe had grown into a formidable force. At its public unveiling in the spring of 1935, the Luftwaffe comprised thirty-four *Staffeln* – roughly equivalent to a squadron in the RAF – and numbered more than 18,000 men. Four years later, there were more than 270 *Staffeln*, seventy of them fighter units, nearly 100 bomber and twenty-two dive-bomber formations.[27]

The world was indeed impressed. Aviator Charles Lindbergh, who had famously flown single-handedly from the New World to the Old, toured the Reich, its aviation factories and airfields extensively in the mid-30s, claimed the Luftwaffe was 8,000 aircraft strong. As Hitler threatened Czechoslovakia in the final days of September 1938, Lindbergh warned that 'German air strength is greater than that of all other European countries combined,' and was getting stronger. The Reich, he continued, 'now has the means of destroying London, Paris and Prague if she wishes to do so.' France's leaders shared Lindbergh's fears. 'French cities would be laid in ruins,' one air force general predicted, while a French minister warned 'towns will be wiped out, our women and children slaughtered'. In Britain the government prepared to deal with 20,000 casualties a day should the Luftwaffe bomb their cities.[28]

The Luftwaffe revelled in the image it had created. An internal report in the spring of 1939 declared the Reich's air force more potent than any other in Europe. It was better armed, better trained, better equipped, better led. When front-line commander Hellmuth Felmy warned that the Luftwaffe was not the sword Hermann Göring proclaimed it to be, he was brushed aside. 'I have not asked for a memorandum weighing the possibilities of success and pointing out our weaknesses,' Göring snapped. 'These things I myself know.' Of course he did not. The minutiae of Luftwaffe strengths and weaknesses did not trouble the Iron Man; he preferred to retreat to his country estate of Carinhall – named for his late first wife – northeast of Berlin where the delights of hunting, art, even an impressive model railway, all proved much more enticing than the affairs of state. The naysayers were right; the Luftwaffe in 1939 was an impressive weapon of war, but it was also deeply flawed. It lacked aircrew and ground crew. It lacked instructors and training schools. It lacked aircraft. In six years, the Reich had created an air force from scratch but, as Erhard Milch testified at

Nuremberg, 'it would have been impossible for any soldier in any country to build an air force equal to the tasks with which we were faced from 1939.'[29]

The massed phalanxes of the panzer divisions and the squadrons of the Luftwaffe could – and were meant to – bedazzle. But at the heart of the German Army in 1939 was not Guderian's armour, nor Göring's bombers, but man and beast. 'Even in the age of the increasing mechanisation of warfare, infantry form the backbone of the modern army and remain the queen of the battlefield,' declared Gerd von Rundstedt, Germany's senior field commander in 1939. All but eight of the fifty-four divisions earmarked for battle in Poland were infantry or mountain infantry – and all but four of those relied on the horse as their principal means of transport, demanding more than half a million animals in all. Siegfried Knappe was dismayed when his train pulled past the barracks in Jena which were to be his home as he began his training as an artilleryman. There were stables – and horses. He prodded the middle-aged man sitting next to him. 'You mean they still pull the artillery with horses?' They did, the gentleman assured him. 'Suddenly the artillery lost all its glamour and appeal.' Knappe had imagined a world of motorised artillery. Instead, he would be leading a horse-drawn battery into battle. 'I wanted to turn around and go back home.'[30]

The ordinary German soldier, the *Landser*, endured sixteen weeks of basic training. Electrician William Lubbeck arrived at the barracks of 47th Infantry Regiment in Lüneberg, near Hamburg. He collected his *feldgrau* tunic, stone-grey trousers, helmet and boots, was subjected to a quick lesson on saluting, then joined his training company. By German standards, the Lüneberg barracks were good: eight men to a room, running water, communal showers and toilets – which the men had to clean. The men learned drill first, marching in order, and, of course, the *Paradeschritt* – goose step. The men rose at 5am to shave, wash, tidy their barracks, make their beds – or, in the case of Knappe, to muck out the stables. After a simple breakfast of bread and coffee, there were lectures, drill exercises in the parade square, marching, sports, marksmanship. The men assembled daily at 1.30pm on the parade ground for inspection, before training resumed until the evening meal around 6.30pm. Even then the day was not done and the exhausted trainees would fall into bed around 10pm. The regime was harsh. '*Schweiss spart Blut*' ('sweat saves blood') their instructors imparted. A non-commissioned officer, one *Stabsgefreiter* (staff corporal) Weizsacker, made a point of driving Siegfried Knappe and his comrades particularly hard. 'All we could do,' the soldier recalled, 'was hunker down and endure his abuse.' But sweat *did* save blood. The men were drilled repeatedly on cleaning, loading and firing the 98K Mauser, the *Landser*'s standard-issue rifle, and told repeatedly to dig a foxhole whenever they could. Such advice would save many lives.[31]

In the autumn of 1937, Siegfried Knappe was selected as an officer cadet where the training was rather less brutal, but no less intensive. The officer spent the majority of the day in the classroom studying tactics, military history, topography, reading maps, plus three hours in the field, chiefly on infantry exercises. There was sport: swimming, fencing, running, boxing, horse riding. And there were social graces to learn: dances, the art of 'drinking socially without getting drunk'. Compared with basic training at Jena, life at the five

Kriegsschule – military schools – was 'quite pleasant'. It was also exceptionally thorough. By the end of their nine months of training, each new *Leutnant* could, in theory, lead an infantry battalion on the battlefield. Bruno Steinbach from Dortmund volunteered for the mountain infantry, the *Gebirgsjäger*, aged twenty-one in 1935. He relished the spartan regime of officer training at the *Kriegsschule* in Hannover. 'The school I am passing through is hard,' he recorded in his diary, 'but I am glad that nothing has been spared me. There can be no tiredness – you must train your will to the utmost. Your body must obey your will. Hunger, thirst, pain have to be silenced if the will demands it.' Why did Steinbach put himself through such hardship? To be an officer. 'What did I see in the officer? I saw a leader, who penetrated the enemy with the men entrusted to him, I saw the warrior who can fight – and die – for a great, worthwhile good. I would like to stand in front of my men as a *Leutnant* and set an example to them which they can model themselves on in every respect.'[32]

Yet for all the ardour, for all the energy, for all the billions of Reichsmarks lavished on the Wehrmacht in six years of National Socialist rule, the German Army was an uneven beast. Four-hour-long parades were all well and good but, observed infantry division operations officer *Major* Siegfried Westphal, 'the brilliant façade could not, however, hide from any German expert observer the grave inherent weaknesses.' The rapid expansion of the Army had come at a cost – and not merely a financial one. 'Quantity was to come before quality,' wrote Westphal. The Officer Corps had grown sixfold since 1933, while in the space of a dozen years the number of artillery regiments had ballooned from seven to more than 100. The consequence of such expansion was a dilution of the nucleus of the German Army: fewer than one in ten soldiers in a division was a regular soldier; the rest were reservists or conscripts, while only one in six officers was 'a thoroughly-trained professional soldier'; the rest were Great War officers, reservists, new recruits. 'Despite all their enthusiasm for soldiering, despite all their zeal, it was not possible to pick up the knowledge and experience that the nucleus had collected in years of careful training,' wrote Westphal, a professional soldier with twenty-one years' experience. 'A war-worthy army cannot be improvised,' he noted. 'Thorough training needs time and consistency. Neither were available.'[33]

What the German soldier lacked in training and expertise, he would make up for with his zeal and National Socialist ardour, Adolf Hitler believed. For the army marching before him that Thursday was very much *his* Army. Not only had Hitler been the driving force behind its expansion, but he also had an army which was loyal to him. Not to the Reich, not to the German *Volk*, not to position of Reich Chancellor, but to the person of Adolf Hitler alone. Every soldier, sailor and airman had pledged to 'show unconditional obedience to Adolf Hitler, the Führer of the German Reich and people, Supreme Commander of the Wehrmacht, and that at all times I will be ready, as a brave soldier, to give my life for this oath.' But the German Army's loyalty to Hitler and his regime went much deeper than the oath. The German soldier was not allowed to be 'politically active', he could not be a member of any political party. He was expected to be a *nur Soldat* – pure soldier. And yet, within four months of the

National Socialists seizing power, defence minister Werner von Blomberg told fellow officers: 'There remains only one thing: to serve the National Socialist movement with complete devotion.' Over the next five years, Blomberg and his staff bound the 'apolitical' Armed Forces to the regime. The Nazi eagle and swastika were incorporated in the soldier's jacket and helmet; the *Hitlergruss* – Nazi salute – was to be given by men when not wearing headgear; military libraries should be furnished with copies of *Mein Kampf* and take the Nazi Party organ, *Völkischer Beobachter*, daily; letters should end with 'Heil Hitler'; every officers' mess was to display a *fitting* portrait of the Führer; portraits and busts of the Kaiser and the Royals were to be relegated to side rooms and the Kaiser's birthday was not to be celebrated; Jews were banned from the armed forces, unless they had served in the Great War or their fathers had died for the Fatherland in that conflict; the German soldier could only be of true German blood – and he could only marry a woman of true German blood; officers and Party members should meet socially, National Socialist speakers should be invited to address the men, and at least two hours should be devoted each month to lectures on political issues to ensure the army adopted 'National Socialist ideology'.[34] Just how much the Wehrmacht had adopted 'National Socialist ideology' was evident on Adolf Hitler's fiftieth birthday.

Soldiers, sailors and airmen unable to attend the great parade in Berlin gathered on their parade grounds. In Keil, in Münster, in Berchtesgaden, in Königsberg, the men of the Wehrmacht were reminded of the greatness of the *Volk* and their Führer by their commanding officers. In the Silesian town of Liegnitz, today Legnica in Poland, *Generalleutnant* Erich von Manstein addressed his 18th Infantry Division. 'Today we thank God that He gave the German *Volk* this great son, that he held his hand over him – the heroic front-line solder – through all the storms in the World War, shielded his life during the years of struggle and so visibly blessed his rule as Führer of the Reich.' The Führer, Manstein continued, had made a defenceless nation strong again, he had led the Reich 'from disgrace and impotency to greatness'. He had marched into the Rhineland, into Austria, the Sudetenland, Bohemia and Moravia, the Memelland:

> If it seems that a hostile world wants to build walls around Germany, to block the path of the German Volk to their future, to prevent the Führer from completing his work, then today we soldiers pledge to our Führer: we will protect him from all forces which attempt to stop his work; we will carry out his will wherever he leads us!

The Führer's work was not yet complete, *Generalleutnant* Gotthard Heinrici told his 16th Infantry Division's in Münster. 'We are still in the middle of developments,' he continued. 'In these very days we have seen how the world would like to join forces to question the right of the German people and the Führer to their successes. We know that they will not succeed if the German people follows its Führer united and faithfully.' And in the square by the gymnasium in the Alpine town of Sonthofen, 1st *Gebirgsjäger* Division's ruthless commander Ludwig Kübler assured his mountain infantrymen there was no need to fear for the future. 'If Adolf Hitler leads Germany it will be invincible against the entire world. We German soldiers are nevertheless ready to keep our solemn oath.'[35]

In Danzig too they celebrated on 20 April, but in their Führer's absence. The port was 'decorated as never before'. Illuminated portraits of Hitler were placed in windows – a demonstration of 'the unbreakable bond between Adolf Hitler and *German* Danzig to the entire world'. The city's leader, Albert Forster, was not there to witness this demonstration of loyalty; he was in Berlin with Nazi Party grandees paying homage to their leader. Forster presented Hitler with an elaborate casket containing a scroll proclaiming him an honorary citizen of Danzig. Long after night enveloped Berlin on this public holiday, Adolf Hitler stood on the chancellery balcony overlooking the Wilhelmstrasse. Twenty-one platoons of the old guard, veteran Nazis, including a guard of honour formed by men from Danzig and beyond, marched under torchlight, as their leader took the salute.[36]

After the theatrics, Adolf Hitler returned to politics on Friday, 28 April, when he summoned the deputies of the Reichstag. Since he had last gathered his cronies, he had marched into Czechoslovakia and Memel. But his foes too had been lining up against him: Britain had voiced her formal support for a defensive alliance with Poland, while across the Atlantic Roosevelt called for peace in Europe. Ostensibly, this latest oration by Hitler was a tirade against the American President for meddling in affairs which did not concern him. But, he told his delegates, he could not overlook recent developments. He banished the Anglo-German Naval Agreement to the history books, then turned his attention to Poland. One issue, and one issue above all, had to be resolved – and that was the fate of Danzig. Danzig was a German city. It wanted to be part of Germany once more. Poland would not allow it. In view of continued intransigence in Warsaw, and Poland's touting for allies in a possible war against the Reich, Hitler declared he had no choice but to tear up the non-aggression pact with the Poles. 'Those who should be blamed are the conjurors of Versailles,' he declared. 'Either through malice or recklessness, they placed one hundred powder kegs across Europe, each one with a fuse it is virtually impossible to extinguish.'[37]

Poland's response was more measured, more erudite, more succinct. At mid-day on 5 May, Jozef Beck rose before the *Sejm*, the Polish Parliament. His spoke for just thirty minutes – a week before Hitler had rambled on for five times as long. He spoke calmly, with quiet determination. He rejected all the German charges with sound arguments. He would not give up Danzig or allow motorways and railway lines to be driven across the Corridor – not, at any rate, for some vague assurances from Hitler. The time had come, he told the delegates of the *Sejm*, to stand up to Germany.

Peace is precious and desirable. Our generation has shed blood in several wars. Surely it deserves a period of peace. But peace, like almost everything else in this word, has its price, a high price, but not infinitesimal. We Poles do not understand the concept of 'peace at any price'. There is one thing in the life of men, nations and states which is priceless – honour.[38]

It was what the Polish people wanted to hear in the spring of 1939. The streets of Warsaw were deserted as Beck spoke. The foreign minister captured the mood of his people perfectly. Few Poles sought to appease Hitler; even the slightest concession to Germany was seen not merely as a sign of weakness but as a nail in Poland's coffin.[39]

In Berlin, they also listened to Jozef Beck's short speech. The Führer, the *Deutsche Allgemeine Zeitung* observed, had given Warsaw 'a great opportunity to drown the powder keg of Poland and Warsaw. Poland has chosen.'

Adolf Hitler had also chosen. He had chosen war, he told his senior commanders. The heads of all three armed forces and their deputies gathered in the study of the New Reich Chancellery on 22 May. Time and again he came back to the constant theme of his policies from the *Kampfzeit* – the period of struggle before 1933 – to the present day: Germany's need for land in the East, *Lebensraum*, living space. Eighty million Germans needed room to breathe. The greater their domain, the greater the nation. 'It is not Danzig that it is stake,' the Führer explained. No, what mattered was expanding Germany's living space in the East. 'Land in the East' meant Poland. Poland, a mortal foe of Germany, a long-standing enemy of Germany. 'There is no question of sparing Poland,' he said unequivocally. 'There will be war.' He would do all he could to keep Britain and France out of any war between the Reich and Poland. But such a war would come – and it would be a conflict 'of life and death'. And if it must come to another European conflagration, then so be it. 'The idea of getting out cheaply is dangerous,' Hitler told his audience. 'There is no such possibility. We must then burn our boats and it will no longer be a question of right or wrong, but of to be or not to be for 80,000,000 people.'[40] Before the summer faded, Adolf Hitler would burn his boats.

Notes

1. Schenk, *Hitlers Mann in Danzig*, p. 114.
2. DGFP, D, v, Doc.119.
3. DGFP, D, v, Doc.126 and Watt, pp. 70–1.
4. *Völkischer Beobachter*, 31/1/39.
5. Author's papers and KTB Engel, 18/2/39.
6. Based upon DGFP, D, iv, Doc.228, Keitel, pp. 78–80, Schroeder, p. 88 and *Hitler's Table Talk*, 13/1/42.
7. DGFP, D, v, Docs.399, 402 and Domarus, iii, p. 1515.
8. Lipski, pp. 503–4.
9. Hartmann, Christian and Slutsch, Sergei, 'Franz Halder und die Kriegsvorbereitungen im Frühjahr 1939. Eine Ansprache des Generalstabschefs des Heeres,' VfZ, Band 45, 1997, pp. 476–95.
10. Sword, pp. 112–18.
11. DGFP, D, vi, Doc.115.
12. *Völkischer Beobachter*, 20/4/39.
13. Uhl and Eberle, *Hitler Book*, p. 42.
14. Based on Schroeder, p. 94 and *Völkischer Beobachter*, 20/4/39 and 21/4/39.
15. Based upon Bradley, *Generaloberst Heinz Guderian und die Entstehungsgeschichte des modernen Blitzkrieges*, p. 33, 77, 90, 153, 171 and Guderian, *Panzer Leader*, p. 24.

16. Bradley, *Generaloberst Heinz Guderian und die Entstehungsgeschichte des modernen Blitzkrieges*, p. 193 and Macksey, pp. 54–5.
17. Guderian, *Panzer Leader*, pp. 29–30 and Bradley, *Generaloberst Heinz Guderian und die Entstehungsgeschichte des modernen Blitzkrieges*, p. 176.
18. Macksey, p. 61, Bradley, *Generaloberst Heinz Guderian und die Entstehungsgeschichte des modernen Blitzkrieges*, pp. 23, 173–4.
19. *Generalmajor* Heinz Guderian, 'Die Panzertruppen und ihr Zusammenwirken mit den anderen Waffen', 1936. Cited in Bradley, *Generaloberst Heinz Guderian und die Entstehungsgeschichte des modernen Blitzkrieges*, p. 208.
20. Guderian, *Achtung! Panzer!*, p. 212.
21. Irving, *Göring*, pp. 87–8.
22. Irving, *The Rise and Fall of the Luftwaffe*, p. 35, Suchenwirth, *Command and Leadership in the German Air Force*, p. 131, and SRGG1225 and SRGG1231 in NA WO208/4170.
23. Suchenwirth, *Command and Leadership in the German Air Force*, p. 8.
24. Galland, p. 72.
25. Maier, *Germany and the Second World War*, vol.2, pp. 35–6.
26. *Times*, 28/4/37, Maier, *Guernica*, p. 160 and Oven, *Hitler und der Spanische Bürgerkrieg*, p. 413.
27. Murray, p. 34; the figures are based on Hooton, pp. 276–9.
28. Cable from Joseph Kennedy, 22/9/38, in FRUS, 1938, I, pp. 72–3 and Corum, James S, 'Inflated by Air: Common Perceptions of Civilian Casualties from Bombing', Unpublished paper, Maxwell Air Force Base, Alabama, April 1998.
29. Taylor, *Munich: The Price of Peace*, p. 866 and IMT, viii, p. 259.
30. Knappe, pp. 99–104.
31. Westwood, *German Infantryman*, pp. 9–12, Knappe, p. 104 and Lubbeck, pp. 55, 57.
32. Knappe, pp. 117–22 and 'Aus den Briefen und Aufzeichnungen Bruno Steinbachs', *Die Gebirgstruppe*, Heft Nr.2–4, 1957, pp. 283–84.
33. Westphal, pp. 36–9.
34. Carsten, p. 397, O'Neill, pp. 119–20 and Noakes, Jeremy (ed), *Nazism*, p. 641.
35. Kopp, Roland, 'Die Wehrmacht feiert: Kommandeurs Reden zu Hitlers 50 Geburtstag', *Militärgechitchliche Zeitschrift*, Vol.62, 2003, pp. 512 and 522 and Hürtner, Johannes, 'Es herrschen Sitten und Gebräuche, geanuso wie im 30-jährigen Krieg: Das erste Jahr des deutschen-sowjetischen Krieges in Dokumenten des Generals Heinrici,' VfZ, Vol.48, No. 2, p. 343.
36. Schenk, *Hitlers Mann in Danzig*, p. 108.
37. *Völkischer Beobachter*, 29/4/39.
38. Beck's speech in author's papers.
39. DGFP, D, vi, Doc.355.
40. DGFP, D, vi, Doc.433.

CHAPTER THREE

Is It War or Peace?

The blow must be struck. We must act now or go under.

– ADOLF HITLER

Men, this madman really is waging war.

– OBERST FREIHERR VON UND ZU GILSA

IN THE forest of Zoppot, the spa resort half a dozen miles north of Danzig, thousands of people enjoyed Wagner's *Ring of the Nibelung*; Erna Schlüter from Hamburg State Opera was mesmerising as Brünnhilde, while Wilhelm Schirp of the German Opera House in Berlin was the embodiment of Hagen. Danzig architect Otto Frick won the competition to design a new opera house with an auditorium holding 2,000 people. On the seafront the new *Kraft durch Freude* (Strength through Joy) hall for holidaymakers, was opened; in years to come, workers enjoying state-sponsored holidays would also be able to stroll out over the Baltic on a pier. The beaches and baths of the suburb of Heubude, on the banks of the Mottlau river, brimmed with Danzigers looking to escape the stifling heat. Steamers ploughed up and down the Bay of Danzig ferrying day trippers to the spas and beaches. August 1 was the busiest day of the season – it was also the hottest.

The city's newspapers, the *Danziger Vorposten* and *Neueste Nachrichten*, juxtaposed trivial articles – five winners of the Reich's business competition hailed from the port, including a confectionary producer; three world records were set in Berlin's Olympic Stadium; a new exhibition had opened in the House of German Art – alongside affirmations of Danzig's resolve to defend herself, of her leaders' meetings with the Führer, and continuing tension between Poland and Germany – a brownshirt shot and killed by a Polish border guard and Polish boy scouts imprisoned for a month for accidentally straying across the frontier.

Great War veteran Heinrich Dombrowski strolled up the heights in Zoppot, where Danzig's elite lived in fine mansions and villas. The vistas were magnificent. It was why Dombrowski came here with his family. 'It's not saying too much to regard Danzig's environment as one of the most beautiful and attractive places on earth,' he mused one summer's afternoon. 'Lakes, mountains and forest in happy union filling any nature lover with incredible pleasure.' Like most of the port's residents, Dombrowski, a reserve infantry officer, followed political events acutely. The newspapers were filled with 'all manner of alarming reports'. And like most Danzigers, Heinrich Dombrowski preferred to enjoy high summer on the Baltic. 'No-one wants to believe that dark thunderous clouds are gathering on the political horizon, that in the near future the harsh storm of war could burst.' But it was impossible to ignore those gathering clouds. As he enjoyed his summer stroll, Dombrowski spied constructors at work in the roads around the villas and spas of Zoppot: the men were building tank barriers.[1]

In Danzig itself, Joseph Goebbels had already stoked the fires of war. The propaganda minister escaped the oppressive heat of the capital to spend the weekend of 17 and 18 June in the free city, ostensibly to celebrate the city's annual cultural festival. From the moment he touched down at the airport in the suburb of Langfuhr, Goebbels was lauded by the Danzig populace. Greeted by a smiling Albert Forster, the minister was driven straight to the *Staatstheater* for a performance of dance by the German State Theatre. A crowd 'spontaneously' gathered outside; their cries could be heard inside the auditorium. When the performance was over, the diminutive minister stepped out on to the balcony to address the multitude – again 'spontaneously'. Caught up by the emotion of the day, Goebbels struggled to speak. His words were frequently drowned out by screaming Danzigers. They chanted: '*Ein Volk, ein Reich, ein Führer!*' – one nation, one empire, one leader. They applauded, cheered. They shouted down Polish claims to their city with cries of 'pfui', whistled, or yelled: 'The Jews and the Poles want to get their hands on Danzig!' And above all they declared: '*Wir wollen heim ins Reich!*' We want to go home to the Reich. And they would go home to the Reich, Goebbels assured them.

> I stand here on the soil of a German city, before me are ten thousand Germans, and all around are countless examples of German culture, German customs, German art and German architecture. You Danzigers speak the language of Germans as we in the Reich do. You come from the same race and the same nationality; you are joined with us in a community with a shared destiny! And so you want to go home to the Reich!

The Poles, Goebbels proclaimed, wanted East Prussia and Silesia. They wanted to push their border westwards to the Oder. 'You wonder why they don't ask for the Elbe, to say nothing of the Rhine,' the minister quipped. The Danzigers laughed. 'Polish nationalists declare that they want to smash us Germans to pieces in a coming battle for Berlin.' The Führer would not allow that to happen. 'The National Socialist Reich is not weak but strong!' he continued. 'It is not powerless. Today it possesses the most impressive armed forces in the world!' For that reason, Goebbels assured his audience, they could 'look to future with safety. The National Socialist Reich stands at your side as you stand at its!' As the strains of *Deutschland, Deutschland über alles* died down, the propaganda minister was driven through the city to a reception in Zoppot. There was still time before bed for a trip around the Bay of Danzig in a boat. In the distance the lights of the Polish port of Gdynia, glittered in the June night. 'For how much longer?' Joseph Goebbels asked his diary.[2]

Long before Joseph Goebbels had arrived in Danzig, the Army General Staff had finalised their plans for the destruction of Poland – destruction, not invasion. The Poles would be dealt a series of 'powerful, surprise blows' from which they would never recover; they would not even be permitted time to complete mobilisation. For the Poles, unlike the Czechs, unlike the Austrians, would fight, 'fight for the existence of their state'. A handful of officers, notably the former head of operations on the General Staff, Erich von Manstein, had been picked to draw up the plan of attack in secret. The men knew that the Poles would stand and fight, rather than abandon their territory along the German border.[3] In doing so, the Poles would play into the Germans' hands, allowing the Wehrmacht to scythe through them. To smash Poland, the German Army would split its forces into two large army groups, North and South. South, under the venerable Gerd von Rundstedt, would strike from Silesia towards Warsaw and across southern Poland through Galicia to Lemberg; the austere Fedor von Bock's Army Group North would slice through the Polish Corridor and southwards from East Prussia towards the Polish capital. As plans of war go, *Fall Weiss* was simple. And as simple plans go it was remarkably effective.

The Army busied itself in the summer of 1939 with planning and training for the coming war with Poland. The *Kriegsmarine* was racked by petty intrigues and professional misgivings. The latter were provoked by the increasingly likely, and worrying, prospect of war with England – Germans almost exclusively referred to *England* rather than *Grossbritannien*. Repeatedly *Grossadmiral* Erich Raeder, the Navy's elderly and reserved Commander-in-Chief, told his staff that the German Fleet was ill-equipped for war against the Empire. Repeatedly Raeder's staff agreed with his assessment. The *Kriegsmarine*'s two battleships, three 'pocket' battleships, smattering of cruisers and fifty-seven U-boats were no match for Europe's strongest navy. The *Grossadmiral* knew it better than any man; 'war with England would mean *Finis Germania*,' he confided in his submarine commanders.[4] But in the critical summer of 1939, Erich Raeder's counsel was not sought by Adolf Hitler, for the admiral was out of favour at the Nazi court. A deeply religious, conservative man, the sixty-three-year-old *Grossadmiral* had quarrelled with Hitler about the marriage of his naval adjutant, *Korvettenkapitän* Alwin Albrecht. Albrecht was a fine, upstanding officer, but his wife had a past. 'A strikingly good looking woman,' Grete Albrecht had apparently enjoyed life to the full in Kiel. She had numerous male friends, one very wealthy one. She attended lavish parties where revellers shed most, if not all, of their clothes. Naval wives talked. This was not conduct befitting the wife of a respected naval officer. The high-minded Raeder agreed and demanded Hitler relieve his adjutant – or relieve his *grossadmiral*. As it was, Albrecht resigned, or was dismissed, from the *Kriegsmarine*, immediately given a senior rank in the *Nationalsozialistisches Kraftfahrkorps*, the Nazi's motoring organisation, and Erich Raeder spent the summer months of 1939 in the doghouse.[5]

At least the Luftwaffe's stock was high. It was justly feared across Europe, not least because of its achievements in Spain. Having helped secure a victory for Franco after three years of civil war, the 'volunteers' of the *Legion Condor* returned home to the Reich on the liner *Wilhelm Gustloff* before being afforded a parade through Berlin on 6 June. As it had done six weeks earlier, Berlin turned out in force to greet its heroes. Children were given the day off school. Girls from the *Bund Deutscher Mädel* – the Nazis' female youth movement – gently fixed flowers in the belts of 18,000 veterans, mostly Luftwaffe men wearing khaki-brown uniforms and field caps. The veterans goose-stepped down the East-West Axis past the gaudy tribune still standing from Hitler's birthday celebrations. They continued through the Brandenburg Gate as huge Spanish and swastika flags billowed beneath the arches in the gentle summer breeze. The men came to a halt in the Lustgarten, Frederick the Great's huge parade ground now in the shadow of the modern Berliner Dom cathedral. They formed up in front of the Kaiser's old palace, while 330 *Hitlerjugend* held 330 silver placards, each bearing the name of a *Legion Condor* 'volunteer' lost in Spain and each surrounded by a garish, golden laurel wreath. From a white dais Hitler – relatively briefly – addressed his 'hardened soldiers', thanking them for 'teaching our enemies a lesson'. The Führer was followed on the podium by his corpulent deputy. 'For the first time since the World War, German soldiers have returned home – but this time they could bring their flags home triumphantly,' Göring proclaimed. 'My comrades, you return to a greater Germany than the one which you left a few years ago. Greater Germany has arisen!' The Luftwaffe Commander-in-Chief spent much of the summer in his lodge *Carinhall* northeast of Berlin or cruising in his yacht *Carin II* – both drew their names from his first wife. He also spent much of the spring and summer of 1939 sulking and out of favour with his master; Göring had been uneasy about the occupation of Czechoslovakia and infuriated that his Führer had decided to act against Poland without consulting him. Perhaps a display of the Luftwaffe's latest weaponry might restore his position at court. On the afternoon of 3 July, the Führer and his entourage headed to the air force's research base at Rechlin, sixty miles outside Berlin on the banks of Müritzsee. The fighters He100 and Me109 both put on impressive displays, the former especially so. An overloaded He111 bomber lifted into the air with the aid of rockets. The star of the show, however, was the He176, a rocket-powered aircraft, making its maiden flight in front of Germany's leader. The Führer was impressed, but Göring's deputy Erhard Milch urged caution. '*Mein Führer*, the things which you are seeing here are things which will not be ready for use in front-line units for another five years.' Hitler did not listen. 'We are going to get a war,' he told the Luftwaffe officers. 'I don't know when. Come what may, this war must end in victory. Whether it lasts one, two or ten years, doesn't matter. It must be won.'[6]

The visit to Rechlin was a rare foray into the world of the military during the summer of 1939 for Adolf Hitler. He did little, too, to address the affairs of state. Instead, he spent the summer at his retreat in the Bavarian Alps, the Berghof, and his apartment in Munich, indulging his passion for the arts. He celebrated the 'Day of German Art' in Munich and graciously renamed the city's Adolf Hitler Platz Mussolini Platz in honour of the Italian leader's visit two years before. He toured the grounds of the *Reichsparteitag*, the annual Party rally in Nuremberg, to observe progress ahead of this year's gathering of the faithful, *Reichsparteitag des Friedens* (The Reich Party Day of Peace) due to begin on 1 September. He made a pilgrimage to the annual Wagner festival in Bayreuth. A fanfare sounded by his faithful SS bodyguard, the *Leibstandarte*, greeted him at the opening performance – *Der fliegende Holländer* (*The Flying Dutchman*), not performed since 1914 when war had forced its cancellation. There was more Wagner to enjoy in the days to come – *Tristan and Isolde* and *Die Walküre* – and a chance to relive the frivolous days of youth with a childhood friend, August Kubizek. The Führer signed postcards for Kubizek to sell in his native Austria. He gave his companion a tour of Wagner's house. The two stood over the composer's grave and paid their respects. And Kubizek reminded him of a fateful performance of Wagner's *Rienzi*, which the two men had witnessed more than thirty years before. Afterwards the pair had climbed the Freinberg, the mountain overshadowing Linz, where the young Hitler had expounded on his world vision. Now, he recounted the story at length. After three decades, it had assumed almost mythical proportions. 'In that hour,' he declared, 'it began.'[7]

Reservists reported for duty in the Reich as they did every summer. *Feldwebel* Hubert Hundreiser broke off his studies as a forestry undergraduate at the University of Munich to join his East Prussian comrades in 311th Infantry Regiment on summer exercises. If war was imminent, it wasn't apparent to Hundreiser and his fellow non-commissioned officers. There was a bit of rifle practice, but the men spent most of the summer swimming, playing sports, and on guard duty. Theology student Hans P, a Berliner, lined up with his company before their commander. The men's division was preparing for a large exercise, but Hans' company commander was angry, fed up with 'misunderstandings and idiotic rumours'. The exercise, he stressed, had nothing to do with the political situation. 'We are perhaps further away from war than most people believe,' the officer assured his men.[8]

Most Poles in Danzig had convinced themselves that war was coming. The mood of the Polish minority in the free city was dangerously fatalistic, the League of Nations Commissioner Carl Burckhardt noted. And war to the free city's Polish inhabitants, the Swiss diplomat observed, 'would mean the republic's last hurrah. People are beginning to convince themselves of an inevitable catastrophe.'[9]

To bolster Polish morale, there were rallies, demonstrations, gatherings, church services celebrating Polish strength, celebrating Polish history. Maps were published in newspapers and on postcards outlining Poland's historical claims to German soil as far west as Bremen and Würzburg. The anniversary of victory at Grunwald – Poland's defeat of the Teutonic Knights in 1410 – was cause for celebration across the land. There were memorial services in the cathedrals of Warsaw and Krakow. Poles demonstrated in front of Grunwald monuments, sang the anti-German anthem *Rota*. In Bydgoszcz, nationalist politicians addressed a rally, proclaiming the imminence of a 'new Grunwald'.[10]

Grunwald was not the only anniversary Poles commemorated in the summer of 1939. On 6 August, twenty-five years after Marshal Pilsudski and a band of legionnaires set out from Krakow to stir up revolutionaries in Russian-ruled Poland, anywhere between 100,000 and 150,000 Poles, some dressed in colourful national attire, met on the Blonia, the 120-acre common in the heart of the city. Krakow was in a festive mood. Decorations and illuminations abounded. Orchestras performed. The celebrations reached their climax on the Blonia with a speech by the nation's military leader, Marshal Edward Smigly-Rydz. Smigly-Rydz was not a great orator. His phrases were awkward; his was not the language of the common people. Today, the common people did not mind; the crowd applauded, cheered, cried 'We want Danzig'. Edward Smigly-Rydz was not about to abandon Poland's demands on the city. Danzig acted as 'the lungs of our economic life'. His country, he declared, sought peace, but it would fight if forced. 'An act of violence must be answered by force.'[11] Four days later, Germany responded.

On a stifling high-summer night, between 30,000 and 40,000 Danzigers crammed into the Lange Markt, the spiritual and governmental heart of the city since the Middle Ages. Perhaps twice as many again who could not hear Albert Forster in person listened to loudspeakers erected around the Hanseatic port. History grants little men their hour sporadically. Albert Forster was a little man and the summer of 1939 was his hour. The thirty-seven-year-old voice of Danzig was no Danziger. He hailed from Franconia in southern Germany, where he had fallen under the spell of the Nazi Party in 1923. He was, he readily admitted, 'a Hitler man'. His belief in his Führer was unshakable. In discussions he was immovable; like his master, he screamed and raged if he did not get his way. Adolf Hitler rewarded Forster for his loyalty by appointing him *Gauleiter* – Nazi district leader – of Danzig in 1930. The former bank clerk quickly set about invigorating the Party in the free city; within three years, the Nazis were the largest party in Danzig's senate and by the mid-30s they were the unquestioned political masters of the port.

In private, Albert Forster could be witty and entertaining, strumming his guitar after dinner with friends. He may – or may not – have been homosexual, despite his marriage to Gertrud (she bore him no children). In public, however, Forster was every bit as cold and ruthless as his official portrait, with deep-set eyes and arrogant expression, suggested. His hatred of the Jews – 'this foreign rabble, this dirty and greasy race' – was surpassed only by his ambition. For like his master, he knew Danzig was a pawn in a much greater game. 'If only war would come,' he once sighed to Hitler's staff. 'I wouldn't be a mere *Gauleiter* of Danzig. No, I'd be *Gauleiter* of the whole of West Prussia as soon as we'd chased out all the Poles.'[12]

To the people of Danzig, however, he was their leader, their voice. Albert Forster was an outstanding public speaker. He knew how to whip the masses up into a frenzy, and tonight in the free city's historic heart was no exception. 'The people of Danzig have endured these rabble-rousing Polish speeches for long enough,' he declared. The *Gauleiter* held up Polish newspapers and picked out choice quotes. 'The Poles do everything they can to stoke the fires of hate against all things German,' he explained. Poles talked openly of war, they talked of seizing Silesia and East Prussia, or drawing the new Polish-German boundary along the Oder. In Teschen (today Cieszyn) for example a politician had declared: 'Poland has not merely to defend something, it must conquer something.' There had been rallies where banners proclaimed: 'Forward across the Oder!' A Polish youth leader had received an inflammatory telegram, Forster revealed. 'We firmly believe that the coming war, a war for a greater Poland, will end in a new Tannenberg.' And now Poland's military leader had spoken: 'Soon we will march against Germany, our traditional foe, to finally draw its fangs.' The Danzigers booed. Cries of '*Pfui*' – rubbish – echoed around Lange Markt, rebounding off the Artushof – the great trading hall which could trace its history back six centuries – the 400-year-old city hall, and the similarly historic Grüne Tor gate. Forster continued to quote Smigly-Rydz. 'The first step on this march will be the occupation of Danzig. Only when Danzig and East Prussia have returned to the Polish mother country will Germany be persuaded to conclude a special agreement in the East. Prepare yourselves for the day of reckoning with arrogant German blood! The hour of revenge is near!' The crowd booed once more. There would be no hour of Polish revenge, Albert Forster assured them. 'Whatever happens, we will thwart any attack upon this hallowed German soil.' Danzigers wanted nothing more than to return to the bosom of the Reich. The masses applauded. And now Forster brought his speech to and end with the cries of 'Sieg Heil' ringing in his ears: 'May the day not be far off when we gather again here not for a protest rally, rather to celebrate Danzig's reunion with the Reich.'[13]

Barely twelve hours later, Albert Forster arrived at Danzig's airport where the four engines of Hitler's personal aircraft, a Focke-Wulf Condor, were idling. Already aboard was Swiss diplomat Carl Burckhardt, the League of Nations' High Commissioner in Danzig whose duty it was to preserve the free city's independence. Burckhardt had little time for the hot-headed *Gauleiter*. Reason was impossible with him; as far as Carl Burckhardt was concerned, Albert Forster was little more than Hitler's puppet. As the Condor turned over the Bay of Danzig and began to climb, Forster leaned forward and treated Burckhardt to tales of the days of the *Saalkämpfen* – the beer hall scraps with the communists, when he had grabbed a stool hurled at his Führer and thrown it back with equal force. The aircraft passed over Prague. The *Gauleiter* seemingly became seized by some nationalistic frenzy. Anyone who opposed the Führer's will, he warned Burckhardt, would be dealt with like Czechoslovakia, perhaps even more forcefully, for Hitler had acted with unheard of clemency towards the Czechs.

In his master's presence at the Kehlstein, the Führer's tea house atop a 5,500ft mountain close to his Bavarian retreat, Albert Forster was strangely silent. His master was not. His master was in a bellicose mood. He banged the table, laughed hysterically, railed at the British and French who blocked his plans at every opportunity, and became so worked up at one point he was unable to speak. All he wanted, he stressed, was a free hand in Eastern Europe. Germany needed grain and wood. If the Poles stopped 'threatening' Danzig, if they put an end to the 'misery' of the German minority in Poland he would be reasonable. So far, Hitler told his Swiss guest, he had not unleashed the full force of his propaganda machine. He had ordered newspapers not to report more sensational attacks on ethnic Germans in Poland, such as castrations, but his patience was at an end. If the Poles insulted him, if they attacked Danzig, he would strike – and strike hard. 'If there's even the slightest incident,' he warned Burckhardt, 'I will smash Poland without warning so that there won't be any trace of her afterwards.'[14]

The day after Carl Burckhardt was entertained in Hitler's tea house, Count Galeazzo Ciano found himself in the Great Hall of the Berghof being subjected to one of the Führer's interminable lectures. Hitler had little time for the Italian Foreign Minister – Mussolini's son-in-law; he was more playboy than statesman. Ciano, in turn, had little time for Hitler and even less for his foreign minister, the humourless, pompous and arrogant Joachim von Ribbentrop, a silent witness as his Führer outlined his plans, his hands sweeping across a large table covered with maps. It immediately dawned on Ciano that he was not here to be consulted. 'He has decided to strike and strike he will,' the dispirited Italian confided in his diary. Indeed he had. The Polish question had to be solved, the Führer explained, 'one way or the other by the end of August'. Hitler was in full flow when an aide burst in to hand him a short message from the embassy in Moscow. Months of tacit diplomacy had paid off: the Soviets wanted to see a German negotiator.[15]

Since the turn of the year, Hitler had been quietly wooing his sworn enemy. And his sworn enemy had been inclined to be wooed. At the eighteenth Communist Party Congress in March, Josef Stalin had signalled his willingness to listen to the Reich, launching a stinging attack on the Western democracies. He would not, the Soviet dictator told his Party comrades, 'give the warmongers, who are used to having others pull the chestnuts out of the fire for them, the opportunity of dragging our country into war'. He further signalled his intentions by dismissing his Jewish foreign minister, replacing him with Vyacheslav Molotov. That move, said Hitler, was decisive. Throughout the spring and summer of 1939, German and Soviet diplomats thrashed out a trade agreement between the two nations. But Adolf Hitler wanted more than a simple trade agreement as his foreign minister explained to the Soviet chargé d'affaires in Berlin, Georgi Astakhov. 'We believe there is no reason for enmity between our countries,' Ribbentrop explained. Of course, the ideologies of National Socialism and communism were diametrically opposed. But if the two nations could agree not to meddle in the internal affairs of the other, 'then further rapprochement is possible'. As for Poland, Danzig would soon be German once more. Ribbentrop had already written off the Poles as a military force; a campaign against them would be settled in a week to ten days. And if it came to war with the West, the Reich Foreign Minister boasted, there was nothing to fear. 'We believe in our strength,' he stressed with exaggerated emphasis, then added. 'There is no war which Adolf Hitler could lose.' Ribbentrop finally returned to the subject of Nazi-Soviet relations. He urged Astakhov to pass on his personal greetings to the Soviet leadership. Above all, the German asked repeatedly, he wanted to know whether Moscow was interested.[16]

Moscow *was* interested. It gave its answer ten days later – as French and British officials arrived in Russia to persuade the Soviet Union to join them in an alliance *against* Germany. The race was on: to conclude a treaty with the Russians before the Allies – and before the attack against Poland was unleashed.

Back in his adopted city, Albert Forster unveiled his 'secret weapon', Danzig's 'home guard' – the SS *Heimwehr Danzig* – a 1,300-strong paramilitary unit whose motto encapsulated their mission: *Lieber sterben als polnisch werden* – death is preferable to becoming Polish. On the sprawling Maifeld, the *Gauleiter* presented the *Heimwehr* with its flag in a symbolic ceremony, watched by more than 50,000 Danzigers whose 'hearths and homes' the new unit would safeguard. 'Let us make sure that the swastika, the symbol of light and the sun [*sic*], always flies before our whole German people in the future,' Forster told the ranks of the *Heimwehr*. 'We will then, no matter what may befall us, be the victor in the end.' The *Heimwehr*'s commander *Obersturmbannführer* Hans-Friedmann Goetze – like two-thirds of his men *not* a Danziger – accepted the standard willingly. 'We want to fight for what is holy to us. We can say honestly and proudly: we are ready for action.'

Two days later Forster addressed a rather smaller gathering, 3,000 Nazi Party faithful, in the suburb of Langfuhr. 'One day the measure of our patience will be exhausted and then woe to those who have so sorely tried us,' he told his audience. 'There is a storm coming, but we are sure that when it has passed, the Führer will march triumphantly into your city.'[17]

Interested though they were, the Soviets had shown little haste in clinching a treaty with National Socialist Germany. For more than a week Hitler and Ribbentrop had awaited an invitation from Moscow. It took a personal letter from the Führer to his Soviet counterpart to hurry Moscow along. At nightfall on Monday, 21 August, the telephone rang at Ribbentrop's villa retreat near Salzburg: Molotov expected to see him in the Russian capital in two or three days to conclude a treaty of friendship and non-aggression. Ribbentrop immediately called his master a few miles away at the Berghof. 'Marvellous! I congratulate you,' a delighted Führer proclaimed. He put the receiver down and hammered the wall with his fists in joy, exclaiming: 'I have the world in my pocket!' Hitler was still beaming as he sat down to supper with his entourage. The meal was interrupted by an aide who handed him a teletype from the Foreign Ministry, a letter from Stalin. 'The peoples of our countries need peaceful relations,' the Soviet leader wrote. 'I hope that the German-Soviet non-aggression pact will bring about a decided turn for the better in relations between our two countries.' He read the letter, paused for a moment, then thumped the table so hard that the glasses shook. 'I have them! I have them!' he shouted, his voice trembling with excitement. The meal resumed. It was only afterwards that Hitler gathered his entourage, holding up Stalin's telegram as he explained: 'We are going to conclude a non-aggression pact with Russia.' There were audible gasps. With the Great Hall still buzzing, Hitler took his official photographer Heinrich Hoffmann by the arm. He wanted events in Moscow recorded for posterity. But more than that, he wanted Hoffmann to convey a message to Stalin. Staring at the Alps through the huge window which dominated the room, he confided in his photographer. 'That man in the Kremlin always sees diplomats. You shall go there as my friend and give Stalin my warmest greetings. He will appreciate it.' Hoffmann nodded. Hitler seized his hand and grasped it firmly. 'Shake Stalin's hand and wish him all the best.' The Führer and his adjutants then retired to watch newsreel footage of Stalin reviewing his troops. All who watched agreed that the imminent pact had eliminated a powerful potential enemy in the east.[18]

Before midnight, news of the impending agreement was broadcast to the world on German radio. By morning, it would dominate the newspapers. 'The Führer has played a masterstroke,' Joseph Goebbels enthused in his diary. Robert Coulandre, the shocked French Ambassador in Berlin, agreed. 'We have been outplayed!' he lamented. 'The last thread by which peace hangs has been torn.'[19]

Outside the Nazi Party headquarters – the 'Brown House' – in Munich's Königliches Platz two naval officers waited. Dressed uncomfortably in civilian clothes, *Generaladmiral* Conrad Albrecht, in charge of German naval forces in the Baltic, and Admiral Hermann Boehm, Commander-in-Chief of the Fleet, had spent a pleasant night in the Four Seasons hotel, where they had not signed the customary registration forms. It was now 9am on a steamy Tuesday in Bavaria. News vendors stood in the street proclaiming the headline of the day, the 'world sensation' – the pact between Germany and Russia. A young man approached the two admirals, showed his credentials, then said he would drive them to the Berghof, seventy miles southeast of Munich.

For the next ninety minutes, the staff car swung around the mountain roads of the Bavarian Alps, through the charming market town of Berchtesgaden, and finally up a steep driveway to the gleaming white Berghof. Once a pleasant mountainside chalet, the Haus Wachenfeld, it had been extensively rebuilt in the mid-1930s and re-titled the Berghof – mountain court. It was an apt title. It was the second seat of government in the Third Reich, where the Führer greeted world leaders and where his court lounged around into the small hours of each morning to listen to Hitler's endless monologues on random subjects.

All morning limousines pulled up the driveway to the Berghof, disgorging upwards of fifty senior officers, each one in civilian clothes. Only Hermann Göring misunderstood the meaning of the word 'inconspicuous'. The Luftwaffe Commander-in-Chief arrived at the Obersalzberg dressed in a gaudy hunting jacket – breeches, an open white shirt and a green waistcoat adorned with yellow buttons. An ornamental dagger hung from a gold-encrusted red leather belt, which struggled to contain his ample girth.

At mid-day, as an Alpine storm brewed outside, the assorted generals were ushered into the magnificent Great Hall, the most magnificent of the sixty rooms in the Berghof. Only the finest paintings – Gobelins and a Titian – and colourful tapestries lined the walls, while rugs imported from Persia were laid on the floor. The room was dominated by an enormous window comprising ninety panes of glass which looked out over the Alps towards Salzburg half a dozen miles to the north. Today, most of the furniture had been cleared away, save for a Bechstein grand piano, a bust of Wagner, and an imposing marble table beneath the huge window. Fifty wooden chairs, arranged in two rows, were set out for the guests, who now took their seats.

They quickly rose as Hitler strode in, wearing his brown Party uniform. For the next two hours, he would treat them to a *tour d'horizon*. There would be no discussion. The generals and admirals sat in silence as their Führer explained his decisions. 'I have called you here so you can see the environment in which I make my decisions.' And his decision, he began, was to attack Poland. War with Poland, he told his audience, 'had to come sooner or later'. Eighty million Germans had to have what was their right. Their future had to be safeguarded. If Germany waited, her enemies would merely grow stronger. 'It is easy for us to make decisions,' he proclaimed. 'We have nothing to lose; we have everything to gain.' He had hoped to strike first against the West, *then* turn against the East. But events had turned out differently. Now was the time to strike at Poland. 'The hour is favourable for a solution. The blow must be struck. We must act now or go under.' The West, he assured his military leaders, would not intervene; Britain would not be ready to wage war for three or four years and France, with her outmoded weaponry, had no stomach for a fight. Besides, Hitler declared, 'our enemies have leaders who are below average. No personalities. No masters, no men of action.' As for the East, his pact with Stalin ensured if it came to war, Germany would not have to fight on two fronts as she had done a generation earlier. 'Now Poland is in the position in which I wanted her.' He would deal with the Poles swiftly, ruthlessly, remorselessly. Hitler expected his men to demonstrate *grösste Härte* – the greatest severity. 'Close your hearts to pity. Act brutally.' It was not enough to simply occupy Poland. Her army would be smashed, destroyed, 'utterly annihilated'. Some propaganda stunt would serve as the *casus belli*, irrespective of whether the world would believe it or not. One hundred and fifty concentration camp prisoners would be dressed in Polish uniforms and ultimately sacrificed. 'The victor is not asked whether he told the truth or not after the event. In starting and waging war, it is not what is right which matters but victory.' There would be no *Blumenkrieg* – a flower-bedecked occupation as with Austria or Czechoslovakia – this time. This time, the guns would sound. 'The Army must see battle for real before the big showdown in the West.' Poland would allow the Wehrmacht to 'test its tools'. For six years, Hitler's policies had restored Germany's status as a world power. Now it was time for the Wehrmacht to prove itself. 'My only concern is that some swine might suggest mediation at the last moment.' But there was little time for that – *Fall Weiss* would be unleashed at the weekend. 'I have done my duty,' the Führer concluded. 'Now you do yours.' Walther von Brauchitsch stood up. There was no speech, no address. He simply said: 'Men, now to your posts.'[20]

The generals and admirals filed out of the Great Hall. Erich Raeder buttonholed Hitler. He feared for his cadet training ship bound for Danzig Bay. It would lie directly under the guns of Polish batteries in Gdynia. 'Well, if the old tub goes down, there's no harm done,' the Führer quipped. The *Grossadmiral* was furious. There were 300 cadets aboard, the lifeblood of the future Navy. Hitler simply brushed him aside.

Some officers such as Fedor von Bock left the Berghof buoyed. Brauchitsch tried to exude a feeling of confidence. The Luftwaffe generals joked among themselves. But most departed sombre, Hitler's Army adjutant Gerhard Engel observed as he eavesdropped on conversations, was sombre, 'not because of Poland, rather what might arise from it'. Few were convinced that Britain and France would not intervene this time. 'This fool wants war!' Gerd von Rundstedt remarked in characteristically blunt fashion, while Walther von Reichenau, usually one of Hitler's most ardent supporters in the Officer Corps, commented: 'That man is terribly mistaken if he believes this war will be over in a few weeks. This will be no six-week war, it will be a six-year war.' Hermann Boehm departed the Berghof thoroughly dispirited, A few days later he was summoned to Kiel by Otto Schniewind, the Chief-of-Staff of the *Seekriegsleitung*, the German Naval Staff, for a final pep talk before the invasion of Poland. 'We in the *Seekriegsleitung* do not expect England to intervene!' Hermann Boehm raised his hand. 'I expect it!' Otto Schniewind cut him down. 'In Berlin they're rather better informed than you at the front.' Undeterred, Boehm raised his hand again. 'I am still convinced of it.'[21]

As the generals and admirals dispersed from the Berghof, Joachim von Ribbentrop and a retinue of thirty diplomats, interpreters, press officers, and two photographers, climbed into two four-engined Focke-Wulf Condors in Berlin and headed east for Moscow, via an overnight stop in Königsberg. The mood on the aircraft was tense; the Soviets might have already signed an agreement with the British or French. Or perhaps the negotiations would drag on endlessly. And almost every man on the aircraft felt unease at striking a deal with Moscow – 'the enemy of European culture and a bitter adversary', recalled Peter Kleist, Ribbentrop's expert on eastern Europe.[22]

The air shimmered in the mid-day heat as the two Condors touched down on the runway in Moscow the following afternoon. Swastika flags fluttered gently next to the airport sign over the terminal, flanked by the Soviet hammer and sickle. A guard of honour from the Red Air Force was lined up on the standing, while a military band played the German national anthem followed by the *Internationale*. The deputy Soviet Foreign Minister Vladimir Potemkin greeted Ribbentrop, watched by the German and Italian Ambassadors. After a hasty inspection of the guard, the Reich Foreign Minister climbed into a limousine and headed into the heart of the Soviet capital to the former Austrian legation. Ribbentrop's stay there was brief; around 6pm, the thick-set head of Stalin's bodyguard, Colonel Nikolai Vlasik, collected the German diplomats. The ZiS limousines rolled through deserted Muscovy streets cordoned off by security troops. The German Ambassador, Count Friedrich von der Schulenburg, pointed out the sights to Ribbentrop as their car passed through Red Square, then turned through one of the Kremlin gates and pulled up in front of a fairly nondescript side door. The Germans were ushered inside, up a stairway and into an oblong room where Josef Stalin and his Foreign Minister, Molotov, were waiting.

Joachim von Ribbentrop had learned nothing from his time in London. There was little time for pleasantries. It was time, he told the Soviet dictator, to put German-Soviet relations on a new footing. 'You have poured bucket loads of shit over us,' Stalin responded in his typically coarse fashion, 'but that is no reason that we cannot be friends again.' The four men – Ribbentrop and his ambassador, Stalin and Molotov – plus their interpreters proceeded to re-draw the map of Europe. Finland, Bessarabia in Romania, Latvia and Estonia to the Soviet Union, Lithuania to the Reich. The two hitherto sworn enemies promised to refrain from acts of violence aimed at each other for ten years to come. What they did not declare publicly, however, was their intention to divide Poland between them... should Poland's situation dramatically change.

The deal struck, the festivities began. Josef Stalin stood up. 'I know how much the German *Volk* love their Führer. So, I would like to drink to his health.' Germans and Russians arose, clinked their champagne or vodka glasses against the Soviet leader's tumbler – filled not with vodka but water. Schulenberg immediately toasted Stalin's health, then Molotov raised his glass: 'It was our great Comrade Stalin who began this coup in political relations. I drink to his health!' The official photographers were waved in to record the historic moment. In the small hours of 24 August, Joachim von Ribbentrop, a Nazi Party badge pinned to his lapel and a white handkerchief poking out of the top pocket of his dark suit, sat down to put his signature to the German-Soviet Non-Aggression Treaty – to the world, the Nazi-Soviet Pact – followed by Molotov, watched by Stalin in his light grey tunic buttoned up to the neck. The deal done, the Russian dictator walked over to Heinrich Hoffmann. 'Excellency! I take great delight in expressing the personal, cordial greetings of *Herr* Adolf Hitler,' the photographer told Stalin. 'He asked me to shake your hand in his name.' Only the German Ambassador, Count von der Schulenburg, did not enjoy these grotesque celebrations. 'This treaty will lead us into the second world war and bring ruin upon Germany,' he muttered to a confidante.[23]

A note was slipped to Adolf Hitler as he dined late that night at the Berghof: the treaty with Russia had been signed. He stood up immediately and told his entourage simply: 'We've won!' As 23 August became 24 August– Moscow was two hours ahead of Berlin – the party moved on to the terrace of the Berghof. Across the valley the Untersberg mountain glowed red and the sky itself shimmered in every colour of the rainbow. It was rare to see the Northern Lights this far south and it cast a red hue over the faces and hands of those strolling on the terrace. Hitler's guests fell silent, lost in thought. This augured a bloody war, Hitler's Luftwaffe adjutant Nikolaus von Below warned. 'If it must be so, then the sooner the better,' the Führer responded.[24]

Across the Reich garrisons were emptying. As August 1939 drew on, troops, panzers, guns, horses, kit were entrained. For some there were ceremonial departures with bands playing and loved ones tossing flowers to the departing warriors. For most, however, the departure was a low-key affair. The men of 1st Light Division drove through the drab industrial city of Wuppertal in the dark to the Oberbarmen station, where a train was waiting for them. The only sound that night was the monotonous drone of the division's vehicles pounding the city streets. The few civilians about stared at the passing armour with questioning glances. The soldiers responded with a friendly salute. Before dawn, 1st Light had been loaded on to its trains. The locomotive jerked. The train began to move to the east. 'Where are we going?' the men asked themselves.[25]

The answer invariably was Silesia, West or East Prussia. To reach the latter meant a journey by sea – the Poles would not allow German armour to roll through the Corridor either by train or road. To many soldiers, taking a steamer to Königsberg was an adventure. They hoped to sample the nightlife of St Pauli and Hamburg's Reeperbahn before sailing and enjoyed a free 'cruise' through the Kaiser Wilhelm Canal into the Baltic. The men exercised, sang, played cards, talked and enjoyed the relatively comfortable surroundings of the steamships. It was certainly much more interesting than a billet at the vast exercise ground of Gross Born, roughly half-way between Stettin and Danzig. The establishment was barely twelve months old; two villages had been flattened to make way for the sprawling base, home to the German Army's artillery school. Today, however, it was dominated by panzers of General Heinz Guderian's XIX Army Corps, which began rolling into Gross Born in the third week of August. Guderian's mission was simple: to slice through the Polish Corridor, reach the Vistula, trap and destroy the bulk of the enemy army defending this narrow strip. A rapid victory would earn him eternal glory and Germany's highest distinction, *Pour le Mérite* – the Blue Max – his superiors assured him. But Guderian had more pressing concerns. The campaign against the Poles was a personal crusade. Sacred soil, the historic estates of the Guderians, his birthplace at Kulm (today Chelmno) all lay under the Polish yoke, and he had been chosen to liberate them. His two sons were under arms. 'Once again, the hand dealt us means we must live in a time of war and must come to terms with it,' he wrote to his wife Gretel from Gross Born. 'Be a brave soldier's wife – as you have been so often – and set an example to others.'[26]

Life in Gross Born was tedious – conferences, discussions, drill, inoculations, gas mask tests. And it was impossible to hide the build-up of such an armoured force – one panzer and two motorised infantry divisions – from the enemy; Polish radio soon reported the arrival of 3rd Panzer – 'the Berlin blood division' – at the exercise ground.[27]

Theology student Hans P spent most of August 1939 fifty or so miles south of Gross Born, near the town of Schneidemühl (today Pila) close to the western border of the Polish Corridor. His company commander had assured the Berliner to discount all rumours of conflict, but Hans and his comrades knew war was coming. The infantrymen stood on the frontier and looked to the east. Every now and then they could see Polish troops patrolling, staring back at their impending foe through binoculars. 'In a few weeks there will no longer be a border here,' Hans mused, 'the land over there will be as German as it is here.'[28]

It would, for Adolf Hitler had already ordered his army to prepare to strike before dawn on Saturday, 26 August. More than one and a half million Germans were under arms or mobilising, over fifty divisions in all. In southern Germany a mountain infantryman, a *Gebirgsjäger*, and his comrades were ordered to gather in a classroom in their barracks. 'What's happening?' they asked as their senior non-commissioned officer walked in. 'We're off!' he replied curtly. 'Nothing more should remind us of our peaceful civilian lives,' the *Gebirgsjäger* wrote enthusiastically. 'Thoughts of war push everything else into the background. Tomorrow we're off, there's rejoicing in our ardent hearts.'[29] In anticipation of the impending clash of arms, Fourteenth Army commander Wilhelm List, charged with taking Krakow and destroying enemy forces in southern Silesia, issued an order of the day to his men:

> Soldiers of Fourteenth Army!
> The Führer calls!
> We follow him with boundless faith, obedience and unswerving loyalty!
> So forwards! With all our might!
> We will strike the enemy!
> Long live the Führer!
> Long live Greater Germany![30]

All that was needed now was the final order from Berlin to attack.

The sound of gunfire echoed across the Bay of Danzig. It was followed quickly by the strains of the *Deutschlandlied*, the German National Anthem. It was a little after 9.30am on Friday, 25 August. Sailors tossed lines to two harbour tugs – *Danzig* and *Albert Forster* – which gently guided the 13,000-ton warship up a canal barely 300ft wide. A large crowd stood on the quay in the suburb of Neufahrwasser, three miles from the heart of Danzig. Some women waved handkerchiefs, others raised their right arms to give the *Hitlergruss*, youngsters furiously waved small swastika flags, others climbed on their parent's backs and also raised their arms in salute. A handful of motorboats and cutters buzzed around in the canal. On the upper deck of the leviathan, the sailors, dressed in their whites, stood rigidly to attention as the tugs nudged the warship alongside, opposite a salt silo adorned with swastika banners. *Schleswig-Holstein* – '*SX*' to her crew – was here ostensibly on a goodwill visit, a commemoration to mark the twenty-fifth anniversary of the loss of the cruiser *Magdeburg* in the Gulf of Finland. No-one was fooled. *SX* was in the free city to stiffen the resolve of Danzigers and to turn her four 28cm guns and secondary armament against Polish positions if necessary.

The guns of the ship were in full view; there was no hiding them. But below decks, out of sight, were 225 men of a Naval stormtroop company. Opposite *SX's* berth lay a Polish ammunition depot on a narrow spit of land, the Westerplatte, guarded by a handful of small forts and bunkers. When the order came, they would storm the depot.

The mood this fine August day was festive. As the venerable battleship tied up, a huge crowd milled around on the quay, bands and street performers entertained the people. A procession of Great War veterans, SA brown shirts and political leaders, led by Albert Forster filed aboard. The crew were lauded in the streets, where large swastika flags swayed from buildings and huge banners were stretched from one side to the other: 'Sailors of our Führer, welcome to German Danzig'. Only one man did not relish the visit to the free city: *Kapitän zur See* Gustav Kleikamp, *SX's* Commanding Officer. Publicly, he was filled with confidence and determination. Danzig's fate would probably be decided during the battleship's visit. Defending it, he told his crew, 'must fill us with pride'. Yet privately, Kleikamp was nervous, depressed. 'I have a terrible mission which I cannot reconcile with my conscience,' he confided in Carl Burckhardt during a reception at the diplomat's home.[31]

As *Schleswig-Holstein* came alongside in Danzig that Friday morning, Adolf Hitler – now back in Berlin after his Alpine summer – strode up to his press secretary Otto Dietrich, eager for the international cuttings and transcripts from foreign news broadcasts.

'Have you the latest news from London and Paris about the impact of our treaty?' the Führer asked. 'What do you know about the cabinet crises?'

'What cabinet crises do you mean, *mein Führer*?' a baffled Dietrich inquired.

'The cabinet crises in London and Paris, of course. No democratic government can survive such a defeat and disgrace as our Moscow treaty has inflicted.'[32]

There was no such news.

It was hardly surprising, then, that Propaganda Minister Joseph Goebbels found his Führer 'serious yet composed'. The Führer issued orders, dictated proclamations to the German people and the Nazi Party, declared his determination to wage war 'for months and years, if necessary'. Goebbels was in awe. 'What responsibility now rests on his shoulders. Only he can bear it.'[33]

A roll of drums echoed around the Chancellery's Courtyard of Honour as Hitler and a small staff sat down to lunch. An SS guard of honour stood stiffly to attention as British Ambassador, Sir Nevile Henderson, arrived to hear the Führer extend an olive branch one final time. For an hour, the upright yet meek Henderson was subjected to one of Hitler's monologues railing against British and Polish intrigues. How dare an Empire totalling more than forty million square kilometres try to impose its will on a nation of just 600,000 square kilometres. 'It is quite clear who it is who desires to conquer the world,' the Führer sneered. He wanted no 'bloody and incalculable war' with Britain for such a conflict 'would be bloodier than that of 1914–1918'. But the Polish problem had to be solved – and would be solved; there had been twenty-one incidents on the Polish-German frontier overnight. Such an intolerable situation could not persist, for he was, Hitler told the ambassador, 'a man of great decisions'. He was willing to negotiate, but his patience was running out. This was his final offer. It was an offer, Nevile Henderson suggested to London, worth considering.[34]

Barely had the Briton left Hitler's official residence than news was presented to the Führer that Britain and Poland had signed a treaty; the Empire would 'aid Poland if her independence should be threatened.' The blow was compounded by Italian procrastination; still his ally would not commit to war alongside the Reich. The 'man of great decisions' was suddenly shaken. The telephone in Franz Halder's office in Zossen, home of the Army High Command, rang repeatedly. The attack might have to be postponed, Hitler's staff warned. What was the latest moment the order to attack could be given? 3pm, Halder curtly told them. At two minutes past three – with no word yet from the Italians – the order to unleash *Fall Weiss* came. In field headquarters along the German-Polish border, teleprinters chattered into life. The message from Zossen was terse: *Fall Weiss. Y-Tag: 26/8. X-Uhr: 0430.* The invasion of Poland would begin at 4.30am the following day.

It was dusk by the time reservist *Leutnant* Albrecht Herzner left the command post of 7th Infantry Division in the Slovakian village of Rakova to join his men.

Herzner had spent the afternoon briefing *Generalmajor* Eugen Ott and his staff about his daring plan: to seize the strategic Jablunka Pass by *coup de main*.

At the western end of the Beskids, one of the many smaller chains in the Carpathians, the Jablunka mountains straddle the Polish, Czech and Slovak borders. And here, at their lowest point, more than 1,700ft above sea level, the main railway line from Vienna to Warsaw passed through a tunnel, two tunnels actually, each 300 yards long, running parallel.

Albrecht Herzner's plan was daring – and simple: clamber over the mountains, seize Mosty – the first village north of the pass – and its station, and overcome the guards at both ends of the tunnel. Until a year ago, this land had been Slovakian, but the Poles had taken advantage of the Munich agreement to seize the Jablunka Pass. Now, Slovaks would reclaim the pass.

But the Slovaks were not Slovaks. They were ethnic Germans. In mid-August, several dozen *Volksdeutsche* arrived at the German Army exercise ground in Neuhammer for training. They were a mixed bag, men aged anywhere from their late teens to mid forties, some wearing caps, some wearing hats, all dressed in jackets, all wearing swastika armbands on their sleeves and all sporting some form of firearm. Herzner was as irregular as the men who served under them. He was a devout Christian; he wore the uniform of the fabled 9th Infantry Regiment, yet he served in the Wehrmacht's intelligence and espionage arm, the *Abwehr* – literally 'defence'; and like many members of that organisation, dabbled with the anti-Hitler resistance movement in the armed forces.

And now Albrecht Herzner struggled through the growing gloom of this Friday evening to find his seventy men and lead them into Poland.[35]

In Schloss Schönwald, a Silesian castle half a dozen miles from the Polish border, a staff officer handed Wolfram von Richthofen a brief message: *Ostmarkflug, 26 August, 0430 Uhr*. It was a little after 6.30pm. Richthofen had barely ten hours to get his specialist dive-bomber and ground-attack units in position. A cousin of the Red Baron, *Generalmajor* Wolfram von Richthofen was arguably the ablest of the Luftwaffe's commanders – and he knew it. Supremely self-confident – his voluminous diaries reveal he was *always* right and other generals invariably wrong, whatever the situation – and supremely agile for his forty-four years, Richthofen was one of the few German generals with combat experience. But his breadth of experience extended far beyond the heavens. He had fought with the Hussars in the Great War, then trained as a fighter pilot before serving in his cousin's legendary 'flying circus', *Jagdgeschwader 1*, in the final months of the war, scoring a respectable, but not outstanding, eight victories. Post-war he earned a degree in engineering, then re-enlisted in the rump of the German Army. The 1920s and early 1930s were spent in a mix of aerial and ground appointments, before being sent to Spain with the 'volunteers' of the *Legion Condor*. Richthofen first served as its Chief-of-Staff, and ultimately as its commander, leading it to victory in the spring of 1939. His experiences in Spain convinced him that the Luftwaffe's future lay in close, direct support of the ground troops; they also earned him a new title and command, *Fliegerführer zur besonderen Verwendung* – Air Commander for Special Duties. A specialist group of dive-bomber and close-support aircraft was placed under Richthofen; it would be the aerial punch for the armour of XVI Corps, smashing its way to Warsaw. Now as the sun set, the Silesian general watched as those panzers rumbled past the castle which served as his temporary headquarters. It was, he confessed, 'a strange feeling. Everything points to the fact that really serious things are happening.'[36]

Really serious things *were* happening in Berlin. Word had come from the Italians. Benito Mussolini was inclined to wage war, but his nation was not. It would be three years before Fascist Italy could enter a war against Britain and France. 'I consider it my bounden duty as a loyal friend to tell you the whole truth,' the *Duce* told Hitler. 'Not to do so might have unpleasant consequences for us all.'[37] Germany would have to face the Western Allies alone.

The Führer was thunderstruck. He summoned Walter von Brauchitsch immediately and told the Army's Commander-in-Chief to put a stop to the invasion of Poland, to put a stop to one and a half million men crossing the frontier before dawn. 'I swear I will stop the attack ordered for early tomorrow before it reaches the border,' the general assured him. 'Give me eight days to complete mobilisation as planned and to carry out the deployment so that more than 100 divisions will be at my disposal. That will buy you time for your political game.' Brauchitsch was a picture of composure, but his officers were already on the move to the General Staff's wartime headquarters in Zossen, twenty miles south of Berlin. The General buttonholed his liaison officer Nikolaus von Vormann and ordered him to make for Zossen immediately and prevent hostilities. Vormann jumped into the first car he found waiting outside the Reich Chancellery. 'To Zossen as fast as you can,' he told the drive. 'Don't stop for any red lights. Ignore the laws of the road.' Within an hour the *Oberst* was standing before Franz Halder, Chief of the General Staff. The order from Berlin left him dumbfounded. 'That is so astonishing that I ask you to remain here while the orders are issued,' he told Vormann. 'I want to make sure that I heard correctly.' Halder picked up the telephone and began issuing orders. 'The war is called off. The border must not be crossed.'[38]

The telephones rang and the teleprinters chattered all night. The airwaves crackled. Messengers were dispatched on motorcycles, racing through the warm August night. In one instance a Fieseler Storch reconnaissance aircraft was sent out to find and stop a motorised column heading for the Polish border. Each means of communication bore the same instruction: stop the attack. A staff officer rushed up to Wolfram von Richthofen, who was still mesmerised by the panzers rolling along the Silesian lanes. '*Ostmarkflug* is off,' the officer told him. Richthofen immediately issued orders to his commanders. 'Not a soul must take off tomorrow, not a single machine' he told his staff. 'Otherwise we shall be blamed for having started the war!'[39]

In the monastery of the Holy Cross at Neisse (today Nysa) forty-five miles south of Breslau, the telephone rang. The headquarters of Army Group South buzzed with activity, as it had done all afternoon. The phone call from Berlin stopped them in their tracks. 'Do not, repeat *not*, commence hostilities. Halt all movements.' The army group's Chief-of-Staff, the brilliant but outspoken Erich von Manstein, blanched. 'How could any man reach such a decision and then cancel it again in the space of a few hours?' he asked himself. Now, however, was not the time for rhetorical questions. Now was the time to stop the attack on Poland. The concerted efforts of Manstein and his comrades worked. Army Group South was halted before it entered Poland.[40]

Since late afternoon the armour of 3rd Panzer Division had been rolling out of the exercise ground at Gross Born towards its jump-off positions on the Reich border. The division's commander, Leo Geyr von Schweppenburg sat in his makeshift command post, near Preussisch Friedland, enjoying a sandwich with his operations officer. A breathless adjutant approached Geyr, handing him orders to halt all movements immediately. Geyr managed to stop his men invading the Corridor, but the halt order provoked widespread disappointment; the soldiers of 3rd Panzer Division yearned for action. 'They had had enough of the Poles,' their general recalled. 'The men were ready to give them a proper thrashing.'[41]

In a guesthouse south of Johannisburg (today Pisz) on the border between East Prussia and Poland the staff of 1st Cavalry Regiment were discussing their impending reconnaissance patrols. The telephone rang. 'The thing's off,' a voice from headquarters reported. The men should be called back to their jump-off positions. 'Have the patrols already set off?' the officer inquired. 'Of course,' the cavalry commander responded brusquely. 'Orders. Counter-orders. Disorder', he fumed. An hour later a breathless *Leutnant* burst into the guesthouse. The patrol was back. 'One non-commissioned officer is missing,' the *Leutnant* reported. His commander shook his head. 'First one thing, then another.'[42]

As Albrecht Herzner fought his way over the mountainous, heavily-forested terrain to the west of the Jablunka Pass, 7th Infantry Division tried to stop his raid. But in the mountains, radio contact was impossible. Messengers sent by Ott throughout the night could not find Herzner and his band of saboteurs; they either got lost in the undergrowth or were captured by Polish border guards. By the small hours of 26 August, these irregulars – *Kampforganisation Jablunka*, Jublanka combat organisation – were on Polish soil, ready to pounce on the station at Mosty and to seize the tunnel.

What happened next was confused and confusing. Few accounts of Herzner's raid agree. But one thing is certain: the Poles were surprised and the station at Mosty was seized. More of Herzner's men seized the southern entrance of the tunnel after a brief but fierce fire-fight, then began to advance through the 300-yard tunnel. Herzner meanwhile commandeered a train waiting to carry steelworkers to a nearby plant and sent it down the track towards the tunnel with two of his men aboard to make contact with 7th Infantry Division.

It was now that Herzner's plan began to unravel. The driver slammed his brakes on several hundred yards short of the tunnel – the Poles had ripped up a section of track and started to fire at the train, seemingly from all sides. Herzner's two messengers panicked, jumped out of the train and ran for the wooded mountains – using four Polish railway workers as human shields. As for Herzner and the rest of his force, most, including the *Leutnant*, ran up the mountainside. Some fell into the hands of two battalions of Polish mountain infantrymen ordered to the Jablunka Pass to bolster the garrison.

The sound of small arms fire had carried through the Beskids as far as Rakova, but Eugen Ott and his staff were powerless to intervene. Powerless, that is, until a volunteer wearing a blood-soaked bandage staggered into the command post in the middle of the morning. Neither Eugen Ott nor his operations officer *Major* Paul Reichelt wanted anything to do with the affair and ordered junior officer Heinrich Kreisel to drive to the border to negotiate. There Kreisel found General Josef Kustron, commander of *25th Mountain Infantry Division*. Kustron was in a foul mood, indignant that he was not negotiating with a general and indignant that his interpreter failed to translate his words precisely.

'Is it war or peace?' he asked Kreisel.

'Peace,' the German replied.

'Why is it, then, that armed men from the German side have attacked Polish territory and committed crimes?'

'Evidently we are dealing with Slovakian guerrillas,' said Kreisel.

Kustron shook his head. 'These guerrillas are led by an officer wearing the uniform of Germany's 9th Infantry Regiment.'

'9th Infantry Regiment does not belong to our division.'

'So what happens now?' asked Kustron.

Kreisel suggested an exchange: the 'Slovakian volunteers' for several Polish railway workers arrested in Slovakia for 'spying'. The Polish general agreed – as long as the insurgents were punished. Kreisel assured the Pole he would do all he could to ensure they would be.

It was mid-day on 26 August before Albrecht Herzner, still hiding in the forests on the slopes of the Jablunka Pass, finally made contact with 7th Infantry Division by radio. 'I am very sorry, but with the best will I cannot help you,' Paul Reichelt told him. 'You must see to it that you get yourself out of this difficult situation.' Herzner did. He dressed some of his men in Polish uniforms to slip through the lines into Slovakia, while he and the bulk of his 'combat organisation' waited until nightfall to sneak over the border in small groups. But Albrecht Herzner had proved the Jablunka Pass could be seized. The only question was whether the Poles would be so accommodating a second time.[43]

There were numerous incidents that night along the entire Polish-German frontier as German patrols crossed the border. At least four border posts in Silesia had been fired at; in one instance, German troops had tossed hand grenades inside. A border guard, one Edmund Piatkowski, had been shot dead as he patrolled the Silesian frontier. Telephone links with Poland were severed. The Poles protested. German diplomats in Berlin promised an explanation. It never came.[44]

As messengers and signallers hurried through the night to prevent the German Army from invading Poland, the officers of 9th Infantry Regiment gathered for a farewell dinner in the garrison town of Potsdam, the historic retreat of the Hohenzollerns just outside Berlin. The regimental band serenaded the men from the terrace as they enjoyed a fine meal in the company of their guest of honour, Prince Eitel Friedrich, second son of Germany's last kaiser. At the evening's end, the prince raised his glass. 'May this regiment be as brave in the coming clash of arms as the First Foot Guards Regiment!' he toasted, followed by a lacklustre 'heil' for the Führer.

The next day officers and men fell in, ready to depart. A generation before, Kaiser Wilhelm II had stood in Potsdam's Lustgarten to bid farewell to the 9th Infantry's forerunner, the First Foot Guards. From 8,000 soldiers the song *Ein feste Burg ist unser Gott* (A mighty fortress is our God) reverberated around the parade ground. And now, a quarter of a century later, stood three rows of steel helmets 'a united front in the military and also the spiritual sense', *Leutnant* Hans Fritzsche recalled.

> They all bore the same uniform and the regimental number. The war threw them together in a common fate. And yet it affected each man differently. One man had a girl, another did not. For one, war was a welcome flight into uncertainty at the front, for others it meant a heartrending departure from loved ones. The possibility of death for each man was certain. What the years of war had planned for them, they did not know. Almost all were heroic and only a few survived.

Their regimental commander, *Oberst Freiherr* von und zu Gilsa, would not be among the survivors. Perhaps he knew it as he confided to his colleagues. *'Mensch, dieser Wahnsinnige macht ja wirklich Krieg'* – Men, this madman really is waging war.[45]

A dozen miles away in the Berlin suburb of Spandau, the reservists of 23rd Infantry Division reported for duty. There was little enthusiasm for war among the men or the civilians, but that did not mean that the infantrymen were unwilling to serve. On the contrary, they were determined to prove themselves as soldiers 'for the Führer, *Volk* and Fatherland,' one soldier remembered. 'Each one of us is filled with Germany's strength and confidence in victory, without having any illusions about the bitterness of the struggle.' Their commander, Walter Graf von Brockdorff-Ahlefeldt issued a curt but stirring order of the day:

> Soldiers of the 23rd Division!
>
> Our Führer has summoned us. We will follow him at the risk of our own lives.
> From the youngest soldier to the divisional commander we will make good our deeds with our honour. The glory of our regiment should be no less than the glory of our fathers' regiments.[46]

But scratch beneath the surface, look beyond talk of glory, beyond the resolve to defend the Reich, and it was clear that 23rd Infantry was far from an elite unit, as one platoon leader realised. Most of his men were reservists. Few had seen action in the Great War – and those that had had barely raised arms since. 'The general level of training leaves a lot to be desired,' he complained. They struggled to load vehicles, to pack their horses and kit on to trains. 'Will we be allowed to give the men even the most rudimentary training, or will we go to war in such a state?' the officer wondered. At least the men's morale was high, the platoon leader observed. 'Given political events, they are confident "things will turn out all right".'[47]

Adolf Hitler emerged from his private quarters in the Reich Chancellery at 10am on Saturday 26 August, apparently untroubled by the chaos his decision to halt *Fall Weiss* had caused along the entire German-Polish frontier. As his armies drew back from their jump-off positions, the Führer had spent the evening talking with his cronies until the small hours before retiring. Now, this Saturday morning, he asked a few questions about the West, then retreated into his study with von Brauchitsch, Keitel, Göring and Ribbentrop. Hitler reappeared for lunch, where conversation was dominated by anecdotes of deeds in the Great War and irrelevant present-day issues. It was all, Nikolaus von Vormann observed, 'insignificant and empty, intended solely to relax the situation'. After half an hour of such trifles, the Führer disappeared once more.[48]

The Reich Chancellery was a hubbub of activity in this final week of August: British Ambassador Nevile Henderson met with Hitler almost daily, so too his French counterpart Robert Coulandre; Goebbels, Göring, Ribbentrop, von Brauchitsch, were perennial visitors, as were SS leaders and senior party functionaries. Some came to the Reich Chancellery merely to show their faces, others were desperate for news. Those who were not there and ought to be were quickly summoned on the telephone, before vanishing behind the imposing doors of Hitler's study where an SS honour guard put a sign on the latch: do not disturb. On the afternoon of the twenty-seventh, Reichstag deputies filed into the Chancellery. They had been called to Berlin for a sitting of parliament which had promptly been cancelled. Now, finally, their Führer apprised them of the situation. This was not one of his finest speeches. Days of tension and late nights had taken their toll; Hitler appeared tired, harassed, his voice was hoarse. He had, however, lost none of his resolve. He was, he told his Reichstag representatives, like Frederick the Great, willing to stake everything on a single card. At the very least he wanted Danzig and the Corridor. If he didn't get that, 'then war – war with the most brutal and most inhuman means'. War would, of course, be bitter, perhaps even hopeless, he continued, but going down with honour was preferable to capitulation. And as long as he was alive, there would be no talk of capitulation. 'If any of you believe that I am not acting solely out of love for Germany,' he declared, 'then he has the right to shoot me down.'[49]

At mealtimes and in the evenings, the Führer spoke at length while his long-suffering entourage listened without interrupting. His mood swung between strong feelings of friendship towards Britain and war at all costs. He was increasingly conscious of his own mortality. 'I am now fifty years old and in possession of my full faculties,' he told Nikolaus von Vormann. 'The problems must be solved by *me*, and I cannot wait any longer. In a few years' time I might not be physically – and perhaps also mentally – able to act.' He condemned his weak-willed military leaders for trying to talk him out of war. 'Frederick the Great would turn in his grave if he saw today's generals.' In any event, the Wehrmacht he had created needed to earn battle honours, 'otherwise a glorious Army would have lost its meaning'. And above all, he wanted war with Poland.

He did not want war with Britain or France. 'If they are stupid enough to join in that is their fault and they will have to be destroyed.'[50]

Perhaps war might yet be avoided. When a tired and harassed Nevile Henderson was ushered into Hitler's spacious brown marble study late on the twenty-eighth, he presented the Führer with one final proposal for a conference to resolve the Polish question. And this was Britain's final proposal, the British Ambassador, explained; if anyone in Germany doubted that Britain was prepared to fight on Poland's behalf, they were sorely mistaken. 'Our word is our word and we had never and would never break it.' The issue, said Henderson, was not Danzig and the Corridor. The Empire was determined to oppose force with force. With Lenbach's portrait of Bismarck staring down at him, the Führer now subjected Henderson to a tirade about the Rhineland, Austria, Czechoslovakia. He talked of annihilating Poland, bemoaned the plight of ethnic Germans, condemned the Poles as unreasonable, provocative, insolent. For his part, Henderson said he had done all he could to spare Europe conflict and bloodshed. The choice between peace and war now rested solely with the Führer. Adolf Hitler chose war; even before Nevile Henderson had suggested a conference, he had issued orders for the German Army to strike Poland before dawn on Friday, 1 September.[51]

By now, hundreds of thousands of German soldiers were deployed close to the Polish border. For many these final days of peace were almost idyllic. The Bavarians of 10th Infantry Division found the people of Silesia particularly welcoming. They housed them in their spare rooms, in their inns, on their estates. The men responded by helping the Silesian farmers gather their crops. 'Our soldiers lived well,' the divisional commander Conrad von Cochenhausen joked. 'Even the Silesian beer tasted like our Bavarian beer – apart from the glasses being too small and the price being rather high.'[52]

In East Prussia, junior officer Fritz Fillies and his company bivouacked in a forest near the border village of Neufliess, a couple of dozen miles north of Mlawa. Day after day the men hid in camouflaged positions on the frontier, observing the Poles in a hamlet a few hundred yards to the south. Sometimes Fillies' company stood watch during the day, sometimes by night. Life across the border went on as normal. Dogs barked, Polish farmers wandered around their pastures, milkmaids moved about the stalls, their pails clattering. On some days the late summer sun penetrated the forest which hid Fillies and his comrades from prying eyes. On others, recalled Fillies, 'it rained in torrents, and the forest and sand, meadows and fields soaked up the water they had gone without for so long. The horses turned with their tails towards the direction from which the rain and wind came from and feasted as they always do in such weather.' And on one day the Poles had shot down a Luftwaffe reconnaissance aircraft which flew into their airspace. 'Since then,' wrote Fillies, 'it had been as quiet as a mouse in our border zone.'[53]

Even though its Army was poised on the Polish frontier, preparing to deliver the mortal blow to Germany's mortal foe, the German public was convinced it was Poland, not the Reich, threatening the fragile peace of Europe. It was hardly surprising. The tone of the German press was inflammatory, sensationalist. 'All of Poland in war fever,' the Nazi Party organ *Völkischer Beobachter* screamed on the twenty-sixth. The Polish Army was 'ready to strike'. Mobilisation proceeded apace. Trains, vehicles, men, all rolled towards the western border. Polish troops encircled Danzig. Polish anti-aircraft guns fired at German civilian aircraft. 'Poland is stoking the fire to turn it into an inferno,' the *Völkischer Beobachter* warned. Every day, the Nazi Party mouthpiece claimed, Poland's newspapers were 'beating the drums of war. The psychosis of hate within the Polish Army has reached its climax.' There were rallies and speeches, newspaper articles almost daily – all aimed at the Reich. 'We are marching against the enemy!' a gathering in Poznan was told. 'We are living in fantastic times. We have begun the road to glory.' The newspaper of the Polish Army, *Polska Zbroyna*, celebrated the might of the nation's armed forces: 'If Poland is attacked, she will fight on her enemy's soil and drive him to the gates of his capital.' And in Warsaw, the daily *Depesza* threatened: 'German blood will flow in the coming war in rivers the likes of which have never been seen.'[54]

And then there was the plight of the German minority in Poland – real and imagined. Headlines in the Reich's press grew increasingly hysterical. 'The flood of terror rises'. 'Mass Polish attacks on Germans.' 'Fresh victims of Polish terror.' 'Life made hellish for Germans.' 'Mass deportations to central Poland.' On the latter story, the German newspapers were at least correct: *Volksdeutsche* were being evicted from their homes in border areas, some out of Polish fear, some out of Polish hatred. Ethnic Germans around Soldau (today Dzialdowo) near Mlawa had been 'rounded up like a flock of sheep' by the Poles and marched off, 'spurred on by rifle butts', the German consulate in Thorn reported. A pregnant woman was beaten to death, a four-year-old girl had been killed by a Polish soldier. But what the German newspapers did not report was the Reich's flagrant violation of the Polish frontier. Almost daily, for weeks, months, Luftwaffe aircraft had been flying into Poland's airspace to take reconnaissance photographs; there had been thirty-two such incidents on 27 August alone. 'How completely isolated a world the German people live in,' American correspondent William Shirer observed. 'All the rest of the world considers that peace is about to be broken by Germany. Here in Germany, in the world the local newspapers create, the very reverse is being maintained.' But it wasn't just ordinary Germans who were hostage to the Nazi propaganda machine. *Oberst* Nikolaus von Vormann fell victim to it, too. In Warsaw, they talked of marching on Berlin, there had been widespread looting, Germans murdered, the Polish Army was mobilised, ready to strike at any moment, the liaison officer recorded in his diary. 'The border was on fire.' It would only take the slightest incident, the *Oberst* mused, and the guns would thunder of their own accord. And if the slightest incident did not occur, Adolf Hitler had one planned anyway.[55]

SS *Sturmbannführer* Emanuel Schaefer was at work in his office in the headquarters of the *Geheime Staatspolizei*, the Gestapo, in the town of Oppeln, fifty miles southeast of Breslau. The telephone rang. It was Berlin. It expected Schaefer to drive to the nearby airfield at Neustadt the following evening. Reinhard Heydrich, icy head of the Reich's internal security service, the *Sicherheitsdienst* or SD, would be waiting for him there.

The Gestapo official did as ordered. At 6pm the following day a Junkers 52 set down on the deserted airfield. As it rolled to a stop, Heydrich stepped out carrying a briefcase and his coat. He laid them both on the wing of the aircraft, then greeted Schaefer. '*Der Führer braucht einen Kriegsgrund.*' The Führer needs a reason for war. In a guesthouse, the Haus Oberschlesien, in the border town of Gleiwitz, Heydrich expanded on the sentence which had taken Emanuel Schaefer aback at the airfield: he would create a reason for war by feigning a Polish attack on a customs house in the village of Hochlinden (today Stodoly) thirteen miles southwest of Gleiwitz. Schaefer felt uneasy. Heydrich calmed the Gestapo man down with the same words Hitler had imparted in him. 'As soon as the panzers roll, no-one will talk about it any more.'[56]

Reinhard Heydrich had spent most of August preparing the *casus belli* Adolf Hitler had promised his generals at the Berghof. The customs house at Hochlinden was just one reason for war. There would be others: a forestry building in Pitschen, near Kreuzberg, a railway halt in West Prussia, and a radio station. The world would hear a Polish rabble make an inflammatory broadcast: the time had come for a clash between German and Pole; it was the duty of every Pole to strike down a German. The radio station mission fell to *Sturmbannführer* Alfred Naujocks, a trusty hand and a member of the SD since its creation, plus half a dozen men. They would strike in the Silesian border town of Gleiwitz, ninety miles southeast of Breslau.

To merely stage an attack, however, was not enough for Reinhard Heydrich, or for the world. There had to be proof 'for the foreign media as well as for German propaganda'. Proof meant Polish dead. Except that the dead would not be Poles, they would be concentration camp prisoners dressed in Polish uniforms – Heydrich had requisitioned 150 uniforms from German intelligence. The prisoners – given the codename *Konserven*, canned goods – would be drugged, dumped at the scene of the attacks, then shot. And then the press would take photographs and the world would have its proof.

Few SS men had any misgivings about the raids they were about to lead. At the SD training school in Bernau, a dozen miles northeast of Berlin, SS *Obersturmbannführer* Otto Hellwig held court at the dining table. He had invited his men for a celebratory drink before leaving for Hochlinden. Hellwig explained the plan of action: the men gathered around the table would be the first Germans to set foot on Polish soil and see action in the coming conflict. 'Comrades, on this table which we are sitting at, a piece of world history will be made.'[57]

In the Reich's capital, a few hundred Berliners waited silently outside the Reich Chancellery hoping for a glimmer of news. Inside, world history *was* being made, hour by hour, day by day. The building's principal occupant was exhausted, his nerves strained by two weeks of intense negotiations. No less weary was Sir Nevile Henderson, driven into the Courtyard of Honour at dusk on the twenty-ninth for yet another bruising encounter with the Führer. Ever the optimist, Henderson fixed a red carnation in his buttonhole as usual; he only removed it if the situation was *truly* serious. But tonight's meeting was particularly stormy. Hitler agreed to meet a Polish negotiator – as long as he appeared in Berlin the following day. That, said Henderson, sounded rather like an ultimatum, at which point Hitler and Ribbentrop rained verbal blows down upon the beleaguered British diplomat. Uncharacteristically, Henderson bit back, shouting at Hitler. But perhaps it *was* an ultimatum. If his Army had to deal with Poland, it had to deal with Poland *now* – before the rainy season arrived, the Führer explained. 'My soldiers are asking me: Yes or no?' As if to reinforce the point, the British diplomat found the ante room filled with senior officers as he left the Führer's study, including von Brauchitsch and Keitel. Stepping into the staff car idling in the courtyard to carry him the 300 yards to the British Embassy, Nevile Henderson was filled 'with the gloomiest forebodings'.[58]

Most Berliners already knew what Nevile Henderson had slowly come to realise: war was imminent. Rationing had been introduced across the Reich: 700 grammes of meat each week, eighty grammes of *Ersatz* (substitute) coffee, eighty grammes of cheese, 150 grammes of cereals, and rationing to the ordinary Berliner spelled war, American journalist William Shirer noted. It even extended to the Reich Chancellery much to the chagrin of the Führer's entourage, whose breakfasts were now accompanied by *Ersatz* coffee and a sliver of butter. Nor was it the only sign of war in the dying days of August 1939. Anti-aircraft batteries were already being moved in to defend Berlin's most important sites. The festivities at the Tannenberg Memorial in East Prussia, celebrating the 25th anniversary of victory over the Russians, were cancelled, so too 1939's Nuremberg Rally – the rally of peace – due to begin on 1 September. In Danzig, shopkeepers closed their stores, women and children clambered into lorries for evacuation to East Prussia, while those left behind waited for 'the big event'. In Berlin, an *Oberst* took a break from drafting orders for *Fall Weiss* to sit in the Kurfüstendamm, one of the city's busiest streets, and watch 'street life stream past me. Something is pressing on people,' he observed. 'They are somewhat depressed and thoughtful.'[59]

The mood in Berlin was echoed across the Reich, in the largest cities, in the smallest villages. The German people wanted Danzig back in the Reich, but not at the cost of another European conflagration. 'The desire for peace is stronger than that for war,' one secret report from Upper Franconia, near Nuremberg, warned. The *Blumenkriege* of Austria, the Sudetenland and Czechoslovakia convinced the German public that their Führer would once again pull a rabbit out of the hat. 'The people know all too well that sooner or later a clash with Germany's enemies must be reckoned with,' a Party leader near Regensburg in Bavaria recorded. 'Although no-one wants war, the majority of the populace awaits coming developments with calm out of faith in the Führer and the Wehrmacht and goes about its work undisturbed.' William Shirer was rather blunter in his observations. 'Everybody against the war. People talking openly. How can a country go into a major war with a population so dead against it?'[60]

At least, Berliners comforted themselves, things were worse 300 miles to the east. A mob dominated the streets of Warsaw; the Polish capital was gripped by worsening panic; the stations were crammed with civilians trying to flee the city, the banks were under siege from anxious investors determined to withdraw their savings, and the grocery stores were under siege from Varsovians hoarding food.[61]

Or that was how the *Völkischer Beobachter* saw life in Warsaw in the final days of August 1939. Varsovians viewed life in their city rather differently. In fact, many preferred to ignore the imminence of war, as Wladyslaw Szpilman, a pianist on Polish radio, observed. They deluded themselves, he recalled, with 'an inherent belief, in defiance of all logic, that although war was bound to come, its actual outbreak would be delayed, so they could live life to the full a little longer. After all, life was good.' Apart from a blackout and Warsaw residents hurrying around carrying gas masks, life in the capital continued as normal. Civic leaders holidayed as they did every summer. Behind the darkened windows of cafes and bars, bands still played, revellers still drank, danced and sang patriotic songs. Wherever they looked, Poles saw posters and banners affirming their nation's determination: We won't give away what is ours, We shall repel the invader. 'The slogans of government propaganda are blindly believed,' German Ambassador Hans Adolf von Moltke reported to his masters in Berlin. Poles were told they stood on the eve of a great victory, that the German people were starving, that Germany's armed forces were more bluff than blood, that the Western Allies would come to Poland's aid. The word of the clergy reinforced the word of the government. In a deeply religious land, the clergy exerted particular influence. There were instances of services praying for victory over Germany, of some ministers proclaiming Poland stood 'on the precipice of a holy war' against the Reich, Moltke telegraphed. Prayers for peace ordered by the cardinal of Poznan, Augustyn Hlond, were turned into prayers for victory by his ministers. In short, the diplomat realised, the Polish people were in the grip of war fever. 'The old hatred of everything German and the conviction that it is Poland's destiny to cross swords with Germany are too deeply rooted to allow passions, once inflamed, to die away so soon,' he warned Berlin.[62]

Polish confidence was unassailable. The Polish soldier was imbued with the spirit of the offensive, of taking the fight to the enemy. 'No-one wanted to hear anything about retreat, let alone think about it,' one officer recalled. The confidence was infectious. It did not just affect the men, the non-commissioned officers, the junior officers, but staff officers, commanders, political leaders, ordinary Poles. A soldier marching through the capital's streets with his company in late August, bound for the railway station and a waiting troop train, was cheered on by patrons of Warsaw's finest restaurants: 'Young men, on to Berlin!' 'We are with you!' A drunk stood outside the exclusive Moulin Rouge club handing out glasses of cognac to the soldiers. 'Get Hitler!' he urged them. The men eventually reached the marshalling yard where they found rail trucks daubed with a slogan, clearly legible in the pale August moonlight: *Do Berlina* – On to Berlin![63]

The Polish General Staff was rather more realistic. *Do Berlina* was fine as a national slogan, but if it came to war with Germany, Poland's generals knew, the army would be on the defensive, not offensive. For fifteen years, the Polish Army had directed its gaze eastwards – and planned its defensive doctrine accordingly. But from 1935 onwards, the growth of German military strength forced it to look west as well. It did not like what it saw: the German soldier would outnumber his Polish opponent almost two to one. As was its duty, the General Staff drew up plans to counter such a threat, concentrating its armies in north-west Poland, defending the Corridor, Warsaw and the Vistula valley. The Reich's swallowing of Czechoslovakia fundamentally changed Poland's plight. Now she faced threats not merely from Pomerania, East Prussia and Silesia, but from the Slovakian frontier as well.

The plan devised by Poland's leaders to deal with these threats, Plan *Zachod* (West), or simply Plan Z, was to hold the frontier as long as possible with armies bearing the names of the cities or regions they were to defend – *Pomorze* (Pomerania), *Poznan* (Posen), *Lodz*, *Krakow*, *Modlin* and *Karpaty* (Carpathians) – to give the rest of the Polish Army time to mobilise, then withdraw to the line of the country's great artery, the Vistula. Plan Z was never intended to defeat the Wehrmacht; it was meant to buy the Polish Army time to complete mobilisation and buy the French time to strike on the Western Front... providing the Polish Army could hold the frontier... and providing the French Army was prepared to strike.

And there was another major flaw with Plan Z. Poland lacked the means with which to execute it. No nation in Europe save the Soviet Union spent more of its wealth on defence than Poland. It was still not enough. In 1938–1939 more than one billion zloty were devoured by the *Polskie Sily Zbrojne* – Polish Armed Forces; in the same period the Wehrmacht received thirty times as much. In 1939, Germany's defence spending was more than fifty times greater than Poland's. The Poles had neither the means nor the industrial capacity to match the motorisation of the Wehrmacht or the technology and engineering of the Luftwaffe. They did, however, try. To this day the popular image of the Polish Army in the 1939 campaign remains that of cavalry charging panzers. It is an image created in part by the German propaganda machine and in part by Poles looking for heroes in a world without them. In reality, the Polish Army if not embracing armoured warfare, did at least experiment with it. There were nearly 1,000 armoured vehicles of one form or another in the Poles' arsenal in 1939, chiefly more than 550 small tanks, or tankettes – caterpillar-tracked armoured scouting cars – bolstered by three dozen British-built light tanks. The brightest hope was the new 7TP medium tank, a match for German Panzer Mk IIIs in speed and firepower, but only a smattering had begun to reach front-line units by August 1939. There were also ten relics of the 1920 war with the Soviet Union: armoured trains, strange beasts which carried artillery in turrets, tankettes on a transporter to scout for them, and stormtroops in a wagon to act as infantry support. And then there were the cavalry, 70,000 men – eight brigades in all, echoes of a bygone age of warfare, but not cavalry in the traditional sense. These horsemen did not ride into battle sabres drawn or lances lowered, charging at the enemy; they dismounted and fought like infantrymen with rifles, pistols and machine-guns.

The cavalry were the elite of the *Polskie Sily Zbrojne*, but the backbone, as with the Wehrmacht, were the infantry, thirty divisions in all. Outwardly they were a match for their German foe: 16,000 men in every division, each man dressed in an olive green-brown jacket and trousers. The men wore a rucksack containing clothes, kit including an entrenching tool, blanket or tent, and carried a standard-issue Mauser rifle. But in training, firepower and mobility, Polish infantry lagged behind the Wehrmacht. Around one in three Polish riflemen was not fully trained. He was outgunned by the German who possessed more and heavier field and anti-tank guns. Worse still, the Polish infantry division relied even more than its German equivalent upon the horse to haul its wagons and weapons.[64]

The Polish Air Force, *Polskie Lotnictwo Wojskowe* – technically part of the army – was the poor relation of its country's armed forces; for every fifteen zloty spent on defence by the Polish Government, the air force received just one. It showed. Of the paper strength of almost 2,000 aircraft, fewer than 400 were fit for battle. Numbers told only part of the story. The principal fighter, the high-wing P11 monoplane, could neither fly as high nor as fast as the Messerschmidt Me109 (it could, however, outmanoeuvre it). It was also outnumbered by its foe: there were barely 130 P11s; there were almost 450 Me109s deployed on the Eastern Front. The Polish bomber force was no less outdated. The mainstay of the fleet was an antiquated reconnaissance aircraft-cum-light bomber, the P23 *Karas* (Carp). The modern twin-engined medium bomber, the P37 *Los* (Elk), was the ace up the sleeve, faster than any Polish fighter and with a substantial bomb load. The Elk, however, was only slowly reaching front-line units; by the end of August 1939, just three dozen had been delivered.[65]

The wheels of mobilisation in Poland slowly began to turn on 24 August – but only along the threatened western frontier with the Reich; general mobilisation was delayed for fear of providing Adolf Hitler with the *casus belli* he was grasping at. And as the wheels turned, so Plan Z began to come apart almost immediately. Even on the train journey to join his unit in the Silesian industrial town of Chorzow, a reserve officer in *75th Infantry Regiment*, found the mood among the men depressed; they openly expressed their misgivings about the impending conflict. In Chorzow itself, the road to the barracks was lined with soldiers' wives weeping and crying. At the barracks, old uniforms and worn-out boots were distributed, plus the odd warm meal. The regiment was ordered to make a twenty-five-mile night march to the industrial town of Oswiecim – Auschwitz to the Germans – a major rail junction in Silesia. They were sent on their way with no food, no pay and no leadership. *75th Infantry Regiment*'s war would only get worse.[66]

Other Polish servicemen relished the prospect of war. They believed in, no, expected victory. 'I went to war entirely convinced that it would end in the defeat of the enemy, that our aces would give the insolent Luftwaffe a thorough drubbing,' recalled Bohdan Arct, who reported for duty at an airfield in northeastern Poland. In a few weeks, Arct predicted, he would take off his air force uniform in triumph and return to his day job as an artist. His confidence was mirrored by fighter pilot Lieutenant Skalski, based in Torun – Thorn to the Germans – in the Corridor. Skalski willingly overlooked the shortcomings of his P11 fighter and joked about the might of the Luftwaffe. War excited him. 'I secretly hoped that it would begin as soon as possible.'[67]

The telephones in the offices of 75–76 Wilhelmstrasse, home to the German Foreign Ministry, rang repeatedly and the teleprinter chattered incessantly on Wednesday, 30 August. The monarchs of Belgium and the Netherlands offered their services as mediators; Sir Nevile Henderson was doing all he could to find a Pole to come to Berlin to negotiate, but time was against him; the Soviet Union was holidaying so the non-aggression pact with Germany could not be ratified by its leaders. And at 5.30pm, a ministry official received a call from John von Wühlisch, German chargé d'affaires in Warsaw. Since the beginning of August, Wühlisch had been holding the fort in the Polish capital. His ambassador, Hans Adolf von Moltke, had returned home to Germany on summer leave – then been forbidden to return to Poland by Ribbentrop. Von Wühlisch calmly and dutifully filled in for his master, recording the mood in the Polish capital and its press. That mood grew ever darker, the consul noted, as August 1939 faded. There were still rallying cries in the newspapers – 'Our nerves have remained victorious during the war of nerves and will remain so during the test of a proper war' the *Gazeta Polska* proclaimed – but the Polish press also spoke openly now of the 'decisive hour upon which we are entering'. And as he wandered the streets of Warsaw on the afternoon of the thirtieth, Wühlisch noticed placards and notices being posted around the capital: the Poles were ordering general mobilisation.[68]

In Upper Silesia, Gestapo *Kriminalsekretär* – criminal secretary – Karl Nowak was called into his superior's office. Sat at the desk, however, was not Nowak's boss but an SS *Sturmbannführer* with a junior SS man hovering over him, both dressed in *feldgrau*. Nowak was to accompany a Gestapo inspector on a secret mission. 'You won't say anything about what you see to anyone, not today, not in 100 years,' the *Sturmbannführer* warned him. Nowak and the inspector drove to the village of Hohenlieben (today Lubie), ten miles north of Gleiwitz. There, the inspector left Nowak. He returned perhaps ten minutes later dragging a smallish man with dark blond hair, scruffily dressed – a 41-year-old Pole, an agent for a farm machinery firm, a veteran of the third and bloodiest Silesian uprising. His name was Franz Honiok.[69]

For a fortnight, SS *Sturmbannführer* Alfred Naujocks and his half dozen men had been holed up in two hotels in Gleiwitz. Naujocks had spent his two weeks in Silesia perfecting his plan. He had reconnoitred the radio station – an imposing brick building on the road to Tarnowitz flanked by two accommodation blocks, surrounded by a wire fence; the entire site was dominated by the 350ft transmitter. He had selected the time for the attack: 8pm – it would be dark, yet not too late to give the impression that the 'insurgents' were criminals, and most Silesians would be at home listening to their radios. When the order came, Naujocks and his men, all dressed in old civilian clothes, would storm the station, fire a handful of shots, make their broadcast – a Polish-speaking *Volksdeutsche* from Gleiwitz would accompany the raid – then leave. The plan, thought Naujocks, was perfect. Naujocks did not know that barely anyone would hear his broadcast.

After a frantic day of diplomacy desperately trying to find a Pole to come to Berlin, it was almost midnight as Sir Nevile Henderson entered 78 Wilhelmstrasse, the old Foreign Ministry, where he was shown into Bismarck's former office.

Perhaps it was the hour, perhaps it was the strain of days of negotiations, or perhaps it was deliberate, but Joachim von Ribbentrop was in a foul temper and in no mood for conciliation as the British ambassador played for time. 'Time is up,' the German Foreign Minister curtly told him. 'Where's the Pole your Government was to provide?' It had been impossible to find a Polish negotiator in twenty-four hours, Henderson protested. Perhaps, he suggested, Germany might try speaking directly to the Polish Ambassador in Berlin. 'That's out of the question after what has happened,' Ribbentrop snapped. The British diplomat now began to lose his composure. His face reddened, his hands shook as he struggled to read through his government's official reply to the Reich in spite of the constant interruptions. With the note read, Sir Nevile Henderson added a personal postscript: he had information proving that Germans were committing acts of sabotage on Polish soil. 'That's a damned lie,' Ribbentrop screamed. Henderson wagged his finger at the foreign minister. 'Damned' was not the language he expected from a statesman. Ribbentrop leapt out of his chair. So too Henderson. The two men glowered at each other for a few moments before sitting down. Ribbentrop rattled through a document containing sixteen points by which the Polish crisis might be solved – notably the cession of Danzig to the Reich and a plebiscite in the Corridor. Might he have a copy of the paper, Nevile Henderson inquired. 'No,' Ribbentrop told him brusquely, tossing the document on to the table. 'It is out of the date anyhow.' A dejected Nevile Henderson stumbled out of the office convinced 'the last hope of peace had vanished'.[70]

As Joachim von Ribbentrop and Nevile Henderson argued, a few yards along Wilhelmstrasse Adolf Hitler was issuing the order, this time irrevocably, for unleashing *Fall Weiss*. Poland's attitude had become 'intolerable', political solutions to the crisis had been 'exhausted'. He had, therefore, 'decided upon a solution by force'. And so the machinery of war began to turn methodically as it had done six days earlier. The orders rattled off the teletypes in every command: in Pomerania, in East Prussia, in Silesia, in Slovakia. A *Hauptmann* on the staff of X Corps, charged with thrusting towards Lodz, relished the challenge to come. For days he had endured news of attacks and atrocities against ethnic Germans across the border. 'They do not want to negotiate,' he wrote firmly in his diary. 'They have mobilised against Germany.' Before dawn on 1 September the 'counter-attack' would be unleashed. 'It is a liberating feeling,' he continued. 'From now on all work takes on a deep, serious meaning. We should demonstrate what we have learned in peacetime.' A young officer in 94th Infantry Regiment was equally enthusiastic: 'Tomorrow, it at last goes off. Tomorrow the theories of our soldierly trade will be put into practice, bloody practice.'[71]

In Danzig, the band of the *Schleswig-Holstein* performed martial music while sailors took part in a parade of flags almost daily. A singular thought dominated the mind of the bandmaster, *Oberleutnant* Willi Aurich: his musicians had to be ready for a concert to be broadcast on local radio on Sunday, 3 September. As crowds of Danzigers heaved to and fro on the quayside, assault troops moved among them to board the aged battleship; the men wore sports clothes to avoid raising suspicions. 'Our situation seems to be getting more tense,' Aurich observed. 'Hopefully there'll soon be a decision!' There would. Danzigers knew it. Danzig's small Polish population knew it. Brownshirts marched through the streets singing the Nazi anthem, the *Horst Wessellied*. Crowds chanted: 'Hang the Jews. Put the Poles up against the wall!' Postman Franciszek Mionskowski was knocked to the ground by SS foot soldiers while his colleague was threatened. 'Away with you, clear off to Poland,' an SS man sneered. 'It doesn't matter. Tomorrow you're going on an eternal journey!' A couple of boys grabbed eight-year-old Stefania Koziarowska: 'Polish pig, get out of Danzig!'[72]

The telephone in Alfred Naujock's hotel room rang around 4pm on Thursday, 31 August. 'Call back,' Reinhard Heydrich said brusquely, then put the phone down. Naujocks did as ordered. The SD chief answered, again curtly. 'Grandma's dead.' Naujock's replaced the receiver. The attack would proceed that night.[73]

Afternoon was turning to evening as Polish Ambassador Josef Lipski was ushered into the Foreign Ministry in Wilhelmstrasse after spending the day trying to see Joachim von Ribbentrop. His government was prepared to discuss the proposals Ribbentrop had furiously tossed on his table in front of Sir Nevile Henderson.

'Have you the authority to negotiate?' Ribbentrop asked Lipski icily.

'No,' said the Pole.

'Well then there is no point in our continuing this conversation.'

Josef Lipski left Ribbentrop's study. The meeting had lasted barely five minutes.[74]

Rifleman Karl Schönfeld and his comrades moved up to their jump-off position in Pomerania. The men were melancholy, almost distant. 'Every one of us stands or wanders around with thoughts which are utterly new, thoughts of his father and mother or his wife and child,' he recorded in his diary. The last day of August was drawing to a close. 'In the West there's a wonderful sunset. Nature is enjoying the most beautiful peace. It all contributes to our melancholy mood.' Officers moved among their men, acting as a reassuring presence.

'Well, Schönfeld, any worries?'

'*Nein, Herr Hauptmann*!' Schönfeld lied. Why had he lied, he wondered. To appear brave? Perhaps. And perhaps every man in company would have given the same answer, whether he believed it or not.[75]

Day was turning to night as Alfred Naujocks invited his men to his hotel room. For the first time he informed them of their mission. In thirty minutes' time they would seize the nearby radio transmitter and broadcast in Polish. The men put on scruffy Polish clothes, removed all forms of identification, and climbed into two cars.

Just before 8pm, five shadowy figures entered the main building and began rounding up the radio station's staff, firing a few shots into the building's ceiling. The employees were handcuffed and led to the basement. Now the broadcast could begin. Except that it couldn't. There was no microphone. Gleiwitz was only a relay transmitter, not a station for broadcasting. Finally, one of Naujocks' team found a 'weather microphone' – used to warn listeners of possible meteorological interference. Shortly after 8pm the people of Gleiwitz and surrounding towns heard their evening listening interrupted by a confused, chaotic Polish babble. '*Achtung, achtung*! This is Gleiwitz. The radio station is in Polish hands. The hour of liberation has come!' As the men leaned over the microphone, the door to the transmission room was flung open by the station manager in his shirtsleeves. The raiders aimed their guns at him and he fled to raise the alarm. It was time, Alfred Naujocks decided, to leave. The *Volksdeutsche* spoke into the microphone one last time in Polish. 'Long live Poland!'

As he stepped out of the building, Naujocks noticed a body slumped next to the entrance. The *Sturmbannführer* walked over and examined the man. His face, his entire head was covered in blood. It was Franz Honiok, arrested barely twenty-four hours earlier. Naujocks left the body and rejoined his men. They had to escape before the police arrived. The whole affair had lasted just thirteen minutes.[76]

On a forward airfield close to the Polish border, Luftwaffe correspondent Peter Supf watched 'an endless chain' of vehicles moving up to the frontier. Panzers, trucks, guns, men. Children stood outside farmhouses and waved furiously at the passing soldiers. Their parents were not so enthusiastic. They remembered the last war, Supf observed. 'This drive to the front in the half-light between day and night, between war and peace, how often would it be repeated?' the reporter mused. 'Today to the East, tomorrow to the West. How many more times would these children's hands wave at the soldiers, the brave soldiers?'

The half-light became night. 'A blood-red moon rose above the distant pine forest,' wrote Supf. 'It first looked as if the forest was on fire. Then the glowing disc rose higher and higher. A strange, magical red tint was cast across the land. Did the blood red of this August moon herald war?'[77]

In a forest near the village of Preussenfeld (today Podrozna) thirteen miles northeast of Schneidemühl, an armoured reconnaissance unit carried out final checks on their vehicles. They played football to pass the time, without really paying attention to the score. 'There's an incredible tension lying over all of us,' war correspondent *Rittmeister* (captain) *Freiherr* von Esebeck observed. 'Will we see action at all?' The tension was soon lifted. 'Tomorrow morning we're off!' Esebeck wrote enthusiastically. 'From 0445 Hours, there will be shooting. There will be no more mercy.'

The engines of the motorcycles and armoured cars idled, then gently revved. In the darkness, the columns wove through the West Prussian forests, along narrow tracks, the motorcycles first, the armour following, until they stopped just short of the Polish border.[78]

A stone's throw away from Esebeck and his comrades, Berliner Hans P and his company left their billets and marched through the night to Preussenfeld. It took an hour for the troops to reach their jump-off positions. The men dozed for a couple of hours, ate, drank coffee and waited for dawn to come.

Back in his hotel room, Alfred Naujocks felt rather pleased with himself. The attack had gone like clockwork. He picked up his telephone and called Berlin to report to his master. But Reinhard Heydrich was far from pleased. 'You're lying. I waited the entire time!' Heydrich had tuned into his radio to the Gleiwitz frequency at 8pm and he heard nothing, no Polish insurgents seizing control of the airwaves. Gleiwitz was only a sub-station, re-transmitting programmes from Breslau on the same frequency. Anyone in Berlin who tuned into Gleiwitz merely heard Breslau.[79]

In East Prussia junior officer Fritz Fillies and his company commander, one *Oberleutnant* Helmut Betzler, wandered around their bivouac. The men, the horses, the guns, all were ready. The two officers talked with their men. None were troubled. They were men 'full of expectation, confidence and readiness, filled with a great, deep inner resolve'. A light rain fell, clearing the humid August night somewhat. Betzler and Fillies discussed poetry, then crawled into his tent to catch a few hours' sleep. 'It felt good under the canvas,' Fillies recalled. 'We slept, and *Oberleutnant* Helmut Betzler did not know that this would be his last good sleep.'[80]

Two Gestapo agents knocked on the door of Carl Burckhardt. Telephone lines were down, they told the League of Nations Commissioner to Danzig. The diplomat must not leave his house, they continued, and must remain at the disposal of Albert Forster.[81]

The staff of 45th Infantry Division stood outside an outbuilding on the edge of Huklady, a good twenty miles from the Czech-Polish border. There was only one topic of conversation among the officers, and the men convinced themselves this impending war would not spread. The divisional adjutant had remained silent throughout until the talk drew to a close. 'We should not deceive ourselves, gentlemen,' he warned his comrades. 'We are on the eve of a second world war!' His fellow officers vehemently rejected his observation.[82]

One and a half million German soldiers were now drawn up along the Polish frontier – more than fifty divisions in all, fourteen of them armoured or motorised. Few men had any doubts about the impending victory of German arms, and fewer still doubted the justness of their cause. On the East Prussian-Polish border, *Generalleutnant* Kuno-Hans von Both gathered his closest staff around him. His 21st Infantry Division was raised in Prussia, east and west; now it was being called upon to re-take sacred soil, to fight 'for the honour and existence of the Fatherland'. East Prussia was in danger, ethnic Germans were suffering 'frightful persecution', this was a land torn from the Reich 'by treason' in 1919, Both told his men. 'This is the living space of the German people. Our struggle and our lives belong to this people and its leader, our supreme commander Adolf Hitler.' One hundred and seventy miles to the southwest in the headquarters of X Corps in Trebnitz (today Trzebnica), north of Breslau, a *Hauptmann* anxiously waited for dawn. 'We would like to unleash our troops and teach the Poles the necessary respect for the German Reich with our weapons, to put right the injustice of 1919 and reclaim an ancient cultured German land. Above all we would like to avenge the persecution of *Volksdeutsche* and offer them protection.' And in the Tatra mountains, on the Slovakian-Polish border, Austrian infantryman Wilhelm Prüller fumed. 'It's unthinkable for us as the greatest European power to sit back and watch the persecution of *Volksdeutsche* without doing something,' he fumed. 'It is our duty to right this wrong. If we fight, then we know that we are serving a rightful cause.' And if it did come to a fight, it wouldn't last long, Prüller assured himself. 'The Poles won't be able to withstand our attack.'[83]

The ordinary German soldier, the *Landser*, was nevertheless warned not to underestimate his foe. The Polish soldier, intelligence experts on the General Staff explained, was filled with a strong sense of pride and an even stronger sense of nationalism. He was arrogant, irrational, easily excitable and often consumed by blind hatred and fanaticism. In uniform, the Pole was brave, patriotic, determined. He was also unthinking, willing to endure heavy losses. In battle, he needed constant leadership from his officers who took their lead from French and German military theorists – except that they had not been as thoroughly trained. Those officers were imbued with a spirit of nationalism; they told each man he should 'regard himself as defender of the faith and as a warrior against the advance of all things Teutonic'.[84]

There were twenty-six infantry divisions and around a dozen cavalry, mountain infantry and armoured brigades filled with such warriors against all things Teutonic, fully or partly ready for battle as Friday September 1 began. The Pole was outnumbered two-to-one on the ground. His comrade in the air faced even worse odds; the Luftwaffe enjoyed a four-one numerical superiority. Not half Poland's armed forces had been mobilised.[85]

On the cusp of 31 August-1 September a couple of trucks lurched through the Silesian countryside. They came to a halt in a forest a few miles from Hochlinden. Around sixty men leaped out, donned Polish uniforms, collected suitable weapons, and were led down a path through the trees to the edge of the wood. It was here, in the small hours of September 1, that the men were briefed. Only Polish was to be spoken from now on. They would sing the Polish national anthem, anti-German tunes. They would curse the Reich and all it stood for. 'Long live Poland.' 'Down with the Germans.' And they would raze the customs house to the ground.[86]

Aboard the *Schleswig-Holstein*, Willi Aurich was woken shortly after 1am by the commotion outside his cabin. The bandmaster got out of bed, put on his clothes and went up on deck. Swinging from a crane were motorcycles while other equipment for assault troops was being offloaded on to the jetty.

Shrouded in the East Prussian darkness, a column of vehicles pulled out of the barracks in Elbing (today Elblag) a little after 2am for the short journey to a railway station outside the city. The trucks pulled to a stop. An official from the German Railways, the *Reichsbahn*, directed the men of 41st Pioneer Battalion to a goods train waiting on the tracks, sixty-five trucks long. It took twenty-five minutes for two platoons of pioneers to clamber into the first third of the train. And then, at 3.08am precisely, the 'goods train' pulled out of Elbing and headed west. After eighteen miles the train halted in Marienburg, the last stop before it left the Reich and crossed into the territory of the Free City of Danzig. A Polish engine replaced the German locomotive hauling the train, but its driver and fireman were not Poles, they were SS men in Polish railway workers' uniforms. With the engine coupled, the train continued its journey westwards towards the Vistula. Another locomotive pulled on to the same track behind the goods train, an armoured train.[87]

It was pitch black in the Jablunka Pass. War correspondent Leo Leixner struggled to follow the terrain of the Beskids under the dim light of a torch. He struggled, too, to listen to a regimental commander briefing his men on the impending assault on the vital mountain crossing. At midnight, 7th Infantry Division had finally bivouacked. But no man slept. 'The night is in so much turmoil,' the journalist wrote in his diary, then corrected himself. 'No, our hearts are in so much turmoil.'[88]

Alfred Lessnau was sleeping soundly in the station house in the village of Szymankowo – Simonsdorf to the Germans – the first stop for any train travelling through the land of the Free City of Danzig from East Prussia to the Reich. The word 'free' meant little to Lessnau and other Poles working in Szymankowo. For months they had been subjected to intimidation. In recent days it had worsened. The local German populace had become brazenly hostile, even talking of butchering the Poles in the village. Before dawn the Germans would be as good as their word.

For twenty minutes SS *Sturmbannführer* Karl Hoffmann and his band of 'Polish' insurgents waited in a meadow, a couple of hundred yards from the customs house at Hochlinden. Hoffmann waved his men forward, crawling or crouching down, until they were one hundred yards from their target. SS *Unterscharführer* Josef Grzimek looked around him. The Polish border lay no more than 300 yards away. The lights were still on in the nearest village. The villagers were singing, talking, laughing. There was, Grzimek recalled, 'complete calm'. That was until Karl Hoffmann fired his pistol several times. It was precisely 4am. The 'attack' had begun.

The next few minutes were chaotic. The men shouted and swore in Polish. They fired their guns wildly. The 'defenders' fired back wildly. Hoffmann's men stormed the building. They smashed the windows, kicked in the doors, tiles flew off the roof. Scrambling for cover on the floor they found a police captain and an SS trooper. Then came the 'counter-attack': SS men dressed in the uniforms of German border police. The 'insurgents' were captured to a man and led out of the wrecked building towards waiting trucks. Josef Grzimek stumbled in the dark. He noticed the outline of several motionless bodies on the ground. Grzimek bent down. The men wore Polish uniforms and each one had a shaved head. Perhaps, he wondered, they were comrades struck down by reckless fire. Grzimek tried to stand one of the bodies up. The corpse was rigid.[89]

Erich Hoepner was awake a little before 4am in the town of Bunzlau in Silesia. The affairs of XVI Corps could wait. First, the panzer general had a personal duty to perform – a final letter home before war raged. 'In an hour the attack begins,' he wrote to his wife Irma. 'We want to hope that we'll all see each other again safely, but that everything turns out well for Germany too. The Polish question *must* be solved once and for all.'[90]

Notes

1. 'Mit der 6 Kompanie die Schöpffer Regiments von Elbing bis Warschau: Tagebuch eines Kompanieführers aus dem Polenfeldzuge', in BA-MA RH37/3094.
2. *Danziger Neueste Nachrichten*, 19/6/39 and TB Goebbels, 18/6/39.
3. Ia No.91/39 Estimate of the situation by Working Staff Rundstedt, 7/5/39 in NOKW 2584 and KTB AGr Süd, 25/8/39, cited in Elble, p. 38.

4. Padfield, p. 181.
5. Raeder was right. Within two years, the Albrechts were divorced. The former adjutant died – or committed suicide – defending Berlin in May 1945. KTB Engel 12/7/39–20/7/39 and Irving, *The Warpath*, pp. 212–14.
6. *Völkischer Beobachter*, 7/6/39 and Suchenwirth, Command and Leadership in the German Air Force, pp. 85, 231n.
7. Kubizek, pp. 254–6 and Hamann, p. 302.
8. Hundrieser, pp. 12–13 and Hammer, I und Neiden, Suzanne zu, *Sehr selten habe ich geweint*, p. 13.
9. Burckhardt, p. 317.
10. *Völkischer Beobachter*, 18/7/39.
11. *New York Times*, 7/8/39.
12. Uhl and Eberle, *Hitler Book*, p. 42.
13. VB, 12/8/39.
14. Burckhardt, pp. 339–45.
15. DGFP, D, vii, Doc.43, Ciano's Diplomatic Papers, pp. 299–303 and Ciano Diario, 12/8/39.
16. Besymenski, pp. 142, 206–9.
17. Michaelis, *SS Heimwehr Danzig*, p. 13 and New York Times, 20/8/39.
18. Read and Fisher, p. 225, Hegner, p. 335 and Speer, p. 234.
19. Author's papers and TB Goebbels, 23/8/39.
20. The account of the conference on 22 August is based on the author's papers, DGFP, Series D, Docs.192–193, KTB Halder, 14/8/39, KTB Groscurth, 24/8/39, Irving, *Warpath*, p. 242, Hermann Boehm, 'Zur Ansprache Hitlers vor den Führern der Wehrmacht am 22 August 1939', VfZ, Band 19, 1971, pp. 294–302 and Baumgart, Winfried, 'Zur Ansprache Hitlers vor den Führern der Wehrmacht am 22 August 1939', VfZ, 1968, pp. 140–9. With Joseph Goebbels, who was at the Berghof that day but not at the conference, Hitler was rather more circumspect. Poland, he told his Propaganda Minister, would not cause Germany too many problems. 'More difficult is the question of whether the West will intervene. That he cannot say at the moment. It depends on the circumstances.' TB Goebbels, 23/8/39.
21. Müller, *Das Heer und Hitler*, p. 411, KTB Engel, 24/8/39, Boehm, 'Zur Ansprache Hitlers vor den Führern der Wehrmacht am 22 August 1939', VfZ, Band 19, 1971, p. 300.
22. Kleist, p. 35.
23. DGFP, D, vii, Docs.228, 229, Hegner, pp. 337–8, 342–3, and Wegner (ed), *From Peace to War*, p. 195.
24. Toland, p. 752, Speer, pp. 234–5 and Below, p. 28.
25. Paul, *Brennpunkte*, p. 21.
26. Straub, Walter, Oberst, *Das Panzer Regiment 7 und 21 und seine Tochterformationen im Zweiten Weltkrieg*, KTB XIX Pz Corps, 31/8/39 and Guderian to his wife, 24/8/39, in Bradley, *Generaloberst Heinz Guderian und die Entstehungsgeschichte des modernen Blitzkrieges*, pp. 215–16.
27. Geyr von Schweppenburg, 'Einsatz der 3 Panzer Division in Polenfeldzug' in BA-MA RH27-3/243.
28. Hammer, I und Neiden, Suzanne zu, *Sehr selten habe ich geweint*, p. 15

29. Oberjäger Prechtl, 'Mobilisation' in Erlbenisberichte: Aufmarsch, Durchmarsch durch die Slowakei. BA-MA RH 53-18/144.

30. Tagesbefehl AOK14, 24/8/39. BA-MA RH20-14/77.

31. KTB *Schleswig-Holstein*, 25/8/39 in NHB 713, Mulligan, *Lone Wolf*, p. 38 and Burckhardt, p. 351.

32. Hegner, p. 274.

33. TB Weizsäcker, 24/8/39, and TB Goebbels, 26/8/39.

34. DGFP, D, vii, Doc.265 and DBFP, 3rd Series, vii, Docs.283, 284, 286–288.

35. Schindler, pp. 20, 45–6.

36. KTB Richthofen, 25/8/39, in BA-MA N671/4.

37. DGFP, D, vii, Doc.271.

38. Schindler, p. 25 and Vormann, pp. 39–43.

39. Bekker, p. 20 and KTB Richthofen, 25/8/39, in BA-MA N671/4.

40. Manstein, pp. 31–2.

41. Geyr von Schweppenburg, 'Einsatz der 3 Panzer Division in Polenfeldzug' in BA-MA RH27-3/243.

42. Heusinger, pp. 58–9. The body of the dead man and his light machine-gun were picked up by the Poles and handed to German authorities the next day.

43. Schindler, pp. 49, 69–71, 77–80, 98–9.

44. DGFP, D, vii, Doc.330.

45. Paul, *Das Potsdamer Infanterie Regiment 9*, p. 129–30, 138.

46. 'Infanterie Regiment 67 (23 ID) in Polenfeldzug' in BA-MA RH37/5024.

47. Oberfähnrich K, Zugführer, Tagebuchnotizen als Beitrag zur Geschichte des Infanterie Regiments 68 in BA-MA RH37/4975.

48. Vormann, pp. 43–45.

49. Vormann, pp. 43–45, 51 and TB Groscurth, 28/8/39.

50. Vormann, p. 55, TB Weizsäcker, 29/8/39 and KTB Engel, 29/8/39.

51. DGFP, D, vii, Doc.384, DBFP, 3rd Series, vii, Doc.455 and KTB Halder, 28/8/39.

52. 'Die 10 Division im polnischen Feldzug,' speech by von Cochenhausen in Regensburg, 31/10/39 in BA-MA RH26-10/544.

53. Fillies, pp. 13, 17, 29.

54. *Völkischer Beobachter*, 17/8/39, 26/8/39 and *Bromberger Blutsonntag*, p. 80.

55. The account of Polish 'atrocities' is based on Bromberger Blutsonntag, pp. 80, 82–3, DGFP, D, vii, Doc.359 and Shirer, *Berlin Diary*, p. 172 and Vormann, p. 53.

56. Spiess, Alfred und Lichtenstein, Heiner, *Unternehmen Tannenberg*, pp. 20–2, and Runzheimer, Jürgen, 'Die Grenzzwischenfälle am Abend vor dem deutschen Angriff auf Polen', p. 115.

57. Spiess, Alfred und Lichtenstein, Heiner, *Unternehmen Tannenberg*, pp. 55–6.

58. DGFP, D, vii, Doc.421, DBFP, 3rd Series, vii, Doc.490 and Henderson, pp. 264–7.

59. Vormann, p. 50, *New York Times*, 29/8/39 and TB Wagner, 23/8/39 in Wagner, p. 92.

60. Kershaw, *Hitler Myth*, p. 142, Broszat (ed), pp. 525–6 and Shirer, Berlin Diary, p. 191.

61. 'Der Mob beherrscht die Strasse in Warschau' in *Völkischer Beobachter*, 27/8/39.

62. Szpilman, p. 22 and DGFP, D, vi, Doc.754.

63. Drescher, pp. 36–8, 68.

64. Zaloga and Madej, pp. 46–55.

65. Zaloga and Madej, pp. 97–9.

66. Polnische Reserve Offizier, 'Die andere Seite!', Anlage zum KTB 5 Pz Div in BA-MA RH 27-5/2.
67. Zamoyski, pp. 18–21.
68. DGFP, Series D, vol.vii, Docs.415 and 451.
69. Spiess, Alfred und Lichtenstein, Heiner, *Unternehmen Tannenberg*, p. 80.
70. Schmidt, pp. 150–4, Henderson, pp. 269–73 and DGFP, D, vii, Doc.461.
71. Based on Directive No.1 for the Conduct of the War in author's papers, plus Tagebuchaufzeichnungen über den Feldzug in Polen beim X Korps, von Hauptmann Kretzschmar in BA-MA RH24-10/554 and Rossino, p. 195.
72. Schenk, *Post von Danzig*, pp. 44, 52, 56.
73. Spiess, Alfred und Lichtenstein, Heiner, *Unternehmen Tannenberg*, p. 131.
74. Schmidt, p. 154.
75. Dollinger, *Kain, wo ist dein Bruder?*, p. 20.
76. Spiess, Alfred und Lichtenstein, Heiner, *Unternehmen Tannenberg*, pp. 131-2, 143, 146.
77. Supf, *Luftwaffe schlägt zu! Der Luftkrieg in Polen*, p. 12.
78. Guderian, *Mit den Panzern in Ost und West: Erlebnisberichte von Mitkämpfern aus den Feldzügen in Polen und Frankreich 1939/40*, pp. 16–17.
79. Spiess, Alfred und Lichtenstein, Heiner, *Unternehmen Tannenberg*, p. 149.
80. Fillies, pp. 32–4.
81. Burckhardt, p. 352.
82. Gschöpf, p. 72.
83. Based on Tagesbefehl 21 Infanterie Division, 1/9/39, cited in Rossino, p. 27, plus Tagebuchaufzeichnungen über den Feldzug in Polen beim X Korps, von Hauptmann Kretzschmar in BA-MA RH24-10/554 and KTB Prüller, 30/8/39.
84. OKW WFA/WPr(IVa) 1180/39 in KTB 17 Infanterie Division, Polenzeldug Anlagen, BA-MA RH 26-17/77 and OKH 330/39 'Die Polnische Kriegswehrmacht', 1/8/39 in KTB 10 Infanterie Division Anlangen, BA-MA RH26-10/476.
85. Zaloga and Madej, p. 44.
86. Spiess, Alfred und Lichtenstein, Heiner, *Unternehmen Tannenberg*,, pp. 160–2.
87. Schindler, p. 145.
88. Leixner, p. 10.
89. Spiess, Alfred und Lichtenstein, Heiner, *Unternehmen Tannenberg*,, pp. 163–5.
90. Bücheler, p. 80.

CHAPTER FOUR

A Very Beautiful September Day is Beginning

It's a wonderful feeling now to be a German

– WILHELM PRÜLLER

The marauders' attack will be smashed against the steel wall of our heroic army.
– DOBRY WIECZÓR KURIER CZERWONY

'WE ARE two miles from the border and ready to go.' Just short of the Slovakian-Polish frontier to the west of the Tatra Mountains – part of the Carpathian spine of central Europe – infantryman Wilhelm Prüller jotted down a few lines to his 'dearly beloved Henny'. Prüller briefly glanced at his watch. 4am. Up for three hours already, he thought. It was now Friday 1 September. In forty-five minutes, the Wehrmacht would put an end to the war psychosis which had seized the Reich and Poland throughout the spring and summer of 1939. Wilhelm Prüller's only concern was for his wife, his family, his home in the pre-dawn hours of tension. 'Keep on being the wife you always were, be assured that I love only you, and that I live only for you.' Prüller's 4th *Leichte* Division comrades sat around in lorries telling filthy jokes, waiting for the signal to move forward. 'We've just got paid,' Prüller continued in his diary. 'One hundred Czech crowns. A joke. In two hours we may not even be in this world.'[1]

More than 300 miles to the north, the 'goods train' carrying the engineers of 41st Pioneer Battalion drew into Szymankowo, an armoured train still behind it. Even in the dark, the sight of the armoured train was unmistakeable; signal men directed it on to a side track. The 'goods train' continued sluggishly through the station, but the senior customs official, Stanislaw Szarek, was suspicious. Leaning out of the window of the station, he sent a warning flare arcing into the September night. As the train passed the window, there was a volley of shots from a carbine. Szarek slumped over the window ledge. The 'goods train' continued westwards.

The flare fired by Stanislaw Szarek gave a reddish hue to the banks of the Vistula, barely five miles to the west. Here, at Dirschau – Tczew to the Poles – two 1,000-yard bridges spanned Poland's great artery: an eighty-year-old road bridge, and a newer one which had carried trains to and from East Prussia since the last decade of the 19th Century. For months the Poles had strengthened their defences on either side of the river, rolling out barbed wire, installing concrete blocks, preparing the bridges for demolition.[2]

A cool wind blew in from the Frisches Haff, the huge lagoon almost stretching from Elbing in the west to Königsberg in the east. The breeze brought with it a dawn mist, hanging barely 150 feet above *Major* Erich Munske's airfield in Heiligenbeil, thirty miles southwest of the East Prussian capital. This Friday morning, Munske stepped out on to the field where the Dornier 17s of his *Gruppe* – roughly equivalent to an RAF wing – were standing, their engines idling. 'Under this strange, pale light, everything seems to have been unnaturally enlarged – the hangars over there seem like mountains, the aircraft behind us like huge prehistoric birds,' Munske observed. 'They've been standing there with their propellers running for ten minutes already, and the air trembles with this metallic bird song.'

The airfields of eastern Germany buzzed with activity this Friday morning, despite the patchy fog shrouding much of eastern Prussia and Poland. 'I have done my best in the past few years to make our air force the largest and most powerful in the world,' a bombastic Hermann Göring declared in his order of the day. 'Born out of the spirit of German airmen in the First World War, inspired by faith in our Führer, the Luftwaffe today stands ready to carry out every order of the Führer with lightning speed and unimaginable might.'[3]

Erich Munske and his comrades had been alerted ten hours earlier, but there was little they could do about the mist they awoke to in the early hours of 1 September. Still, orders were orders. The *Major* called over the commanders of his three *Staffel* – each approximately the size of a British squadron. Their orders: attack airfields in Mlawa, Modlin, Kutno, Thorn and Graudenz – and any other valuable targets which might present themselves. 'Gentlemen,' the *Major* concluded, 'off at 4.26am. One aircraft every twenty seconds! Understood?' The *Staffel* leaders clicked their heels, nodded and then headed for their bombers. 'The next minute, the engines roar, the aircraft follow each other down the airfield, leap up and immediately disappear in the white mist.'[4]

There was a light mist too hanging over the airfield at Nieder-Ellguth, a good fifty miles east of Breslau. It was not enough to trouble *Hauptmann* Walter Sigel. Sigel and his *Gruppe* inspected their Ju87 dive-bombers – the infamous 'Stukas' the world would come to know – ahead of their first mission. Tall, with swept-back hair, barely two weeks before the thirty-three-year-old *Gruppe* commander had witnessed the death of twenty-six comrades when a demonstration of close-formation dive-bomber attack had ended in tragedy in the fog at the Neuhammer ranges. Today, Sigel told himself, mist and fog would not hold him back. Around 4.15, the Ju87s lifted off from the airbase and turned to the northeast. Their objective lay barely twenty-five miles away.

In the Schloss Schönwald in Silesia Wolfram von Richthofen had woken before 4am. He breakfasted well, then waited for his staff car to take him to his command post on the airfield at Grunsruh (today Bodzanowice). By the time the car pulled into the airbase, the air crackled with gunfire. 'Things must be serious,' Richthofen told himself. Poland would be no *Blumenkrieg*, there would be no political settlement this time; this was a 'very real war'. But the time for philosophical thoughts was past. He had an air campaign to direct. Or perhaps not. His staff had done their work thoroughly. The aircraft took off 'like clockwork'. There was little to do now except wait for the first reports to come in from his airmen.[5]

On the western edge of the Polish Corridor, *Freiherr* (Baron) von Esebeck waited in a forest with an armoured reconnaissance unit. None of the panzer men slept, preoccupied as they were with impending events. Esebeck glanced at his watch. 4.30am. 'The sky in the east begins to change colour,' he observed. The pitch black night began to give way. The faint light revealed a light mist covering the West Prussian terrain.[6]

The crew of the pre-dreadnought battleship *Schleswig-Holstein* were waiting anxiously. The night had passed uneventfully. Shrouded in darkness, the ship's boats were readied. Marine stormtroops clambered into them ready to assault the Westerplatte, the Polish ammunition depot little more than 600 yards distant. The marines disembarked under the cover of night before the battleship lumbered into position. At 4.30am the *Matrosen* – the ordinary German sailor – closed up at action stations. The 28cm main turrets of *Schleswig-Holstein*, known simply as *SX* by her men, swung around to train on the Westerplatte. *Kapitän zur See* Gustav Kleikamp clutched an order of the day from Erich Raeder, Commander-in-Chief of the *Kriegsmarine*. 'The hour of the decision finds us ready to respond for honour, right and the freedom of our Fatherland,' the *Grossadmiral* proclaimed. 'Aware of our glorious tradition, we will wage this struggle with unshakable faith in our Führer and in the firm belief in the greatness of our people and our Reich!' Gustav Kleikamp added his own postscript. 'Our ship has the mission to participate in the defence of Danzig. This task must fill us with pride.'[7]

By the time the sailors of *Schleswig-Holstein* had closed up, *Oberleutnant* Bruno Dilley and his Ju87 had already been roaring low over the Vistula delta for four minutes. Three days earlier Dilley, a dashing former police officer cadet who had transferred to the Luftwaffe in 1935, had celebrated his twenty-sixth birthday. Now he led a *Staffel* of three *Stukas* on its first mission of the campaign against Poland. Four minutes after take-off, the meandering Vistula, Poland's great artery, was in view – but only sporadically in the fog. Follow the Vistula as far as Dirschau, a few miles south of Danzig, Dilley remembered his orders, and destroy the railway bridge. Hopping over the countryside at tree-top height Dilley and his two comrades from *Stukageschwader* 1 – StG1 – spied their target eight minutes into their flight. Dilley lead the way. At 4.34am he pressed the trigger and released his stick of bombs. They spread across the railway embankment which led to the Dirschau bridge, hoping to smash the demolition wires which the Poles had set up. All three *Stukas* hit their target. Hitler's war had begun – eleven minutes early.

In the small farming town of Wielun, sixty miles east of Breslau, school children Stanislaw Kubalczyk, Józef Musia and Zofia Burchacinska were startled out of their sleep by a strange howling noise. It lasted maybe four or five seconds. Then a loud explosion. And another. And another. And the chatter of machine-guns. 'There was hell over Wielun,' Kubalczyk observed. 'Shooting, smoke, whining, crying – all this combined created a frightful scene.'

Above Wielun, this town of 16,000 inhabitants, Walter Sigel's Stukas were picking out their targets, such as they were. All Saints' Hospital was clearly distinguishable – a huge red cross was daubed on its roof. The bombs fell regardless. Windows smashed, a building collapsed, a crater the size of half a house was torn in the hospital's grounds. 'There was debris everywhere and under the debris, we heard moaning,' Dr Zygmunt Patry recalled.

Schoolgirl Zofia Burchacinska dashed into Wielun's market place, barefoot and still wearing her nightgown. The nave of the 17th-Century church was wrecked. Everything was wrecked. A man, covered in blood, stumbled out of a side road. 'Help, help!' he begged. Eight-year-old Josef Musial also felt drawn to the heart of the town, dragging his sister with him. 'It was badly destroyed,' Musial remembered. 'Everywhere lay corpses and body parts torn off: arms, legs, a head.' Other residents dashed for the fields, chased as they did so by strafing Stukas.

It was all over in a matter of minutes. There had been no warning, no air raid sirens. More than 1,600 townsfolk had perished; 160 buildings – the hospital, the school, the hotel, the synagogue, the market square, shops businesses – had fallen victim to an attack officially against fortifications *outside* Wielun.

At the foot of the Tatra mountains, southwest of Krakow, a young *Gebirgsjäger* waited for Friday to dawn. In the darkness this rich land of fruitful meadows was hidden. Only the mountain peaks were lit faintly by the first rays of 1 September. The mountain men waited silently, until their *Hauptmann* ordered them to gather round. The metallic sound of his harsh voice was the sole noise in those pre-dawn minutes. 'The miracle which I spoke about yesterday has not occurred,' the officer told his company earnestly. 'The Führer has decided to talk with Poland in the language which for a long time now this nation has been trying to talk with us.' As the *Hauptmann* finished, 200 *Gebirgsjäger* cried 'Sieg Heil'; the exhortation rebounded off the faces of the Tatra slopes and echoed a thousand fold. At that moment day began to destroy the night. 'The first rays of sunshine light up the peaks before us, wonderful, magnificent to look at,' one soldier wrote enthusiastically. 'A sign for the beginning of the Polish campaign!'[8]

The 'goods train' from Marienburg stopped at a signal outside the station in Lisewo, the last halt before the Dirschau bridge. From the driver's cab, the imposing turrets which formed the gateway to the bridge were clearly visible. At 4.42am the signal changed. The engine moved out slowly. In the cab, a pioneer *Leutnant* implored the driver: 'Head for the bridge at full speed!' As the train gathered speed, the driver and the officer peered through the round windows in the cab. Barriers had been laid across the track. The train ground to a halt one hundred yards from the eastern end of the Dirschau bridge, drawing fire from Polish troops which wounded the fireman. There was a shrill whistle from the locomotive and the platoons of engineers jumped from the train, looking for cover.[9]

1st Panzer Division staff officer Johann Graf von Kielmansegg, nervously studied his watch. 4.43am. 'I light a cigarette – when it goes out, the war will be on,' he recalled. 'Another two minutes before the war begins. It's a strange and provocative feeling to experience a historic moment, whose significance cannot be predicted, so consciously, so directly!' Kielmansegg studied the terrain on the opposite bank of the small river, the Lisswarthe, fifty miles east of Breslau: a few small single-storey farmhouses, and marshy, damp fields. Far from ideal panzer country.[10]

Seventy miles southwest of Danzig, anti-tank gun officer Alexander Stahlberg strained his eyes. The twenty-seven-year-old officer lay barely thirty feet from the frontier with three comrades of 2nd Motorised Division. 'Nothing moved,' Stahlberg recalled. 'It was as silent as a graveyard. Only a dog could be heard howling in the distance.' The dawning day began to cast a faint light on the Pomeranian countryside. Darkness gave way to a broad meadow, German and Polish border posts and, in the distance, a few trees and the roofs of homes in a village. 'I searched the area intently, my heart beating so hard that I had difficulty in looking through my binoculars,' the officer wrote. 'Nothing indicated that anyone over there was expecting the attack.'[11]

On the East Prussian-Polish border about ten miles northeast of Mlawa, a young *Feldwebel* and his comrades of 11th Pioneer Battalion huddled around their officer. The engineers had spent the night removing barricades on the border – 'protecting us from surprise enemy attacks' – before grabbing a couple of hours' sleep. The first rays of sunlight were streaming from the east, silhouetting the trees of a small forest next to the pioneers' makeshift billets. The men were apprehensive. 'What personal fates, personal experiences, difficulties and hardships, highs and lows, lie in store for the individual no-one can know or even roughly guess at,' the *Feldwebel* recorded in his diary. 'We are all young men and only know of war from books, films and from the stories of our fathers.' The *Leutnant* read out a proclamation from Adolf Hitler.

Germans in Poland are being persecuted by bloody terror and are being driven from their homes. Numerous violations of the frontier – something no great power can tolerate – are proof that the Poles are no longer prepared to respect the Reich's frontiers.

To end this madness there is no other course of action left to me than to meet force with force.

The pioneers nodded in agreement. The *Feldwebel* summed up the thoughts of his comrades: 'With weapons in our hands and acting on the Führer's orders, we will protect our rights and put right the disgrace of Versailles in battle.'[12]

SS police commander Johannes Schäfer stood in front of Danzig's central railway station. From here he would direct the occupation of Polish 'strongpoints' in the free city: the station, the signal box, the post office. He observed his fellow Danzigers scurrying to work – or returning from it – as usual on this Friday morning. 'Then the sky was suddenly shaken by the thunder of cannons.' The handful of civilians dashed for cover, terrified.[13]

The thunder came from the guns of *Schleswig-Holstein* three miles to north. At 4.47am Gustav Kleikamp gave the order: '*Los!*' – open fire. For the next seven minutes the guns boomed, unleashing sixty-seven 28cm and 15cm shells and 600 rounds from the 20mm pom-pom guns. Trees were sliced in half, every window in the barracks shattered instantly, wooden buildings on the Westerplatte disintegrated, then went up in flames as fuel barrels were ignited by the shells impacting. 'It's as if all hell is let loose, thunder and lightning, huge fountains of earth and flames crash among the fortifications,' naval correspondent Fritz Otto-Busch observed. '*Schleswig-Holstein* soon resembles a mountain, spewing flames enveloped in a brown-yellow dust and clouds of smoke. Sheets of flame, metres long, shoot forth continuously; machine-guns and flak hammer away.' Busch watched as thick clouds of black smoke began to rise above the Polish fort. The harbour ferry terminal went up in flames, followed by the shipyard next to it, then the trees in the small copses which littered the small spit of land; slates came crashing down from the roofs of homes in Neufahrwasser, dislodged by the shockwave from the booming of *SX*'s guns. 'Iron, steel, stone, wood and soil fly through the air, climb and then rain down back to earth,' a mesmerised Busch recorded. 'Time stands still, spellbound eyes only see the bright glow of fire, flames and rubble hurled sky-high, ears buzz from the sound of heavy shells firing and landing, from the rattling of machine-guns and crashing and barking of flak.' On the upper deck of the old warship, empty shell cases were piled high, while a pungent, sulphurous cloud surrounded the turrets; within the gun crews 'work like devils, dripping with sweat, their faces beaming'.[14]

Polish airwaves crackled with a short message: 'SOS, I am being attacked'. There was no time to encrypt it. The defenders of the peninsula donned gas masks and waited for the Germans to come.

Johannes Schäfer took the booming of the battleship's guns as his signal. His SS troops swept into Danzig's central station, dashing from the side streets. The building was taken without a shot being fired. Not so the signal box. The Polish railway workers fired back with rifles. Surrounded, they were soon overcome. Schäfer arrived to see his 'prize', stepping over the bodies of dead Poles, lying in pools of their own blood, at the signal box's entrance.[15]

The roar of *Schleswig-Holstein*'s guns woke the staff of the Polish post office in Heveliusplatz. The director ran through its corridors yelling: 'Get to your posts! Get to your posts!' Almost simultaneously, the building was rocked as an explosive charge went off, ripping a hole in a fence which separated the post office's courtyard from the neighbouring police station. Rifle fire from a house in a nearby street strafed the post office as armed police tried to force their way inside through three different entrances. The three-score defenders responded with three Browning light machine-guns and pistols, hurling grenades at their attackers. Police and SS *Heimwehr Danzig* troops forced their way into the lobby of the parcel depot until they were driven back by a combination of pistol fire and grenades. The first abortive assault on the post office had cost the Germans two dead and half a dozen wounded.[16]

Near the small town of Kreuzberg (today Kluczbork) *Hauptmann* Johann Graf von Kielmansegg noticed that zero hour came and went almost without incident. The pioneers and infantry crossed the river in whatever boat they could find and secured the opposite bank. It was a good ten minutes before the Poles responded with the weak rattle of rifle fire. Then the crash of explosions, and in the distance, small white clouds rose in the early morning sky; the Poles had blown up bridges in the division's first objective, Panki.[17]

On the edge of the Polish Corridor, fifty miles northwest of Bromberg, Alexander Stahlberg had waited for the hands on his watch to reach 4.45. As they did, there was a crescendo of artillery fire from his left. But ahead, in the Corridor, nothing stirred.

'Our infantry began to move up, carrying their rifles under their arms as if they were going hunting,' Stahlberg observed. 'Not a shot was fired.' The men advanced to the dull rumble of the artillery. 'Column after column rolled by for well over an hour,' the officer recalled. 'I looked at the soldiers' faces, seeing and hearing no excitement, no cheers; they were silent, their faces generally expressionless.'[18]

Panzer reconnaissance company commander Hans von Luck crossed the Polish border some fifty miles west of Krakow. Luck and his comrades in 2nd *Leichte* Division had watched the bombers of the Luftwaffe roar overhead, then moved off at 4.50am. There was no opposition. 'We marched into Poland,' he later wrote. 'Far and wide there was not a single Polish soldier in sight – although they were supposed to have been preparing for an "invasion" of Germany.'[19]

In the Tatra mountains, the mist began to turn to light rain as Wilhelm Prüller moved up to the Polish border. Excitement had replaced his apprehension, as the panzers rolled past him into Poland. 'The row of tanks has no end. A quarter of an hour, tanks, tanks, tanks,' he scribbled in his diary. 'It's a wonderful feeling now to be a German.'[20]

In Moravia, *Schütze* Karl Fischer had been awake at least two hours. Every five minutes, Fischer glanced at his watch. 'The two hours before an attack are an eternity,' Fischer lamented. 'If only we had something to do, but we lie pressed to the ground and must wait – nothing but waiting.' Finally the order to attack was given. Ahead, Fischer watched his 132nd Infantry Regiment comrades begin the march towards Krakow. The machine-gunner manned his weapon and aimed at a ridge in the distance from where he expected a Polish counter-attack to come. The Poles did not respond.

Fischer's comrade nudged him.

'Listen, Karli, for a couple of minutes we've been at war! Can you imagine that?'

'No!'

'Me neither.'[21]

It was just before 5am when the first naval infantry moved off against the Westerplatte, advancing 500 or so yards before the Poles brought fire to bear on the German troops. A second group of shock troops succeeded in breaching a wall, but it was as far as the men got. Once more, Polish fire poured down on the attackers. 'Wild machine-gun fire bursts out, rifle shots rattle, and hand grenades explode,' Fritz Otto-Busch observed. Barely ninety minutes after the assault began, the company broke off its attack and pulled back. Its losses had been too great. 'We knew nothing about the enemy,' *Feldwebel* Heinz Denker recalled bitterly. 'We possessed only an old 1:1000 map, without the pillboxes marked on it. We immediately noticed that the ship's barrage had been ineffective. The huge 280mm shells needed to travel 600 metres to explode. In fact, they had travelled just 400 metres.' The only useful purpose the projectiles served in many cases was to provide cover for the attacking marines.

Walter Sigel brought his Junkers 87 down on the tarmac at Nieder-Ellguth shortly after 5am. One by one, his *Gruppe* followed him. After debriefing his crews, Sigel compiled his after-action report. 'Objective destroyed,' he wrote. 'Fires observed. No particular enemy movements seen.'

The fog enveloping East Prussia and much of northern Poland was almost 10,000 feet high. Erich Munske and his comrades climbed above this 'mountain of fog' and a radiant sun finally appeared. 'Sometimes there's a gaping hole in the cloud, then we can see a bit of the world far below like on the surface of a well, a village with a small, pointed steeple, the chessboard-pattern fields, small grey-green forests.'

Now over Poland, and with the fog clearing, Munske's *Gruppe* descended as it approached Graudenz, eighty miles from Heiligenbeil on the east bank of the Vistula. The flight had taken little more than thirty minutes. Below, glimmering in the September sun, the tracks of a railway line and a train getting up steam. 'The locomotive and wagons are covered with green foliage, men wave noisily from the windows with their caps and hats – a military train with Polish reservists. They have not recognised us – they believe we are friendly.' For a second, Munske had qualms about attacking these unsuspecting Polish troops. 'But tomorrow these unsuspecting soldiers would bear arms and would not hesitate if they saw the son of a German mother in front of them,' the pilot convinced himself. The bombs were unleashed. The reservists jumped out of the carriages and ran across the fields for cover 'like chickens pursued by a hawk'.

The *Gruppe* flew on towards Graudenz and its airfield; still, there was no activity below. Only after Munske and his formation had obliterated the hangars did Polish flak fire back. The shells fell short.[22]

To the southeast of Erich Munske's bomber *Gruppe*, the Bug bridges spanning the river between Warsaw and Brest-Litovsk and airfields were the target of *Oberleutnant* Pritzel and his Heinkel He111. Unlike at Graudenz, the Poles were alert. Below the flash of muzzles. Seconds later, Pritzel noticed 'red-hot shells racing towards us. They look like red mice dragging a long, fiery tail behind them.' But the rest of Poland early on this Friday morning was at peace. 'The broad plains of this land lie bathed in sunlight,' Pritzel noted. 'A peaceful picture: fields with large herds of geese in them, people working, and dark woods extending far and wide. Now and then, a small village, hard to make out because the old thatched roofs blend in with the terrain.' Roaring high over the Polish steppe, Pritzel spied a goods train steaming along the main line from Warsaw to Bialystok. The instructions of the pilot's *Hauptmann* were still ringing in Pritzel's ears: 'Don't get involved in unnecessary battles.' But the opportunity was too good to pass over. A few short bursts from the machine-guns and a blast of steam shot up from the locomotive, which promptly ground to a halt. The crew jumped from the engine and darted for a nearby forest.[23]

Roaring low down the Vistula valley, barely twenty feet above the ground, *Oberleutnant* Möckel guided his *Staffel* of Do17s from *Kampfgeschwader 77* towards an airfield at Krakow. 'We don't need the map to tell us we're flying over Poland,' Möckel observed. 'Sweeping uncultivated plains, bleak fallow fields, between them squalid farmhouses, lie under us. The tattered villagers run frightened to the side or raise their pleading arms towards us.' The Dorniers hopped over copses and forests, swept along clearings, down forest paths, then along the Vistula. Finally Krakow loomed into view, and then the airfield. It had already been visited by the Luftwaffe – fire and smoke rose above the base. Now on his bomb run, Möckel climbed to 160 feet to arm his bombs. 'In front of us we can make out a flight of Polish fighters neatly laid out on the edge of the field,' the officer noted. Bombs tumbled out of the aircraft's dorsal. At the same time, 'red fireballs' raced up from Polish anti-aircraft guns, while the Dorniers' machine-guns rattled away furiously in response. Overhead, too high – they were not expecting a low-level attack – Polish fighters circled; too late, they began to turn their attention to the Dorniers only to be swept away by twin-engined Bf110 Zerstörers.[24]

Northeast of Mlawa, the engineers of 11th Pioneer Battalion had waited for their comrades in 11th Infantry Division to cross the Polish border before deciding to move off. Forty-five minutes after zero hour, the pioneers marched, first on dirt tracks, then across fields and meadows. *Is this war?* the engineers asked themselves. 'It is very still,' a *Feldwebel* noted in his diary. The men marched in silence, their helmets slung off their ammunition cases. 'Occasionally we hear a light gun firing, also the sporadic rattle of a machine-gun somewhere, several kilometres in front of us.' The land was empty. The Poles had gone, abandoning their farms. A few pigs and chicken ran around, and dogs, mad and frightened.[25]

The armour of 3rd Panzer Division tentatively rolled through thick fog into the Polish Corridor. The mist thwarted any hope of Luftwaffe support. It also thwarted effective artillery support. The German guns ignored orders and fired blindly into the fog. Accompanying 3rd Panzer Brigade in his command truck, General Heinz Guderian shuddered as one shell crashed fifty yards in front of his vehicle; a second crashed fifty yards behind it. The panzer general ordered his driver off the road. Unnerved by the artillery fire, the driver plunged the half-track straight into a ditch, wrecking it. It was an inauspicious beginning to Heinz Guderian's campaign.[26]

A light rain dripped off the tall beech trees in a forest near Preussenfeld, a dozen miles northeast of Schneidemühl. The trees provided natural cover for the vehicles of 8th Machine-Gun Battalion. A few shafts of light from the east penetrated the forest. The battalion commander gave the order to mount the vehicles and start them up. The engines growled into life, giving off a reassuring warmth on a chilly late summer's morning. The men looked at each other, looked at their watches, looked at their weapons, lost in thoughts. Then: *Kompanie marsch!* The soft growl of the engines turned into a screech as the trucks began rolling through the trees. At the edge of the forest, the battalion joined a country lane. There was no sight of the enemy, only German infantry and German baggage columns moving east towards the frontier. The mist of early morning began to give way to sunshine as the machine-gunners reached the *Reichsgrenze* – the border between Germany and Poland. The barrier was already smashed, the Polish eagle standard lay by the side of the road, the customs house was scarred by fighting. 'That is the Polish border,' a machine-gunner recorded in his diary. He corrected himself. 'The former Polish border – which now, and for ever more, belongs to the past, the past which Versailles forced upon us, that so-called peace treaty.'[27]

In the village of Mosty at the northern end of the Jablunka Pass, Lieutenant Witold Pirszel was roused by a loud explosion. The reserve officer ran to the window and saw three German bombers flying low over the mountains, accompanied by the sound of shots firing and shells crashing. Pirszel hurriedly dressed, rounded up his men and ran towards the railway tunnel. There he found a lieutenant with his troops falling back and German soldiers deployed across the valley and advancing. In the six days since the abortive raid to seize the tunnel, Pirszel's engineers had placed twenty charges in the parallel tunnels and around their exits – twenty tonnes of trotyl in all. With communications to his superiors cut, the officer took it upon himself to order the tunnel demolished. An almighty explosion shook the valley. The tunnel collapsed. The road above collapsed into the gaping hole. It would be six months before trains again rolled through the Jablunka Pass.[28]

Fifteen-year-old Gerhard Blottner was shaken awake by his aunt. 'Wake up, wake up, it's war!' The schoolboy didn't want to believe it. Still half-asleep, Blottner peered out of the window of his aunt's home in the town of Bojanowo, forty miles north of Breslau. Poles were shuffling past, almost aimlessly. Some bore guns. Most did not. There was a distant rumbling, followed by the crash of shells. There were no air raid shelters in this small Silesian town. People took shelter in their cellars, or their neighbours. The homes shook. Why are they firing at us? the young Blottner asked himself. Bojanowo was as much German as it was Polish. 'The shells struck German homes just as they did Polish ones – and killed German and Polish civilians,' the youngster astutely observed. Bojanowo became a ghost town; no-one ventured into the streets. They waited in their cellars for the Germans to come.[29]

The first strains of light were beginning to pierce the haze devouring Warsaw this Friday morning. It was still early, 6am to be precise, and most of the capital's inhabitants had yet to rise, let alone realise that the war threatened all summer had engulfed their nation. A 'terrible howling' swept across the city as the air raid sirens sounded, and a jarring, tinny voice screamed out of loudspeakers: Air raid warning for Warsaw. One Varsovian peered through her window. 'The city is dead, traffic has come to a halt, vehicles stop in the roads,' she wrote.

> People look for shelter in entrances and houses. We wait nervously for what is going to happen. Despite the seriousness of the situation, there's a certain element of defiant curiosity in me. How will this war be with these new, unknown methods of fighting? We look for the aircraft above us. But up there over our heads is spread only the clear, dark-blue sky of a Polish autumn. A very beautiful September day is beginning.[30]

Marta Korwin had barely arrived home at her flat in the heart of Warsaw. The carefree hospital secretary had spent the night dancing. Now she found herself on the rooftop of her apartment block as a fire watcher. Rather than watch for fires, Korwin was mesmerised by the spectacle. 'Some planes went down, leaving trails of smoke behind,' she recalled. Korwin rejoiced. They had to be German aircraft falling from the sky.[31]

As the sirens sounded across Warsaw, Heinz Borwin Venzky and his comrades in 3rd *Geschwader* Panzer Reconnaissance *Abteilung* prepared to roll into Polish Upper Silesia. Infantry and pioneers had already cleared the way for the armour, whose first objective was a little known industrial town thirty miles away. To the Poles it was Oswiecim; to the Germans, Auschwitz. Venzky and his comrades moved off at 6am promptly. The first village the panzers entered was devoid of enemy troops. It was, however, filled with overjoyed *Volksdeutsche*, celebrating liberation. They handed the soldiers flowers and cigarettes, then the armour drove on. Another former German village. Then another. 'Everywhere indescribable jubilation,' Venzky recorded in his diary. 'We look at ourselves, look at the machine-guns ready to fire which are now adorned with flowers. Is this war?'[32]

Berliner Hans P, a former theology student, crossed the border into the Corridor at 6am precisely. His company commander repeatedly told him to ignore the rumours of war. Even now it seemed unreal, unreal until he marched past a Polish customs house on the border a dozen or so miles northeast of Schneidemühl. The smell of gunfire and hand grenades lingered; the Polish customs officials had been 'smoked out'. Hans and his comrades were now on enemy soil, alert to the dangers of enemy soldiers and 'a hostile and spiteful civilian population'. He recorded in his diary:

> We moved on into enemy territory exactly as we had exercised in peacetime a thousandfold, the infantry regiments soon left us behind. And yet a change advances with us all, almost automatically. If we thought of a journey in peacetime as a pleasant excursion, more or less, when we could eat or sleep after enjoying the beautiful countryside, then now suddenly each one of us became wide awake, weapon in our hands at the ready, ready to leap down from the vehicle in a flash at the sight of strong enemy fire and take up position.[33]

The Dirschau bridges still stood. Perhaps the bombs of Bruno Dilley and his fellow Stuka crews had worked and destroyed the fuses leading to the demolition charges. The pioneers had finally moved their armoured train up to bring its heavy guns to bear on the Polish positions. And then, a little after 6am, as the pioneers worked their way along the track on to the eastern end of the bridge, a tremendous explosion rocked it. Poles and Germans were thrown into the air, the stone foundations crumbled and collapsed into the river, dragging the steel arches with them. Half an hour later, the western end of the bridges disappeared in a cloud of smoke and dust. The pillars collapsed, taking the spans, track and roadway into the Vistula with them.[34]

Just west of 1st Panzer Division, near the village of Kostau, forty-five miles east of Breslau, the men of the SS Infantry Regiment *Leibstandarte Adolf Hitler* moved forward to seize crossings over the River Prosna. The SS men had been told to expect light resistance on the border, allowing for a rapid breakthrough to the River Warthe, one of Poland's main waterways, by dusk. The only real threat, the regiment had been told, would come from militia. But as *Hauptsturmführer* Kurt Meyer drove into the village of Gola, he found not militia but Polish troops, well hidden, in houses, trees, ditches:

> Machine-gun fire strafes the street and brief fiery flashes of exploding shells show us our target. The armour roars into the village of Gola at full speed. The bridge over the Prosna – already prepared for demolition – is captured by our assault troops and falls into our hands undamaged. In a few minutes, the village is occupied. Startled Polish troops clamber out of their positions and move towards us, their hands raised. They cannot believe that the war is already over for them, barely ten minutes after it began.

The men of the *Leibstandarte* needed no motivation to attack. Loyal Nazis to a man, they believed the stories of Polish atrocities and hated the *Diktat* of Versailles. Meyer continued:

> Each one of these magnificent soldiers is convinced of the justness of the struggle and has no compunctions about giving his all, whatever the consequences, for the right of his Volk to live. That said, there are no rousing hurrahs drifting across the battlefield. Loyal young men fulfil their duty and make unequalled sacrifices with serious expressions. For these men the struggle against the Poles is no war of aggression, rather it is the end of an outrageous miscarriage of justice. They want to expunge the rape of the German Volk at Versailles.[35]

Gola fell with little opposition, the *Leibstandarte* drove on through the early morning half-light towards the next village, Boleslawice. A scouting party was sent forward. Barely out of sight of its comrades, the reconnaissance patrol was subjected to 'wild, irregular fire'. Shots bounced off walls and roof tiles. The SS men stopped in their tracks, until a platoon of infantry stormed the village. *Obersturmführer* Hubert Meyer formed up his platoon and led it into the village. The SS men moved 'very timidly', the officer recalled. 'Those were not cardboard practice targets out there any more.' Meyer soon realised his men were being fired upon not by Polish soldiers, but by armed civilians. 'The spell had been broken. We noticed that not every bullet finds its mark.' Shortly afterwards Boleslawice fell to the *Leibstandarte*.[36]

The sleep Alfred Lessnau had been enjoying in the station house at Szymankowo was brutally interrupted as German police, border guards and SA volunteers burst into the building, dragged him out of his bed and beat him repeatedly. The rest of the station staff – the duty officer, the cashier, the signalman, workers, customs officers, more than twenty men and women in all – were beaten or shot in revenge for the destruction of the Dirschau bridges. The corpses were dragged over the road outside the station and tossed into a ditch. The SA men erected a sign: Here lies the Polish minority.[37]

In Danzig, the crucible of this fledgling conflict, the gardeners of the suburb of Oliva pushed their carts laden with flowers to the market barely a mile away in Langfuhr, once the heart of the city's Jewish community. They did so to the echo of gunfire from the harbour, five miles to the east. Danzigers rushed past them. 'The Westerplatte is on fire,' they told the gardeners, who continued on their way as if nothing was happening.

The Westerplatte was indeed on fire. And it remained firmly in Polish hands. But Gustav Kleikamp was not prepared to give up the attempt to seize it after a single assault. A second attempt would be made, but not before a much heavier barrage. *SX*'s guns opened fire once more, for thirty minutes without end; there was a brief pause, then the muzzles of the old battleship flashed again.

Just before 9am, the marines moved off once more, this time supported by sixty armed SS personnel, the *Heimwehr Danzig*. Painfully slowly, the troops advanced over barbed wire, trip wire and branches brought down by *Schleswig-Holstein*'s bombardment. At first the Poles were slow to react, but once again the machine-guns opened up. Not once did the attacking troops see an enemy soldier; the defenders were too well hidden in their bunkers and gun positions camouflaged with turf.

Nevertheless, the attackers continued probing, despite snipers in the Westerplatte's trees picking off the hapless German troops. But there were simply not enough marines and SS men to take the Polish fort. The second assault withered around mid-day. The Westerplatte would not fall by a *coup de main*.

Albert Forster did not wait for the Westerplatte to be subdued to declare the free city part of the Reich once more. And the Reich, Hitler told him, welcomed the great port back into its fold 'with a heart brimming with joy'. Bells sounded in the city hall, in the tower of the venerable Marienkirche, and throughout the port. 'The hour for which we have been longed for twenty years has come,' a breathless Forster told Danzigers. 'As of today, Danzig has returned home to the Reich. We thank the Lord that he has given the Führer the strength and opportunity to free us from the evil of the Versailles *Diktat*.' The *Gauleiter* wasted no time in dismantling the vestiges of international administration in the newly 'liberated' Danzig. The committee which had overseen harbour affairs was promptly disbanded. The swastika was draped on railway engines, from public buildings, on the town hall, on the façade of Danzig's central station alongside a banner inscribed with a Hitlerian slogan: Resistance doesn't exist for capitulating but for breaking![38]

Northeast of Mlawa, junior officer Fritz Fillies crossed the East Prussian-Polish border and overcame weak resistance around the village of Wasily Zigny. Mist shrouded the landscape. Enemy artillery fire was scattered at best as Fillies led his company through a swamp. A breathless messenger rushed up to the officer, guiding an infantry gun to dry ground. Fillies took the runner to one side. In a calm, soft voice, the messenger told him that the company commander, an *Oberleutnant* Betzler, was gravely wounded; his final instructions had been for Fillies to take over from him.[39]

Before 9am, pioneers had thrown a temporary bridge across the Lisswarthe for 1st Panzer Division to enter Poland. The artillery rolled first, followed by the panzers. 'It's not the Polish soldier, whom until now we have not seen at all, who offers the first steadfast resistance, rather the Polish land,' von Kielmansegg observed. The terrain on the east bank of the Lisswarthe was deep, loose sand, climbed sharply and was wet. Tractors were called up to haul many of the vehicles. For much of this first morning, 1st Panzer Division struggled to deploy around Panki. It presented an ideal target to the Poles, but the Poles never came.

It was late morning before the division began moving out of Panki in earnest. If the Poles had not appeared to 1st Panzer yet, they at least made their presence known. Every road, lane, path seemed to have been mined; barriers and obstacles had been thrown across them; all the road and rail bridges had been blown up. The division finally made headway along an ill-suited dirt track towards the town of Klobuck, its objective for the day, eight miles to the east. The Poles, thought Kielmansegg, obviously believed the track was *'panzersicher'* – panzer proof. But then, before 1 September 1939, the panzer men had never tried to move their armour down such a track. A few Poles tentatively clambered out of their hiding places and watched the panzers roaring past. An elderly Pole, with a reasonable grasp of the German language, stood in front of his cottage. 'So many Germans, so many Germans, and not one is on foot!' he muttered repeatedly.[40]

The war was perhaps three hours old when rifleman Karl Schönfeld crossed the Polish border in Pomerania. Schönfeld and his comrades jumped up and down, danced and sang, but their mirth vanished just a few hundred yards into Poland. The first Polish prisoner. Then the first German wounded. And then the first dead. Poles. Five of them. Perched in trees. Lifeless. A few yards on more dead, two Poles on the edge of a copse. 'The horror of this sight unnerves us,' Schönfeld recorded in his diary. 'There lie men who were killed by the hand of man. It's not murder, it's war! I thought about the mothers who once gave birth to these men and I imagined the pain my mother would feel if she knew her child lay dead somewhere.'[41]

Polizeioberst Willi Bethke was baffled. Danzig's Polish Post Office should have been in German hands by now. It was not. Instead, the building had turned into a 'fire-spewing volcano'. It was time to try new tactics, Bethke reasoned. He evacuated every home within a 200-yard radius of the post office, brought up an armoured car, and called on the postal workers to surrender within two hours or face being blown up. The Poles had no intention of surrendering. They had supplies. They had suffered few wounds. And the Polish Army would soon come to their rescue from the east.[42]

A few blocks away Jewess Dora Anker returned to her apartment. Like most Danzigers, Anker had been woken by the roar of *Schleswig-Holstein*'s guns. And like most Danzig housewives, she hurried straight away to the grocery stores to hoard food. She found the door of her apartment guarded by an SS trooper, while two Gestapo men turned the flat upside down, convinced the Ankers had hoarded guns and money. Anker's husband waved his visa at the Gestapo officials. 'The Jew expects to go to Palestine during wartime,' they sneered and laughed, carry the family's iron coffer containing all their savings out of the door.[43]

Berliner Hans P had been on the march for little more than an hour when his company entered the village of Gross Elsingen (today Podrozna). He found not the 'hostile and spiteful civilian population' he had feared, but delighted ethnic Germans. They lined the street, handing the *Landsers* flowers, crying: '*Heil*'. The villagers had all but abandoned hope of being liberated, having been oppressed for weeks by the Poles, they told the soldiers. That morning the Polish soldiers had pulled out. The villagers summoned their courage once more. 'Now their delight knew no limits,' wrote Hans. 'Only a few Polish inhabitants remained behind in their houses, apparently disinterested.'

On the edge of the village, the soldiers ran into a farmer who offered them sausages and cheese. The *Volksdeutsche* was overjoyed. The fleeing Polish troops had seized his horses and ridden off to the east that very morning. They had been overtaken by German armour. The horses were returned to their owner.[44]

In Warsaw, pianist Wladyslaw Szpilman hurried to the headquarters of the state broadcaster. The schedule had been disrupted by the German invasion, but music would be still be played between the air raid warnings, communiqués and official announcements. 'Paperboys selling special editions ran breathlessly down the streets,' Szpilman observed as he made his way to the radio station. The newspaper *Dobry Wieczór Kurier Czerwony* – Red Good Evening Courier – proclaimed: 'The war for the freedom of our people has begun. The marauders' attack will be smashed against the steel wall of our heroic army.' Elderly cityfolk stopped at roadside pillars where an appeal by Poland's president Ignacy Moscicki had been hastily pasted. Attacked by 'our traditional foe', Moscicki called upon 'the whole nation to rally around its commander-in-chief and the armed forces to defend their freedom, their independence and their honour'. He expected his compatriots to give the Germans 'a worthy response as has been the case more than once in the history of relations between Poland and Germany.' He concluded: 'Blessed by God in the struggle for the holy and just cause and as one with the Army, the entire nation – its ranks united – goes into battle for total victory.' An old man read the appeal. 'They attacked us, without warning,' he grumbled, shaking his head. 'There was no panic,' Szpilman noted. 'The mood swung between curiosity and surprise.' Before the musician could reach his destination, the sirens sounded. 'The street rapidly emptied,' he recalled. 'Women scurried to the shelters in alarm. The men did not want to go down; they stood in doorways, cursing the Germans.'[45]

A couple of miles south of Wasily Zigny Fritz Fillies' company marched through another farming village, Duczymin, and its 'narrow and extremely dirty streets'. Before the rifle company lay northern Poland, 'a flat valley extending almost as far as the horizon, with small bushy forests and the odd hilltop where fruit trees usually stood'. In the gardens of Duczymin, the infantrymen found the residents of Wasily Zigny taking shelter, offering fruit and butter as a gesture of goodwill. But the farms themselves were empty, abandoned. Most Poles had fled. Small *panje* wagons, crammed with every household item had been left in the courtyards; Polish troops had commandeered the farmers' horses and ridden off southwards.

Fillies studied his map. A mile or so away lay a larger village, Krzynowroga Wielka. 'Now the unpronounceable names had begun. One man pronounced it one way, the next man another way, but they both meant the same thing,' the junior officer observed.[46]

Since 6am, German radio had been broadcasting news and communiqués every ten minutes. The first editions of Friday's papers were all but torn from the hands of street vendors. There was only one topic of conversation on the trams and trains as Berliners went to work. Or so the Nazi propaganda machine would have the German people believe. An apathetic Berlin public trudged to work, CBS radio correspondent William Shirer observed as he drove through the heart of the capital. The overcast sky captured the mood perfectly. Luftwaffe crews were installing flak guns on the East-West Axis. No-one Shirer saw was buying the special editions.

Those special editions were filled with alarming headlines: 'Polish insurgents cross the German border', 'German police throw Polish hordes back across the border', 'Attack on German guards – the Poles were beaten back', 'Poland opens fire'. The raid at Gleiwitz, the Nazi newspapers explained, 'was evidently the signal for a general attack by Polish guerrillas in German territory'. A raid on a railway halt in West Prussia had been thwarted by machine-gun fire. The fields around the Silesian village of Pitschen, near Kreuzberg, had seen the fiercest fighting. Two hundred Poles, so the newspapers reported, had been engaged by border police on the Reich's soil after dark the previous night. After a brief fire-fight, the Poles had fled, leaving behind two dead – 'one a soldier'. At least one German border guard had also been killed. At Hochlinden, the fighting had raged for half an hour before the Polish insurgents were driven away and the customs house re-taken; at least fourteen Poles had been captured. 'Because it was dark, the precise number of dead and wounded is not yet known.' In fact, the number of 'Polish' dead at Hochlinden *was* known. It was precisely six. But they were not Poles. [47]

In the courtyard of the Schloss Ehrenforst, an imposing country home fifteen miles northwest of Gleiwitz, twenty SS men who had taken part in the early-morning 'attack' against the customs house at Hochlinden found a couple of trucks waiting for them. The vehicles rolled through the Silesian lanes until they came to a forest just outside Hochlinden. The men's commander ordered them out, thrust spades into their hands and told them to bury six corpses, *Konserven* – canned goods – he called them. Six bodies dressed in civilian clothes were hauled out of the second wagon and tossed on to the floor. The men's faces were disfigured, smashed in by axe or similar blunt object. An SS platoon leader detailed to bury the corpses felt distinctly uneasy. No-one had been shot during that morning's 'attack', he pointed out to his commander. Where had the corpses come from? The SS officer told him not to worry. The dead were inmates from the Sachsenhausen concentration camp, brought from Oranienburg alive and killed on the border. The burial party resumed their work. They dug shallow graves, threw in the bodies and covered them with twigs.[48]

A little before 10am on this grey, overcast Friday in Berlin a column of black cars pulled slowly out of the huge underground garage beneath the New Reich Chancellery into Voss Strasse for the brief journey to the *Krolloper* on the southern edge of the Tiergarten. The Wilhemstrasse was lined by a cordon of brownshirted SA guards. The roads were empty. So too the pavements, save for a few Berliners going about their usual business. The column passed slowly through the Brandenburg Gate where there was a faint ripple of applause then drew up outside the opera house. Inside, hastily summoned *Reichstag* deputies – Party functionaries – waited for the Führer to address them. Gone was Hitler's traditional brown shirt; that morning he had donned a *feldgrau* smock 'which fitted every bit as loosely and badly' as his usual attire. He would wear it, he declared, 'until victory is ours or I do not survive the outcome'.

The speech lasted barely an hour, following a well-trodden path. The *Diktat* of Versailles, Polish atrocities, Polish provocations, the Reich's right to live, to breath. The Führer had endured all this silently for months on end, but since the Polish 'attack' on German soil last night, he could bear it no longer. 'Since 4.45am we have been returning fire. From now on, bomb will be met by bomb.' He addressed fellow National Socialists as 'the first soldier of the Reich'. The Führer continued:

> I will wage this fight against whoever is our enemy until the security of the Reich and its rights are safeguarded…
>
> I expect no more of any German than I myself was prepared to do for four years. As a National Socialist and a German soldier I embark upon this struggle with a determined heart. My life has been one long struggle for the German Volk, for its rebirth, for Germany.

This, Hitler told his audience, would be a struggle unlike the last one a generation earlier. 'There's one word I've never known – capitulation! I would like to assure the world of just one thing: there will never be another November 1918 in Germany's history.' There was a brief adulatory from Göring, then Hitler left the *Krolloper*, climbed back into his black Mercedes and returned to his chancellery through streets 'almost devoid of people'.[49]

Gefreiter Wilhelm Berchtolds and his comrades of 179th Infantry Regiment huddled around their radio to listen to Hitler's *Reichstag* speech. No man had any doubts about invading Poland, as they listened to the Führer recount a string of 'transgressions': 'Ethnic Germans persecuted and murdered throughout Poland, Polish soldiers across the border in six different places…' No, Berchtolds and his comrades thought, 'the hour has come for us to fight for Germany'.[50]

The wagons of 8th Machine-Gun Battalion rolled into the village of Tlukomy, fifteen miles northeast of Schneidemühl. The *Volksdeutsche* populace stared in disbelief at the German soldiers. Women stood in the doorways of their homes, tears streaming down their faces. Young mothers lifted up their children so they could wave at their 'liberators'. 'They cannot yet believe that all the deprivation and servitude is at an end, that they are now part of us, that from this day forth they are under the protection of our arms,' one machine-gunner observed.

On the edge of the village, the men set up a radio and gathered around it to listen to the *Reichstag* address. 'My comrades listen breathlessly,' the gunner recorded in his diary. 'It's a strange feeling to hear the voice of the man to whom we owe everything, who has summoned us, and now as we stand on enemy soil, who speaks to us as if he were in our midst.'[51]

This was a day Hamburg schoolteacher Luise Solmitz had 'so dreaded and feared'. The conflict just beginning would make the Thirty Years' War look like 'a Sunday School outing', the fifty-year-old confided in her diary. 'A butchery is beginning such as the world has not yet experienced – a world full of blood and atrocity.'[52]

The second of SS *Heimwehr Danzig*'s two armoured cars pulled up on the edge of Heveliusplatz. Albert Forster climbed out. Today was the crowning moment of his political career, the day when Danzig came *Heim ins Reich* – home to the Reich. Newspaper reporters, journalists from state radio, the *Reichssender Danzig* and cameramen from the newsreel *Ufa-Tonwoche* were here to record this moment of triumph for posterity. But the battle for the post office was not running according to plan and the police officer leading the assault lacked the imagination to force the Poles to surrender. He suggested simply blowing the building up with high explosives. Forster forbade it. He brought up a howitzer and two field guns then exhorted the postal workers to surrender. Again they refused. The three guns smashed holes in the post office's façade, already pockmarked by machine-gun and rifle fire. The defenders were shaken, some were wounded, some were losing hope, but still they do not walk out into the square with their hands raised. *Polizeioberst* Willi Bethke changed his tactics again, summoning a mortar from the battle for the Westerplatte. The results were almost farcical. Faulty sights ensured mortar rounds began falling all around Heveliusplatz, threatening not the post office but the Germans attacking it. After a handful of rounds it was withdrawn from the fight.[53]

The ranks of 309th Infantry Regiment had yet to cross the Polish border. They hauled their kit from a train in Schneidemühl, the last major town before the border, and readied their weapons. It was almost mid-day when the *Landsers* moved off. Schneidemühl was in a festive mood. The swastika flag hung outside almost every house to celebrate Danzig's return to the Reich. Townsfolk rushed up to the marching soldiers, handing them flowers, sweets, fruit, tomatoes, cordial, cigarettes. The regiment continued eastwards under the September sun. As they neared the border the tarmac road turned to gravel. Vehicles racing past kicked up clouds of dust which enveloped the marchers, drowning out their cursing. At a German customs house, the men came to a halt. A few hundred yards away lay a Polish customs building, the red and white barrier emblazoned with the Polish double eagle pushed aside. There was little left of the customs house itself. Charred beams reached for the sky, bricks and rubble lay around. The regiment paused briefly to survey the scene, then continued eastwards. In the first villages beyond the border, swastika flags welcomed the infantrymen once more. Liberated *Volksdeutsche* struggled to contain their enthusiasm. *Gefreiter* Erich Müller watched as his company commander greeted the ethnic Germans with three loud 'Sieg Heils'; the company joined in enthusiastically. And then the regiment resumed its relentless march eastwards. 'As we continued our march we saw a fertile land with small farms on both sides of the road, bordered by small woods,' Müller recalled. 'All this is German once more and will remain German for eternity. We soldiers of Adolf Hitler will see to it.'[54]

Marching into Polish Upper Silesia southwest of Katowice, infantryman Werner Flack observed 'rabble-rousing appeals to take up the struggle against the Reich, images of Poland's glistening weapons, guns which threaten the heavens, aircraft which roar over the black barrels in huge squadrons' pasted on the sides of houses. The Poles glowered at the *Landsers* strutting past them. *Volksdeutsche* women hurried out of their homes and picked flowers from their gardens, handing these 'bouquets' to the marching soldiers. 'A young infantryman fixes a daisy from the hands of an old woman to his chest,' Flack noted. 'The vehicles are bedecked, the drivers, the guns, the horses.' Other ethnic Germans dashed into the shops, then emerged holding huge buckets filled with sweets, chocolates, biscuits, cigars, cigarettes, apples, and pears. Cries of 'Sieg! Sieg!' echoed along the road. Young girls waved at Flack and his comrades, tossing flowers. A 'pretty girl' handed Flack a dahlia, which he fixed in a buttonhole. 'Totally unsoldier-like, I raise my hand and wave back.' The infantrymen marched onwards. The waving hand of the pretty girl was swallowed up by the crowd.[55]

A few hours after being handed command of his company, Fritz Fillies received his baptism of fire along a stream in front of the village of Krzynowroga Mala, sixteen miles east of Mlawa. Fillies and his deputy decided to call on artillery fire to suppress anything they spotted through their binoculars – usually small puffs of smoke rising from machine-guns in Polish foxholes.

Each time it was as if you were slamming your fist on a table. *Wumm*! Pause. *Wumm*! *Wumm*! Pause. *Wumm*! Then four rounds, one rapidly after the other. *Wumm*! *Wumm*! *Wumm*! *Wumm*! Our light infantry shells, 7.5cm calibre, boomed briefly when fired, and when they came down over there a loud crash. Crash, crash! The shells of the heavy platoon made a bang. Bang, bang! It was a real symphony of noise. Sometimes Polish bullets whizzed by and bursts of machine-gun fire shot over us. 'Mies!' That's what it sounded like. After that we called them *Miesmacher* – killjoys.

The battle for Krzynowroga Mala was not a one-sided affair, however; Polish batteries joined in this hellish concert, but unlike the German fire, their artillery shells mainly exploded among poplar trees.[56]

By mid-morning, infantryman Karl Schönfeld had marched into his first burning village in the Corridor. 'There are fresh images of war constantly appearing before our eyes,' he wrote. 'I can't take it all in so quickly – there's no time for contemplation and reflection. We have to be on our guard so we're not suddenly attacked.' Soon the first enemy shells began to crash into the ground to the left and right of Schönfeld and his comrades. 'Now we can see that we're in action.'[57]

Having performed on Polish radio, Wladyslaw Szpilman left the broadcasting centre to grab some lunch. This was the first day of war, and yet life seemed to be continuing as normal. 'There was a great deal of traffic in the thoroughfares of the city – trams, cars and pedestrians,' the pianist remembered. 'The shops were open, and since the mayor had appealed to the population not to hoard food, there were not even queues outside them.'[58]

On the edge of the village of Wilkowiecko, a dozen miles north west of Czestochowa, tank commander Willi Reibig re-grouped with his company. The men of 4th Panzer Division had been thrown off balance, first by the ferocious resistance of the Poles then by a collision with enemy tankettes and cavalry in the burning ruins of Mokra III – an encounter which surprised the Poles as much as it did the Germans. Reibig's commander, Georg-Hans Reinhardt, was unimpressed. He ordered his panzers to storm Mokra again. Reibig followed his company commander along a country lane towards the woods which surrounded the village. As the German armour reached the treeline and a railway embankment, the Polish guns opened fire. 'There's crashing and smashing like mad,' Reibig wrote. There was little he could do. The angle of the lane meant only some of the enemy could be brought under the guns of his Panzer Mk III. The tank ahead of him nervously edged through a railway underpass. It was immediately engulfed in flames. 'Damned bandits!' Reibig snapped. Field batteries were drawn up to pound the embankment. The armour fanned out, struck the Polish defenders from the rear. By early evening, elements of 4th Panzer Division had pushed a couple of miles beyond Mokra. The day's objectives had been reached. But the day's drama for the division was not yet over.[59]

Acrid smoke still hung over the town of Wielun. The flames still flickered. Through the odd breaks in the black clouds, Romuald Szczecihski spied black dots seven, perhaps eight, thousand feet above. And there, high above *Major* Oskar Dinort had his gaze fixed firmly on the target. Dinort was every bit as ferocious as his piercing eyes and harsh nose suggested. Too young – just – to serve in the Great War, Dinort had joined the rump of the German Officer Corps in 1919 as an infantryman, then transferred to the clandestine air force in the mid-20s. Now, aged thirty-eight, a consummate pilot, commander of a dive-bomber *Gruppe*, Dinort seized his chance to prove himself in battle. Fog had shrouded the land for most of the morning, but in the early afternoon it cleared slightly. The *Gruppe* took off to compound Wielun's misery.

Nearly 8,000 feet above the market town, the fires from the morning still burned. Smoke cast a pall over the fields and shimmering streams, glinting in the occasional afternoon sun. German fighters buzzed over Wielun, safeguarding the approaching Ju87s. Dinort glanced through the cockpit glass. To this day, Poles and Germans dispute whether there were Polish troops in the town that fateful Friday, but Oscar Dinort was certain black figures were moving below – 'troops, wagon columns and mounted units'. There was a town, too, 'a town full of people'. Such thoughts quickly disappeared. There were soldiers down there, Oskar Dinort convinced himself, and he was, after all, only attacking soldiers.

I do all the things I've practised a hundredfold already, and then I push the aircraft over on its left wing and go into the dive.

The airbrakes screech, the blood in my body drains away, I've seen it all a hundred times, I've felt it a thousand times, but never as sharply, never as intensely as today. The target, the live target, grows in size in the windshield.

1,200 metres altitude. A single press on the release button on the joystick. A shudder goes through the aircraft. The first bomb is falling!

Bring her under control. Turn. Get away. And now, a glance below.

The bomb was well-aimed, right on the road. Smoke rises, and the black snake which was creeping along the road stops.

Far below, Romuald Szczecihski cowered, convinced the Luftwaffe was determined to raze Wielun and spread fear and panic among its inhabitants. To Szczecihski there was no rhyme nor reason to the German bombing, no concentration. The bombs were spread across the entire town. Not the churches nor the hospital, daubed with a huge red cross, were spared. 'The entire town lay in ruins and was in flames,' he recalled. He was surrounded only by the shattered shells of buildings and 'masses of dead and wounded'.

Still, Oskar Dinort was not done with Wielun. He dropped another stick of bombs on a farm apparently teeming 'with troops and teams of horses' and a final stick, 'the heaviest', on the market square. 'A fountain of flames, smoke and splinters, higher than the tower of the small church. And as we bank, a last look: there's nothing more to be seen of the Polish cavalry brigade.' And then home, home across the Silesian countryside, basking in the gold-green rays of the late summer sun. 'At the junction of a country lane, a couple of riders, possibly a group of stragglers, latecomers, looking to join up with their brigade – the brigade in Wielun which we have sent to its death.'[60]

With the dust barely settled around the collapsed Dirschau bridges, the men of 41st Pioneer Battalion received fresh orders: cross the Vistula and seize the opposite bank. The pioneers struggled to drag their small rubber boats across the 800-yard-wide flood plain. German artillery pummelled the town of Dirschau across the water while the pioneers rowed their boats back and forth, ferrying an entire company to the left bank. The men dug in on the eastern bank, a stone's throw from a Polish bunker. They were too close, however, for the German guns to turn their attention to the enemy fortifications without hitting their own men. Having crossed the Vistula, the pioneers were ordered to return to the right bank and watch the battle from afar.[61]

This first day of war had been frustrating for 7th Panzer Regiment. In fact, so far, there had been no war: the German armour was being held in reserve in a small copse near the village of Wetzhausen, half a dozen miles north of the fortress town of Mlawa. The infantry of *Panzer Division Kempf*, a hodgepodge of SS men and regular Army troops led by the man who gave this *ad hoc* unit its name, Werner Kempf, had struggled to make headway against strong Polish field positions. Early in the afternoon, Kempf order 7th Panzer forward. The tanks rumbled forward eagerly, roaring through the village of Kucklin – the German front line by mid-afternoon – and on towards Mlawa. But now the panzer attack began to unravel. The tanks ran headlong into tank barrier composed of railway track embedded in concrete, fixed at an angle to thwart the attacker. There was no way the regiment's inadequate Panzer Is could overcome the obstacle. They sought a way around it. And as they did, driving in front of the barrier in search of a gap, they presented their vulnerable sides to Polish anti-tank guns. Losses mushroomed. Panzers almost ran into each other in the confusion. Even when the German armour found a way around the barrier, they blundered straight into another one: an anti-tank ditch 10ft deep, 20ft wide and at least 500 yards long. The men of 7th Panzer Regiment had overcome one barrier; they could not overcome a second. With seven panzers knocked out and more than four times as many damaged, the regiment broke off the battle and fell back. 'The attack,' Werner Kempf conceded to his masters, 'was a disaster. Terrible losses of panzers, numbers unknown. An attack here is hopeless.'[62]

As the day drew on, Alexander Stahlberg and his 2nd Motorised Division drove ever deeper into the Polish Corridor 'as if we were on manoeuvres'. There were few signs of war yet. 'Here and there people were standing at their doors, but for us the exercise was without incident.' Only once on this first day of the campaign was he threatened. An obsolescent Polish biplane clattered towards Stahlberg and his colleagues, its two crew and the red-white Polish national emblem clearly visible. A German fighter pounced on this anachronism. 'After a single burst of fire, the biplane caught alight and plunged to the ground.'[63]

The 'attack' against Alexander Stahlberg's anti-tank unit was the exception, not the rule, on Friday September 1. For most Germans marching or rolling into Poland, the Polish Air Force simply failed to materialise. 'To a large extent the enemy air force remained unseen,' Albert Kesselring noted in the war diary of *Luftflotte 1*. Only an attack on Warsaw in the late afternoon provoked any real response from the Poles, who sent up two fighter squadrons to ward off the assault. Ten planes were lost, twenty-four more were in no state for further action. The first aerial battle over Warsaw severely shook the Polish crews. 'The only thing we were left with after this first encounter was a profound bitterness. In our mind's eye we could only see the beautiful modern shape of the enemy's fighter planes,' one Polish pilot wrote later.[64]

Far to the southwest, 1st Panzer Division was faring much better. By late afternoon, it had occupied Klobuck – now ablaze in numerous places – and begun to re-group for the next day's advance. It had moved a dozen miles that first day, hardly an auspicious start, but Kielmansegg and his colleagues felt satisfied; to them, it was if they had driven three dozen miles into Poland. 'Surely the Poles could not have believed that we would advance so far if you bear in mind everything which opposed us – the terrain, the barriers, destruction and demolitions, the roads in a state which hitherto would have been regarded as impassable, and not least the enemy himself,' the staff officer recorded.[65]

After a sluggish beginning, the trucks of 8th Machine-Gun Battalion had raced eastwards along the main road from Schneidemühl to Bromberg. By late afternoon they were just fifteen miles from their objective, moving through the town of Naklo nad Notecia – Nakel to Germans. It was deserted, the streets empty, the doors locked. Slowly the inhabitants emerged until the welcome for the machine-gunners became almost rapturous. 'Anglaises, Anglaises,' they cried out. 'The Poles believed in English help so effectively and did not believe that German troops could enter their town at all,' one *Leutnant* observed. The residents who realised their mistake sheepishly returned to their homes as quickly as possible. Others got down on their knees and begged for their lives. 'They are extremely surprised when they are not shot dead immediately,' wrote the *Leutnant* in his diary. 'Is there a more vivid picture of the incitement of a people?'[66]

Beneath Danzig's Heveliusplatz, pioneers were burrowing a tunnel through the cellar of a police station. With the hastily-dug tunnel complete, the engineers fixed an explosive charge at the far end and withdrew. At 5pm, the square was rocked by a huge explosion. For a few seconds a paralysing silence hung over Heveliusplatz, then the machine-guns opened fire, followed by the howitzer and the light infantry guns – all directed at the post office. Huge chunks of masonry fell off the building's façade, the iron poles in front snapped. Still the defenders fired back sporadically, but some were now toying with surrendering – though they could find no white cloth. Others in the post office were resolved to fight and die. They would soon have their wish.

Having commandeered a new vehicle, Heinz Guderian was chastising his men for their timidity. The day's objective was to cross the River Brahe, roughly one third of the way between the eastern border of the Reich and East Prussia. Guderian's staff insisted his troops needed a rest; they could not cross the Brahe today. As the panzer General fumed, a young *Leutnant* accosted him. 'Herr General, I've just come from the Brahe. The enemy forces on the far bank are weak.' Guderian nodded. 'The advance has only stopped because there's no-one to lead it,' the junior officer implored. 'You must go there yourself, sir.' Guderian did. He sent motorcycle infantry across the river in rubber boats to seize the opposite bank – and the bridge over the Brahe. By nightfall, the panzers were across the river.[67]

Hans von Luck's reconnaissance regiment had torn into Poland with the same drive. 'Where were the Polish troops?' he asked. Now ten miles inside Poland and no opposition. As afternoon turned to dusk, Luck's company finally ran into the enemy, a line of Polish mortars and machine-guns dug in on a hill. Luck formed his unit up for an attack as mortar shells splattered the terrain. 'Suddenly a round of machine-gun fire hit *Privat* Uhl, not far from me. He was dead at once,' Luck wrote. 'This was no longer a manoeuvre, this was war.' The company attacked anyway, but was brought to a halt by Polish artillery fire.[68]

In his command post on the heights near Opatow, Georg-Hans Reinhardt had a right to feel satisfied. His division had overcome the initial shock of fierce Polish resistance at Mokra. By nightfall its spearheads stood a good couple of miles east of that nest of enemy opposition. But while their general was confident, resolute, the men of 4th Panzer Division were still jittery. A motorcycle messenger riding across the battlefield and a handful of infantryman were accompanied by the cry: *Feindliche Panzer* – enemy tanks. A few damaged panzers withdrawing for repairs and a terse message from a rifle regiment – *Alarm* – added to the confusion. The baggage column – the field kitchens and ammunition trucks – was the first to panic; then two field batteries turned about and scurried westwards, even some armoured vehicles headed back across the battlefield. 'All too easily there's a sudden, unexpected, contagious collapse,' the division's chronicler observed. Only *der lange Reinhardt* stood firm. Half a mile behind his command post he and his staff rallied the men. The panic stopped.[69]

On the Vistula, the pioneers of 41st Pioneer Battalion watched as a bomber squadron tossed bombs on the Polish troops holding out around Dirschau at dusk. It broke the defenders' will. The Poles began to pull out of the town. By midnight, the pioneers had a four-tonne ferry running across the Vistula downstream of the ruins of the Dirschau bridges.

In the Bay of Danzig, Gustav Kleikamp was reviewing the second failure to storm the Westerplatte. His marines told him they could not take the peninsula. But Friedrich Eberhardt, the police 'general' in charge of the SS troops supporting the assault, refused to accept defeat. He was determined to see his men storm forward again the following day. Kleikamp disagreed. He took the SS officer forward to meet the men he expected to take the peninsula. As dusk descended upon the Gulf of Danzig, a wounded soldier limped back to German lines. Only with the onset of darkness had the marine thought it safe to crawl back. He was one of eighty-two Germans killed or wounded on the Westerplatte on the first day of Hitler's war. 'We were assured by Danzig's police that the Westerplatte would be taken in ten minutes,' fumed *Oberleutnant* Willi Aurich, *SX*'s bandmaster, now serving in the battleship's sick bay. 'In ten minutes, the Westerplatte was a pile of ruins – that's what tonight's newspapers reported. Their report was somewhat premature.'[70]

Willi Bethke had tried a simple assault – and failed. He had brought up armoured cars – and failed. He had used field guns – and failed. He had fired mortar rounds – and failed. He had tried to blast a way into the post office using an explosive charge – and failed. Almost desperate, the police officer called upon Danzig's fire service to bring up a railway wagon filled with petrol – petrol which was promptly pumped into the cellar of the post office. A hand grenade was tossed in. Five Poles were burned alive in an instant, six more were so hideously scarred that they succumbed to their injuries a few days later in hospital. This was an episode which did not feature in the weekly newsreel or propaganda accounts; 'other military means' had been employed to force the surrender of the Polish Post Office. Willi Bethke called it 'fumigation'.

One by one, the defenders of the post office filed out, led by director Jan Michon, brandishing a white bath-towel. 'There are the Polish dogs! Down with them! We take no prisoners!' echoed around the square. Michon was felled by a shot to the stomach. His postmaster Jozef Wasik, shortly behind Michon, was either shot dead or burned alive by a flamethrower. The remaining postal workers, their hair singed, their faces blackened, staggered outside, were lined up against a wall and driven to a school building converted into a makeshift prison.[71]

The picture as night enveloped Poland on this first day of battle was confused. The Germans had no accurate information about the strength of the Polish Army or where it lay. The only surprise had been how few forces defended the Corridor. Still, the Wehrmacht held the field of battle. At the day's end, German radio announcers read out the first official record of the war. *Das Oberkommando der Wehrmacht gibt bekannt* – the High Command of the Wehrmacht reports. The communiqué was drafted personally by Hitler:

> On the orders of the Führer and Reich's Chancellor, the Wehrmacht has assumed active defence of the Reich. On Friday morning, in accordance with their mission to halt Polish aggression, troops of the German Army passed all German-Polish border checkpoints to launch a counter-offensive.[72]

The Luftwaffe had flown more than 2,000 sorties – half directed against the Polish air force and its bases that day. Some twenty-eight airfields were attacked, 100 aircraft were claimed to be wrecked on the ground for the loss of just twenty-five German aircraft. But the Luftwaffe's objective of smashing the enemy air force on the ground remained unfulfilled. Those Polish aircraft caught on airfields were for the most part not front-line models. 'The Luftwaffe did exactly what we expected,' one Polish air force major wrote later. He continued:

> It attacked our airfields and tried to wipe out our aircraft on the ground. It seems quite naïve of the Germans to have believed that during the preceding days of high political tension and with their own obviously aggressive intentions, we would leave our units sitting at their peacetime bases.[73]

In Warsaw, Roman Umiastowski gripped the microphone in his hand. The forty-six-year-old lieutenant colonel headed the propaganda section in the Polish High Command. Never had he addressed his comrades at a graver hour than on this evening. His language was more florid than that used by Adolf Hitler in his terse communiqué, but Umiastowski was no more honest with his address:

> We are ready. Wherever the enemy has attacked, he has run into a wall of our resistance against which his attacks have been smashed. We are not merely defending ourselves successfully, we are also attacking. Two brigades of Polish cavalry have crossed the border of East Prussia and are pressing forward continually to rescue our brothers in the Masurian Lakes and Ermland. Soldiers! Fight heroically! You are fighting for a just cause! The moment of the victory is at hand.[74]

As Umiastowski broadcast to his people, Poland's Foreign Minister Jozef Beck was haranguing French ambassador Léon Noël, enraged by British and French vacillation. 'We are in the thick of war,' he blustered. The point was not lost on Noël. 'The atmosphere,' he reported to his masters in Paris, 'is no longer one for conciliation.'[75]

William Shirer made his way to the radio studio to make his regular broadcast to America. Today, of course, was anything but a regular day, and yet for all their melancholy, for all their indifference to this new war, Berliners were determined to enjoy a Friday night out. 'The cafes, restaurants and beer halls were packed,' Shirer noticed.[76]

The Polish landscape this Friday evening was bathed in the red glow of towns and villages burning. Polish evening sun, one *Landser* callously called it. 'The night sky is lit with red strips,' an officer in a signal unit with 1st *Leichte* Division advancing on Wielun wrote. 'Black smoke rises. There are scenes of the devastating fire of war which later we will see even more often.' For many German soldiers this bloody hue was intoxicating. The SS *Leibstandarte* bivouacked in a field near the town of Wieruszow, barely ten miles inside the Polish border. As the sun dipped beneath the horizon, Kurt Meyer turned to look westwards. Darkness shrouded the battlefield, but did not hide the misery, now illuminated by countless fires. 'The horizon is marked by burning villages and dense smoke rolls over the violated earth,' the SS man recorded in his diary. 'In silence, we sit behind the remains of a wall, trying to make sense of this first day of battle.'[77]

The men of 4th Panzer Division were also mesmerised by the sight of the fires tinting the horizon red, until the war dragged them back to reality. 'A sudden cry,' panzer man Willi Reibig recalled. '*Polish cavalry on the left*! We grabbed our weapons again.' It was a false alarm. The panzer crews watched as herds of riderless horses searching for their masters galloped past.[78]

The people of Bojanowo were still hiding in their cellars, awaiting the arrival of German soldiers as night descended upon the Silesian countryside. That Friday evening there was only one sound, a distant, terrible roar, carried by the wind from the neighbouring village. German farmers had abandoned their crofts and fled across the border, fearing for their lives. They left behind their animals, including the cows still in their stables, waiting to be milked. They cried in pain.[79]

In the Corridor, the men of 20th Motorised Infantry Division still could not believe they were at war. 'This was no exercise where everything ran like clockwork,' one *Landser* recalled. 'Here they were shooting back.' And 'they' were taking their toll of the 20th Infantry as they struggled to reach the River Brahe. 'There could be no thought of sleep – emotions were too mixed up,' the infantryman wrote. 'News of the first dead comrades had stirred the men to the depths of their souls. No-one spoke about it, yet somehow each man felt it.'[80]

7th Panzer Regiment found itself in the same jump-off positions from where it had set off early that afternoon 'certain of victory'. The panzer men's mood that evening was downbeat. But it was also determined. 'We have received our baptism of fire but not achieved success – that is bitter,' wrote *Hauptmann* Walter Straub, on the regimental staff. 'But the regiment has not been beaten. It was given an impossible task.' The men sat around their panzers and chewed over this bitter first battle long into the night despite their exhaustion. 'There is so much to discuss,' Straub recalled. 'That well-known soldiers' song *Ich hatt einen Kameraden* has suddenly become a reality.'[81]

Danzigers were possessed by no such melancholy this night. Their city was cloaked in darkness, but they ignored the blackout. They poured on to the city's streets, through Langgasse and the Lange Markt. The façades of Danzig's basked in the moonlight, swastika flags hanging in front of homes swayed in the night breeze. Before midnight, the crowds had faded away leaving Danzig's historic alleys empty. On the stroke of twelve, the bells in the town hall sounded. 'The chimes begin and echo around the alleyways which are now quiet, around the old proud houses, the churches, gates, towers, warehouses, shipyards and ships,' one Nazi reporter recorded. 'Danzig is German again. We thank the Führer.'[82]

Johann Graf von Kielmansegg returned to Panki in his staff car, passing men of the labour service, the *Reichsarbeitsdienst*, and pioneers building a steel road behind the front for the panzers to trundle down. In Panki, he found a spartan billet in the classroom of the village school. 'I lie my sleeping bag down on the floorboards of the classroom. Through the windows I see the glow of fire from the still-burning post office. Messengers come, the telephone rings, the corps' order for tomorrow has to be passed on to the front, quickly, because dawn of 2 September is approaching. I don't sleep much during this first night of the war.'[83]

Carrying a 30lb pack in full battledress, Wilhelm Prüller and his comrades struggled to march more than six miles into Poland in the heat. 'We're 103 kilometres from Krakow,' he wrote excitedly in his diary. 'Everywhere we see torn-up roads, trenches, tank traps hastily thrown up. Destroyed bridges make us take long detours across fields. The blown-up bridges and torn-up streets continue to slow up our advance. But all the Poles' efforts are to no avail. The Wehrmacht is marching! If we look back, or in front of us, or left or right: everywhere the motorised Wehrmacht!' The company finally rested at 9pm. The field kitchen handed out pork soup and tea, as the men settled down for the night in a field. Exhausted, Wilhelm Prüller ate, then fell asleep immediately. His rest did not last long. The crack of rifle fire echoed in the darkness. The Austrian and his comrades were ordered to scour the countryside. They found nothing. The men finally got their heads down again at 1am. It was now the second day of Adolf Hitler's war.[84]

Notes

1. KTB Prüller, 1/9/39.
2. Schindler, pp. 107–8.
3. Tagesbefehl, 1/9/39. Author's papers.
4. Kesselring, Albert (ed), *Unsere Flieger über Polen: Vier Frontoffiziere berichten*, pp. 53–4.
5. KTB Richthofen, 1/9/39. BA-MA N671/4.
6. Guderian, Heinz, *Mit den Panzern in Ost und West*, pp. 16–17.
7. Busch, *Unsere Kriegsmarine im Polnischen Feldzug*, p. 7 and Mulligan, p. 38.
8. BA-MA RH53-18/144.
9. Schindler, pp. 145–6.
10. Kielmansegg, pp. 14–16.
11. Stahlberg, p. 117.
12. Liere, *Pioniere im Kampf: Erlbenisberichte aus dem Polenfeldzug 1939*, pp. 5–6.
13. Schenk, *Hitlers Mann in Danzig*, p. 125.
14. Fritz-Otto Busch, *Unsere Kriegsmarine im Polnischen Feldzug*, pp. 17–21.
15. Schenk, *Hitlers Mann in Danzig*, p. 125.
16. Schenk, *Post von Danzig*, pp. 60–61.
17. Kielmansegg, pp. 14–16.

18. Stahlberg, p. 117.
19. Luck, p. 28.
20. Prüller, p. 13.
21. Schimak, Anton, Lamprecht, Karl and Dettmer, Friedrich, *Die 44 Infanterie Division: Tagebuch der Hoch und Deutschmeister*, p. 25.
22. Kesselring, Albert (ed), *Unsere Flieger über Polen: Vier Frontoffiziere berichten*, pp. 53–5.
23. Ibid, pp. 14–18.
24. Eichelbaum, H (ed), *Schlag auf Schlag: Die deutsche Luftwaffe in Polen*, pp. 14–17.
25. Liere, *Pioniere im Kampf: Erlbenisberichte aus dem Polenfeldzug 1939*, pp. 6–7.
26. Guderian, *Panzer Leader*, p. 68.
27. BA-MA RH37/7535.
28. Schindler, pp. 84–6.
29. Anon, *Wach auf, es ist Krieg! Wie Polen und Deutsche den 1 September 1939 erlebten*, p. 15.
30. Drescher, pp. 102–3.
31. Korwin-Rhodes, p. 8.
32. Venzky, p. 11.
33. Hammer, I und Neiden, Suzanne zu, *Sehr selten habe ich geweint*, Schweizer Verlag, Zurich, 1993, p. 20.
34. Schindler, p. 146.
35. Meyer, *Grenadiere*, pp. 7, 9.
36. Leibstandarte, vol.1, p. 93.
37. Schindler, pp. 123–4.
38. Domarus, iii, p. 1746, KTB *Schleswig-Holstein*, 1/9/39 Anlagen in NHB 714, *Deutsche Rundschau*, 9/9/39 and Schenk, *Hitlers Mann in Danzig*, pp. 127–8.
39. Fillies, p. 36.
40. Kielmansegg, pp. 16, 18–19.
41. Dollinger, *Kain, wo ist dein Bruder?*, p. 21.
42. Schenk, *Post von Danzig*, pp. 61-2.
43. Schenk, *Post von Danzig*, pp. 71-2.
44. Hammer, I und Neiden, Suzanne zu, *Sehr selten habe ich geweint*, Schweizer Verlag, Zurich, 1993, pp. 20–1.
45. Drescher, p. 130 and Szpilman, pp. 24–5.
46. Fillies, pp. 42, 44.
47. Shirer, *Berlin Diary*, p. 197, *Völkischer Beobachter* and *Berliner Börsen Zeitung*, 1/9/39.
48. Spiess and Lichtenstein, *Unternehmen Tannenberg*, pp. 174–5.
49. Vormann, pp. 69–70 and Reichstag speech of 1/9/39 in the author's papers.
50. Rossino, p. 197.
51. BA-MA RH37/7535.
52. Evans, *The Third Reich in Power*, pp 704, 705.
53. Schenk, *Post von Danzig*, pp. 63–4.
54. March of 309th Infantry Regiment based on the accounts of Rudolf Pahl, Erich Müller and Kurt Schmoll in Hoffmann, Oberleutnant Dr. (ed), *Infanterie Regiment 309 marschiert an den Feind*, pp. 25–6, 30, 31–3.
55. Flack, pp. 20–2.
56. Fillies, pp. 52–4.
57. Dollinger, *Kain, wo ist dein Bruder?*, p. 21.

58. Szpilman, pp. 26–7.
59. Reibig, pp. 16–17 and Neumann, *Die 4 Panzer Division 1938–1943*, p. 30.
60. Kesselring, Albert (ed), *Unsere Flieger über Polen: Vier Frontoffiziere berichten*, pp. 116–18 and *Grösste Härte*, p. 71. Dr Oldwig von Natzmer, the Nazi official sent to restore order in Wielun, recorded his impressions of the town five days after the raids. 'The smell of burning hurts our eyes and noses. The trees of an old avenue stretch their bare branches into the singed air. Here and there a fire is still flickering... In the streets lie rubbish, stones, overturned streetlights and telephone poles. Only the market and the road out of town are free... In daylight we can clearly make out the effect of the bombs. The heart of the town is completely destroyed. Here the houses have burned down and collapsed, smashed and blown apart by bombs. Every now and then rafters stick up into the air like fish bones. Electricity and telephone cables hang down in chaotic fashion – you have to be careful not to trip over them. Bomb craters have smashed the streets and squares, properties upturned, large and small duds lie in the roads... Out of the stone heaps of collapsed homes we see crushed beds, closets wrecked, torn clothes. And then there is a sweet smell. Corpses must still be lying beneath the stones...In the new market place, two houses are still standing. In the old market place, the post office is standing, behind it the town hall, although its tower has suffered a bomb hit, and the district council office. Wielun had 16,000 inhabitants. All but 200 of them have fled.' See *Grösste Härte*, p. 71.
61. Schindler, pp. 146–7.
62. Straub, Walter, Oberst, *Das Panzer Regiment 7 und 21 und seine Tochterformationen im Zweiten Weltkrieg*, in author's papers and KTB I AK, 1/9/39. Cited in Jentz, i, p. 93.
63. Stahlberg, p. 118.
64. Bekker, p. 35 and Zamoyski, p. 22.
65. Kielmansegg, p. 19.
66. BA-MA RH37/7535.
67. Guderian, *Panzer Leader*, pp. 70–1.
68. Luck, pp. 28–9.
69. Neumann, *Die 4 Panzer Division 1938–1943*, pp. 31–32.
70. Stjernfelt, p. 85 and Schenk, *Post von Danzig*, pp. 77–8.
71. Schenk, *Post von Danzig*, pp. 65–7.
72. OKW Communiqué, 1/9/39.
73. Bekker, p. 37.
74. Drescher, pp. 131–2.
75. *French Yellow Book*, No.343, pp. 330–1.
76. Shirer, Berlin Diary, p. 199.
77. Fillies, p. 55, Paul, *Brennpunkte*, p. 28 and Meyer, *Grenadiere*, p. 9.
78. Reibig, p. 2.
79. Anon, *Wach auf, es ist Krieg! Wie Polen und Deutsche den 1 September 1939 erlebten*, p. 15.
80. Asmus, *Die 20.Inf.Div.(mot) Chronik und Geschichte*, Band 2, p. 25.
81. Straub, Walter, Oberst, *Das Panzer Regiment 7 und 21 und seine Tochterformationen im Zweiten Weltkrieg*, in author's papers.
82. Schenk, *Post von Danzig*, pp. 78–9.
83. Kielmansegg, p. 20.
84. KTB Prüller, 1–2/9/39.

CHAPTER FIVE

Pluck the Enemy Capital Like a Ripe Fruit

My faith in the panzer divisions was always boundless!

– ADOLF HITLER

Warsaw will be defended to the last breath and, if it falls, the enemy
will have to step over the corpse of the very last defender.

– LIEUTENANT COLONEL WACLAW LIPINSKI

JOHANN Graf von Kielmansegg had grabbed what sleep he could on the floor of the village school in Panki. He was up before dawn this Saturday morning. He washed himself vigorously in the school's water fountain, then climbed into his staff car to return to the front line. As he did, he watched three bombers coming in low from the east. The Luftwaffe returning from its first raid of the day, Kielmansegg thought. Something dark fell from one of the bombers then three, four, five explosions. Lumps of earth flew through the air. Another stick of bombs fell directly over Panki, but it did not halt 1st Panzer Division. Only poor roads and the odd demolition hindered the armour's advance. There was little sight of the enemy. The race to Warsaw had begun in earnest.[1]

Everywhere on the first day of battle German troops had punctured the Polish lines: in Pomerania, in the Corridor, in Silesia, in the Carpathians. In places the enemy had offered battle, but invariably the invader had skirmished briefly with his foe, and his foe had fallen back. Only on the Westerplatte, where this fledgling conflict had begun, did the sense of success elude the attacker. Every attack against the peninsula had been repulsed for the cost of just four dead. Henryk Sucharski, the garrison's commander, was pleased. Battle-hardened veterans had stiffened the resolve of his younger troops. In each man there was a feeling of 'having won the first battle'. With dawn on the second they waited for the attacker to come once more. But he did not…[2]

There had been little darkness by the banks of the Brahe. All through the night flares had raced into the sky above the bivouacs of 3rd Panzer Division around the hamlet of Hammermühle, forty miles north of Bromberg. Blazing farms lit up the valley 'like burning torches'. Wild rifle and pistol fire persisted throughout the night. Two Polish officers in a large Mercedes, its headlights on full beam, accidentally drove through the German picket line and were immediately taken prisoner and marched off into captivity. But if the panzer men believed they were dealing with a shaken, demoralised, beaten enemy, they were sorely mistaken.

With first light, the Poles swept forward – infantry and cavalry, elements of two divisions and one brigade – determined to crush the German bridgehead. The 3rd Panzer's commander Geyr von Schweppenburg and his staff fled, dashing back over open ground to find shelter as Polish shells and machine-gun fire chased them. The defence of the bridgehead was leaderless; Geyr had little idea where his men were.[3]

Geyr's superior Heinz Guderian was not a man to be unnerved. The attack on 3rd Panzer did not unduly trouble him. But the timidity of 2nd Motorised Infantry Division on the armour's left flank did. Like the panzers, the infantrymen were set upon by enemy horsemen, the *Pomorska Cavalry Brigade*. *Generalleutnant* Paul Bader warned his corps commander he would be forced to fall back. Guderian exploded. Had Bader ever heard of Pomeranian grenadiers being overrun by enemy cavalry, he asked. No, Bader sheepishly replied, he had not. His division would stand firm. Still Guderian was unconvinced. His mistrust was well founded. When he visited the division's staff that morning it was, he recalled, 'all at sea'. There was only one solution. The panzer General took charge, leading the regiment which had withdrawn in the face of Polish cavalry back to the positions it had held.[4]

Hundreds of miles to the south in the Carpathians, the *Landsers* of 7th Infantry Division had already marched half a dozen miles. Some men had spent an unsettled night billeted in a Polish restaurant; its owner reluctantly served the invaders a few glasses of rather stale beer before the men settled down on hay in the adjacent stable. About to doze off, the *Landsers* were startled by the crack of infantry fire. For an hour, the soldiers swept through the neighbouring meadows on a mild, bright moonlit night, then rested for a couple of hours. Well before dawn, the division was on the move again, unhindered, in silence. Where is the enemy? the men asked themselves. He had gone and so too the few villages who inhabited this mountainous landscape. All that remained were cattle. Only as the infantrymen approached the heights of Barania, beyond the village of Szare, did the enemy appear, sending artillery shells raining down on the men. As the morning mist began to disperse the German guns opened fire on the slopes of Barania. The Poles fell back. The German troops stormed through a brook then up the hill. At the top they enjoyed a warm meal, pork they were told, and looked down the valley towards Polish bunkers defending the village of Wegierska Gorka, a handful of miles to the north.[5]

Some thirty miles away, Heinz Borwin Venzky's armoured reconnaissance unit drove past Polish field fortifications on the road to the Upper Silesian town of Auschwitz. Panzers and infantry had stormed the bunkers at dawn; the tell-tale markings of caterpillar tracks were still visible on the road and in the fields. 'Dead Poles lie around everywhere,' Venzky wrote as his unit rolled past the battlefield for a good half hour. Some dead looked as if they were sleeping peacefully; others were a bloody mess. Wounded Poles crouched apathetically by the side of the road. Bloody scraps of uniform and dented steel helmets were scattered around. Shot-up anti-tank guns were stuck in ditches. Under one smashed limber, Venzky spied a dead Pole. 'From a pale face, his empty, wide-open eyes stare towards heaven.'[6]

Auschwitz was also the objective for one Polish reserve officer, marching with his column towards the town against a tide of dejected, panicking soldiers. The remnants of three divisions were falling back in chaos. Fear of German panzers had gripped every man. There was talk of an enemy breakthrough barely a dozen miles away. The officer and his men continued towards Auschwitz, but as they approached the town they were attacked from behind by German armour. The column scattered; the men abandoned their kit and, in some cases, their guns and ran for Auschwitz. The roads were crammed with retreating military vehicles and refugees. The staff of 6th Division forced their way through by brandishing pistols. They attempted to rally the men and succeeded in forming a new line in Auschwitz itself. But how long would it last?[7]

4th Panzer Division was finding Saturday, 2 September, no easier than Friday, 1 September. Shortly before mid-day Willi Reibig drove over the previous day's battlefield north of Czestochowa – Tschenstochau to the Germans – as he moved into position to attack. A Polish field kitchen had been overrun on the first day of the war. Dead Poles lay scattered around it, with wood and coal still littering the field. A bit further on Reibig came across a wrecked field howitzer, ammunition and shell cartridges, more dead. A hideous sweet smell drifted across the battlefield, hardly surprising under the heat of the September sun. Reibig's panzers crept slowly along, then as the ground opened up before them, the crews sighted dismounted Polish cavalry resting in a copse, and immediately opened fire. The panzers opened fire. 'The Poles run away as if giant fists have waded in,' he recalled. 'Columns of smoke rise over the forest like fiery pine trees. What has not stayed down, dashes in great bounds and disappears behind a hill.' The panzers pursued the horsemen into the wood, yet Reibig and his comrades found fighting among the trees unnerving. It wasn't natural panzer country; it was difficult to manoeuvre, to sight the enemy amid the undergrowth, to avoid incoming Polish shells. 'With a strange *piijüh, piijüh,* the shells whistle past us,' wrote Reibig. 'These hardly worry us – for what whistles has already passed and can do no harm. The bullet which you don't hear is the one which hits you.' It was the crack of rifle fire striking at the trees which gnawed at the men's nerves. 'We curse this damn bush war where we can never bring our full might to bear properly.'[8]

As 4th Panzer battered its way forward, its right-hand neighbour, 1st Panzer, was racing for the River Warthe – the only substantial natural obstacle on the road to Warsaw. A reconnaissance unit pounced on a train packed with reservists. The soldiers fled into the surrounding woods, but were soon rounded up; none expected the Germans to be so deep inside Polish territory after less than thirty-six hours of war. The Poles had no time, too, to blow the bridges over the Warthe. All three fell undamaged into 1st Panzer's hands and by 2pm, the first Germans were across the river far to the northeast of Czestochowa. Poles hampered the division's onward move. Not the Polish Army, but civilians, refugees in their hundreds, clogging the roads with horses, carts, but mostly on foot. 'There are also unintentional moments of comedy,' Johann Graf von Kielmansegg observed, 'like when an old farmer's wife moved along with a cackling chicken under her arm and a gigantic alarm clock in her other hand as her sole possessions.'[9]

On the east bank of the Vistula, the right arm of the German pincer squeezing the Corridor was lumbering towards the city of Graudenz. The East and West Prussians of 21st Infantry Division had been given wildly optimistic orders on the first day of battle – to smash any Polish forces northwest of Graudenz, then seize the city and the bridges over the Vistula, more than a dozen miles from the division's jump-off position. Still, they had given it their best shot, punching their way over a small river, the Ossa, to within four miles of Graudenz. The second day of September dawned with the Vistula valley shrouded in thick fog. Under a blanket of artillery fire 45th Infantry Regiment tried to force its way through the Polish defences on the Ossa. It was cut down by a devilish hail of shell, mortar, machine-gun and rifle fire. 'Medics here, medics there,' recalled squad leader Karlheinz Herzberg. 'Cries of: "Medic", "Mother", "Mama", "Help" were drowned out by commands and orders. In the haze an olive-green helmet appeared sporadically and then vanished. In the bright morning after gaining a few hundred metres of ground the order to dig in arrived.' The regiment dug in, but still the enemy's shells continued to crash down. Incompetence now came to the attackers' aid. The Polish command decided its two divisions blocking the road to Graudenz should swap places. As *16th Division* began pulling out of the line, there was all manner of chaos as communications broke down and troops ran into each other. Their commander, Colonel Stanislaw Switalksi, lost his head and ordered a general retreat a dozen miles to the southwest. At times, particular among the rearward columns, the withdrawal turned to panic. Switalksi was promptly sacked, but the damage had been done. Only Graudenz's small garrison and the militia – the *Obrona Narodowa* – stood between 21st Infantry Division and the town.[10]

A few dozen miles to the west, 9th Infantry Regiment was rushing towards the Brahe to help Geyr von Schweppenburg and his beleaguered panzer division. The regiment force marched along the few roads which ran through a land studded by copses and lakes and which were now crammed with supply columns, hundreds of vehicles, limbered carts, unable to move. As *Oberst* Werner *Freiherr* von und zu Gilsa, the regimental commander, pushed his men east from Pruszcz down a railway line towards the village of Klonowo, half a dozen miles away, Polish troops swarmed out of the copses and south, over the rail line. They were thrown back. At dusk, the Poles came again – and again they were repulsed. Von und zu Gilsa feared a renewed attack. His men had not eaten for more than a day, they were exhausted by marching and fighting, but above all they were running out of ammunition. Inexperienced in battle, the men had swiftly devoured what supplies they carried with them – they had left the ammunition columns behind on the clogged roads. If the Poles came on again in force, supported by artillery, there was a chance they would smash their way through Gilsa's lines and reach the banks of the River Brahe, barely a mile to the south, where all manner of vehicles were waiting to cross the makeshift bridge thrown across the river by 3rd Panzer.

But the Poles did not come. They did not come because Geyr and his men had weathered the storm and renewed their thrust to the Vistula. The sun beat down mercilessly. The roads were poor and usually only suitable for single-file traffic.

Signs of Polish disintegration spurred the German armour on. Frequently the lanes were blocked by enemy columns which had bumped into each other in the chaos of battle, or by carts and trees struck by the stukas. By the side of these roads were abandoned ammunition and baggage wagons, the cadavers of horses, dead Poles.[11]

On the Westerplatte still they waited. Throughout the morning and into the afternoon, plans for a concerted raid on the Polish depot by dive-bombers had been postponed and delayed. In *Schleswig-Holstein*'s sick bay, bandmaster Willi Aurich was tending to the wounded from yesterday's fighting. 'On the bed opposite me lay two grey-black bodies, only one of which moved slightly from time to time and gave out awful, loud groans,' he recalled. An hour before dusk, Aurich moved to the upper deck. A shipmate pointed to the sky. High above the Bay of Danzig three dots appeared. The dots multiplied. Six, nine, a dozen. For forty minutes they peeled off, one by one, sixty dots in all. The sirens screamed as the Ju87s of *Sturzkampfgeschwader* 2 plummeted towards the peninsula, then dropped 150 bombs upon the stubborn fortress. Observers on the *Schleswig-Holstein* saw clouds of smoke and dust tumbling into the sky – and just one section of wall crumble under the weight of the attack. 'The heavens darken with rising smoke,' Aurich recorded. 'On board everyone is full of confidence that this must be the end for the Westerplatte.' For a moment, the sailors thought they saw a white flag hoisted above the depot, only for it to be quickly hauled down again.

They *had* seen a white flag. Henryk Sucharski had lost his mind. The forty-year-old was a career soldier, a veteran of the Italian Front with the Austro-Hungarian Army in the Great War. But two days of intense bombardment had shattered the commander's nerves, his deputy Captain Franciszek Dobrowski observed. 'He was shaking and blubbering, his lips were foaming.' Sucharski ordered the white flag hoisted and began burning all his secret papers. His officers mutinied. The Westerplatte's doctor was summoned. Henryk Sucharski was strapped to a bed, a stick thrust between his teeth. The white flag was lowered, and resistance resumed.[12]

Willi Reibig's armour eventually emerged from the undergrowth only to run into fierce Polish resistance in front of the village of Kocin Nowy, eight miles north of Czestochowa, which was promptly set ablaze. By the time Reibig passed through it, the first inhabitants were nervously returning home. They stood, staring at the ruins of their cottages. Those who could still find a cellar untouched by fire or artillery were branded 'the happy ones' by the panzer men. Other refugees appeared, people who had fled the border villages with the imminence of war and headed for the forests. Now they emerged, wailing, shaking from fear. That evening, Reibig wandered back through the German lines. 'I noticed a lovely smell,' he remembered. A calf – wounded in the fighting – had been slaughtered by an enterprising *Landser*. 'A piece of dry bread and one piece of fried meat was an exquisite meal after the day's exertions,' wrote Reibig. 'After eating, calm gradually descended, and I hit the sack and tried to sleep. But before I slowly crossed into the land of dreams, yesterday's and today's experiences once again flashed before my eyes. Another hot day had drawn to a close.'[13]

Fifteen miles to the east, Graf von Kielmansegg settled down in his billet, a doctor's house in the village of Gidle on the right bank of the Warthe. The bulk of his division was across the river. No German unit had punched its way further into Polish territory.

It was twilight before 7th Infantry Division was in position to attack the bunkers at Wegierska Gorka. The soft blue hue in the heavens contrasted with the red of countless fires in the valley of the River Sola. Luminous green tracers raced towards the embrasures of the concrete fortifications. A thousand gun barrels roared – machine-guns, rifles, field guns. A flamethrower was sent up to clear out one particularly troublesome bunker. The way was cleared into Wegierska Gorka, although little remained of the Carpathian village which now burned fiercely. Set against the yellow-red glow of the flames, the advancing *landsers* were easy targets for Polish sharpshooters hiding on the hillside. But beyond the blazing ruins, the infantry were plunged into darkness, stumbling through a brook, scrambling up a hill whose slopes were covered by trees in pitch blackness – so dark it was barely possible to see the man in front.[14]

For some this was still a *Blumenkrieg*. The soldiers of 309th Infantry Regiment settled down in the homes and barns of German farmers. There had been no contact with the enemy.

It had been an exhausting, blazing, muggy Saturday in the Corridor. The night was cool. The men were tired and, above all, hungry and thirsty; the division's supply columns were still far to the rear, unable to force their way through the traffic jam on the Brahe. In desperation, a few men grabbed their rifles and crawled over the fields in the darkness to milk any cows they could find. Leo Geyr von Schweppenburg shared the men's exhaustion. But he also knew that his panzers stood a hair's breadth from the Vistula. As far as the *Generalleutnant* was concerned, the enemy was cut off. The battle of the Corridor had been won.[15]

Long before first light the following morning, Sunday, 3 September, Geyr von Schweppenburg ordered his armour to race along the left bank of the Vistula and begin clearing out the pine woods, marshes and scrubland of the Tucheler Heath. The Poles struck back, trying to force their way southeastwards towards Schwetz by the banks of the Vistula. They threw infantry and cavalry down the main road. 3rd Panzer's artillery opened fire. It took a terrible toll. Limbers and baggage carts were overturned, horses ran around wildly and Polish soldiers threw away their guns and hurried across the fields in panic. Geyr threw in his infantry to complete the rout; by nightfall, more than 800 prisoners and fifteen guns had fallen into his hands. The road to Schwetz was a graveyard of wrecked vehicles and smashed guns. As for Schwetz itself, German armour dashed past it and continued north along the Vistula valley. The closer the panzers drew to Graudenz, the louder the sounds of battle drifting across the Vistula became and the brighter the fires burning in the town; 21st Infantry Division was fighting in the suburbs of Graudenz. They seized the railway yard. But they fell short of taking Graudenz. With darkness descending – and with the threat of fighting in the streets by night – 21st Infantry withdrew.[16]

By first light that Sunday, staff officer Johann Graf von Kielmansegg was already at work in the courtyard of a doctor's house in Gidle. Many of the village's residents had stayed behind – convinced the panzer troops were English; some had even handed the soldiers flowers. Kielmansegg's commanding officer, Friedrich Kirchner paced up and down the courtyard with his operations officer, Walther Wenck, discussing the situation. The deceptive tranquillity of this Sunday morning was shattered by the drone of aircraft. Luftwaffe formations had already roared overhead in both directions all morning long, but this time there was a loud cry. 'Look out, bombs!' Kirchner and his closest staff jumped into a hastily-dug trench, as the bombs straddled the doctor's house. All missed their true targets – the Warthe bridges – but the attack was one of fifteen suffered by 1st Panzer's columns that day, proof that the Polish Air Force had deliberately avoided battle on the first two days of the campaign – rather than being driven out of the sky. The division moved its command post repeatedly, finally settling in a forest. 'We finally feel safe to some extent in a forest, when right next to us a blazing Polish aircraft crashes into the forest and sets it ablaze,' wrote Kielmansegg. 'Once more we have to run. But a success all the same!' There was a begrudging admiration for the Polish airmen who 'carried out their orders with great courage and also considerable skill. A shot-down Pole was one of numerous prisoners who said nothing during interrogation, despite his wounds.'[17]

There was little sign of enemy aircraft twenty or so miles to the west of Kielmannsegg. In fact, there was little sign of *any* enemy as the artillery of 19th Infantry Division moved their guns across the Warthe. The fighting had long since passed. Soldiers bathed in the river. And on its bank, a naked *Landser* armed with a bayonet tried in vain to catch a goose.[18]

In Berlin, Paul Schmidt moved quickly through the corridors of the Foreign Ministry in the Wilhelmstrasse, carrying several sheaths of typescript paper handed to him minutes earlier by Sir Nevile Henderson. Britain's Ambassador to Germany had arrived punctually at 9am – as he said he would. The supercilious Ribbentrop could not possibly see Henderson. He asked his interpreter, Paul Schmidt, to receive the British envoy. And now Schmidt hurried through the heart of Berlin's government quarter to the Reich Chancellery bearing an ultimatum from the British.

The mood for the past two days in the Chancellery had been upbeat. London and Paris beat their chests and threatened ultimata, but that was all they were – threats. They had buckled at Munich, they would buckle again now, twelve months later. But the mood this Sunday morning was dark. A procession of Party bigwigs gathered in the Führer's outer office. The Führer sat at his desk, his Foreign Minister by the window. Schmidt quickly translated the ultimatum. Germany had until 11am to agree to cease hostilities and withdraw its troops from Poland, otherwise it would be at war with the Empire. Hitler thought for what seemed like an eternity, then turned to Ribbentrop: '*Was nun?*' what now? Ribbentrop was crestfallen. 'I assume the French will present us with a similar ultimatum within the hour,' he said quietly. At mid-day, French Ambassador Robert Coulandre duly obliged. He gave Hitler until 5pm to comply.

The Führer had no intention of complying. He summoned his three military commanders, then paced up and down a room overlooking the Chancellery garden, dictating four appeals – to the soldiers in the East, in the West, to the German people and to the Nazi Party. Walther von Brauchitsch strolled into Hitler's office quietly confident. His army was on the verge of a great victory in the Corridor; the enemy was completely on the back foot. The war in Poland, he told his Führer, would be decided in a few days. Luftwaffe Commander-in-Chief Hermann Göring was deeply shaken, however. 'If we lose this war, then God have mercy on us,' he muttered. Erich Raeder, the Navy's elderly head, tottered out of the Reich Chancellery ashen-faced. Hitler had repeatedly assured the *Grossadmiral* there would be no war with the Britain until 1944. Faced with the overwhelming might of the Royal Navy, the men of the *Kriegsmarine* 'can do no more than show that they know how to die gallantly,' Raeder lamented.[19]

A fanfare blasted out over the loudspeakers erected around the Wilhelmplatz in central Berlin at mid-day. Several hundred Berliners were enjoying a Sunday lunchtime stroll on a glorious early autumn day. They stopped and listened to the announcer declare that Britain had declared war on Germany. American journalist William Shirer studied their faces. Berliners were dumbfounded, depressed, silent. Like their Führer, they had expected the 'Polish thing' to be settled in a few weeks. Few believed the Polish war would become a European war. But now it had. There was, Shirer observed, 'no excitement, no hurrahs, no cheering, no throwing of flowers, no war fever, no war hysteria.' Berliners 'just stood there as they were before. Stunned.'[20]

The downbeat mood in Berlin was not shared by Varsovians. Around mid-day loudspeakers across the Polish capital crackled into life. Britain had declared war on Germany, they proclaimed. 'It was an electrifying moment,' hospital secretary Marta Korwin remembered. 'Warsaw overflowed with joy.' Varsovians rushed out into the streets to celebrate, they laughed and cried with joy, they converged on the British Embassy, ignoring calls to disperse as German bombers roamed overhead. 'Roly' Sword, Britain's military attaché, stepped out on to the balcony to acknowledge the crowds below him which stretched for miles down the Nowy Swiat. Sword raised a glass to the throng, then urged Jozef Beck, the Polish foreign minister, to join him in a toast to the two nations. The foreign minister shook his head. *'Non, le moment est trop triste pour ma patrie.'* – no, this is too painful an hour for my country.

Jewish schoolteacher Chaim Kaplan was not among those celebrating. He knew Britain could not help his country directly. He knew Britain could not spare his beloved Warsaw from German air raids – there had been four on 2 September alone. He feared for Poland's future. 'She is at the mercy of the full force of war with a cruel, barbaric enemy who is armed to the teeth.' And he feared for humanity. The German-Polish war, he wrote in his diary, had become a world war – 'a bloodbath of nations'.

There was little jubilation, too, among the first refugees arriving in Warsaw that Sunday. Carts crammed with entire families moved wearily through the streets; the more agile struggled on bicycles with personal possessions dangling in bags from the handlebars. 'They had fled to the "safety" of the capital of the country,' Korwin observed, 'but only found more German bombers over Warsaw.'[21]

In Silesia, 1st Light Division crossed the Warthe northeast of the ruins of Wielun, still smouldering from the raids on the first day of the war. News reached the men that they were now at war with Britain and France as well. 'Now this war has become a World War and it will last at least four years,' a reservist officer said to himself.[22]

Austrian infantryman Wilhelm Prüller spent his first wedding anniversary, 3 September, marching down the road to Krakow. He continued marching, resting, marching some more, preparing for battle, all Sunday and into Monday. Battle rarely came. There was sporadic shelling, the odd fire-fight, a few German dead, more wounded, but rarely did the enemy offer battle outright. 'They continue to withdraw,' he fumed. 'They should face and fight us in a decent and manly way – but not a bit of it.'[23]

Had he known the enemy's plight, Wilhelm Prüller might not have been so frustrated. Everywhere the *Army of Krakow* was falling back. This was not an orderly retreat. It was chaos. The line the staff of *6th Division* had tried to hold at Auschwitz crumpled almost immediately. All Sunday one Polish reserve officer and his men marched wearily eastwards. At dusk they trudged into Skawina, seven miles from Krakow. The horizon to the southeast glowed red: the town of Wadowice, barely a dozen miles away, was obviously ablaze. Civilians panicked. Soldiers panicked. All rushed towards Krakow in disorder. Command broke down. Officers were unable to give orders. Whenever soldiers asked where they should go the answer was always the same: to Krakow.[24]

All over the lower slopes of the Beskids and the Upper Vistula valley the scenes were identical: *Landsers* marching forwards, Polish soldiers and civilians retreating. The men of 132nd Infantry Regiment found themselves showered with gifts from ethnic Germans. 'It's raining sandwiches, milk stands in pails by the side of the road – we can fill our canteens to our heart's content,' one delighted *Landser* wrote. 'There's fruit by the ton. And everywhere there are cheerful faces, the hands of young women waving and eyes looking on longingly.' The joy of the liberated *Volksdeutsche* contrasted sharply with the plight of the Poles. *Oberleutnant* Heinz Borwin Venzky's armoured reconnaissance column passed small carts crammed with goods, hauled by mules which could barely move any more. Some people walked barefoot, carrying their shoes in their hands, others carried large bundles, worried expressions etched on their faces. Woman cried. Old men shuffled along. They had fled in the face of the invader. Now the invader had overtaken them and they wandered forlornly towards their homes. Few expected to find them still standing, for the landscape was littered with villages and towns in flames, set ablaze either by German artillery or by the infantry, which torched every settlement where they encountered resistance. By night, wrote Prüller, 'the whole countryside was red with fire'. War reporter Leo Leixner was spellbound by the 'fantastic sight' of Krakow and the landscape of the Upper Vistula under the pale glow of the moon. But it was not only the Polish land given a blue-green tint by the moon; the marching troops were also illuminated. Four cavalry who had ridden on ahead to reconnoitre were picked off by Polish troops. 'We don't know whether to thank the moon because it shows us the way, or curse it,' wrote Leixner. When the cavalry failed to return, the troops decided the moon was their foe. 'Damned light, horrible night.'[25]

By nightfall, Adolf Hitler had recovered his poise. The Allies had declared war, but they would not fight, he explained to his Propaganda Minister. No, in the West there would be nothing more than a 'potato war'.* Joseph Goebbels was unconvinced, but he stood behind his Führer. 'We will fight and work towards victory one way or another.' The two men shook hands and parted company. Shortly before 9pm, a series of staff cars pulled out of the Reich Chancellery and into Berlin's empty, blacked-out streets. They drew up less than half a mile away outside the Anhalter Bahnhof. 'Twenty-five years ago I was sucked into the First World War covered with flowers accompanied by stirring regimental music through an enthusiastic crowd of people,' Army liaison officer Nikolaus von Vormann recorded in his diary. 'Today the streets, shrouded in total darkness, were deserted.'

Waiting for Hitler and his entourage at a sealed-off, dimly-lit platform was a ten-carriage train, with two flak wagons added for protection, the *Sonderzug* (special train). The stationmaster watched the Führer and his party climb aboard, then blew his whistle. The wheels of two large, dark-green locomotives slowly turned and the train moved gently out of the station and headed northeast. There was no thought in Adolf Hitler's mind of withdrawing from Poland. His troops were bearing down on Warsaw; Danzig was German again; Fourth Army was on the verge of cutting off the Polish Corridor. Yet Hitler knew that news of the Anglo-French declaration of war would unsettle many of his men – Germany was now fighting a conflict on two fronts. The Führer sought to reassure his Army swarming across Poland. 'I know that you are aware of the magnitude of the task before you, and that you are doing your utmost to speedily throw down the adversary as a first step,' he told them. They should not worry themselves about the Western Front. The West Wall would 'shield Germany' from the French and British onslaught. The *Sonderzug* continued through the night. At four minutes before 2am on 4 September, it drew into Bad Polzin (today Polczyn-Zdroj) 140 miles northeast of Berlin and stopped.[26]

All through the night a column of staff cars drove steadily through Prussia towards Bad Polzin. When Adolf Hitler stepped off his train the next morning he found nearly eighty vehicles waiting for him and his entourage. A large beige open-top Mercedes pulled up for Hitler, shepherded by two armoured cars. The Führer climbed in, accompanied by his adjutants and his valet Heinz Linge. The Mercedes set off almost immediately, followed by two cars with half a dozen men of Hitler's bodyguard, the *Führer Begleit Kommando* – Führer Escort Command. Three more Mercedes drew up for senior Wehrmacht officers, Hitler's personal photographer Heinrich Hoffmann, physicians and various adjutants, followed by another two armoured cars. The rest of the motorcade – more than seventy vehicles – was dedicated to the golden pheasants of the Nazi

---

* The War of the Bavarian Succession in 1778–79 became known as the 'potato war'. The opposing armies spent little time fighting but plenty of time picking potatoes.

Party, the weasely *de facto* Party chief-of-staff Martin Bormann, the sycophantic von Ribbentrop, the head of the Reich Chancellery Hans Lammers, and others. The dignitaries jostled for position, each one determined to be ahead of his rival in the interminable column.

The Führer's motorcade snaked through Pomerania. The Mercedes threw up huge clouds of dust on the sandy roads, enveloping everything – especially the Party bigwigs, much to the amusement of the military adjutants. *Volksdeutsche* stood by the roadside. Some held hastily-made banners, others hung out black-white-red flags hidden during two decades of Polish rule. Whenever the Mercedes drew to a halt, soldiers surrounded Hitler's car – there were no barriers, no cordon to hold them back. The Führer was in his element, at ease as he had never been before nor would be again. He shook the hands of his soldiers, who cried out, yelled, smiled, laughed, joked. The motorcade visited the command posts of Fourth Army in Komierowo, twenty-five miles northwest of Bromberg, then to II Corps in Pruscz, half a dozen miles from the Vistula, and finally to the command post of 3rd Infantry Division in Topolno on the left bank of the Vistula, fifteen miles northeast of Bromberg. In glorious sunshine, the Führer looked across the Vistula valley. 'What this means to me!' he enthused. Here, seven centuries before, Hermann Balk, the first *Landmeister* (ruler) of the German order of knights in Prussia, had begun the German colonisation of the land beyond the Vistula. To Nikolaus von Vormann the vista was intoxicating. 'The view of the land of Kulm stretched far and wide, land fertilised with German blood,' the officer recalled. To the southeast, perhaps twenty-five miles away, was the Teutonic fortress of Thorn, birthplace of Copernicus. And just half a dozen miles to the northeast were the historic towers and spires of Kulm itself. The panzers, von Vormann observed, were rolling through the city. This was the land where Nikolaus von Vormann had been born nearly forty-four years earlier. This was not the time to think about the future. A single thought dominated the *Oberst*'s mind. 'A grave injustice in the Versailles *Diktat* had finally been put right,' he remembered. 'Historic German land had become German once more.'[27]

A single thought also dominated the minds of the men of 3rd Panzer Division: reach the Vistula at Graudenz. The drive was relentless. Any panzers which broke down were abandoned by the wayside, their crews left to repair them on their own. The enemy offered little resistance. Polish troops simply raised their hands as the German armour rolled past them – the panzers didn't even stop to round up prisoners. Elsewhere, a short burst of fire from a panzer's machine-gun prompted Polish soldiers to emerge from their hiding places and surrender.

Across the Tucheler Heath, the scrubland, copses, marshes and lakes between Bromberg and Danzig, the German Army was rounding up the remnants of the 'Corridor Army' – the *Army of Pomorze*. Just north of Schwetz artilleryman Emil Falckenthal watched as infantry razed the village of Skarszewy to the ground after Polish troops offered stubborn resistance. Upwards of 300 Poles fell into German hands, but some escaped, setting a farm ablaze as they withdrew. In a stable seventy cows bellowed in fear, straining at their leashes as the flames ripped through the building. Falckenthal and his comrades braved the acrid smoke to save what they could, but only the pigs could be rescued. 'Everything else burns, perishing in the searing flames,' he wrote. That afternoon the artilleryman reached the edge of Grupa Dolna, opposite Graudenz. From a hillside cemetery, the gunner could see the Vistula valley laid out before him and there, just three miles away, the towers of Graudenz – now in German hands after 21st Infantry Division had marched in almost unopposed – twinkling in the sunlight. The bridge over the Vistula still stood, only partially demolished by the Poles; three of its huge iron-arch spans had collapsed into the river. And right in front of the artillerymen, the red steeple of the church at the Polish Army's exercise ground in Grupa itself, where 20,000 enemy soldiers were now trapped.

A few miles upstream, the *Army of Pomorze* was making a final desperate attempt to force the Vistula near Schwetz. Having brushed past 23rd Infantry Division, a cavalry column, accompanied by infantry and vehicles, moved along the left bank in the direction of a dam, hoping to use it to cross the Vistula – unaware German infantry had beaten them to it. As the Poles moved through a field, German heavy machine guns opened fire from little over a mile's range. Some men gave themselves up instantly, some made a dash for the dam, most were mown down. The sandbanks leading to the Vistula were littered with dead Poles; a makeshift ferry, crammed with fleeing troops, suffered a direct hit from a German field gun. A few Polish troops took shelter in a farmhouse, from where they took a heavy toll of an infantry company. Only when the farmhouse was ablaze and the building surrounded did fourteen Poles emerge and raise their hands. 3rd Panzer spent the rest of the day clearing out the scrub on the Vistula's left bank. By the day's end, 450 prisoners had been brought in, 100 vehicles captured and the cavalry regiment had ceased to exist. A few miles to the north a Luftwaffe reconnaissance aircraft found two regiments of *ulans*, the fabled Polish cavalry, and another cavalry brigade trying to make for the Vistula. Bombers soon appeared over the heath and tossed their bombs. The cries of wounded horses and men echoed around forests, cavalry squadrons galloped between the trees, scores of riderless horses ran around wildly. The principal road across the heath, from Tuchel to Schwetz, was littered with the detritus of a destroyed army. It was, one *Unteroffizier* recalled, 'a depressing, fateful scene. Baggage wagons are piled up in chaotic heaps, their horses dead next to them, still in their harnesses, mountains of ammunition piled up as well as countless guns, bayonets, gasmasks, all manner of equipment hastily discarded.' Guderian's men began to round up Polish prisoners, thousands of them, plus innumerable field guns and other military equipment. That evening, gunner Emil Falckenthal examined the exhausted, expressionless faces of weary prisoners, sat in a circle around their officers. A dejected young lieutenant who spoke a little German shook his head. 'I do not understand the reason behind this war,' he confessed. 'Of course, it's wonderful to fight for something great – to give up your life for high ideals, but that's not the case in Poland any more. So we can't fight any more – we must lose. Poland will cease to exist!'

Heinz Guderian spent the evening with the men of 3rd Panzer, convinced the fighting in the Corridor was all but over. His passion for the tank, for armoured warfare had been vindicated. His men had boundless confidence in their weapon. But there was a dark cloud. Britain and France were now involved. 'A new world war is beginning,' the panzer General wrote to his wife. 'It will last a long time and we must stand our ground.'[28]

The infantry of Eighth Army, protecting the left flank of the thrust on Warsaw, were a good day or two behind the panzers and motorised divisions. Now, in the early afternoon of the fourth, the foot soldiers began to arrive on the Warthe between Lodz and Kalisz. Conrad von Cochenhausen climbed between the gravestones up a hill to the north of the town of Sieradz. Through his binoculars the *Generalleutnant* looked eastwards across the valley of the Warthe, the last major natural obstacle between his 10th Infantry Division and the industrial metropolis of Lodz, thirty miles to the northwest. The view through the binoculars was far from encouraging. To be sure, the enemy was silent – there was no movement in his positions on the far bank of the Warthe. But the terrain was formidable. From Sieradz, the ground sloped gently to the river, which had been spanned by rail and road bridges until the Poles had blown both up. The Warthe here was nearly 200ft wide, its waters flowing freely, if not violently. And beyond them the Poles were obviously dug in on a dam which dominated the marshy, flat east bank of the Warthe. Further east still a smattering of bunkers and a forest where the enemy would clearly be lurking. All in all, thought Cochenhausen, you could not imagine more difficult terrain to attack over.[29]

A few miles south of Sieradz, an *Oberleutnant* and his men in 17th Infantry Division marched wearily through the burning sand on the dust tracks. The terrain was monotonous, the few cottages they passed filthy. And now, in the distance, basking in the sunshine of late afternoon, the village of Stronsko, its red-brick church towering over the surrounding copses. With the setting sun, the men rested in a forest of pine and birch trees which offered welcome shade. Field kitchens began serving the evening meal. Artillery began firing sporadically at the right bank of the Warthe. Through binoculars, the men could see the Poles digging in. The men moved up to the river's edge during the bright moonlit night, hastily digging slit trenches to protect themselves should the Polish artillery open up. But the Warthe valley was bathed in a milky-white fog as dawn approached. The enemy remained silent.[30]

Shortly before 8am on the fifth, the German guns opened fire on a twenty-mile front straddling Sieradz as three divisions attempted to storm the Warthe behind a wall of steel and iron. Ten miles north of Sieradz, Wolf Oeringk and his 24th Infantry Division comrades moved towards the river near the village of Glinno, where pioneers were already at work ferrying infantry across the Warthe in inflatable boats. The river here split into four arms – some could be forded, some could not. Polish shells hissed and fizzled as the infantry crossed the first arm by boat. The men struggled through muddy, marshy terrain before reaching the next arm, which they waded through, and the third. The *Landsers* sank to their knees in mud, holding their rifles high. Then the final arm, the widest, only passable in boats, and then only two or three men at a time. Machine-gun fire kept the Poles pinned down, while two German rifle platoons cowered on the steep far bank, unable to move. Oeringk watched as the enemy troops attempted to wipe out the tiny German bridgehead – and promptly fell under a hail of machine-gun bullets. And above the Warthe, on the high ground on the right bank, tall, dark clouds of smoke rose above Glinno.

It took Wolf Oeringk barely thirty minutes to cross the Warthe. It took Conrad von Cochenhausen's men nearly five hours to subdue the Polish troops dug in on the right bank. The *Generalleutnant* and his staff had planned the assault down to the finest detail: artillery would pound the bunkers and dug-outs close to the water's edge, then switch to the enemy's rear defences. There was nothing to be done about the terrain. Marshes and swamps restricted the attack to a strip of land barely 300 yards wide. The Poles poured withering fire on this narrow strip, but once 10th Infantry finally got a foothold over the Warthe, it quickly rolled up the Polish defences, even seizing an enemy battery still firing. A good half dozen miles beyond the river, the advancing *Landsers* found enemy infantry and artillery columns decimated by German howitzers, pounding away from the left bank. The battle for Warthe was over.

After a rest, Wolf Oeringk's *Feldwebel* ordered his men on to the east. It was dark now, but fires on both sides of the Warthe lit the way down an endless, sandy road. 'The air is mild and filled with the smell of burning,' Oeringk recorded in his diary. 'The awful reality of this war strikes us – coupled with the expectation that at any moment we could be shot out of the darkness.' There are still Polish soldiers everywhere, he thought. But then came the comforting howl of German shells racing over the marching men's heads. At the day's end the infantry entered Glinno. The village was still ablaze.[31]

While Eighth Army's infantry battered its way across the Warthe, 1st Panzer Division was rolling into Petrikau – to Poles Piotrkow Trybunalski – a town of 15,000 residents sixty miles south of Lodz, while the rest of the division struck onwards to the north. For the first time, the German armour ran into Polish tanks; at least half were shot-up, the remainder took to their heels. The defenders of Petrikau, however, proved more stubborn; they continued to offer resistance beyond dusk as the *Landsers* cleared out the town house by house. That night, with the remnants of the elite *19th Division* streaming back towards Warsaw having been routed around Petrikau, Johann Graf von Kielmansegg's column of panzers rounded up countless Polish troops, startled by the Germans' rapid advance. Suddenly, a truck, its headlights on full beam, nervously edged out of a side road. Seeing the panzers, its occupants jumped out and tried to flee; all were captured, including the divisional commander – a Brigadier General Kwaciszewski – and his entire staff. 'A good capture at the end of a good day,' Kielmansegg observed succinctly. But then, the general no longer had a division to command. 'Who was not taken prisoner and what did not fall into our hands as booty, what did not lie dead on the battlefield, were merely the shattered remnants,' the German staff officer recorded.

Poland's *19th Division* no longer existed; her *29th* was still battle-worthy and still a threat to 1st Panzer. Roused just before dawn on 6 September, Johann Graf von Kielmansegg grabbed his steel helmet and carbine as cries of '*Naprzod, naprzod*' – forward, forward – filled the air south of Petrikau. He continued:

We take up position in a rather deep ditch on the edge of the estate and hear, or rather feel, for the first time what it means to be under direct machine-gun fire. There's a slight whizzing, whistling or singing, the shaking of the striped blades of grass and bushes, the rustling of branches, all this causes new, but brief sensations.

The fighting reached its climax around the village of Milejow, as the Poles swept out of the forests and copses which had shielded them from the Luftwaffe's prying eyes on the fifth and fell upon 1st Panzer's right flank, bound for Petrikau. 'Every man defends himself exactly where he is,' Kielmansegg wrote. Staff officers, infantry, engineers, panzer crews, artillerymen, all were thrown into the battle, which dragged on throughout 6 September and into the seventh. The Polish attacks first halted, then turned about. The enemy, Kielmansegg observed, 'disappears in the direction whence he came, leaving behind countless dead, many prisoners and considerable material, among it a complete battery. In places, so many Polish dead lie in the smallest area that even veterans of the World War say that they have rarely or never seen anything like it.'[32]

The scenes were identical behind 1st Panzer's route of advance. Everywhere 'a scene of desolation' one soldier recalled. 'Burned-out houses and ruined farms, weapons, vehicles and horse-drawn carts abandoned by the roadside. And everywhere, the dead. Horses, men, their bodies bloated, distorted, covered by flies, the smell unbearable.'[33]

Such was war, mused XVI Corps' commanding officer Erich Hoepner – *der alte Reiter*, the old cavalryman. 'It's rather interesting here,' he wrote to his wife, 'but it's not always nice. We oldies didn't expect to have to go to war again – now we must get used to it once more.' Erich Hoepner very quickly 'got used to it'. After six days' relentless advance, his corps, spearheaded by 1st Panzer Division, was within touching distance of the Polish capital. 'Without enemy resistance I could be there in two hours,' he boasted.[34]

The enemy already stood at the gates of Krakow. Scenes in the great mediaeval city were chaotic. Its citizens were leaving by any means they could after a German air attack. Polish troops entering the city found those inhabitants who had stayed behind plundering the department stores. The Helwetia chocolate factory had also been raided; bars were handed out to soldiers as they marched hurriedly through Krakow. As the first German armour rolled into the city's suburbs on the sixth, the last Polish troops pulled out to the southeast. The road to Weliczka, eight miles from the heart of Krakow, was 'a picture of misery', one Polish officer recalled. The withdrawing troops had been attacked by the Luftwaffe. So hasty had been the retreat there had been no time to bury the corpses of soldiers and cadavers of horses. When a single German aircraft appeared over the small town of Brsesko, on the main road to Rzeszow, all form of order and discipline disintegrated. Drivers abandoned their cars and trucks and took shelter in homes. The town was completely clogged with traffic. When the aircraft eventually disappeared, the drivers gingerly returned to their vehicles; their officers horsewhipped them for deserting the column.[35]

Northeast of Krakow, the relentless advance of 5th Panzer Division through the valley of the Vistula brought the armour to the town of Staszow. Townsfolk lined the streets in silence as the panzers rolled past. 'They were told that these colossuses had just enough power to trundle past the Führer's dais in the parades in Berlin,' Heinz Borwin Venzky gloated. 'Someone had told the Polish soldier that the stupid Germans had only fixed armour to their foremost panzers, the rest were merely cardboard dummies which they could easily withstand.' For half an hour 5th Panzer's armour thundered through Staczow. An exhaust backfired; the inhabitants fled from the streets terrified, before tentatively returning when they realised there was nothing to fear.[36]

The sun continued to beat down on the gravel roads of Pomerania. Wednesday 6 September was another glorious day in the Corridor. The beige Mercedes roaring along the main road between Tuchel and Schwetz once again left an impenetrable cloud of dust behind it. The car came to a stop outside the village of Plewno where Heinz Guderian was waiting for it. A radiant Adolf Hitler climbed out. 'My dear general, what you and your men have achieved!' he greeted the panzer man. 'My faith in the panzer divisions was always boundless!' Guderian glowed with pride. He ran through the deeds of his Corps to the Führer, then accompanied Hitler to his Mercedes to begin a tour of the front. Soldiers and *Volksdeutsche* applauded and crowded around the car. Smiling, Hitler raised his hand. The jubilation ceased. The men fell silent. 'Soldiers! You have put Berliners' minds at rest,' he declared. 'The Poles won't get to Berlin. What has been fought over with German blood remains German.'

A dozen miles away, *Generalleutnant* Leo Geyr von Schweppenburg had drawn up a panzer regiment and armoured reconnaissance cars from his 3rd Panzer Division along the main road from Schwetz to Graudenz. Geyr was anxious. His men were not lining the road merely to greet Hitler; they were there for their Führer's protection. 'There were still armed Poles everywhere – in the bushes on the road which the Führer drove down,' he recalled. One of his ordnance officers dragged a Polish soldier from the undergrowth shortly before Hitler was due to arrive.

The Führer was still enthralled by his tour of the battlefield. The road from Plewno to Schwetz was littered with wrecked Polish batteries. 'Our dive bombers did that?' he asked Guderian. 'No, our panzers,' the General told him. As the motorcade approached the left bank of the Vistula, the outlines of the towers and steeples of Kulm, half a dozen miles to the south, were clearly visible. 'In March last year I had the privilege of greeting you in your birthplace,' the panzer General told his Führer. 'Today you are with me in mine.'

Shortly before mid-day, Hitler's Mercedes turned on to the road to Graudenz. The Führer stood up to acknowledge the soldiers lining the route. He stopped briefly to greet 3rd Panzer's commander with an earnest handshake. 'General von Geyr, your division has achieved wonderful things.' Geyr told him his men had merely done what had been asked of them. 'No,' Hitler insisted, 'it has done more than its duty.'

The motorcade continued towards Graudenz to the strains of a regimental band. Hitler asked Guderian about casualties. Just 150 dead and 700 wounded in the four divisions under his command, the general responded. And for that his Corps had destroyed perhaps three enemy infantry divisions and a cavalry brigade, and taken thousands of prisoners and captured hundreds of guns. The Führer was astonished; his regiment alone had suffered far heavier casualties in the Great War. The few losses, Heinz Guderian explained, were due to the potency of his panzers. 'Tanks are a life-saving weapon,' he declared. He neglected to mention the Poles barely possessed any...[37]

It was around 11pm when the Führer returned to his train and stepped into the command wagon. Nikolaus von Vormann had spent the day in the carriage monitoring the latest reports from the front, feeding the relevant ones to Hitler such as news of the fall of Krakow. The Führer's first concern, however, was not for the East, but the West. What was happening on the Western Front? he asked breathlessly. 'Nothing new,' Vormann responded rather flippantly. 'The Potato War continues.' The officer was equally smug about the state of affairs in the East. The German Army was on the verge of encircling large Polish formations in front of Warsaw and had already left the *Army of Poznan* 'hovering in thin air'. Poland's leaders could no longer direct their armies. 'All that's left is a rabbit hunt,' von Vormann declared. 'Militarily, the war is decided.' Hitler stared at his liaison officer, took Vormann's hands in his, shook them heartily and left the carriage without saying a word.[38]

On the Westerplatte, Henry Sucharski was still strapped to a bed in his bunker. His men were still being pounded daily by German bombs and shells – and they were still holding out. The incessant bombardment had inflicted few casualties, but it had wreaked terrible destruction on the peninsula. 'Enemy artillery fire literally ploughed the land, overturned trees, the men in the guard posts were thrown up in the air like feathers,' one junior officer wrote. Shrapnel and lumps of concrete were blown into the mess, serving as a makeshift hospital, exacerbating the wounds of already-injured men, while the Westerplatte's sole doctor struggled to care for them without the aid of an operating table or even bandages.

The uninjured were barely any more able to defend the peninsula. 'The barracks are unrecognisable after all the damage,' one young officer recorded in his diary. 'In the cellar, soldiers lie along the walls, overly tired, the wounded on stretchers. The only light comes from a candle. Hygiene is beneath all contempt, the air is awful.' At night there was no hope of sleep. Random bursts of gun and machine-gun fire every few minutes kept the defenders awake.

By mid-morning on Thursday, 7 September, it had become too much for the men of the Westerplatte. Shortly before 10am, the white flag was raised for the second time over the depot. On this occasion, it would not be hauled down.

After days of sobbing and uncontrollable shaking, Henryk Sucharski had recovered some of his composure. He summoned his men in front of the wrecked barracks. The troops were reluctant to surrender. 'Someone will still rescue us here,' they pleaded with their major. 'We can endure for one more day.' For the first time, the major told his men about the plight of their comrades, that the Germans were at the gates of Warsaw, that Poland was being overrun. There was a brief prayer for the fifteen dead, followed by a soldier's hymn,

'Peaceful calm, comrade'. And then Henryk Sucharski crossed the German lines to capitulate.

To the Germans, Sucharski appeared 'utterly exhausted', his men 'scruffy, extremely sullen and demoralised'. The peninsula had cost the Reich nearly 400 casualties, but its defenders were treated with respect. As the garrison marched into captivity, German soldiers stood stiffly to attention and saluted.[39]

After five days almost continually retreating, the anonymous Polish reserve officer who had originally set off towards Auschwitz now found himself with three men and a field canteen near the village of Radomysl Wielki, a good sixty miles east of Krakow. Once again the Germans were there first. Artillery shells began crashing down on the village and reports reached the exhausted men that German armour had taken the village. The officer turned north, aiming for Szczucin, eighteen miles away on the right bank of the Vistula. 'There was no leadership,' he recalled. 'Everyone acted on his own initiative.' The Polish Army was disintegrating around him. The men were demoralised; they threw away their guns. Horses collapsed out of exhaustion. In the sandy terrain the field guns became bogged down. The officer overheard a sergeant complain: 'I can't force anyone to go on any more; each man does what he wants because none of this makes any sense. The men have nothing to eat and no ammunition to continue to fight with.' Later that day, Thursday, 7 September, the reservist was captured by 5th Panzer Division.[40]

For a week, the armour of 1st and 4th Panzer Divisions had punched through the heart of Poland down the road to Warsaw. Now, with barely seventy miles to go to the Polish capital, their paths separated: 4th Panzer would head on to Warsaw, its comrades would smash their way through to the Vistula to the south of the city, thwarting any relief of – or escape by – its garrison. Although their objectives differed, the methods of the two panzer divisions' leaders were identical: relentless pursuit. 'Forward to the Vistula!' demanded *Major* Walter Wenck, 1st Panzer's operations officer. 'What remains behind, remains behind. As long as we have the strength, the enemy will be attacked.' *Generalmajor* Georg-Hans Reinhardt expected his men 'to be first to reach the enemy's capital. We have not merely hit the enemy, but driven him back in confusion in front of us. But still we have not reached our objective. Our objective is Warsaw. Forward to Warsaw!'[41]

Reinhardt's men began the day in the town of Bedkow, seventy miles from Warsaw. By mid-morning, they had already reached the objective for the day, Czerniewice, fifty-five miles from the capital. The armour was now on the highway to Warsaw. The pace of the advance accelerated. The Pole wasn't resisting now. He wasn't retreating. He was fleeing. By early afternoon, 4th Panzer had rolled through Rawa Mazowiecka, eight miles down the road to Warsaw; the town had been flattened by the Luftwaffe to clear the way. By nightfall, Reinhardt was in Babsk, forty miles from his objective. That evening, one of his men surveyed the scene on the road to Warsaw. The world was aflame. 'As far as the eye can see, every village is burning, every farm, even the smallest haystack, near and far,' he wrote. 'The flames hiss and crackle, whoosh towards the night sky. A shower of sparks shoots up when a roof collapses, crashing down, or a house wall caves in. There's an acrid, stinging smell of burning and thick clouds of smoke spiral across the sky.'[42]

In the forests and copses around Tomaszow Mazowiecki, 1st Panzer Division was enjoying little of its neighbour's success; the terrain and the enemy conspired against it. 'Our exhaustion is probably already so great that it could hardly be endured any longer under normal circumstances,' Johann Graf von Kielmansegg wrote. 'Here, with the fulfilment of victory at hand, we barely notice it.' If 7 September had been relatively frustrating for 1st Panzer, Friday the eighth passed by in a blur of Polish place names as the division rushed to cross the Vistula south of Warsaw. At 7.35am Nowe Miasto, thirty-seven miles from the Vistula; forty minutes later, Mogielnicka, twenty-nine miles from the river; by 10am, Grojek, fifteen miles; and at 11.15 Chynow, just five miles from Poland's great artery. 'The road presents a picture of a flight in panic,' Kielmansegg wrote. He continued:

> The road is strewn with all kinds of abandoned pieces of equipment, including steel helmets, rucksacks, coats and gas masks. Vast quantities of ammunition, left loose or packed in boxes, have been thrown out of cars. At times we have to stop to clear the road of all this material so we can continue. The closer we get to the Vistula, the more vehicles are left on the road, especially field kitchens and panje wagons loaded with all kinds of things. Most of the horses haven't been unharnessed and have dragged the carts into the fields to graze. Among torn sacks of rice and flour there's an open medical case with valuable surgical equipment. Loaves of bread in their hundreds, countless brown cubes of ground coffee, all covered with dust and dirt, mostly crushed by vehicles driving over them – it's impossible to give the slightest inkling in words of this Polish road of flight.

The number of prisoners grew by the hour. 'The deprivation and horror of the last few days is clearly etched upon their faces,' the staff officer observed. 'For them, the war is over.'[43]

In the early afternoon, near the town of Gora Kalwaria, 1st Panzer arrived at the Vistula. The bridge had already been destroyed by the Germans and Poles in turn; the withdrawing Poles had also destroyed the final floating bridge before being wiped out or taken prisoner. Motorcyclists thrust into the water with inflatable boats and forged a weak bridgehead on the east bank of the Vistula.

The advance of 4th Panzer Division was no less relentless, no less exhilarating that Friday. The panzers passed through burning villages and destroyed bridges, leaving Polish stragglers behind in the copses and forests. And everywhere, the remnants of a defeated opponent. 'Panic must have broken out among the enemy,' Willi Reibig concluded. 'Each man looked to save himself in a wild flight. Were they so filled with fear in the face of our panzers? All the better then if they're already shaken morally, we'll have easier battles. Bits of equipment, field kitchens, baggage wagons, cases of ammunition, guns, rifles and ammunition lined our route of advance in large quantities. Between them, bomb craters on the left and right of the road.' Another road sign. *Warszawa 70 kilometres.*

'We'll soon achieve that,' Reibig was convinced. Tenth Army commander von Reichenau now decided it was time 'to pluck the enemy capital like a ripe fruit' before the enemy could respond. The men of 4th Panzer Division would soon learn that Warsaw's fruit left a bitter taste.[44]

In his headquarters in the heart of the Polish capital, the commander of the city's defensive zone, General Walerian Czuma ordered Warsaw be turned into a fortress. Here at the walls of the great city the 'ravaging of Polish soil comes to an end'. In a rousing order of the day, he continued: 'We have taken up a position, from which there can be no more steps back. The enemy can receive just one answer now: "Enough! Not one step further!"'[45]

Warsaw's inhabitants and troops built makeshift barriers from overturned trams, removal vans and furniture, then took up position behind them, or in cellars, or rooftops, or at the windows of tenement blocks. And then they waited for the enemy to come.

Around 5pm, the first German tanks appeared, the armour of 35th Panzer Regiment. The panzers rolled through the 'ugly' suburbs of Ochota – four miles from the city centre – then Rakowiec, three miles from the heart of Warsaw. 'Everyone went into the heart of Warsaw proudly and confident of victory,' Reinhardt recalled. Everyone went in expecting Warsaw to be an 'open' city – undefended. But then the defenders opened fire. Standing with a pair of binoculars at an anti-tank gun position, Colonel Marian Porwit watched as 'an unequal duel of fire raged – so heavily in our favour that the German panzers no longer moved.' Even so the barricades which had been hastily erected were no match for the armour's firepower, Porwit observed. 'They shot up in flames like matches.' But the defenders grew in stature. 'The first burning panzer and destroyed vehicles calm us down, and the soldiers, seeing the excellent results of their weapons and their leaders, gain trust and believe that they do not have black devils in front of them,' one Polish officer recorded. Heinrich Eberbach, 35th Panzer Regiment's commanding officer, ordered his armour off the main road and through allotments to avoid the barriers 'but even there our panzers are shot at from four-storey houses, from skylights, windows and cellars, and from behind more barricades'. As the sun went down over Warsaw, Eberbach reluctantly called off his attack and returned to the road bridge where his attack had begun barely two hours earlier.[46]

After dark, state radio broadcast Walerian Czuma's order of the day. Lieutenant Colonel Waclaw Lipinski, head of the Polish General Staff's information section, added his own postscript. 'Warsaw will be defended to the last breath and – if it falls – the enemy will have to step over the corpse of the very last defender,' he declared. Now the hour had come for Varsovians to demonstrate their love for their motherland. 'Looking around, the Polish soldier should see only calm faces,' the officer continued. 'He should be accompanied by the blessings and smiles of women and when he goes into battle, a cheerful song should sound.'[47]

Panzer grenadier Bruno Fichte spent the night quartered between a sanatorium and houses on the edge of Warsaw. Polish artillery shells rained down on the homes as smoke rose from their chimneys. 'I went into the house,' Fichte recalled. 'It was full of women and children. I asked them to please go down into the cellar and not make fires any more.' The women begged for a warm drink for their children; Fichte fetched warm milk and coffee. His actions were not entirely magnanimous; he wanted to spare the panzers the constant shelling. 'Nevertheless, they treated me like their saviour and kissed my hands.' Fichte and his comrades spent the night re-fuelling, stocking up on ammunition, eating, sleeping, all untroubled by the Poles. In Warsaw 'hundreds of barricades shot up like fungi after a rainstorm' as the garrison prepared for the enemy to renew his thrust into the capital. But to what end? schoolteacher Chaim Kaplan asked himself. 'The streets are littered with trenches and barricades. Machine-guns have been placed on the roofs of houses and a barricade has been set up in the entrance to my apartment block, just beneath my balcony,' he recorded in his diary. 'If there's fighting in the streets then there won't be one stone standing on top of the other in the walls in which I live.'[48]

With the first rays of light on Saturday morning, a ten-minute artillery barrage was unleashed upon the main route of advance into the city centre. And then, at 7am, the regiments of 4th Panzer Division moved off in two groups through the outskirts of Warsaw, closely followed by infantry. Bruno Fichte peered up at the tall tenement blocks looming over the narrow Warsaw streets with a sense of foreboding. But it was only when the advance was well under way that the Poles showed themselves. 'Terrible fire descended upon us. They fired from the roofs, threw burning oil lamps, even burning beds down on to the panzers. Within a short time everything was in flames.'[49]

In Wolska Street in the suburb of Wola, little more than one mile from the centre of the Polish capital, Colonel Marian Porwit watched as a column of panzers edged nervously along. There was a blast from a trumpet and a barrage was unleashed upon the advancing enemy. 'German soldiers jumped out of their panzers on fire, but could find no cover in the narrow street,' Porwit wrote. 'Fuel tanks were set on fire. The panzers and German vehicles were on fire.' Vehicles following behind the first panzers tried to avoid the melee, but instead ran up the pavements and blocked the road.[50]

The city, 35th Panzer Regiment's commander Heinrich Eberbach observed, was defending itself 'with courage born of desperation'. A first then a second barricade was passed, but at terrible cost to man and machine. 'The infantry must fight house by house and clear them out,' wrote Eberbach. 'Bursts of machine-gun fire, hand grenades from above and out of cellars, blocks of stone hurled down from the roofs, make things difficult for them.' Inside his panzer, Willi Reibig heard machine-gun fire clatter against the armour. 'Gun and machine-gun fire sprays out of the houses,' Reibig recorded in his diary. 'An infantry gun is brought to the front by a platoon, and its shells fire directly into the houses. We slowly gain ground. But around me it has already become damned hot.' Over the headphones, there was a cry: 'Eagle in front.' A knocked-out panzer partially blocked the road, but not to prevent Reibig squeezing past. By now, Reibig has passed through four barricades. 'Suddenly, a devastating blow,' he recalled. 'I throw up the hatch, an artillery hit on one of the panzers following us. Polish artillery lays down shot after shot on the road and in front of the barricade.'[51]

It was, one *Feldwebel* – a platoon commander in 36th Panzer Regiment – observed, as if 'all hell broke loose. In front of us one shell landed one after another rapidly.' The *Feldwebel* scanned the streets through his panzer's optics: two Panzer IIs to the rear were ablaze; a Panzer III to the side was struck by an anti-tank shell. A smoke canister exploded, shrouding the street in a grey-black mist, under which the German armour fell back; the attack had been called off. 'We continued through dingy backyards,' the *Feldwebel* continued. 'Our panzer thundered past the corners of houses and grazed walls. Bricks clattered and scraped against our iron hull. All of a sudden, I saw a civilian who jumped out of a corner made a brief movement with his arm. A pineapple hand grenade flew towards us, without causing any damage. He didn't get around to throwing a second one.'[52]

One panzer got as far as Warsaw's central station, then was forced to fall back. Heinrich Eberbach watched as panzer after panzer was shot-up, until his vehicle too fell victim to the furious Polish fire. By mid-morning, 4th Panzer's assault on the capital had ground to a halt. Its commander, Georg-Hans Reinhardt, decided the battle was 'hopeless' and 'with a heavy heart' broke off the attack mid-morning and pulled his panzers back to the edge of the city. His division stuttered out of Warsaw under a hail of Polish artillery shells; damaged and abandoned panzers lined the main road. Exhausted crews assembled, minus their armour, at the jump-off point where the attack had begun with such high hopes five hours earlier.[53]

A shell-shocked Heinrich Eberbach returned on foot. 'At first the number of panzers appearing is terrifyingly low,' he recorded. His regiment had moved off with 120 vehicles at dawn; by mid-afternoon, just fifty-seven were still combat-worthy. The panzers of brigade and regimental commanders had been knocked out, two company commanders had been killed. And yet Eberbach's men were buoyant. 'The combat spirit of the troops was unshaken even though the attack on the city was repulsed,' the panzer commander reported. 'Everyone knew that time worked for us. Their resistance cannot last long after the other divisions arrive.'[54]

Intelligence reports suggested 4th Panzer Division had run into elements of as many as five divisions. Its commander reported in person to his immediate superior XIV Corps' commander Gustav von Wietersheim in the small town of Nadarzyn, fifteen miles southwest of Warsaw's centre. The picture Reinhardt painted was black: a brigade and regimental commander had come back on foot, knocked-out panzers, too few infantry, too little artillery support. The attack on Warsaw could not be carried with the means at his disposal, he told Wietersheim. And at any rate, what was the use of seizing a city 'of little value militarily', Reinhardt argued.[55]

In the centre of Warsaw, Colonel Marian Porwit walked past still-smouldering panzers. The city was deserted, save for its defenders and German dead. The inhabitants were still in hiding, several hundred of them in the cellars of the Akademicki Cathedral. 'Someone told me that fear and unease ruled there because the sound of battle had reached the shelter and asked me to say a few reassuring words,' Porwit recalled. With the sun going down and with no sign of a renewed German assault, the officer found time to visit the cathedral. 'A large crowd gathered around me, and when I told them of the defence against the German attack, the destroyed panzers and the enemy's bloody losses, there was delight.'[56] Varsovians would enjoy a few days' respite from the foe. For to the west of the city that very day Polish troops had unleashed an offensive. Perhaps they might save the capital. And the nation.

Notes

1. Kielmansegg, pp. 20–1.
2. Stjernfelt, p. 104.
3. *Geschichte der 3 Panzer Division 1935–1945*, pp. 18–19.
4. Guderian, *Panzer Leader*, p71.
5. Leixner, pp. 16–18.
6. Venzky, pp. 17–18.
7. Polnisches Reserve Offizier, 'Die andere Seite!' in BA-MA RH27-5/2.
8. Reibig, pp. 21–2.
9. Kielmansegg, pp. 22–3.
10. Allmayer-Beck, *Die Geschichte der 21 (ostpr/westpr) Infanterie Division*, pp. 31–2.
11. *Geschichte der 3 Panzer Division 1935–1945*, pp. 20–21 and Paul, Das Potsdamer Infanterie Regiment 9, pp. 144–6.
12. Schenk, *Post von Danzig*, p. 83, Stjernfelt, pp. 89–91, 107 and author's papers.
13. Reibig, pp. 23–4.
14. Leixner, p. 21.
15. *Geschichte der 3 Panzer Division 1935–1945*, pp. 20–21.
16. Allmayer-Beck, *Die Geschichte der 21 (ostpr/westpr) Infanterie Division*, p. 33.
17. Kielmansegg, pp. 25–7.
18. Hinze, *19 Infanterie und Panzer Division,*, p. 51.
19. Events in the Reich Chancellery on 3 September are based upon Vormann, pp. 73–77, Schmidt's memoirs, and Raeder's memorandum of 3/9/39 in FCNA, pp. 37–8.
20. Shirer, *Berlin Diary*, pp. 200–1.
21. Korwin-Rhodes, pp. 14–15 and Turnbull and Suchcitz, *Edward Roland Sword: The Diary and Despatches of a Military Attaché in Warsaw, 1938–1939*, p. 53.
22. Paul, *Brennpunkte*, p. 30.
23. Prüller, p. 17.
24. Polnisches Reserve Offizier, 'Die andere Seite!' in BA-MA RH27-5/2.
25. Schimak Lamprecht and Dettmer, *Die 44 Infanterie Division: Tagebuch der Hoch und Deutschmeister*, pp. 27, 29, Prüller, pp. 16–17, Venzky, p. 25, Leixner, p. 29.
26. Based on TB Goebbels, 4/9/39 and Vormann, pp. 77–8; Hitler's proclamation to the Eastern Armies, 3/9/39 can be found in Domarus, iii, p. 1784.
27. Vormann, pp. 87–9, KTB Bock 4/9/39 and Gunter d'Alquen, 'Der Führer an die Front' in *Völkischer Beobachter*, 5/9/39.
28. Fighting in the Corridor is based on *Geschichte der 3 Panzer Division 1935–1945*, p. 24, Falckenthal, pp. 29, 31, Buchner, *Der Polenfeldzug 1939*, pp. 52–3, Supf, p. 61, *Unteroffizier* Pries, 'Ich habe stets auf die Panzer vertraut! Der Führer bei seinen Panzermännern,' in Guderian, *Mit den Panzern in Ost und West*, pp. 25–6 and Guderian's letter to his wife, 4/9/39 in Bradley, *Generaloberst Heinz Guderian und die Entstehungsgeschichte des modernen Blitzkrieges*, p. 216.

29. Schmidt, *Die Geschichte der 10 Infanterie Division*, pp. 24–5.

30. *Oberleutnant* Riessner, 'Infanterie voran!' in *Mit dem XIII Armeekorps in Polen*, pp. 11–12.

31. Oeringk, pp. 36–7, 44–5 and Schmidt, *Die Geschichte der 10 Infanterie Division*, pp. 25–7.

32. Kielmansegg, pp. 34–6, 38–41.

33. Lucas, *Kampfgruppe*, p. 14.

34. Brief 6/9/39 in Bücheler, p. 86.

35. Polnisches Reserve Offizier, 'Die andere Seite!' in BA-MA RH27-5/2.

36. Venzky, pp. 33–4.

37. Hitler's tour of the Corridor is based on Guderian, *Panzer Leader*, pp. 73–4, KTB XIX Pz Korps, 6/9/39, Geyr von Schweppenburg, 'Einsatz der 3 Panzer Division in Polenfeldzug' in BA-MA RH27-3/243, and *Unteroffizier* Pries, 'Ich habe stets auf die Panzer vertraut! Der Führer bei seinen Panzermännern,' in Guderian, *Mit den Panzern in Ost und West*, pp. 25–6.

38. Vormann, pp. 95–6.

39. Stjernfelt, pp. 112–14, 120, and KTB *Schleswig-Holstein*, 7/9/39 in NHB 713.

40. Polnisches Reserve Offizier, 'Die andere Seite!' in BA-MA RH27-5/2.

41. Bradley, Dermot, *Walter Wenck: General der Panzertruppe*, p. 115 and *Tagesbefehl* 4 Panzer Division, 7/9/39, cited in Drescher, p. 294.

42. Generalstab des Heeres, *Kampferlebnis aus dem Feldzug in Polen 1939*, p. 46.

43. Kielmansegg, pp. 46–9.

44. Reibig, p. 35 and Neumann, *Die 4 Panzer Division 1938–1943*, p. 49.

45. Drescher, p. 316.

46. KTB 4 Pz Div, 8/9/39 in BA-MA RH27-4/197 and Drescher, p. 243–4, 245, 303.

47. Kabisch, p. 16.

48. Schüddekopf, *Krieg: Erzählungen aus dem Schweigen*, p. 32, Drescher, p. 324, and Dollinger, *Kain, wo ist dein Bruder?*, p. 29.

49. Schüddekopf, *Krieg: Erzählungen aus dem Schweigen*, pp. 32–3.

50. Drescher, p. 333.

51. Drescher, p. 304 and Reibig, pp. 36–7.

52. Buchner, *Der Polenfeldzug 1939*, pp. 82–3.

53. Neumann, *Die 4 Panzer Division 1938–1943*, pp. 52–3 and Buchner, *Der Polenfeldzug 1939*, pp. 82–3.

54. Drescher, pp. 305–6 and KTB Pz.Regt 35, 9/9/39. Cited in Jentz, i, p. 96.

55. Drescher, pp. 248–9 and KTB 4 Pz Div, 8/9/39 in BA-MA RH27-4/197.

56. Drescher, pp. 330–1.

CHAPTER SIX

Much Blood has Flowed

There was bad news followed by more bad news, raining down on us like blows from a club.

– GENERALMAJOR HANS FELBER

Terrible scenes. Groans and screams from the wounded.
Utter confusion among the men. Dejection. Tiredness.

– *POLISH OFFICER*

AFTER eight days continuously on the march, the men of 6th Infantry Regiment arrived in the small town of Piatek, twenty miles north of Lodz. The faces of the soldiers, mostly from Schleswig-Holstein in the north of the Reich, were covered with dust; their comrades in 30th Infantry Division were scattered thirty or forty miles apart along the valley of the Bzura, a small tributary of the Vistula. Perhaps, officers and men alike wondered, they might get some rest in Piatek. Sporadic Polish artillery fire brought shells crashing down in the town, setting several buildings on fire. Beyond Piatek, on the north bank of a non-descript tributary of the Vistula, Polish troops were on the move, hundreds of them, in long unmissable columns, heading east. The *Landsers* were not worried. The Poles were retreating. The shells landing in and around Piatek were dismissed as weak attempts to slow the German advance.

Some twenty miles to the west, the staff of the unflappable *Generalleutnant* Kurt von Briesen pitched their tent in the village of Wartkowice. Their leader's pennant, a red-and-white-striped shield, hung limply in the stifling late summer heat. Come the morning, von Briesen would be where he loved to be: at the front, among his men, when his tent moved to Piatek.

His men skirmished with scattered Polish troops in the valley long into the night. One Pole was captured and sent back to Wartkowice for interrogation by von Briesen's staff. Before dawn, he told them, a regiment of *ulans* – the renowned Polish cavalry – would strike from the north. The onslaught which would strike the men of 30th Infantry Division that morning would be the first act in the sole Polish offensive of the campaign.[1]

Scattered across 5,000 square miles of Greater Poland, 150,000 troops had been bypassed by events for more than a week. The *Army of Pomorze*, charged with defending the Corridor, had been largely crushed by Heinz Guderian's panzers; the *Army of Poznan* had all but been ignored as German soldiers focused on Warsaw. Also ignored were the pleas of the army's commander, Taduesz Kutrzeba, to strike at the enemy. For several days, Kutrzeba had been insisting upon unleashing an offensive southwards into the left flank of the German thrust towards the Polish capital. For days, Warsaw had vacillated. By 8 September, Kutrzeba's blood was up. It was time to strike, he argued. His army would lunge towards Lodz; the *Army of Pomorze* would withdraw eastwards to the sanctuary of Warsaw. But if his men were to move that night, he pressed Poland's embattled Chief-of-Staff Waclaw Stachiewicz, the order to attack had to be given now. Stachiewicz reluctantly agreed – but only if his Commander-in-Chief approved. Obtaining Edward Smigly-Rydz's permission, however, was far from easy. The Marshal fled Warsaw for Brest, 110 miles to the east, on the seventh for reasons he never satisfactorily explained. Telephone communications with Brest had failed completely; the teletype was scarcely better. Smigly-Rydz was finally tracked down that afternoon. It was long after nightfall before the Marshal approved. It would be 11 September before written orders were in the hands of Tadeusz Kutrzeba. But by then the battle in the Bzura valley would be raging.[2]

As its name suggested the *Army of Poznan* had been mobilised in the spring of 1939 to defend its namesake city and the Greater Poland region. Beyond minor skirmishes with German border units and isolated thrusts into Prussia, the Army had seen little action. Nor had its fifty-three-year-old leader. Tadeusz Kutrzeba had served as Chief-of-Staff to his Commander-in-Chief, Smigly-Rydz, in the Great War. The Marshal regarded Kutrzeba highly, as did Kutrzeba's contemporaries. The General was an outstanding staff officer, a theorist, a lecturer, instructor, 'a man of high culture, liked and highly regarded by all – decent and sensible'. But he was not a man to lead fellow men in battle. When faced with a problem, he resorted to the ideas of the classroom rather than the practicalities of the battlefield. 'In decision making he was fickle and he was not up to a crisis,' one contemporary wrote. He was also excessively optimistic. He had no contact with Polish Army intelligence. Instead, he based all his plans on suppositions and a sketch map of German positions a liaison officer had handed him four days earlier. He convinced himself the *Army of Lodz* to the south would tie the Germans down when he launched his offensive. But the *Army of Lodz* was a beaten Army. Its men were hungry, they were demoralised by falling back on roads crammed with refugees. Their commander conceded he could no longer control events; the fate of the *Army of Lodz* rested in the lap of the gods.

Taduesz Kutrzeba was as out of touch with his men as he was with his situation. *26th Infantry Division* was typical of the units about to rush headlong into the Germans on the Bzura. After four days of bitter fighting west of Bromberg, the division had been ordered to head east towards the Bzura – and ultimately Warsaw. Discipline had all but broken down. Commanders were deserting their posts, soldiers commandeering the carts of refugees and carrying women in their cars. In some instances, the infantrymen had marched into villages and arbitrarily executed civilians. Only 'utter ruthlessness' Colonel Adam Brzechwa-Ajdukiewicz, the *26th's* commander, had decided could prevent his division disintegrating. 'A soldier may only shoot in defence of his own life. The death penalty will always be applied to whoever shoots a fleeing civilian in the back.'

And so General Tadeusz Kutrzeba joined battle with men exhausted, disorientated and in some cases demoralised. He had almost no air support to speak of. His actions were based on indifferent reconnaissance and a hastily-drawn, out-of-date sketch map. But he had nine infantry divisions and a couple of cavalry brigades at his disposal – in the region of 150,000 men in all. He had more than sixty armoured cars and light tanks. He had the advantage of surprise. His infantry outnumbered their foe three to one. He enjoyed a twofold superiority in artillery. Above all, Tadeusz Kutrzeba had belief. 'Most of us were up for a fight,' he recalled later. Now was the time to unleash an offensive. 'We had an outstanding opportunity for carrying it out.'[3]

As Taduesz Kutrzeba and his staff conferred under the stars that night, the officers of the German General Staff produced their daily *Lagekarte* (situation map) at their headquarters in Zossen. They carefully plotted the positions of friendly units based on the evening reports flashed back from the front-line: 4th Panzer Division at the gates of Warsaw, 1st Panzer a stone's throw away to the south on the banks of the Vistula, 30th Infantry around Piatek, 24th Infantry slightly to the east. And between Lodz and Warsaw there were eight Polish divisions unaccounted for. The German Army was in the dark. 'Our information about the Poles is truly wretched,' one staff officer fumed in his diary that night. Somewhere between the Bzura and Vistula there had to be countless Polish troops.[4]

The battle on the Bzura began not as Tadeusz Kutrzeba planned it but by accident – and one day too soon. An impetuous Polish regimental commander was convinced the German garrison in the historic small town of Leczyca, twenty miles northeast of Lodz, was weak and could be easily overrun. In the late morning of Saturday, 9 September, the men of *25th Infantry Division* swept across the Bzura and through the swamps on the south bank. For a dozen miles and more Kurt von Briesen's lines crumbled. By mid-day that Saturday scattered Polish artillery fire was falling on the outskirts of Piatek. It was far worse to the west, around the historic small town of Leczyca. Waves of brown Polish infantry struggled across the Bzura under the guns of the Polish artillery then swarmed up the southern bank and fanned out 'like a wave breaking with the tide'. The townsfolk of Leczyca took it as a signal to rise up against the invader. 'Suddenly the town is full of people, emerging from cellars and tunnels,' the history of 30th Infantry Division recorded. 'They are armed, they attack retreating wounded and individual combat vehicles, destroy telephone lines and light signals close to the command post, ignoring the danger from the Polish artillery which begins shortly afterwards.' Leczyca began to burn. The blazing buildings gave the sky a red hue as darkness set in.

The men of 46th Infantry Regiment defended Leczyca to the last round, as horse-drawn columns bearing ammunition ran the gauntlet of Polish infantry and cavalry patrols and struggled through the smoke-choked burning streets of the old town to bring relief. It was not enough; shortly before midnight, the regiment sent a curt, desperate report to von Briesen. 'Situation hopeless. The staff are dug in and defending themselves.' Kurt von Briesen was not a man to panic, but even he was shaken by the day's events. As a bitter Saturday drew to a close he appealed to his superiors: 'Request urgent support. Situation deadly serious.'[5]

What befell Leczyca on 9 September, befell Piatek on the tenth. All through the night, Polish troops had crossed the Bzura, an entire division. At dawn they fell upon the beleaguered town. An artillery barrage plastered Piatek; a salvo landed in 30th Infantry Division's command post, shattering Kurt von Briesen's right arm. His division caved in around him. By mid-day it was withdrawing, and in some cases fleeing. The baggage columns and rear services led the way, streaming southwards along the solitary road to Lodz, all the time watched by a Polish spotter plane directing the fall of the guns. The road became a death trap. Horse-drawn carts made a break over the Bzura plains only to become bogged down, while riderless horses spread confusion and panic among the retreating columns.

A generation ago, Kurt von Briesen's father, a Prussian infantry general, had been killed on the banks of the Vistula, barely forty miles from 30th Infantry Division's current position. His son had no intention of suffering the same fate. Like many senior officers, the fifty-three-year-old *Generalleutnant* held a deep-seated hatred of the Poles. He hailed from Hinterpommern – Trans-Pomerania, east of the River Oder; two decades earlier he led bands of volunteers as they fought to defend their homeland against Polish marauders. As a leader of men in battle, von Briesen was without peers. His men adored him. 'He knew every recruit – the youngest *Leutnants* and the oldest officers swore by him,' a friend wrote. In the autumn of 1939, 30th Infantry Division was arguably the finest unit in the German Army. And now, as his proud division crumbled in the face of the Polish onslaught, came the hour of Kurt von Briesen, the divisional history wrote admiringly. 'He appears, his arm bleeding in the torn uniform, and steps out into the heart of the retreating infantry with his staff.' News of Briesen's resolve spread. His men rallied, turned around, headed back towards the Poles in an attempt to stem the seemingly inexorable Polish tide. The tide won.[6]

By the morning of 10 September, Tadeusz Kutrzeba's counterstroke along the Bzura was in full swing. As they had been twenty-four hours earlier, the Polish infantry were again impatient. They did not wait for the artillery. They swarmed forwards over the Bzura, but the valley's terrain with its marshy plains favoured the defender, not attacker. The Polish guns looked for targets in vain. Their observers could give them none – every telephone line was down and there were no radio communications with the artillery. Kutrzeba expected rapid results from his offensive, but reports reaching him that Sunday morning were discouraging. In the heat of battle, his men had forgotten their peace-time training and attacked the enemy head-on, drawn almost magnetically to town and villages. And so rather than smashing through the German lines, the Poles merely pushed them back. The momentum rested with Tadeusz Kutreba's Army, but the successes, he lamented, 'had been paid for with too much blood'.[7]

Along the middle Bzura, isolated remnants of 30th Infantry Division stood their ground, dug in, and waited for relief to come from the south. North of Piatek, the Poles came forward against men drawn from the SA detachment in Kiel, the *Nordmark*, in seemingly endless waves. 'The machine-guns were repeatedly muddied by the whipped-up sand,' soldier Christian Kinder remembered. 'Nevertheless everyone who could still shoot calmly took aim. The men of this shrunken company shot in almost exemplary calm. Troop after troop of Poles was mown down. But more and more Poles appeared again. Just hold out – that was the thought which filled each one of us!'[8]

The fighting at Piatek was hand-to-hand, but the Poles believed that was in their favour. 'As a rule,' one General later wrote, when it came to such close quarters combat 'the Polish infantryman maintained the upper hand'. In this instance, the Poles were halted eighty yards from the German company's decimated lines. The company was ordered to pull out – but that meant running the gauntlet on the road to Piatek, which was now occupied by the enemy. No, the *Landsers* would hold to the last round, their commander, a seasoned *Hauptmann* ruled. 'A platoon leader drew the *Hauptmann's* attention to the Poles, who were trying to establish themselves in the company's rear,' Kinder recalled. 'Each man could see individual soldiers with their triangular caps. The *Hauptmann* answered him curtly: "Who here sees Poles in our rear? I cannot see any. If you don't believe me, then go there for yourself and find out."' The officer's put-down had the desired effect. The company stood its ground.[9]

Not all Christian Kinder's comrades were so resolute, however. Gerhard M, in peacetime a fire-fighter in the small Baltic port of Flensburg, fell back towards Lodz along the only road not occupied by the enemy. The men were tired, hungry, nervous. 'The Poles are all around us,' the soldier recorded worriedly in his diary. 'I don't think we'll get out of this unharmed.' Gerhard M was convinced he would fall victim to 'little Tannenberg – except that we're the ones who are now encircled'. Suddenly there was wild shooting coming from a row of farm cottages. A few figures in brown tried to flee across the fields as the Flensburger and his comrades stormed the houses. The German column wearily resumed its retreat, only for fresh shooting to flare up in the same farmhouses. This time the *Landsers* received orders to torch every building. 'Out of the flames come the cries of those who can no longer save themselves,' Gerhard M recalled. 'The cattle bellow out of fear for their lives. A dog howls until he's burned alive. But the worst thing is the screams of the people. That's terrible – I can still hear them ringing in my ears today.'[10]

Sounds of victory and defeat drifted across the Bzura battlefield that Sunday. In villages recaptured by the advancing Poles, huge cheers went up as the civilian inhabitants celebrated liberation and fraternised with their countrymen. In Lodz, twenty miles to the south, the dull thunder of the cannon was unmistakable. The 700,000 inhabitants of this great industrial city were convinced the distant rumble of the guns signalled their impending liberation. There was talk of 'the miracle of the Vistula'. People gathered in the streets and city squares. Wild rumours flew through the crowds. There was feverish activity outside the Grand Hotel, the headquarters of XIII Corps, as messengers, ordnance officers and drivers hurriedly came and went. Inside the hotel, the corps' commander, the aristocratic Maximilian *Freiherr* von Weichs, pored over the alarming reports arriving from the flurry of messengers. Weichs hated Lodz – 'an extremely horrible industrial city with no architectural charm'. He did not know that apart from his staff the city was defended by just forty German field police and clerks. Every other soldier had been sent to the front.[11]

Weichs' corps had been marching towards Warsaw when the Poles struck on the Bzura. Ordered to turn around, his divisions were strung out northeast of Lodz. The Bavarians of 20th Infantry Regiment had endured a restless and disconcerting night, frequently interrupted by machine-gun fire. The regiment was on its own, its men scattered around the town of Glowno. It needed at least twelve hours to regroup and launch a concerted counter-attack to throw the Poles back across the Bzura. The Poles would not give the Bavarians twelve hours to regroup. [12]

The road to Zgierz, a small town four miles outside Lodz, was crammed with supply columns carrying ammunition, food, fuel. Infantry hurried on foot, motorised infantry lurched along in trucks, all heading north. Empty ammunition columns, ambulances and Polish prisoners and an endless torrent of refugees headed in the opposite direction. On the southern outskirts of Zgierz could be found the command truck of Eighth Army; the night before its Chief-of-Staff *Generalmajor* Hans Felber had caught just ninety minutes' sleep. As Sunday the tenth drew to a close, the battle just a dozen miles away was reaching its climax. 'There was bad news followed by more bad news, raining down on us like blows from a club,' Felber recalled. The situation was 'extremely black'. Eighth Army's staff were nervous, wavering. But not their Commander-in-Chief. No, Johannes Blaskowitz stood firm, and ordered his army to do likewise.[13]

The fifty-six-year-old *General der Infanterie* hailed from the very eastern extremity of the Reich, an insignificant village thirty miles from Königsberg. As an East Prussian, he abhorred the Polish Corridor. He abhorred the Versailles Treaty. Yet he also abhorred the brutality of the National Socialist regime. 'If the Nazis do anything stupid, we will deal with them with all our force – we will not shrink back from bloody disputes,' he boasted to fellow officers before Hitler seized power. Nazism jarred with his cultured nature; Johannes Blaskowitz was a lover of the finer things in life: opera, theatre, galleries – hence his choice of Dresden, arguably the most artistic of Germany's cities, as his home. Nazism jarred too with his religious beliefs; a devout Christian, the general's last act before bed each night, in peace or war, was to read a passage of the New Testament. It was not for these reasons that Adolf Hitler disliked him, however. Hitler disliked because he lacked ability – he had apparently been too timid during pre-war manoeuvres; the Führer never forgave him.[14] Out of favour or not, Blaskowitz had led German troops into Czechoslovakia that March. In June he had been ordered to prepare to invade Poland. On 1 September, his Eighth Army had crossed the Silesian border and begun the march on Warsaw.

If he was rattled by the bitter struggle his army found itself embroiled in, Johannes Blaskowitz did not betray it. Hans Felber marvelled as his chief took 'tough decisions' to block the Polish thrust. There would be difficult hours ahead. Great demands would be made of the men. But come the morning, Eighth Army would confront the Poles with a continuous front.

Despite all his resolve, Kurt von Briesen had been unable to hold Piatek and its environs. After dark on the tenth, the men of 30th Infantry Division began to break contact with the Poles and fall back southwards. There they found not the salvation of German lines but a Polish ambush. 26th Infantry Regiment disintegrated, its companies scattered in the dark. Small groups of *Landsers* pushed southwards, often without maps and invariably low on ammunition, using the stars and the sounds of battle to orient themselves. They hauled their wounded on farmers' carts, or strips of canvas turned into makeshift stretchers, skirmishing sporadically with Polish troops before finally reaching German lines. By first light on Monday the terrain around Pietak and Leczyca was littered with abandoned German machine-guns and rifles, and German dead. Kurt von Briesen's division had been decimated; what was left possessed 'very little fighting value'.[15]

In his command truck, now moved to Brzeziny, a dozen miles east of Lodz, Johannes Blaskowitz reviewed the morning reports from his divisions and corps. 'We have succeeded in presenting the enemy who has crossed the Bzura with a united front,' the general recorded in his diary. 'The crisis has passed.'[16] Tadeusz Kutrzeba had other ideas.

For sixty miles or more along the Bzura valley from its mouth to the towns and villages north of Lodz, the *Armies of Poznan* and *Pomorze* battered and hacked their way southwards on Monday, 11 September. 'The enemy is in retreat,' Taduesz Kutrzeba declared in a stirring order of the day. 'He is withdrawing from the Warsaw area and is encircled by us. In his rear our fellow countrymen form rebellious gangs. Revolt throughout the Poznan region. Forward to total victory!'[17]

And on they came. Gerhard M and his 30th Infantry Division comrades held a thin line – 'a man every couple of metres' – armed only with rifles, although there was the comforting sound of German artillery booming a few hundred yards behind them. But the crash of the field guns did nothing to deter the enemy. 'An *Unteroffizier* saw them first,' the Flensburger recalled. 'Small brown dots on the landscape.' The horizon shimmered, teeming with Polish infantry. But still the Poles were out of range. Gerhard checked his pockets – each one was stuffed with ammunition – and loaded a couple of clips. At just 300 yards' range, the riflemen opened fire. Suddenly German machine-guns joined the battle. 'In a flash the Polish troops throw themselves to the ground and look for cover.' Gerhard M fired his rifle 'like mad'. For all the German fire, the Poles kept coming, and the men of 30th Infantry kept shooting. Gerhard M watched with admiration as a tall comrade stood up, rifle in hand and fired round after round. 'White as a sheet he is.' Only as the sun began to sink beneath the horizon did the battle wane.[18]

On the heights of Celestynow, half a dozen miles north of Zgierz, *17th Infantry Division* bludgeoned its German namesake. 'I want to act resolutely and with all our might to finally break the enemy's resistance,' its commander Colonel Mieczyslaw Mozdyniewicz told his men. His men were as good as his word; they inflicted upwards of 900 casualties upon the German formation. 'Now the name of Celestynow was added to the bloody fields of this battle at Leczyca and Piatek,' Kutrzeba observed.[19]

Northwest of Lodz, 23rd Panzer Regiment moved up to counter-attack against a stream of German columns pouring southwards. Near the village of Orla the German armour ran into Polish forces. 'Heavy fire, from trees, from behind haystacks, from the left, from the right and from the front, struck our panzers which advanced without halting,' a company commander reported. 'A murderous duel between our panzer and Polish anti-tank guns began. A Polish anti-tank gun, situated behind the corner of a house, was particularly dangerous. Even though one crew after another was killed as a result of our panzer's machine-gun fire, again and again Polish soldiers jumped out of the house to man the gun. The last man to shoot – and die – at the gun was a Polish lieutenant.' After a day of bitter fighting, the panzers withdrew; two had been shot-up, another four damaged or become bogged down.[20]

After dark, Gerhard M and his 30th Infantry Division comrades fell back a couple of hundred yards and settled down in foxholes – two men in each, one always on watch – filled with straw. Gerhard slept with his steel helmet still on; it at least offered a little protection. His fitful sleep was soon interrupted by the roar of artillery. Ours? he asked himself. No, he realised, Polish. The shells soon began crashing down close to the division's makeshift bivouacs. 'We bury our heads in the sand – not that it'll do us any good.' It lasted for at least an hour, perhaps two. But this time the Polish infantry did not come. At dawn on the twelfth, the *Landsers* edged forward nervously. There was no sign of the enemy. But he had been here. The battlefield was marked everywhere by his footprints.[21]

For all the hurrahs, for all the bravado and raw élan shown by the Poles on 11 September, the net result of the day's fighting was as it was twenty-four hours earlier: the German lines had bent, fallen back in places, but nowhere had the attackers achieved the breakthrough they so desperately sought. On the twelfth, Kutrzeba's forces struck to the southwest, towards Brzeziny and Skierniewice to seize the heights east of Lodz. But by mid-afternoon, the attack had bogged down around the town of Glowno. Failure in the south was compounded by a growing threat to the northwest; the pressure from III Corps was relentless, thrusting into the *Army of Pomorze*'s rear. Tadeusz Kutrzeba was forced to make a decision. Threatened in the west, with no hope of breaking through to the south, the only hope for both armies lay now in striking eastwards, to Warsaw, joining hands with the troops defending the capital. But to reach Warsaw, the *Armies of Poznan* and *Pomorze* had to pass through the eye of a needle barely more than a dozen miles wide between the Vistula and the main road to the Polish capital. The terrain between the Bzura and Warsaw was dominated by the Kampinos forest. It was also dominated, Tadeusz Kutrzeba lamented, by the enemy.[22]

The *Armies of Poznan* and *Pomorze* were trapped. Johannes Blaskowitz knew it. He now enjoyed superiority on the Bzura in arms and men.

On an airfield west of Lodz, Johannes Blaskowitz waited for a three-engined Junkers 52 to touch down. At 10am on Wednesday, 13 September, the leviathan rolled to a stop. In a dark grey jacket and brown cap, Adolf Hitler stepped down from the aircraft, greeted the general, then climbed into a beige open-top

Mercedes G4, its engine idling. Eighth Army's commander joined his Führer in the car. Hitler was keen to see the latest city to fall to his all-conquering armies, but Blaskowitz could not guarantee his safety. On the city's narrow streets with row-upon-row of houses, the chances that a Pole might try to assassinate Hitler were too great. The column of Mercedes made a wide detour of the city before pulling up outside Blaskowitz's headquarters on the eastern outskirts.

Inside the Army's command truck, Hans Felber, Blaskowitz's nervy Chief-of-Staff, was worried. The Bzura battlefield was far from safe. The Führer might be in danger. But when Hitler entered, Felber steeled himself. Standing next to his Führer, Felber gave a concise account of Eighth Army's achievements. Hitler nodded, evidently satisfied by the Army's efforts. As he departed, Hitler's slavish Chief-of-Staff Wilhelm Keitel clasped both of Hans Felber's hands. 'Your Army has had the most difficult task up to now,' the normally taciturn general imparted in him. 'We all know that.'

The Führer climbed back into his Mercedes for a tour of the Bzura battlefield. First to 10th Infantry Division, then to 17th Infantry, next to XIII Corps' headquarters and finally to a run-down schoolhouse which served as 30th Infantry Division's temporary command post, where the imposing figure of Kurt von Briesen greeted him. His right arm in plaster squeezed into his *feldgrau* jacket and his chiselled face partially hidden by his steel helmet, Kurt von Briesen explained how his men had fought to the last round at Piatek and Leczyca. The Poles had attacked repeatedly, regardless of their losses. The 30th Infantry had fought bravely, it had prevented an enemy breakthrough, but it had paid a heavy price. 'Our losses are grave,' von Briesen concluded. The Führer listened intently to the *Generalmajor*'s report. Von Briesen had done his best to hide his wounded arm, but there was no mistaking it. The Führer was impressed. 'And you continued to lead?' Yes, the general told him, he had continued to command his division. 'That was my duty.' Hitler turned to his Army liaison officer, *Oberstleutnant* Nikolaus von Vormann. 'That's how I imagined a Prussian general to be when I was a child.'[23]

On the return journey to the airfield west of Lodz, Hitler's convoy raced through the sprawling industrial city at upwards of forty miles an hour. The roads had been cleared of traffic and people. The city was deserted. The Führer turned to his chief adjutant, the jug-eared *Oberst* Rudolf Schmundt, clearly still in awe of von Briesen. 'Schmundt, I'm looking for hard men,' he told him. 'I need fanatical National Socialists. If their ability is somewhat lacking, put a trained General Staff officer at their side. See to it that such officers are brought forward.' Johannes Blaskowitz, however, had made a very different impression. 'He didn't seem to have realised his mission,' Hitler smouldered.

In Eighth Army's command truck, Hans Felber sighed with relief. The day had passed without incident. 'We really thought that the Poles would attack today,' he wrote in his diary. 'Perhaps they will still do so this evening. They're strong enough.'[24]

The Poles did not attack in force on the thirteenth, or the fourteenth for that matter. They were regrouping – a difficult task made even more so by relentless Luftwaffe attacks which harried their movements. The aerial onslaught had the desired effect. The *Armies of Pomorze* and *Poznan* were disintegrating, the attacks on German lines slackening. 'The number of deserters is growing,' a German staff officer observed, 'abandoned guns line the routes of retreat.' In Eighth Army's command truck there was growing satisfaction at a battle won. One or two more days, Hans Felber mused, and the Polish troops between the Vistula and Bzura would be annihilated. Felber did not know his foe, nor did he seek to demonise him – 'that chap', as he politely referred to Kutrzeba in his diary. 'The commander facing us has an amazing brain – he must be their best and youngest leader,' he wrote admiringly. 'He defends himself with the utmost bravura.' The Eighth Army Chief-of-Staff was rather glad that he did. 'It's rather satisfying there's no Bohemian *Blumenkrieg* this time,' he wrote. Too much blood had flowed for that.[25]

Tadeusz Kutrzeba could allow himself no romantic musings. His was a struggle of life and death and death was winning. 'By 14 September, we were encircled,' he later wrote, 'and the noose around our necks would tighten day by day, if Warsaw did not come to our aid.' There was time for one final push. One last time, on the evening of Friday, 15 September, the general rallied his troops. They had already destroyed two German divisions, 17th and 30th Infantry, he told them. 'Now a fresh victory awaits you,' he continued.

We know that we are stronger than the enemy facing us. Summon your strength, smash the Prussian hordes with a single, powerful blow and open the road to Warsaw.

Full of belief and determination, throw yourselves into the battle. Glory awaits you.

Forward for the glory of the Fatherland, avenge the ravaging of our homeland![26]

General Edmund Knoll-Kownacki, commanding an *ad hoc* group of troops, issued an equally rousing order of the day. 'We are attacking a weaker enemy,' he assured his men. It would be a disgrace if they could not break such a foe. 'Once again I stress with the greatest emphasis that our attack must have a "desperado" character.'[27] The Poles would strike towards their capital on the sixteenth. Their attack would come too late.

On the south bank of the Bzura half a dozen miles west of Lowicz, *Leutnant* Arnold Schöneboom crept forward with his platoon. It was still long before dawn on the sixteenth. The only light came from a farmhouse in the distance which continued to burn despite the steady rain. The men of 16th Infantry Regiment had spent most of the campaign kicking their heels, held in reserve in Silesia. But on the twelfth they had been ordered to board Junkers 52 transport aircraft, flown to Lodz and ordered into the front line on the Bzura. For a week Eighth Army had been the anvil battered by the Polish hammer. It was time to reverse the roles. At first light the German Army would begin the destruction of Polish forces west of Warsaw.

The first rays of light gave form to the strange shapes on the far bank of the river. Polish soldiers moved about, unaware they were being observed by

Schöneboom and his men, who were impatient, itching to strike across the Bzura. For forty-five minutes, Schöneboom held his men back. The hands on his watch turned to 4.45am. The last act of the battle on the Bzura began. As German rifles and machine-guns opened fire, Polish artillery responded by pummelling the right bank of the river. Great fountains of earth were tossed up as 15cm shells began landing around Schöneboom's platoon. First one hundred yards away, then seventy. A messenger was knocked to the ground as a shell splinter struck him. Medics raced out amid the inferno to haul him back to safety. To the *Leutnant*'s rear there was a loud rumble, then hissing and howling, as German shells hurtled on their way towards the Polish positions. 'There's a feeling of relief among us,' wrote Schöneboom. 'There's a wall of earth and huge cloud of soil on the opposite bank.' The village of Urzecze, about 300 yards away, went up in flames. It was the signal for the pioneers to strike out across the Bzura in their rubber boats. By 5.30am, 16th Infantry Regiment was on the left bank and rushing through the streets of Urzecze. The village was still aflame, so much so that weapons and ammunition cases warmed as the *Landsers* swept past the fires. The attack stopped briefly on the village's edge when shooting came from a birch wood. A *Feldwebel* grabbed a machine-gun and began spraying bursts of fire into the tree tops. The Poles responded with anti-tank and field guns at the German infantry. The impetus lay with the Germans. The advance continued northwards, ending three miles from Urzecze in Begurja-Dolna, 16th Infantry Regiment's objective for the day. Just short of the village, Arnold Schöneboom inspected a Polish trench. 'Lying in it are some of the best warriors Poland has,' he noted. 'Most of them have been shot in the head.'[28]

The black waters of the Bzura gurgled through the marshes and swamps to the north of Piatek. A light mist hung over the river as a damp dawn, which seeped into the boots and clothes of every man, began to cast the valley in a grey hue. Shortly before 7am the guns of 17th Infantry Division opened fire, bringing shells crashing down on the far bank of the Bzura. Through the reeds and rushes, the German infantrymen heard the crack of rifle fire as the Poles shot back. The pioneers dragging rubber boats down to the Bzura's edge along a dam were shot up, others sank to their knees in the morass. Polish artillery now entered the fray. Yet amid the chaos a company commander, a handful of men and an engineer, struggled to fix duckboards to the remains of the bridge which once spanned the 35ft-wide main channel of the Bzura as sniper fire struck the waters about them.[29]

In the tall church which dominated the village of Kozlow Biskupi, a couple of miles southwest of Sochaczew, Friedrich Kirchner gathered his staff. It was a cool early autumn morning. The rain was still falling outside. The crisp bang of German 10cm field guns was clearly distinguishable above the clatter of machine-gun and rifle fire. Since early morning the armour of 1st Panzer Division had been rolling towards the Bzura along slippery, bottomless roads; engineers had already thrown two bridges across the river during the night. Now Kirchner outlined the division's mission to his commanders: to cross the Bzura and advance on the village of Kiernozia, a good fourteen miles to the northwest. Such a thrust would drive a stake through the heart of the Polish armies, Kirchner explained to his men, but it would not be easy. The Poles were defending themselves desperately. But if 1st Panzer's attack succeeded, Kirchner continued, the Poles' fate would be sealed.

The panzers moved towards the two temporary bridges under constant, if erratic, Polish artillery fire. A few shells straddled the crossing points, but not enough to prevent the armour reaching the left bank of the Bzura. There was no let-up from the heavens. The muddy lanes leading from the river were made passable only by covering them with branches and straw.[30]

On a footbridge north of Sochaczew, the *SS Leibstandarte Adolf Hitler* filed across the Bzura, then fanned out on the opposite bank. As the *Leibstandarte* men approached the hamlet of Bibijampol, hordes of Polish soldiers – the remnants of two infantry divisions – came charging towards them. The Poles were stopped not by bayonet or bullet, but by the *Leibstandarte*'s artillery, which brought its barrels to bear on the advancing soldiers. 'The Poles attack with great determination and prove yet again that they know how to die,' observed *Hauptsturmführer* Kurt Meyer. 'The finest Polish blood mixes with the waters of the river. The Poles' losses are awful.'[31]

In a Feisler Storch reconnaissance aircraft, a *Propaganda Kompanie* reporter watched the Luftwaffe take a terrible toll of the trapped Polish armies. Wave after wave of Stukas and bombers emerged from the clouds and lurched towards the ground, diving 'on the olive-green masses below like mighty birds of prey'. Columns of smoke and flame rose up, as did fountains of sand briefly. In a clearing off the main road from Sochaczew to Wyzogrod, a dozen miles away on the north bank of the Vistula, a Polish anti-aircraft gun unit was bivouacking when a hail of bombs fell. 'Above us bombs continually burst and covered us with a devastating hail of shrapnel and splinters,' the gun's commander later recounted to his German captors. 'We heard the tops of trees crashing, the cries of horses, the groans of men, the roar of stones thrown up in the air. We had still not fired the first salvo from our guns when we were blown away from them by a tremendous shockwave, and those who were not dead, lay half-conscious on the grass, incapable of getting up for minutes on end.' The shells still lay in the barrel; not one had been fired.[32]

Along the lower Bzura and the forests which bordered it, Polish troops were making a final desperate push to break through the German lines and reach their comrades thirty miles to the east in Warsaw. Approaching the battlefield from the west, one Stuka pilot was struck by the deceptive peacefulness of the land. 'Only when we approach the Bzura do we see clouds of smoke and burning farms as well,' he recorded. The dive-bombers found two makeshift bridges spanning the Bzura; the formations broke up to attack the two crossings, then the troops, carts, vehicles and material massed on every road, lane and path leading to the river. The scenes on the ground were chaotic, horrific, as the pilot observed:

There a battery is dashing over open ground towards the bridge over the Bzura, which can no longer be used, and the horses tear into the gently-flowing river without their riders. Soldiers run into the swamp on the

Bzura, shooting wildly, and get stuck there. People, animals, everything is running around in confusion. Horses fall as if they've been struck by a blade, are dragged along, others crash into overturned wagons. There an entire convoy is ablaze. And while we make our second, third attack against this enemy, who is laid low until he can no longer fight, groups of Stukas dive down upon these disintegrating divisions and spread hell, death and ruin with their bombs.[33]

By late afternoon, 17th Infantry Division's duckboard bridge across the Bzura was ready. The *Landsers* dashed across under heavy machine-gun fire, careful not to loose their footing on the unsteady boards. Once across, *Oberleutnant* Riessner mustered his company in a small hollow, then ordered his men to fix bayonets. '"Hurrah!" is the roaring cry from the infantry storming forward,' he recalled. 'The Polish position is overrun.' The enemy had dug in well on the Bzura; some of his foxholes were six feet deep. And some Poles were still in them, too scared or surprised to fight, flee, or even surrender. With dusk falling, Riessner ordered his men to dig in for the night. They grabbed bundles of straw to keep the September cold at bay.[34]

The spearhead of 1st Panzer had reached the outskirts of Kiernozia, but the division was spread out across the valley. More worryingly, 19th Infantry Division following in its wake had been held up in the Bzura forests, and communications were patchy at best. Intelligence officer *Hauptmann* Johann Graf von Kielmansegg drove to 19th Infantry's command post, a manor house a dozen miles from Kiernozia, to confront the division's commander, *Generalleutnant* Günther Schwantes. Schwantes was waiting for him, so too 1st Panzer's general Friedrich Kirchner – and Tenth Army commander Walther von Reichenau. As the officers discussed the fragile situation, two Polish shells crashed outside.

'The whole house shakes, the windowpanes clatter,' Kielmansegg wrote. Reichenau was unfazed, continuing to give out orders. More shells came crashing down, but the army commander stuck to his briefing. 'Outside in the courtyard are dead and wounded,' the staff officer noted in his diary. 'I later removed various splinters from my car. I am convinced that during the whole day no shells fell upon the manor house except for when the three generals were there.'

Late on the sixteenth, Kielmansegg returned to his billet, a country estate at Zlota, ten miles from 1st Panzer's spearhead. It was the most uncomfortable night for the officer and his comrades. The staff had no idea where some of the panzers were and knew others were almost certainly cut off. And the Poles closed the day with a ferocious artillery barrage preceding a night assault. With typical under-statement, Kielmansegg described the situation as 'anything but pleasant'. He continued:

There's nothing you can do against this hail of fire; going to the front again is pointless and at any rate impossible for the time being. There's nothing left to do except decide whether it would be better to be hit in the open or in the house. In the end, the commander of the telephone company and I choose neither and abandon ourselves to our fate on the outer staircase of the house. Nothing happens to us.

What Kielmansegg and his comrades did not know was that the panzers' lunge had gravely unsettled the Poles in Kiernozia and paralysed their leaders.[35]

Having thrust the knife into the belly of the Polish armies on 16 September, 1st Panzer Division twisted it the following day. The division's spearhead had spent the night hidden in a small wood outside Kiernozia. All night long Polish columns had pulled past the panzers on two roads which ran barely 100 yards from the hiding place. In the small hours, the panzers struck 'firing from every barrel', routed several Polish columns and regained contact with the remainder of their division, their fuel tanks almost dry. Reunited, 1st Panzer turned first to the north, then to the northeast, back towards the Bzura. It was as if Pole and German alike were in a race for the river, one seeking salvation, the other annihilation. The panzers came to a halt in the small town of Mlodzieszyn, a couple of miles from the left bank of the river. There was little to do here except round up demoralised Polish troops; the Luftwaffe had taken a terrible toll of the trapped enemy. 'The captured Poles are driven half-insane by fear and throw themselves to the ground – even in captivity – whenever there's the sound of an aircraft engine from somewhere,' Kielmansegg wrote. 'Even Polish officers are visibly shaken and repeatedly express the opinion apologetically that no human being could endure panzers and Stukas...'[36]

On the western edge of the pocket between the Bzura and the Vistula, the men of 8th Machine-Gun Battalion found the Polish Army evaporating before their eyes as they pressed east from the town of Gostynin down the main road to Sochaczew and Warsaw. The Luftwaffe cleared the way for the machine-gunners, dropping their bombs just a few hundreds yards in front of the German troops. 'We realise how overwhelming this must have been for the enemy and how powerless the individual is when he faces his fate as these steel birds overhead,' a machine-gun *Leutnant* wrote. The bombs killed men and horses, tore craters in the road, threw retreating Polish columns into confusion. 'Polish soldiers emerge running from the fields and forests to our left and right to give themselves up,' the gunner recorded in his diary. The road was strewn with abandoned weapons, equipment, vehicles, horses. The battalion pushed on to the southeast, past the villages of Topolno and Czyzew into Sanniki, half-way between Gostynin and Sochaczew. A gathering storm ominously darkened the sky. The craters in the road and the ruined houses were still smouldering. But the inhabitants – and the Polish soldiers – had seemingly fled. Only the church in Sanniki was still standing. Cautiously, the *Leutnant* approached it. In the doorway, he spied a Polish officer leading prayers with his company by candlelight. As the machine-gunner walked into the house of worship, the Polish troops stood up, tossed their guns on to the tiled floor and surrendered without a word.[37]

By mid-day on the seventeenth, 17th Infantry Division had pushed to the edge of the village of Karsznice Duze, fifteen miles west of Sochaczew. As *Oberleutnant* Riessner led his men across the a meadow he spied a Polish column little more than 1,000 yards away on top of a hill making for the Bzura. An infantry gun was hastily unlimbered. The breechblock clanged. The gunlayer hurriedly took aim. *Feuer*! The shell struck the dirt on the heights. Riessner watched figures clad in brown run for cover. Horses reared up. German flares arched over the battlefield as 17th Infantry Division swarmed across the field and fell upon the column. Most of the Poles – 200 men and several officers – raised their hands; two guns, radios and baggage carts fell into the Germans' hands. The *Landsers* continued into Karsznice Duze in a thunderstorm, fighting their way from house to house. Beyond the village, Polish troops took aim with machine-guns and rifles from a wood until 17th Infantry Division drove them out of the trees. The day's battle ended on the edge of the wood in the hamlet of Czerniew. By nightfall, 700 Poles and countless booty had been seized by the division.[38]

As the Poles moved east to attempt their breakout towards Warsaw, the Germans re-occupied the positions they had held four or five days earlier. 26th Infantry Regiment returned to the Piatek-Bielawy road, where it had splintered in the face of the Polish attack. Scattered groups, exhausted, hungry, often wounded, had struggled back to German lines. They re-formed their regiment and returned to the battlefield. The Poles had already dragged many of the German dead from the country road, other *Landsers* had been abandoned where they had been wounded or struck down. German doctors moved among the dead, concluding some had been murdered rather than succumbed to their wounds. Every move the medics took they felt the eyes of Polish civilians, burning with rage, watching them. Occupied, liberated and now occupied once again, it was too much for many Poles to bear. 'Their fanaticism smouldered and the Poles' ancient hatred of their oppressor – whether he came from the East or West – was reawakened,' the historian of 30th Infantry Division observed.[39]

A handful of men from 16th Infantry Regiment stood by the roadside outside the village of Chruslin – on the road from Piatek to Lowicz, a couple of miles southwest of their battlefield the previous day. An elderly *Oberleutnant*, a veteran of the Great War, from the regimental staff read a brief eulogy. The rest of his staff, indeed the rest of his regiment, was still locked in battle to the north. 'We have passed several soldiers' graves these past few days, but these graves upset us particularly. For these are our dead, the regiment's first fallen,' the *Oberleutnant* told his small band of mourners. 'And we could find no better place for their graves than this spot. From here they attacked over the low ground before us, then through the Bzura which meanders through the meadows. From here we can survey the battlefield where they fell.' The dead were *Unbekannter* – unknown soldiers. 'We do not know their names,' the officer declared. 'But we can assume that they are our fellow countrymen.' The men removed their helmets. 'Almighty God, we entrust our fallen comrades and their families to you. Bless our *Volk* and Fatherland.'[40]

Oberleutnant Riessner and his 17th Infantry Division comrades continued to punch their way through the Bzura valley, first northwards, then to the northwest. There were more signs of flight than fight now. Columns of unarmed Poles streamed past Riessner, heading west, their rifles, gasmasks, bayonets and belts scattered. Only near the village of Aleksandrow, a dozen miles west of

Sochaczew, was there determined Polish resistance, initially from behind walls and buildings, then from high ground beyond Aleksandrow. Riessner's platoon commander dashed forward with several men. Dirt flew up as the horses' hoofs galloped over the soft Bzura ground to the top of the hill. Utterly surprised, the Polish soldiers raised their hands. A few continued to resist in a neighbouring copse. The field guns were quickly brought to bear. Shell after shell hissed into the trees. 'It has the desired effect,' wrote Riessner. 'The Poles have an unholy fear of shells. They come running with white pieces of cloth. Gradually, their resistance crumbles.'[41]

Tadeusz Kutrzeba was one of the fortunate ones. He made it to the right bank of the Bzura, crossing the river near the village of Witkowice, three miles from its confluence with the Vistula, mid-morning on the seventeenth. 'Every movement, every grouping, all the routes of advance were subjected to a pounding from the air,' he recalled. 'Hell on earth had begun. The bridges were destroyed, the fords jammed, the columns waiting to cross destroyed by bombs.' Accompanied by two staff officers, Kutrzeba struggled through the Kampinos forest as far as the village of Myszory, three miles from the river. Exhausted, the three men briefly rested under a cluster of birch trees. 'We lay there, unable to stir ourselves until mid-day when the air attacks ceased,' the general wrote. 'All of us remained rooted to the spot, so threatened by death from the Luftwaffe were we.'[42]

The forests of Kampinos cover more than 150 square miles of the Vistula and Bzura valleys. Intersected by bogs, marshes and dunes, and tributaries of the two rivers, the woodland was as unforgiving to attacker and defender alike. Panzer commander Willi Reibig rumbled slowly through a clearing when he spied Polish baggage wagons and troops moving along the edge of the trees. 'Before they can think or carry out an order, our gunfire is landing amid the Polish masses – they are utterly surprised and confused by the sudden appearance of German panzers,' wrote Reibig. 'Machine-guns rattle among the leaderless Polish soldiers who are running around aimlessly, destroying everything in the area and snuffing out any resistance in its infancy. In a short time, everything is a desolate mess of men, vehicles and horses.' For Reibig's 4th Panzer Division comrades, 17 September was a particularly bitter day. The Poles charged the lines of the division's 12th Rifle Regiment with customary élan. Cries of 'hurrah' reverberated around the battlefield. The regiment splintered into small groups which 'defended themselves with the courage of despair – with hand grenades, rifle butts and bayonets and held their ground,' the regimental history recorded. 'Artillery fired to the last round directly at the Polish infantry and cavalry, which had penetrated the fire positions until they were close to the guns.' Even 4th Panzer's staff drew their guns as the fighting reached its climax. 'Cries for help came from all sides, losses increased, elements had all but shot themselves up. But the division had nothing more to give, it could not help, it had committed the last man.'[43]

The woods and copses of Kampinos became the 'grave of the *Army of Poznan*', Kutrzeba recalled. German artillery pounded the forest incessantly from every direction. Command broke down. Discipline broke down. One Polish officer observed a 'panic-stricken mood' among the encircled troops on the seventeenth. The next day they forced the Bzura. 'Terrible scenes,' the same officer recorded. 'Heavy losses, many dead and wounded. Groans and screams from the wounded. Utter confusion among the men. Dejection. Tiredness.' There the diary ends. Only a narrow strip of land between the edge of the forest and the bank of the Vistula offered salvation. Taduesz Kutrzeba and his staff bumped into a weak, poorly-armed rearguard led by a lieutenant who offered to guide his commander out of the forest to safety. The general agreed. After walking for several hours he reached Polish lines twenty miles northwest of Warsaw in the village of Cybulice late on the eighteenth. Waiting for him were the remains of two divisions and stragglers from a handful of other units. Others who escaped the hell on the Bzura were not so fortunate; often they ran into German pickets in the northwestern approaches to Warsaw. Elements of 1st Light Division were drawn up on the edge of Wolka Wegiowa, half a dozen miles from the heart of the capital when squadrons of Polish cavalry came galloping out of the broken terrain and into the German armour. The cavalry were massacred. A Polish regimental commander surrendered to 1st Light's commanding officer, *Generalmajor* Friedrich Wilhelm von Loeper, offering the general his sword. 'Keep your sword,' Loeper told him. 'The fortunes of war have gone against you.'[44]

A good forty miles to the southwest, the Bavarians of 20th Infantry Regiment were still clearing out the pocket, hacking their way through overgrown terrain. The difficult ground made it impossible to stay in contact with the other units of 10th Infantry Division; the regiment was on its own. After dark on the eighteenth, the Poles began surrendering *en masse*. There were too many for the Bavarians to cope with, perhaps 3,000 in all. The booty too was enormous. Abandoned vehicles sunk to their axles in the Bzura sand, guns left, rifles tossed away. And yet every now and then resistance flared up. Some Polish officers rallied their men, offering courage born of desperation 'They're probably determined to give up their lives but not their honour,' one Bavarian officer wrote. 'We cannot deny them our admiration.' In farmhouses and barns, in homes, in clearings, in woods, in countless villages and small towns in the Bzura valley, the final remnants of two Polish armies continued to fight 'in a most gallant fashion'. It could not go on like this, a *Propaganda Kompanie* reporter observed. The destruction of the enemy on the Bzura was only a matter of hours away. 'Such efforts as the Poles did make were only the death throes of a dying army.' That night the staff of 20th Infantry Regiment found an abandoned Polish truck to serve as their billet – 'our worst accommodation in weeks'. There were no houses to stay in; all had been ruined by the ten-day battle. The officers spent a disquieting night in their temporary home. Polish artillery shot constantly, farm houses and buildings burned; the heat caused ammunition dumps to explode, gnawing at the Bavarians' nerves. 'Some Polish horses which have broken free roam through the night in search of water, like eerie, spectral figures,' the officer recorded.[45]

The men of 20th Infantry's sister regiment, the 85th, were possessed by a single thought: Pursuit! To the Vistula! No rest! And it seemed feasible, for the enemy before it on the left bank of the Bzura was disintegrating. Every few minutes

Oberst Heinrich Thoma, the regimental commander, reported the ballooning number of prisoners: 3,000, 10,000, 12,000. Endless columns of dejected Polish soldiers trudged into Germany captivity as far as the eye could see. Shortly before 6pm, Thoma's men reached the shores of the Vistula near the hamlet of Arciechow, half a dozen miles from the confluence with the Bzura. There were yet more prisoners here and a tangled mess of guns and carts stretching along the south bank of the Vistula.[46]

The battle on the Bzura petered out in the late morning of 19 September. Leaderless, exhausted, hungry, demoralised, Polish soldiers poured across the Bzura not to fight but to surrender. 4th Panzer Division alone took as many as 20,000 men prisoner. 'The Bzura valley and the banks of the Vistula present a ghastly picture of fallen Poles, shot-up horses and carts, and all manner of destroyed equipment,' the division's historian recorded.[47]

In Lodz Eighth Army's presses had been rolling all afternoon. On grainy white paper with a thick black and red border, the letters in *Fraktur*, the gothic German typeface then prevalent, an order of the day by Johannes Blaskowitz's was printed and subsequently handed out to the men:

> The ten-day battle on the Bzura has been waged victoriously. An enemy who was cleverly led and who fought with determination has surrendered.
>
> You have grappled the enemy forces left west of the Vistula. You have withstood and thwarted all attempts to break through until fresh forces were brought up. You tightened the ring of encirclement as planned. A victory of decisive importance for the war is yours!
>
> With just pride, you can take the lion's share of this great battle of encirclement. With justification you bear the number of the famous Eighth Army of Tannenberg![48]

Eighth Army's staff had every reason to feel satisfied. They had won *the* battle of the campaign in Poland. 'This is a great event – the outcome is as great as Tannenberg, far exceeding our expectations,' a delighted Hans Felber – awarded the Iron Cross Second Class for his part in the battle – recorded in his diary. 'That Army also bore the number "eight".' Some 180,000 Polish troops had been captured, more than half of them by Eighth Army. At least 17,000 Poles were dead, scattered in the fields and forests, marshes and sand of the land between the Vistula and the Bzura or buried in makeshift graves in towns and villages throughout the valley, in Leczyca, Juliopol, Sochaczew, Rybno, Ilowo and countless hamlets and settlements. Materiel losses, too, were enormous. At least 300 field guns, 3,500 horses, thirty tanks, more than 4,000 trucks and 180 trains fell into German hands. 'If the Poles taken prisoner in the battle on the Vistula were lined up, single-file,' the OKW communiqué trumpeted, 'the line would run for 125 miles. If you added the booty, it would extend 500 miles.' It was 'one of the greatest battles of annihilation of all time'. German losses on the Bzura were bloody, but not on the Polish scale; the losses of 24th Infantry Division – 135 dead and 433 wounded – and 10th Infantry – seventy-three dead and 211 wounded – were representative of the cost of the fighting west of Warsaw in mid-September. No division suffered heavier losses than 30th Infantry. Twenty-nine officers and 766 men were left behind on the battlefield; another 794 soldiers were wounded.[49]

The battle won, German troops began clearing up the battlefield. Thousands of horses roamed around without their masters. Some were shot, most were rounded up and pressed into service hauling German carts and guns. Cattle, too, driven by the Poles from Poznan, also wandered around aimlessly. Binoculars, saddles, harnesses, ammunition, guns, rifles – all proved useful replacements for equipment lost or destroyed in the bitter fighting. Polish wounded lay on straw on panje carts, tended by nurses. Polish prisoners were herded into temporary camps or sent to the rear for processing. There were German prisoners too, several hundred *Landsers* freed from temporary captivity in Polish hands. Most were men of 30th Infantry Division who had been marched around the battlefield by their captors for days on end, seemingly without aim, covering upwards of thirty miles a day. 'They were treated badly and roughly,' a staff officer observed. 'Usually all they had to eat was a thin cabbage soup and occasionally some bread.'[50]

After two days out of the line to recover from the battering it had taken, the men of 30th Infantry Division returned to the battlefield. The inhabitants of the village of Slugi, north of Lodz, had rejoiced when liberated by their countrymen. Now they were sullen and evasive. But the battlefield itself was empty; gone were the bodies of the German dead – among them company commander, the brave yet brutal Joachim Meyer-Quade, and two junior officers – they had been carted away by the Poles and hastily buried in Piatek, five miles to the east. Meyer-Quade was a Nazi hero, winner of the Iron Cross First and Second Class a generation earlier, an *Obergruppenführer* in the *Sturmabteilung* in Kiel, a veteran of the Party from its days of the *Kampfzeit* – years of struggle. 'He always set the example,' Viktor Lutze, the SA's Chief-of-Staff, eulogised in the Nazi organ, the *Völkischer Beobachter*. 'Now he marches to immortality under the standard of Horst Wessel.' For Meyer-Quade's fallen comrades there were no such eulogies, no full pages dedicated to them in the *Völkischer Beobachter*. There were, however, seventeen dog tags, recovered by Bavarian troops now holding the line at Slugi; children playing in a farmhouse found soldiers' paybooks. The men of the *Nordmark* scoured the now silent command post and the lines they had held determinedly. Dead Poles lay where they had been cut down by the Germans' fire. 'The cap of a dead NCO was found, while at the position where the company's final command post had been, the *Hautpmann*'s sword was still sticking out of the piled-up earth,' Christian Kinder recalled. Gerhard M was ordered to bury German dead in Piatek – 'a ghastly place of death' – with five comrades. The town centre was littered with smashed vehicles and the cadavers of horses. And piled high in two ditches, each 300 yards long, were the *Gefallenen*. No attempt had been made to inter them. Faces had turned black and started to decompose. Gerhard picked up guns, rusted machine-guns, spades, bayonets, gunsights, and strips of canvas from this 'field of death', while the rest of the burial party dug graves for six men at a time. The soldiers snapped slats off garden fences to make simple crosses. 'The dead are laid side-by-side with all their kit,' Gerhard remembered. 'Nothing is taken off them – we even leave their steel helmets on their heads.' Dirt was tossed over the fallen until small mounds replaced the hole in the ground. Green branches were tossed upon them and a simple wooden cross thrust into the mound. A pierced steel helmet placed atop the cross completed the grave. It went on like this all day. No man ate.[51]

No man who witnessed the battlefield of the Bzura was not left deeply impressed by what he saw. A *Propaganda Kompanie* reporter wandered along a stretch of the main road between Sochaczew and Wyzogrod – 'the road of lost divisions'. It was littered with wrecked cars, burned-out ammunition limbers, abandoned gas masks, steel helmets, cartridge belts, caps, boots. The smell was acrid, overpowering. 'Bloated cadavers of horses, their harnesses torn, litter the forest earth,' he wrote, 'and among them dead artillerymen, their hands tensed up, their faces look like masks which still depict their last fright.' Such scenes were repeated mile after mile. In a clearing a dozen guns were lined up ready to move. On a secluded forest lane, a handful of light tanks wrecked, burned out, their hulls empty shells. Next to the main road a staff car was turned upside down, letters, photographs, documents were tossed around on the ground. The reporter studied the photograph of an elderly Polish officer at home with his family. His body lay a few feet away on a forested slope. 'It is that same clean-shaven face, only waxen now and without life,' the reporter recalled. 'We look for his dog tag, but there's no indentation on it, a blank piece of metal hanging pointlessly around his chest.' So hastily had the Polish Army been mobilised there had no time to press them. The ford of the Bzura at Brochow, thirty miles west of Warsaw, seemed 'like the apotheosis of devastation'. Polish troops had tried to force the river only to face a wall of steel on the far bank in the form of panzers, while a hail of death fell from the Stukas overhead. Carts, guns, men, horses, all became trapped at Brochow. 'They were destroyed where they drove, rode or stood, at the exits of the forest paths and here, where the columns ran into each other in front of the ford, only to end in utter chaos and wild panic,' the reporter observed. The waters of the Bzura lapped the remains of a shattered army. There was so much debris in the river it was possible for the victors to cross the Bzura without getting their feet wet.[52]

Hans Felber, whose attitude towards the Poles throughout the campaign swung between triumphalism and pity, was visibly moved by his tour of the Bzura battlefield. Eighth Army's Chief-of-Staff was a veteran of the Great War, but this was different. Then there had been dead strewn across the battlefield. But on the Bzura the dead were concentrated at road junctions, on forest lanes, at crossings, in towns and villages where only chimneys were left standing. Elsewhere in the valley, the world was at peace. 'Farmers tend to their fields as if there's no war on,' Felber observed. And where the *Armies of Pomorze* and *Poznan* had made their last stand, a scene of desolation and destruction 'the like of which I never saw in the World War', wrote Felber. 'It wasn't so much the dead – most of them had already been buried – but the vast quantity of equipment scattered around.'[53]

At its height the Battle of the Bzura (Johannes Blaskowitz preferred the 'Battle of Lodz' but was overruled) had drawn in nearly half a million men – nine Polish infantry divisions and nineteen German divisions, including five armoured and light formations. It was, Hans Felber observed, 'the first great battle of this war'. He added rather smugly in his diary: 'Experts around the world will realise the importance of this battle.' Experts around the world would also realise, however, that Eighth Army had been lucky. 'The miracle on the Vistula which the Poles so ardently longed for was tangibly close,' *Oberst* Erwin Jaenecke, Eighth Army's operations officer conceded in a moment of rare candour. Had the Poles co-ordinated their efforts, struck with all their might at a decisive point, they would have sliced through Eighth Army's flank and into the rear of Tenth Army. 'The Poles,' commented Jaenecke, 'did not know how to make use of their moment and so met their fate.'[54]

With hindsight, Tadeusz Kutrzeba agreed. He saw the battle on the Bzura as a lost opportunity, a battle which, he later wrote, 'could have been won by us, or at any rate ought not to have been lost so bloodily'. Instead, a thoroughly demoralised Kutrzeba wearily entered Warsaw on 20 September and was immediately taken to the headquarters of the city's commandant, Juliusz Rommel. The general's physical and mental state shook Rommel; standing before him was a man who was 'utterly wrecked and who had lost self-control'. Rommel said nothing, encouraging his guest to speak. 'I have lost a battle,' Kutrzeba said bluntly.[55]

In Lodz, fresh orders were handed to Hans Felber. The next day, 23 September, Eighth Army would begin redeploying to the east. It had a new mission. The *Geballere* – bashing – of Warsaw. 'I wouldn't like to swap places with its inhabitants,' the Chief-of-Staff confided in his diary. 'It's not a pleasant task for a soldier. But it must be done, if only as a matter of prestige.'[56]

Notes

1. Breithaupt, *Die Geschichte der 30 Infanterie-Division, 1939–1945*, pp. 20–2.
2. Elble, pp. 101–2.
3. Drescher, pp. 531–1, Elble, pp. 100, 108–9, 111–12.
4. BA-MA RH24-10/554 Tagebuchaufzeichnungen über den Feldzug in Polen beim X Korps, von Hauptmann Kretzschmar.
5. Breithaupt, *Die Geschichte der 30 Infanterie-Division, 1939–1945*, pp. 24–5 and *'Seit heute wird zurückgeschossen...' Der Polenfeldzug der 8 Armee* in BA-MA RH20-8/40.
6. Breithaupt, *Die Geschichte der 30 Infanterie-Division, 1939–1945*, pp. 30–1 and Vormann, p. 123.
7. Elble, pp. 131–2.
8. Kinder, p. 28.
9. General Wladyslaw Bortnowski, *Na tropach wrzesnia 1939*, (Following the Tracks of September 1939) Lodz, 1969, p. 209. Cited in Elble, p. 133 and Kinder, p. 30.
10. Breloer, pp. 36–7.
11. Weichs, *Erinnerungen*, Band 3, p. 18 in BA-MA N19/7 and 'Die Armee Blaskowitz in Polenfeldzug' von Oberst Jaenecke in BA-MA RH20-8/46.
12. 'Der 20 (Regensburger) Infanterie Regiment in Polenfeldzug' in BA-MA RH37/6385.
13. KTB Felber, 11/9/39 and 20/9/39 in BA-MA RH20-8/1 and KTB AOK8, 10/9/39 in Elble, p. 140.

14. Stieff letter, 21/8/32. Stieff, p. 71; Macksey, p. 73; Giziowski, *The Enigma of General Blaskowitz, passim.*

15. Breithaupt, *Die Geschichte der 30 Infanterie-Division, 1939–1945*, p. 32 and KTB AOK 8, 11/9/39, cited in Elble, p. 142.

16. KTB AOK8, 11/9/39. Cited in Elble, p. 142.

17. Order of the Day, 11/9/39. Cited in Elble, p. 155.

18. Breloer, p. 39.

19. Elble, pp. 153, 155.

20. Buchner, *Der Polenfeldzug 1939*, pp. 106–7.

21. Breloer, p. 39.

22. Elble, pp. 159–61. Marshal Smigly-Rydz reached the same conclusion twenty-four hours earlier, but had been unable to inform Kutrzeba of his plan..

23. To Keitel, the Führer was even more fulsome with his praise. 'You can't have enough soldiers like him. He's a man after my own heart. He saved Blaskowitz's army by his gallantry and drive.' See Keitel, p. 95.

24. Hitler's visit to Eighth Army is based on Hans Felber's diary entries of 13/9/39 and 20/9/39 in BA-MA RH20-8/1, Eighth Army's diary in BA-MA RH20-8/11, Vormann, pp. 120–4 and Heusinger, pp. 63–5.

25. OKH/GenStdH/Truppenamt, H10-3/93, 14/9/39 in Elble, p. 181, KTB Felber, 15/9/39 and 16/9/39 in BA-MA RH20-8/1 and KTB AOK8, 14/9/39 in BA-MA RH20-8/11.

26. Kutrzeba Order of the Day, 15/9/39. Elble, pp. 182–3.

27. Elble, pp. 181–2.

28. *Leutnant* Arnold Schöneboom, 'Bzura, the Baptism of Fire of our Home Regiment' in the author's papers. Schöneboom was killed in Holland the following spring..

29. *Oberleutnant* Riessner, 'Infanterie voran!' in *Mit dem XIII Armeekorps in Polen*, pp. 22–4.

30. Kielmansegg, pp. 61–3.

31. Meyer, *Grenadiere*, p. 13.

32. Supf, p. 58 and Oberkommando der Wehrmacht (ed), *Der Sieg in Polen*, p. 127.

33. Strohmeyer, pp. 26–7.

34. *Oberleutnant* Riessner, 'Infanterie voran!' in *Mit dem XIII Armeekorps in Polen*, pp. 22–4.

35. Kielmansegg, pp. 63–6.

36. Kielmannsegg, pp. 67–8.

37. BA-MA RH37/7535.

38. *Oberleutnant* Riessner, 'Infanterie voran!' in *Mit dem XIII Armeekorps in Polen*, p. 24.

39. Breithaupt, *Die Geschichte der 30 Infanterie-Division, 1939–1945*, p. 34.

40. Major Engelke, '16 Infanterie Regiment forces the Bzura on September 16th' in author's papers.

41. *Oberleutnant* Riessner, 'Infanterie voran!' in *Mit dem XIII Armeekorps in Polen*, p. 24.

42. Buchner, *Der Polenfeldzug 1939*, p. 116.

43. Reibig, p. 78 and Buchner, *Der Polenfeldzug 1939*, pp. 118–19.

44. Elble, p. 192, Buchner, *Der Polenfeldzug 1939*, pp. 119–20 and Paul, *Brennpunkte*, pp. 42–3.

45. 'Der 20 (Regensburger) Infanterie Regiment in Polenfeldzug' in BA-MA RH37/6385 and Lucas, *Kampfgruppe*, pp. 23–4.

46. Schmidt, *Die Geschichte der 10 Infanterie Division,,* pp. 45–6.

47. Neumann, *Die 4 Panzer Division 1938–1943*, p. 80.

48. Tagesbefehl, AOK 8, 19/9/39 in BA-MA RH20-8/2 Armeebefehle AOK 8, 1/9/39–12/10/39.
49. KTB Felber, 16/9/39 and 20/9/39 in BA-MA RH20-8/1, OKW Communiqué, 20/9/39 and Elble, pp. 199–201.
50. KTB Hauptmann Kretzschmar, 20/9/39 in BA-MA RH24-10/554 and 'Der 20 (Regensburger) Infanterie Regiment in Polenfeldzug' in BA-MA RH37/6385.
51. Kinder, pp. 44–5, KTB *Hauptmann* Kretzschmar in BA-MA RH24-10/554, *Völkischer Beobachter*, 17/9/39 and Breloer, p. 41.
52. Oberkommando der Wehrmacht (ed), *Der Sieg in Polen*, pp. 127–8 and Supf, pp. 58–60.
53. KTB Felber, 20/9/39 and 22/9/39 in BA-MA RH20-8/1.
54. KTB Felber 20/9/39 in BA-MA RH20-8/1 and Oberst Jaenecke, 'Die Armee Blaskowitz in Polenfeldzug' in BA-MA RH20-8/46.
55. Elble, p. 192 and Drescher, pp. 530–1.
56. KTB Hans Felber, 22/9/39 in BA-MA RH20-8/1.

CHAPTER SEVEN

The Lord Struck Them Down With Man, Steed and Wagon

Today we thank God from our hearts that the wish of every Danziger to be able to return to the German fold and share its destiny has been fulfilled.
– BISHOP CARL MARIA SPLETT

I can be particularly proud of my panzers; they have shown how brilliant they are and we owe our rapid and relatively bloodless successes to them.
– GENERAL HEINZ GUDERIAN

HEINZ Guderian was feeling rather pleased with himself. He had liberated his birthplace. He had liberated the Corridor. East Prussia was no longer cut off from the rest of the Reich. He enjoyed his Führer's favour. His theories of armoured warfare had been proven. And now, in the castle of *Graf* (count) Dohna-Finkenstein,[1] twenty miles east of the Vistula, he slept in the same bed as Napoleon; there were still scuff marks on the wooden floor where the Frenchman's spurs had scratched them. The count was away in Berlin; he gave the panzer general free use of his estate to hunt deer. Guderian took the count up on his offer, and bagged a large twelve-pointer.

As their general hunted deer, the men and armour of XIX Panzer Corps crossed the Lower Vistula on pontoon bridges along a thirty-mile front between Käsemark, half a dozen miles from its estuary, to Mewe. For three days the armour of 3rd Panzer Division rolled eastwards in glorious sunshine past the Tannenberg Memorial, through Allenstein, then sixty miles further east to the exercise grounds at Arys (today Orzysz) in the heart of the Masurian Lakes. It was a march of nearly 250 miles 'but no-one minds the exertions,' the division's chronicler wrote. 'Our reception in the villages is indescribable.' Boys and girls rushed up to the vehicles, covered them with flowers and crowded around the soldiers. Their parents handed the passing panzer men newspapers, hot coffee, chocolate, cigarettes, fruit. 'We are welcomed with incredible joy,' wrote artilleryman Emil Falckenthal. 'We are, of course, the victors of the Corridor.' In Arys 3rd Panzer and the rest of Guderian's corps halted, awaiting further employment.[2]

The panzers moved again in the small hours of the ninth to strike southeastwards in the land between the Narev and the Bug towards the fortress city of Brest-Litovsk, a hundred or so miles away. The advance was no less rapid – and no less brutal – than it had been in the Corridor a week before. After a faltering start crossing the Narev, Guderian's armour and motorised divisions sliced through inconsistent Polish resistance. They passed sprawling woods, swamps, heaths, bleak plains which stretched eastwards, and kicked up huge clouds of dust on the sandy lanes. There were few farmhouses, fewer wells and the field kitchens struggled to keep pace with the armoured spearheads. The men called it the *Durststrecke* – the road of thirst. Otherwise, the scenes and experiences on the road to Brest were almost identical to those in the Corridor, gunner Emil Falckenthal observed. Ruined towns, Polish dead, Polish refugees. In Zambrow, seventy miles northeast of Warsaw, the artilleryman raced past 'endless columns of refugees' pushing their possessions on small *panje* carts. 'It's a scene of misery, a scene of the most bitter need,' wrote Falckenthal. Twenty miles further down the road to Brest, Falckenthal and his comrades approached Wysockie Mazowieckie. 'The silhouette of a town emerges from the clouds of dust,' Falckenthal recorded, then corrected himself: 'No, the ruins of a town. There's not a single house standing, just chimneys towering into the heavens like silent witnesses. People wander around in the smoking, smouldering ruins, poking at the embers with long sticks, looking for anything.' The Poles had offered resistance here twenty-four hours before – the Germans claimed they had been set upon by the town's inhabitants. Wysockie Mazowieckie was set on fire. Only the church, the sole building made of stone, was unharmed.[3] 3rd Panzer Division quickly forgot about the rubble of Wysockie Mazowieckie and sped to the southeast in the direction of Brest.

War was still a novelty in Danzig, still a spectacle. Curious Danzigers wandered down to the Heveliusplatz to see the scars of battle for themselves. The front of the post office had been torn away – the rooms in the front of the building were exposed to the elements. Every window was shattered, the shutters hanging limply from their fittings. The pavement and walls around the square were pockmarked where bullets had struck them just a couple of days earlier. But now the city was safe; *keine Gefähr für Danzig* – no more threat to Danzig, the *Danziger Vorposten* promised. And more importantly, Danzig was German once more. 'Today we thank God from our hearts that the wish of every Danziger to be able to return to the German fold and share its destiny has been fulfilled,' the Bishop of Danzig, Carl Maria Splett, declared at his first pastoral since 'liberation'. 'At this historically-important and fateful hour we do not want to forget to thank the Almighty and ask him to give his blessing for the future, Führer, *Volk* and Fatherland.' In a few days trains would be running again across the Vistula – the bridge at Dirschau, eighteen miles south of the city had been destroyed. And then, for the first time in two decades, the city's inhabitants would be able to travel to Stolp and Stettin in West Prussia without the need for visas or passports.[4]

For all the celebrations in Danzig, for all the joy that it had now *Heim ins Reich* – come home to the Reich – war was rather closer to the city than the Nazi leadership would like to admit. Danzig itself was in German hands. So too the Westerplatte, finally. But barely ten miles from the heart of Danzig, just north of the resort of Zoppot, the Reich ended and Poland resumed. For in the woods and marshes between the port of Gdynia and the northern Baltic coast, a mish-mash of Polish troops – militia, marines, a few artillerymen – still held out. Gdynia was the heart of the Polish resistance. Once a mere fishing village, in less than two decades it had grown into a thriving port whose trade outstripped Danzig. To the north of this unattractive concrete city lay marshland, the Oxhöfter Kämpe, whose boggy terrain in places turned into slimy, shallow lakes.

For nearly a week, aged Luftwaffe general Leonhard Kaupisch had mustered a less-than-impressive assault force of SS militia – the *Heimwehr Danzig* – a recently-raised infantry division, police troops and border guards to crush the 18,000 or so Polish troops stubbornly holding on at Gdynia. On 8 September, Kaupisch unleashed his assault. Over the next four days, Kaupisch's corps battered its way through the forests and marshes. The Poles had evidently opened sluice gates or blocked several streams, for the Kämpe had seemingly become little more than one large lake, dissected by a handful of cobbled paths. Each night, SS *Heimwehr* trooper Georg Diehl took a motorcycle into Danzig to a command post. The city's residents waited impatiently outside the headquarters, eager for the latest news from the front. Grateful for the *Heimwehr*'s sacrifices, Danzigers stuffed Diehl's overcoat with sweets and cigarettes to take back to his platoon.

At times Diehl and his comrades waded through chest-high water. It was hardly surprising progress was slow. When the Poles counter-attacked on the twelfth, men in the 207th Infantry Division panicked and fled. But the defenders of Gdynia could not hold out indefinitely. Their front had shrunk considerably during the battle; it now wended for twenty miles from Gdynia in the south to the northern edge of the Kämpe. With the pocket shrinking, the defenders began to evacuate just a dozen miles across the Bay of Danzig to the Hela peninsula, where Polish naval forces continued to resist.

As the Poles pulled out of Gdynia, German troops moved in. At dawn on the fifteenth, they reached the heart of the port and stood in front of the city hall, a drab building surrounding by protective sandbags. A *Propaganda Kompanie* reporter found a week-old appeal to the city's inhabitants posted on a wall. 'We will defend Gdynia to our dying breath,' it proclaimed. 'A new chapter in the history of Gdynia is being written. We will defend Gdynia with our last soldier until ultimate victory. I call on all Poles to stand up to the enemy with the Army if necessary. Each home must become a fortress.' But the port, the journalist quickly realised, was defenceless. It fell into the conquerors' hands largely intact. There was no wholesale destruction of the harbour and its installations – the cranes still worked, there were mountains of coal and other supplies lying about. Gdynia's inhabitants were terrified, convinced anything which fell from a German bomber had been poisoned. Their defenders who had vowed to defend Gdynia to the last man had vanished, some to Hela, some into the marshes of the Oxhöfter Kämpe, others still threw away their uniforms and mingled with the civilian populace.

That evening Georg Diehl and his comrades sat by the waterfront in Gdynia, looking east a dozen miles to the tip of the Hela peninsula. The *Schleswig-Holstein* had been joined by her sister *Schlesien*. The guns of the two aged battleship pounded Hela incessantly. And from afar, Diehl and his friends watched. It was, he thought, like going to the cinema.[5]

The Muchaviec is a pleasant if non-descript river which meanders westwards through the central European heartland to its rendezvous with the River Bug, one of the continent's great arteries. And as it nears the Bug, the Muchaviec splits into two channels which flow past a small island, before the waters of the two rivers merge. Here, 900 years before, Slavs had settled the town of Berestye. Nine centuries later, grain, flax, tar and wood were shipped west from Brest-Litovsk, as it now was, to Danzig first via the Bug, then the Vistula. But trade was not why Brest-Litovsk was renowned. For on the small island surrounded by the arms of the Muchaviec, the Russians had built a central fortress, a citadel, protected by huge outer ramparts on three fronts and a ring of a dozen outer forts. Warfare had moved on since Fortress Brest was conceived and built, but it remained a formidable obstacle.

It was also a valued prize. Not, perhaps, as valued as Warsaw, but valued nonetheless.

Herinz Guderian's foremost armour reached Brest after dark on the fourteenth, boldly proclaiming the city captured (it was not) and reporting that a *coup de main* against the citadel had failed (it had). Before dawn the next morning the assault was resumed. 'Today will see the decision in Brest,' the corps' diarist recorded confidently. The day began promisingly. The forts north of the Bug fell to the panzers after token resistance. So too did Brest's railway station and its railway junction. But the citadel obstinately refused to capitulate. Under the cover of ferocious artillery fire, 69th Infantry Regiment fought its way as far as the ramparts. It was here that the assault began to falter. Tall trees in front of the walls prevented German gunners from directing their fire at the defenders who, in turn, poured fire on the *Landsers* below. Two field guns were brought up to eliminate Polish snipers in the trees, but with little effect. Exhausted, covered in sweat, their faces filthy, the attackers fell back, leaving their dead and wounded behind. Only when night fell did the men of the 69th return to recover their comrades.[6]

Ever impetuous and angered by the failings, Heinz Guderian determined he would direct the assault on Brest in person when it was renewed on the sixteenth. He expected to see his men storm the citadel. As the panzer General waited impatiently in the command post of 20th Motorised Infantry Division, a young medic, one Dr Frahm, was sheltering behind a railway embankment with his company. 'It's a beautiful autumn morning,' Dr Frahm mused as he stared at the thick clouds of smoke hanging over the citadel, obscuring the sky. And then the guns roared. Every one of Guderian's artillery pieces was directed at the ramparts of fortress Brest for the next half hour. 'There's a deafening sound,' Frahm recorded in his diary. 'Right over our heads shells howl over and land beyond the embankment with a loud crash.' The infantrymen and pioneers waited. The guns paused briefly, then laid down five three-minute barrages from every one of the 160 barrels trained on the citadel – a cannonade on a scale Guderian's men had not seen on their march across Poland. The *Oberleutnant* leading the attack checked his watch, placed a whistle in his mouth and blew. The men dashed to the top of the embankment, leapt across railway tracks, then down the opposite side of the bank. They expected a hail of enemy fire.

Nothing. Only a large peaceful park lay in front of them, plus an iron fence to suggest they were closing on the fortress. Kit, bags, stretchers were tossed over the obstacle, followed by the attackers who scrambled over to find themselves in dense undergrowth. There was the hiss of rifle fire from a few long sheds. A few hand grenades later and the shooting stopped. The men continued, out of the undergrowth, through a cabbage patch. Beyond it, more undergrowth, and beyond that, the citadel.

All this was observed by Heinz Guderian. But the panzer commander was not satisfied with the progress. After two and a half hours, he had seen enough; he left the command post and drove directly to the front line. *He* would lead the attack. And it would succeed.

Slowly, the assault gained ground. The fort itself was protected by an outer rampart – already abandoned by the Poles – and a moat, filled with by now black water. Under sporadic, poorly-directed enemy fire, pioneers dragged two inflatable boats to the moat's edge – the rest had been shot-up – then struck out across the muddy water, while flak and field guns were turned against the opposite bank to keep the defenders at bay. Frahm watched the attackers storm ashore:

> The pioneers demonstrate heroic courage storming past a trench, tossing explosive charges into the embrasures as they do, then they climb swiftly up the steep slope of the inner rampart with cat-like agility as the Poles flee in wild panic. They stand at the top, breathless, and finally the broad courtyard of the citadel lies before them with the defenders fleeing across in it; they shoot at will, still standing, and then occupy their foxholes. But they cannot stay here. The Poles press against their flank from an uncaptured part of the rampart and try to bring up a gun. One enemy gun crew after the other is knocked out with the light machine-gun, but fresh olive-green figures always emerge from the casemate forced out by their officers at gun-point. In the end, when the pioneers have fired their last round and used up all their hand grenades, they must fall back. As they pass the trench cleared out earlier, they encounter withering fire: the enemy has re-occupied it using a secret passage. A large number of heroes fall here, their hot weapons grasped by hands growing cold.

Pioneer *Leutnant* Hemmich decided to commit his last reserves. A local White Russian – no friend of the Poles – had guided the officer to a relatively undefended approach to the citadel. The morning's assault had decimated Hemmich's men; all he had left now was a handful of pioneers, a flamethrower and a single rubber boat. Before the pioneers could thrust the boat into the water of the moat it was shot-up by Polish fire. The man carrying the flamethrower threw himself down at the *Leutnant*'s side, fuel pouring from the shattered tank. 'Even though there was only a narrow moat separating us from our objective, we were forced to stop,' the officer regretted. All along the line, the assault on the fortress was faltering. 'Ammunition runs out, one machine-gun after another falls silent, flares requesting help hiss skywards,' Dr Frahm observed. Help came in the shape of the German artillery which laid accurate, destructive fire upon the Poles stopping the defenders in their tracks. The attackers, too, cowered under this barrage. The young Frahm lay in the dirt alongside a gravely-wounded comrade. 'He seemed to be dead, but with each tremendous crash a shudder went through him,' the doctor observed, 'and he opened his eyes for a final, questioning look.'

The sense of failure experienced by the attackers at Brest was not shared by the ranks of 3rd Panzer Division to the city's east. It was racing down the monotonous, grey Bug valley, bound for the town of Wlodawa, twenty-five miles to the south, intent on sealing off an escape route for the fortress' defenders. Few Poles showed their faces, civilians or soldiers, apart from the odd armoured car and retreating enemy columns – quickly shot up. The advance was intoxicating. The panzers roared along at speeds touching 30mph, smashing down telegraph lines in the process paralysing Polish communications. As the sun set that Saturday, German armour rolled into the small town of Tomaszowka, a couple of miles east of their objective. The road between Brest and Tomaszowka was littered with burning villages, abandoned trucks, and scattered Polish columns.

One hundred or so miles to the southeast of Brest, schoolboy Wladyslaw Jacinski had been watching frenetic activity at the railway station in the Polish-Ukrainian border town of Budki Snowidowicze since mid-day. The station lay little more than half a mile away from the fourteen-year-old student's home, just inside Soviet territory. Horses and material had been unloaded all day and long into the night. Odd, thought Wladyslaw, the station has been disused for twenty years.[7]

In Brest, the pioneers received orders to fall back. The young surgeon Frahm was covered in blood and dirt from tip to toe. He had lost count of the men he had treated – it was probably forty. Nearly two-dozen pioneers had fallen in the bloody, fruitless assault. Heinz Guderian was also downcast. The attacks on Brest had miscarried. His adjutant had been mortally wounded by a sniper. The fortress, Guderian recorded in his diary, would not fall without more troops being brought up.

There was no question of falling back for 3rd Panzer Division. They were determined to prevent any Polish troops fleeing south of Brest. A single thought filled each man: if there's petrol in the tank, then we continue southwards. The roads worsened, a pitch black autumn night enveloped the land. The motorcyclists accompanying the tanks abandoned their journey. The panzers alone rattled onwards.[8]

The sound of the telephone's shrill ringing echoed around the ante-room of the Polish Ambassador, Waclaw Grzybowski, in Moscow. Grzybowski spoke briefly then replaced the receiver. He had been summoned to the Foreign Ministry by Vladimir Potemkin, deputy foreign minister, 'on a very important and urgent matter'. Grzybowski was perturbed. It was three minutes to midnight; the Soviet Foreign Ministry *never* worked at this hour.

An hour later the ambassador returned, his fears realised. In a frosty exchange, Potemkin declared that the Polish Government and the Commander-in-Chief had 'skedaddled' to Romania. Grzybowski protested; a diplomat would not use the word 'skedaddled'. Potemkin rasped. There was no longer a Polish Government, so there were no longer any Polish diplomats, merely Poles living in the Soviet Union. The war, the deputy foreign minister went on, had revealed 'the internal bankruptcy of the Polish state'; Poland was disintegrating, its ethnic groups were in danger. The Soviet Union had to protect Ukrainians and White Russians on Polish soil. At 4am the Red Army would march across the border. But there was a non-aggression pact between the two nations, the ambassador argued. No, Potemkin countered icily, 'If there's no longer a government in Poland, then there's no longer a non-aggression pact.'

Foreign Minister Vyacheslav Molotov had been too busy to receive Grzybowski in person. He had been in the presence of his leader and the German ambassador in Moscow, *Freiherr* Werner von Schulenburg. Barely eight hours earlier, Schulenberg had been in Molotov's presence and treated to a *tour d'horizon* by the foreign minister. Ukrainian and Russian minorities in Poland were in danger. The Polish state had collapsed. An unscrupulous nation might try to take advantage of the chaos. The Soviet Union, the Foreign Minister declared, had to intervene. Imminently. 'Perhaps even tomorrow or the day after.' Now, as Molotov looked on, Josef Stalin repeated these same arguments to the German aristocrat. The Red Army would move at 6am – four hours' hence. It was the Soviet Union's 'sacred duty to proffer help to its Ukrainian and Belorussian brothers in Poland.'[9]

The telephone in Eberhard Kinzel's office jangled. It was long before dawn on Sunday, 17 September, and the head of the German Army's intelligence arm dealing with Russia was still groggy as he picked up the receiver. The voice on the other end was weary too. Ernst Köstring had been up all night, struggling to penetrate the impenetrable wall of secrecy enveloping the Kremlin. Köstring, Germany's military attaché in Moscow, had learned little beyond what his ambassador had told him in the small hours: the Red Army would move into Poland at 6am. 'The Russians are on the move,' Köstring curtly informed Kinzel. The news woke the sleepy officer in a flash. 'Against whom?' he demanded in an instant.[10]

In Soviet Sixth Army's forward command post east of the Polish city of Tarnopol, staff officer Sergei Shtemenko waited. 'The atmosphere was tense,' the officer recalled, 'as on the eve of any great event.' The phones rang intermittently all night long, messengers arrived and departed bearing reports. 'And yet,' Shtemenko recalled, 'time seemed to crawl with unspeakable slowness.'[11]

A few minutes before dawn on the seventeenth, the Red Army crossed the Polish frontier along its entire length from the Baltic States to the Carpathian mountains. Some border guards offered resistance, others were bemused. The white flag fluttered on vehicles coming from the east, while Russian soldiers cried out: 'Don't shoot – we've come to help you against the Germans.' The official Soviet organ *Pravda* painted an idyllic picture of the invasion. 'The hatch of a tank will open and our Soviet lads will leap out, laughing and singing songs.' One report fed to Stalin claimed the Red Army was being hailed 'like true liberators'. Ethnic Ukrainians came out of their homes to offer 'apples, pies, drinking water' to the passing Soviet soldiers. In numerous villages, the populace flocked into the streets to meet the 'liberators'. 'Many,' the report concluded, 'weep with joy.' But elsewhere, discipline in some Red Army units disintegrated as they crossed the border; troops dashed into Polish shops and came out with watches, shirts, shoes, anything their paltry wages could buy.[12]

The night at Brest had been terrible. The 'wild, pointless shooting' never ceased, *Leutnant* Hemmich recalled. As Sunday dawned, the pioneer decided to help some wounded comrades across no man's land to a first-aid post. The wild pointless shooting continued – but only from the German side. Hemmich grabbed an *Unteroffizier* and dashed up to the walls of the citadel, then scaled them. At about the same time troops from 76th Infantry Regiment swept over the River Bug, across the sole bridge still standing which led to the citadel of Brest-Litovsk and seized the fortress. All night long the remnants of the garrison had been preparing to break out and flee westwards as the German infantry stormed in; some had already fled, dressed in civilian clothes. Now the German Army surveyed its prize. It realised why Brest had defended itself so stubbornly. Behind walls and ramparts, the Poles had buried several old tanks so that only their turrets stuck out from the soil; they had proved almost impossible to hit. But elsewhere in the citadel, 'there was a terrible scene of destruction,' one *Oberstleutnant* recalled. 'Our artillery had caused widespread devastation.' Encirclement and two days of constant shelling had broken the defenders' spirits. Now eight officers, 1,380 men and one Jewish woman in soldier's uniform surrender. Also seized were a couple of dozen field guns, seven tanks, and 1,200 rifles, plus food and ammunition. That night, a delighted Guderian wrote home to his wife:

> I can be particularly proud of my panzers; they have shown how brilliant they are and we owe our rapid and relatively bloodless successes to them. Gross Born to Brest-Litovsk in seventeen days! I haven't yet calculated how many hundred kilometres that is, but it's a lot.[13]

Anxious faces appeared at the morning conference aboard Adolf Hitler's command train. News of the secret deal struck with Stalin to divide Poland came as a surprise to the Reich's military leaders. The new frontier between Germany and Russia, Foreign Minister von Ribbentrop explained, would follow the Pissa, Narew, Vistula and San rivers. Jaws dropped. But in many cases the German Army was far to the east of such a line, 125 miles further east, protested Alfred Jodl, the senior operations officer on Hitler's staff. The troops, Jodl insisted, must halt and talks begin with the Russians as quickly as possible. The Führer turned to his foreign minister. 'Where can these discussions take place? What do you say, Ribbentrop?' Perhaps Brest-Litovsk, suggested the bumbling diplomat. 'That's madness,' Hitler snarled. 'Brest-Litovsk of all places – with all its memories of 1917 and 1918. Out of the question.'[14]

The *Landsers* of 23rd Infantry Division were marching along the main road to Bialystok accompanied by the men of the labour service, the *Reichsarbeitsdienst*. The division's supply officer watched as a Soviet aircraft flew up and down the column, then suddenly unleashed its bombs, convinced the *Reichsarbeitsdienst* in their brown uniforms were really Poles. Numerous labour service men and soldiers were killed and wounded. Shortly afterwards, the division's staff began distributing leaflets among the troops, a 'formal greeting' in Russian and German, from the Wehrmacht to the Red Army. 'As soldiers we wish to have good soldierly relations with the soldiers of the Soviet Union,' said the greeting. 'We have always held the Russian soldier in high regard.'[15]

In the insignificant Carpathian town of Kuty, 120 miles southeast of Lemberg, a terse message was handed to President Ignacy Moscicki: the mayor of Sniatyn, less than two dozen miles away, reported Soviet tanks rolling through the streets of his town. It was time for the Polish Government to abandon sacred soil. Overtaken by events from the moment the Germans struck, the Polish Government had led a fruitless nomadic existence for a fortnight. Smigly-Rydz and his high command had fled first to Brest-Litovsk, then eventually to Kolomyja, ninety miles south of Lemberg on the edge of the Carpathians. The civilian vestiges of government displaced first to the small town of Naleczow, near Lublin, thence 200 miles to the southeast to Krzemieniec. They were bombed repeatedly on the journey, and again in Krzemieniec itself. As the Wehrmacht sliced through Galicia, the government moved yet again to Zaleszczyki and finally to the border town of Kuty where the River Czeremosz separated Poland from Romania. And there, at 4pm on Sunday, 17 September, the government of the Polish Republic met for the final time and resolved to seek refuge across the border and continue the struggle from abroad. A car bearing Moscicki joined the columns of refugees on foot, cart and vehicle struggling across the Czeremosz. Edward Smigly-Rydz was not far behind him. Polish soldiers seeking sanctuary with the leaders were forced to surrender their weapons to the beleaguered Romanian customs officials. Most chose to toss their guns into the river. The waters of the Czeremosz now forced their way past mountains of rifles, revolvers and machine-guns. In Warsaw, the recriminations began almost immediately. Just a few weeks before the mob in Warsaw had been baying for German blood. 'Lead us to Berlin!' the people screamed. But now the cries of *Do Berlina* – On to Berlin – had died. 'The blood of the masses is boiling,' Jewish teacher Chaim Kaplan observed. 'Everyone is full of rebellion and bitterness, prepared to tear the nation's leaders to pieces.' Pianist Wladyslaw Szpilman bitterly recalled Edward Smigly-Rydz bombastic declaration that he would not let the invader touch a single button on his uniform. 'And nor did he,' Szpilman commented acidly, 'but only because the buttons remained attached to his uniform when he saved himself by escaping abroad.'[16]

The scenes at Kuty were repeated in small towns and villages in the Carpathian foothills as the Polish people sought to escape the invader, be he Russian or German. It was a moment when every Pole realised the magnitude of his country's defeat. People grabbed at the soil, or rocks, or flowers by the roadside, a final reminder of the motherland. They kissed the white-red barrier at the border posts. They fell to their knees in prayer. 'We all had tears in our eyes,' recalled one airman. 'It was a horrible moment.'

What was left of the *Polskie Lotnictwo Wojskowe* rumbled overhead, heading to internment at Romanian airfields in Cernauti and Focsani. The Polish Air Force may have been outdated and outnumbered, but its men had fought bravely and its aircraft had, on occasions, wrought havoc, especially against unescorted German bombers. On 2 September one Polish regiment shot down nine out of a flight of sixteen Do17 bombers without loss, and the fighter brigade defending Warsaw accounted for forty-three Luftwaffe aircraft in the first seven days of the campaign; it paid a high price for its success, however – thirty-eight of its own planes out of action, two pilots dead, two more missing and seventeen wounded. It was the loss of aircraft which was particularly hard to bear; the Polish Air Force had no reserves to draw upon. By 6 September half its fighters were either downed or no longer serviceable. 'Before the war and during its first days we were blindly keen to fight and win,' one pilot based near Warsaw complained. 'After a few days we began to realise that something was badly wrong.'[17]

By 12 September, Hermann Göring was proudly telling his Führer that the battle in the skies was won. 'The Polish Air Force has disappeared from the skies, totally destroyed,' he declared. As ever with the corpulent Luftwaffe Commander-in-Chief it was a boast, and a premature one. But the Polish airman could see that the writing was on the wall. 'A new fighter tactic was being born, together with new methods of combat, which would be put to good use in battle one day, but not over Poland,' one pilot conceded. 'We were the first cadre of fighter pilots to feel the huge might of the modern German Air Force on our necks. Being in the front rank we gained experience at a bloody cost, and we were the first to draw conclusions from it. Gloomy conclusions they were.' By the middle of the month, the *Polskie Lotnictwo Wojskowe* was down to half its front-line strength. 'The supply situation became hopeless,' one Polish airman recalled. 'Aircraft lay around useless in ever greater numbers. There were no more spare parts. Only individual bombers could still carry out attacks.' Perhaps 100 combat aircraft flew across the Romanian border into internment. Three out of every four Polish aircraft which took to the skies in September 1939 had been shot down. The Polish Air Force had been beaten; its pilots, however, would live to fight the Luftwaffe on another occasion.[18]

In the hilly, undulating and frequently wooded terrain between the Bug and Vistula valleys one hundred or so miles southwest of Brest, three German infantry corps were marching eastwards. The Polish Army before them was disintegrating. The battered entrails of three Polish armies were struggling to regroup. Rather than concentrating they were dispersing, breaking up into small groups. They had to be trapped and wiped out.

The heat of the first days of the campaign had been replaced by heavy rain in the day and bitterly cold nights. 'Every inch of my body was shaking with the cold,' Wilhelm Prüller complained. 'There is no more sun during the day – we have to keep our coats on during the day.' Friend and foe alike was exhausted, but the enemy wouldn't surrender, Prüller noted in his diary. Why didn't he? 'The Poles are completely encircled and there's no way out for them. They should surrender for there's no point in their going on with it.'[19]

But go on with it the Poles did. After dark on the nineteenth, they renewed their efforts to escape encirclement. 'A flaming circle of burning villages blazes away under the firmament,' VII Corps' chronicler wrote vividly. 'Flashes from the muzzles flare up through the night.' The defenders brought up heavy machine-guns, mortars, field and anti-tank guns. The Poles fought valiantly, but the line held, while the *Landsers* surveyed the landscape. 'The blazing torches of the burning villages, which flicker and send flames licking skywards, create a beautiful but eerie image.'

One breakout attempt was thus averted in the dead of night, but news soon reached the men that a handful of miles to the south the woods were swarming with Polish soldiers; the *Army of Krakow* was making one last push to smash through the German encirclement. Each *Landser* grabbed as much equipment and ammunition as he could carry and set off for the forest around Tomaszow Lubelski, 110 miles south of Brest, struggling over the marshy ground, crisscrossed with ditches and scrubland.

The Bavarians of 27th Infantry Division led the charge to blunt the Polish breakout, beginning their attack in farmland north of Tomaszow. The Poles dug in behind haystacks in a potato field. Shells started to crash down on the hard earth with a loud thud. Clouds of dust and smoke were thrown up, drifting across the field. German mortars joined in the hellish symphony. The haystacks were set ablaze. A company of men in olive-green uniforms emerged, their hands raised.

It was the signal for the men of the 27th to advance. They were quickly halted as Polish artillery, machine-guns and mortars fought back. The Poles, however, could not take advantage; they were exhausted. Encircled, out of fuel and out of ammunition, Tadeusz Piskor, Commander of the *Army of Lublin*, decided it was time to bring an end to the battle. German radio operators soon picked up a signal: 'Polish military command here. The commander says that he is ready to lay down his arms. If you can hear me, reply on the same frequency!' *Generalleutnant* Friedrich Bergmann, a bald, gruff character with a jowl seemingly chiselled into his harsh face, accepted the offer. 27th Infantry Division's Commanding Officer responded: 'To the Polish command: Surrender of Tomaszow accepted. Show white flags! Step unarmed on to the Tomaszow-Tarnawatka road! German divisional command.' The forests around Tomaszow swarmed with Poles once more, except this time they emerged from the woods to lay down their arms.[20]

This was not the last act in the fields and woods around Tomaszow Lubelski either for the Poles or 27th Infantry Division.

It took three days for Leonhard Kaupisch's men to sweep through the copses and marshland of Oxhöfter Kämpe and round up the last defenders of Gdynia. By early evening on the nineteenth, Kaupisch's troops stood by the shore of the Baltic. Enemy resistance had all but ceased. More than 12,000 Poles had been captured. The only Poles left in the Bay of Danzig now were a few hundred troops on the Hela peninsula.

Across the water in Danzig, the mood was ecstatic. The Führer was coming. *Gauleiter* Albert Forster had called on the city's female inhabitants to don festive clothes. The principal newspaper, *Danziger Neueste Nachrichten*, and German radio urged residents to dress their homes. Householders outdid each other to adorn their properties more fancifully than their neighbours. Garlands and banners were stretched across streets, lampposts and flagpoles covered with flowers. Above doorways and window frames, the eagle of the Reich. And on almost every street corner, a band. Danzig, Albert Forster declared, would 'give the Führer a reception which he has never experienced in any city'.

Hitler's cavalcade reached the edge of Danzig shortly after mid-day. From there it was a seven-mile journey to the heart of the Hanseatic city. Flowers littered the road, the pavements were lined with Danzigers two, three, four deep. 'This is the first time that Adolf Hitler has set upon *this* German soil,' gushed *Völkischer Beobachter* correspondent Gunter d'Alquen.

> Only in this historic hour could he be seen here: only as the liberator, as the victor, as the Führer of the Reich, in which Danzig also enjoys its former place, did he want to come here.
>
> The wall of people along our route becomes denser and more narrow. Men and women – the grave events which have transpired have etched deep furrows in their faces – are relaxed, liberated by a joy which is both serious and jubilant. Now with their own eyes they see the hope of the bleak years, wide awake they experience the turn of events and the gracious stride of fate, which their courage and loyalty through the years has already paved the way for.

The greatest crowds awaited the Führer in Danzig's historic heart, where one of the regime's favoured artists, Benno von Arent, had provided suitably gauche festive decorations. Crammed together, the Danzigers jostled for position, pushing, shoving, in some cases fainting.

Hitler's destination was the Artushof, a magnificent trading hall from the city's Hanseatic days. A crescendo of noise from outside told the audience of the Führer's imminent arrival. For most Danzigers, loudspeakers hastily erected in the city's streets would have to carry the Führer's words. First, however, there was a saccharine introduction from Forster. Tuesday, 19 September 1939, he declared, was 'the happiest moment in the history of this city which goes back centuries, a moment which for many years every Danziger has ardently longed for'.

As Hitler rose to the podium, the hall shook with the sound of hundreds of Party faithful, SA, veterans, Danzigers applauding, chanting. Outside, the distant thunder of *Schleswig-Holstein*'s guns, pounding Polish positions still holding out on the Hela peninsula, rattled the trading hall's windows. 'Danzig,' he told his audience, 'was German, Danzig remained German, and Danzig will be German henceforth as long as there is still a German people and a German Reich.' For more than an hour, the Führer repeated the themes he had addressed on manifold occasions. The injustice of Versailles. The brutal treatment of the *Volksdeutsche*. The antagonism of the Western Powers. And not least Polish aggression:

> Poland chose a fight – and got one. She chose to fight light-heartedly because certain leaders in the West assured her they had clear proof of the worthless

nature of the German armed forces, of its inferior equipment, of the low morale of its troops, of defeatism rife within the Reich, of the supposed divide between the German people and their Führer.

The Poles were persuaded not merely that it would be easy to resist our armies, but even that they could be thrown back.

The Poles had been proven wrong, Hitler declared, reviving a cry from the wars of liberation a century and a quarter earlier. 'Rarely in history has the following sentence been more appropriate: *Mit Mann und Ross und Wagen hat sie der Herr geschlagen* – the Lord struck them down with man, steed and wagon.' The campaign in Poland – the 'campaign of eighteen days' – was almost at an end, the Führer promised. 'What is left of the Polish Army will surrender within a few days and lay down its arms – or it will be smashed.'

After he left the Artushof, American reporter John Raleigh strolled through the streets of liberated Danzig. Tonight was a night of festivities. No blackout here; it had been lifted in celebration of the Führer's visit. Danzigers held torches and candles, waved them, stretched out their hands to give the *Hitlergruss*, the Nazi salute. 'Searchlights shone over the Marktplatz,' Raleigh wrote. 'Coloured lights played over the fountain. The bands continued to blast out military marches.' The decorated houses 'shone and glistened'. The streamers hung out earlier to celebrate Hitler's arrival now danced in the searchlight beams. 'It was the maddest, most barbaric pageant I have ever seen,' a disgusted Raleigh wrote.[21]

After his triumphal entry into Danzig, Adolf Hitler spent the next two days touring the Westerplatte and Gdynia. The latter lacked any of Danzig's charm, his entourage decided. 'The city has no character,' wrote Gunter d'Alquen. 'It has grown unlovingly, without any culture, a mighty heap of stones has been forced upwards. Tenement blocks, industrial buildings, concrete monstrosities around a wide modern harbour.' And now, observed d'Alquen, this port which had set out to strangle Danzig would be known by a new name. No longer Gdynia. Henceforth it would be a Germanic port. Gotenhafen, the harbour of the Goths.[22]

More than 300 miles to the southeast, Polish troops were struggling to fight their way through a German ring forged around the woodland and limestone hills rich with wildlife between Tomaszow Lubelski and Zamosc and to the west. The break-out efforts reached their climax late on 22 September as the weary remnants of three divisions struck out.

From high ground, the men of 27th Infantry Division watched the flash of their artillery in the distance: once, twice, five, six, seven, eight times, each time followed by a clap of thunder. It went on like this all night long. The guns lay silent for no more than half an hour; for the most part, the artillery ceased for no more than a matter of minutes.

By dawn on the twenty-third, the howitzers seemed to have halted the breakout. There was no sign of the men in olive green. 'Suddenly, amid the thunder of our artillery in the early morning there's a strange noise, a shattering roar,' VII Corps' chronicler wrote. Polish artillery was fighting back – and accurately. The shells crashed down among the infantry division's vehicles which promptly disappeared in 'impenetrable clouds of smoke and dust'. Emerging from the smoke came some undamaged wagons making a dash for safety, while riderless horses careered around wildly. The Polish fire shifted; the shells landed among thatched homes until now spared the horrors of war. 'They go up in flames like boxes of matches,' the observer recorded. The shells destroyed more than just vehicles and buildings. On the edge of one hamlet, staff officers stood around the open grave of 14 comrades. A steel hail of Polish shells landed among the mourners, laying them low.

Having weathered the storm, VII Corps struck back. The anvil became the hammer. Around 8am, 27th Infantry crossed to the offensive. It was too much for many of the Polish troops. They threw away their weapons and surrendered. 'The Russians will help us,' some told their captors. 'They are already very near!'

That evening a light rain descended upon the battlefield. In the gloom, lights flickered along the horizon. The men picked up their binoculars. The horizon was in flames as one Polish village after another burned. VII Corps' chronicler was spellbound:

> White flares, which show the positions of the other battalions, fizzle above. In between the artillery shells howl, machine-guns bellow and gun fire whooshes. We can observe the firing and impact of the guns from the heights precisely. We can see how one Polish battery after the other is silenced. A solitary, huge jet of flame shoots into the grey-black sky. An ammunition dump has been hit. Everywhere new fires flicker; no village and no house seems undamaged any more. The Poles fall back.

Fifteen hundred Polish prisoners were brought in that night. Another 6,500 officers and men were rounded up, including one General and three divisional commanders in the succeeding two or three days.[23]

Heinz Guderian did not enjoy his prize for long. News soon reached him that the fortress of Brest-Litovsk was to be abandoned to the Red Army. Preparations for the withdrawal were hurried, so hurried the panzer General complained, 'that we could not even move all our wounded or recover our damaged tanks'. The sole consolation was that the city would at least be handed over to General Semyon Krivoshein – a reserved, self-confident, well-dressed commander and, above all, a proponent of armoured warfare. The two tank men conversed in broken French, shared a meal, toasted their respective armies. And on the fresh, autumnal afternoon of 22 September, they stood side-by-side on a platform as tanks and panzers bedecked with flowers clattered through the streets of Brest. A Russian and a German band struck up tunes in turn. 'It was a scene of rare beauty as the large tanks rattled past the German musicians, engines clattering and belching small exhaust flames,' war correspondent Kurt Frowein observed; the reporter did not comment, unlike Guderian, on how poorly turned-out the Soviet troops were. The Soviet soldiers laughed, waved at their German counterparts, even gave the *Hitlergruss*. With the passing of the final panzer, Heinz Guderian gave a brief speech then ordered the swastika lowered. To the strains of the *Internationale*, a hastily-improvised Hammer and Sickle was raised on the flagpole in the sprawling square. 'For a few brief moments we stood and saluted Brest-Litovsk, won by German arms, as it was returned to its rightful owner,' Frowein wrote sycophantically.[24] With that the Wehrmacht withdrew from Brest. It was not the only city captured by German blood which was surrendered to the Red Army that September, nor the only one to demand further sacrifices in years to come.

Notes

1. Near present-day Kamieniec Suski, five miles north of Susz..
2. *Geschichte der 3 Panzer Division 1935–1945*, p. 27; Kwasny, *Panzer-Regiment 6 im Polenfeldzug 1939*, pp. 24–5; Guderian, pp. 74–5; Falckenthal, p. 38.
3. Asmus, *Die 20.Inf.Div.(mot) Chronik und Geschichte*, Band 2, p. 85 and Falckenthal, p. 43.
4. Urban, p. 296 and *Deutsche Rundschau* (Bromberg), 9/9/39.
5. Michaelis, SS *Heimwehr Danzig*, p. 37, Völkischer Beobachter, 16/9/39 and 23/9/39 and Russ, pp. 131–4.
6. KTB XIX Pz Corps, 13–15/9/39 and Asmus, *Die 20.Inf.Div.(mot) Chronik und Geschichte*, Band 2, p. 91.
7. felsztyn.tripod.com/id18.html.
8. Fighting on the Bug on September 16 is based on Guderian, *Mit dem Panzern*, pp. 62–6, *Leutnant* Nemmich, 'Der Sturm auf Zitadelle von Brest-Litowsk', in BA-MA RH12-5/240, *Geschichte der 3 Panzer Division 1935–1945*, pp. 30–2, Asmus, *Die 20.Inf.Div.(mot) Chronik und Geschichte*, Band 2, pp. 92–3 and KTB XIX PzK, 16/9/39.
9. Piekalkiewicz, pp. 171–2, Watt, Bitter Glory, p. 433, DGFP, D, viii, Docs.78 and 80 and Volkogonov, p. 358.
10. Vormann, p. 133.
11. Shtemenko, p. 19.
12. Bethell, pp. 311, 316, Volkogonov, p. 359 and Moynahan, *Claws of the Bear*, p. 84.
13. The fall of Brest-Litovsk is based on *Leutnant* Nemmich, 'Der Sturm auf Zitadelle von Brest-Litowsk', in BA-MA RH12-5/240, Guderian's letter to his wife, 17/9/39, in Bradley, *Generaloberst Heinz Guderian und die Entstehungsgeschichte des modernen Blitzkrieges*, p. 217, Vortrag von *Oberstleutnant* Friebe, 'Die 20 Div in polnischen Feldzug', 31/10/39 in BA-MA RH26-20/143 and KTB XIX PzK, 17/9/39.
14. Vormann, p. 136.
15. Paul, *Das Potsdamer Infanterie Regiment 9*, p. 150.
16. Watt, *Bitter Glory*, pp. 7–9, 435–7, Bethell, pp. 318–20, Kaplan, p. 22 and Szpilman, p. 44.
17. Zamoyski, pp. 24, 26, 32–33.
18. Vormann, p. 112, Zamoyski, pp. 29, 32, and Buchner, *Der Polenfeldzug 1939*, p. 190.
19. KTB Prüller, 19/9/39.
20. Siebte Armeekorps, *Wir zogen gegen Polen*, pp. 46–9.
21. *Völkischer Beobachter*, 20/9/39, 21/9/39 and Raleigh, pp. 83, 94.
22. *Völkischer Beobachter*, 23/9/39.
23. Siebte Armeekorps, *Wir zogen gegen Polen*, pp. 54–8.
24. Guderian, *Panzer Leader*, p. 82, Piekalkiewicz, p. 196, KTB XIX Pz Korps, 22/9/39 and Asmus, *Die 20.Inf.Div.(mot) Chronik und Geschichte*, Band 2, p. 107. Such amicable scenes were not always repeated. In one instance, Soviet cavalry charged a Wehrmacht infantry unit and left more than a dozen German dead for two of their own. KTB Wagner, 19/9/39.

CHAPTER EIGHT

The Edelweiss Becomes the Scourge of the Enemy

We have provoked this hell
In which the victor of every battle –
Death – reaps his grim harvest.

– GEFREITER HANNS PFEUFFER

BENEATH a blood-red night sky, *Oberjäger* Hans Peinitsch glanced at his map under torchlight to orient himself. A solitary German bomber ignored the bark of Polish flak and dropped five bombs on the heart of the town ahead of Peinitsch. Machine-gun bullets whipped around the mountain infantryman. Shells hurtled over his head. This, said the map, was Neu Sandez – Nowy Sacz to the Poles – a pleasant market town at the foot of the Beskids, one of the lesser mountain ranges in the Carpathians. From here the men of 2nd *Gebirgs* Division would pivot eastwards and begin the long march to the capital of Galicia 180 miles to the east: Lemberg (Lvov in Polish, today Lviv in the Ukraine). But in the first week of September 1939, Lemberg was a dream, a mirage. There could be no thought of Lemberg before the Poles had been dislodged from Neu Sandez and the heights surrounding it.

The Poles were dug in on the edge of the town. The mountain men brought up their artillery to neutralise the enemy guns. The first houses went up in flames – 'just punishment,' thought Peinitsch's comrade Bernard Alois, for an 'incited populace shooting from their homes'. Columns of smoke rose into the night sky. 'There's the dull rumble of shells firing and landing like the beating of a drum,' Peinitsch observed. 'The sky is red far and wide. Advancing troops stand out from the horizon like ghosts.' Shortly before midnight, the mountain troops reached the left bank of the Dunajec. The earlier sounds of battle had died down. Only the sporadic howling of a dog shattered the silence. The autumn moon pierced the clouds of smoke billowing above Neu Sandez. The waters of the Dunajec reflected the weak light allowing the *Gebirgsjäger* to make out the opposite bank. By dawn on the sixth the town had been encircled and captured by German forces. A bright clear September day revealed what was left of Neu Sandez – in many places just smouldering ruins. The door of the road to Lemberg was open.[1]

The men of 1st *Gebirgs* Division had been on the march for three days already. Three days through the mountains and hills of northern Slovakia – more than sixty miles in all, just to reach the Polish border. The pace once the frontier was crossed, thirty miles southeast of Neu Sandez, was no less relentless, no less forgiving. Medics were already treating the first foot sores; men with bandaged feet were expected to march at the double to catch up with their comrades. Ludwig Kübler, the division's commander, set the pace. 'Until now 1st *Gebirgs* Division has marched, indeed marched a lot,' he told his men on 8 September. 'From today and from now on it will run!' The shaven-headed commander of 1st *Gebirgs* Division was as ruthless as his official portrait suggested. The fifty-year-old Bavarian was a born soldier – 'physically strong, skilful, very persistent' his company commander had observed three decades earlier. Rarely for a senior officer, he was regularly photographed with a cigarette drooping out of his mouth. He had fought with distinction on the Western Front – where three of his five brothers fell – as a platoon leader and commander of a machine-gun detachment. But Kübler's men never warmed to him. He had little time for the worries and hardships of his troops; he simply expected them to 'die or be victorious'. As one contemporary observed, 'with him, service came before everything.'[2]

If not elite, then Ludwig Kübler's men were at the very least specialists, distinguishable from the rest of the German Army by a simple badge: the edelweiss. The *Gebirgsjäger*, or mountain infantryman, wore an edelweiss sleeve patch on the upper right arm of his traditional *feldgrau* tunic and a metal badge of the flower on his cap. He preferred a *feldgrau* woollen peaked cap, the *Bergmütze* (mountain cap) to the field caps or steel helmets worn by the rest of the German Army. But it was not uniform alone which distinguished the *Jäger* from the ordinary *Landser*. No soldier was more at one with his environment. Most, though not all, mountain infantrymen hailed from Bavaria and Austria. Their barracks were in the Alps. Their training was in the Alps – 'the school in the mountains', Ludwig Kübler called it. In short, their hearts were in the Alps. 'Out of the struggle with the forces of nature in the mountains, the soldiers' defiant harshness, bold courage and loyal comradeship develops,' wrote Kübler. It was, the general added, 'the best preparation for war.'[3]

The *Gebirgsjägers*' mission was to reach the main road winding east from Neu Sandez through Galicia then cross the San valley and make for Lemberg – 'a proud task,' one staff officer recalled, 'but a distant objective and one demanding super-human efforts'. It demanded marches of twenty-five miles a day or more along roads barely worthy of the name. 'Mountain boots and horses hoofs sink down to their ankles in the dust on the roads,' recalled *Hauptmann* Josef Remold, a regimental adjutant. Grey clouds of dust enveloped the marching mountain infantry. Rucksacks and weapon straps rubbed against the men's sweaty backs. Thirst tormented their throats. 'The joyful song of the *Jäger* has long since faded,' wrote Remold. At least the people of Galicia – ethnic Ukrainians living under Polish rule – were friendly. Convinced the advancing German troops were here to liberate them, villagers flew small flags in their national colours – blue and yellow – from their thatched roofs. Girls attached blue-yellow streamers to their blouses and men pinned the Ukrainian colours in their buttonholes. 'A different type of people lives here – you can see it, even if you only see it briefly in the faces of those coming towards you,' war correspondent Leo Leixner observed.

'Children, bright-eyed and blond, run to the side of the road as we halt our journey; they bring us flowers and fruit from the bountiful gardens – they shower us with them.' Farmer's wives rushed out with thick slabs of bread, or pressed cigarettes into the marching *Jägers'* hands. Huge pails of water were left by the wayside for man and horse. The girls provided a colourful escort for the *Gebirgs* troops through most villages. A few even cried: 'Heil Hitler!'[4]

This wasn't war. It was pursuit. 'We've been marching on Polish soil for four days and still no sight of an enemy aircraft,' one *Leutnant* observed. 'There's no sign of war. The populace has stayed behind – they continue their work or stare curiously at the countless columns of German troops.' It must have been Sunday, the tenth, the officer realised; the women and girls were dressed in their finest clothes.[5]

There were sporadic signs of fighting. The airfield at Krosno, half way between Neu Sandez and Przemysl, had been wrecked by the Luftwaffe. In the town itself a few walls were pock-marked by bullets. The buildings of Rymanov, a few miles east along the main road, were scarred too. The guns of the *Gebirgs* Division's artillery had howled briefly. Houses burned. Roof beams collapsed. A pall of acrid black smoke lingered above the town. Children cried. Women screamed. The mountain men marched onwards. The sun was merciless. Caterpillar-tracked vehicles thundered past the marching soldiers, kicking up great clouds of dust which settled on the narrow country roads ankle-deep. The men tied handkerchiefs to their faces to keep the dust at bay but it was no use. 'Our uniforms are almost white, our faces covered with dirt caused by the sweat and dust,' one artilleryman recalled. 'The sun blazes. Thirst tortures us.' The men stopped at a fountain; the water was so dirty not even the horses would drink from it. Escorted by a handful of *Landsers*, Polish prisoners were sent westwards, fear seared into their faces, convinced they would be ill-treated in German hands. After dark the column came to a halt outside the village of Besko, just east of Rymanov. The men grabbed some straw, lay down alongside their mules and slept as if they were resting in a four-poster bed. The *Gebirgs* artillerymen and *Jäger* were roused before dawn the following day. Gunfire in Besko woke them. Polish snipers were briefly engaged by mountain infantry. The German troops decided to torch the village to end the resistance.[6]

The further east the scars of war became more evident. The main road to Sambor through the San valley was littered with burned-out villages. 'Only individual chimneys and the remains of walls stare sorrowfully over the land,' one officer recalled. 'The smell of burning consumes everything.' The railway station in the village of Stefkowa, a dozen miles southeast of Sanok, had been wrecked; a smashed goods train smouldered on the broken rails. Such scenes were repeated mile after mile, hour after hour. The station in Chyrov, eighteen miles to the northeast, had been reduced to rubble. A bit further on Gradowice. Razed to the ground. A Polish farmer stared vacantly at the German troops. All he possessed now were a couple of cows. His children were overcome by curiosity; they played in the fresh craters created in the Galician earth by German bombs and shells. Further east still in Felsztyn another destroyed railway station, this time the charred remains of a Polish troop train just beyond

might'… The German Army parades before its Führer on his 50th birthday.

(Hugo Jaeger/Timepix/Time Life Pictures/Getty Images)

Danzig, the crucible of war: (*Above*) 'Danzig is a German city and wants to return to Germany'...
Gauleiter Albert Forster (third from the left) inspects Nazi Brownshirts in July 1939 and (*Below*) the
battleship *Schleswig-Holstein* opens fire at the Westerplatte.

Westerplatte burns under the weight of *Schleswig-Holstein*'s fire.

'A fire-spewing volcano'... (*Above and Below*) SS *Heimwehr Danzig* troops attack the Polish Post Office the first day of war.

...pressing, fateful scene'... Abandoned Polish guns, limbers and a dead horse in the Tucheler Heath.

'Utterly exhausted'... (*Above*) German soldiers and sailors escort Henryk Sucharski and the garriso
of the Westerplatte into captivity and (*Below*) German sailors tour the devastated peninsula.

'Terrible fire descended upon us' ... Infantry accompany a Panzer Mk II of 4th Panzer Division during the first assault on Warsaw.

'The apotheosis of devastation'... (*Above*) The detritus of the *Armies of Pomorze* and *Poznan* abandon at one of the Bzura crossings and (*Below*) 'You can be proud to have taken part in a campaign the li of which military history has never seen'... Hitler is hailed by his troops near the River San; on the left of the photograph is future Field Marshal Erwin Rommel, then head of the Führer Begleit Bataillon, the Hitler's army escort.

e quickest possible advance to Lemberg'... (*Above*) German armour rolls along a dusty Galician
d bound for the region's capital and (*Below*) 'Our mood is serious, our enthusiasm
rwhelming'... Exhausted German soldiers dig in on an embankment before Grodek, near Lemberg.

'The happiest moment in the history of this city'... (*Above*) Danzig hails its liberator and (*Below*) 'Returned to its rightful owner'... Soviet tanks roll through Brest-Litovsk during a German-Russian victory parade.

ove) 'And onward we go, the never-ending footsteps, the endless road of war'... German infantry
ches along a sandy Polish track and (*Below*) panzers churn up a dusty lane.

Putting death to the test...
(*Left and Below*) German
infantry storms forward.

'A procession of bombs falls precisely on the target'... A Ju87 Stuka drops a stick of five bombs and (*Inset*) the radio transmitter at Baranowice in Silesia disappears amid a cloud of smoke.

'If we die, then together'... A distraught Polish girl crouches over the blood-splattered corpse of her sister.

'The German sword has struck like lightning' ... The railway bridge at Sochaczew on the Bzura lies in ruins.
(Hugo Jaeger/Timepix/Time Life Pictures/Getty Images)

'Farms everywhere were ablaze'... German infantry advance through a burning farm and (*Inset*) a supply column moves through the flaming ruins of a Polish village.

The shadows of death have hung over Bromberg these past few days'... *Volksdeutsche* victims of 'Bromberg Bloody Sunday' are shown to foreign reporters.

'Polish civilians are dragged out everywhere'... German troops force their way into a house durin the pitiless war against the 'franc-tireur'.

we're in enemy territory I trust no-one!'... Polish 'franc-tireurs' are rounded up by German
iers.

bashed and beat the Poles'... Men of 57th Infantry Division adorn their train before returning
e from Poland.

'A boiling kettle of fire and blood'... (*This page and opposite above*) German troops lie in wait in trenches on the edge of Warsaw before the final assault.

(below) Hitler watches the battle for Warsaw on 25 September from the race course tower at Mokotow ...mpanied by I Corps' Commanding Officer Generalleutnant Walter Petzel (in the glasses) and ...eraloberst Wilhelm Keitel, Chief-of-Staff of the Oberkommando der Wehrmacht (partially ...ured by the field binoculars).

'Broken, shattered, exhausted men'... (*Above*) Polish troops march out of Warsaw into captivity and (*Below*) 'Weapons lay scattered around the city, dumped in a disorderly fashion in public places'... a officer surveys the vast booty left behind.

German soldiers line the bombed-out streets of Warsaw awaiting Hitler's arrival. (Hugo Jaeger/Timepix/Time Life Pictures/Getty Images)

'More ready to strike a blow than ever'... Hitler takes the salute from his panzers in Warsaw.

it on an embankment. Lying around it were the blackened corpses of Polish soldiers. Some bodies had literally been torn to pieces by the Luftwaffe's bombs. The lanes of Galicia offered the Poles no more sanctuary than did its railway lines. 'Dead Poles lie beside the road – their brown uniforms have almost been turned white already by the dust which has drifted over them,' one *Gebirgsjäger* wrote in his diary. He continued:

> Discarded helmets, guns, ammunition, equipment lying behind, then more dead horses, gradually bloating in the heat giving off a sweetish smell, some armoured cars with broken wheels and shafts. Individual, hastily-dug graves with a steel helmet and hastily-erected wooden crosses: the signs of battle left by the pursuit group which is already far ahead.
>
> We come across exhausted, weary prisoners in long columns; they stare at the German *Gebirgsjäger* marching past them with blank expressions. They are just as dirty, just as exhausted and just as weary from exertion as German soldiers.[7]

A single objective kept the men going: Lemberg, capital of Galicia, focal point of Galician cultural life – home to churches, cathedrals and a university – an important trading centre on the cusp of central and eastern Europe, a vital rail hub. Polish troops sought refuge there, just as their comrades on the Bzura and Vistula made for Warsaw. Ludwig Kübler was determined to beat them there. *Schärfstes Vordringen auf Lemberg*! he demanded. The quickest possible advance to Lemberg. The *Jäger* came to know it as the *Sturmfahrt auf Lemberg* – storm on Lemberg. They were mounted in cars and trucks which raced along the Galician lanes at speeds in excess of 40mph. Polish horse-drawn carts scattered as the German vehicles hurtled towards them, Polish soldiers dashed into the fields or raised their hands in groups of three, six, ten or twenty. 'The road is littered with pieces of equipment, discarded weapons and all kinds of vehicles,' one *Gebirgsjäger* officer wrote. 'We see scattered enemy elements in the fields; they were overrun, caught completely unawares, by our incredible tempo. The flag of a Polish regiment has even been abandoned by the Poles fleeing the road in panic and falls into their pursuers hands' as a proud victory trophy.' There was no let-up for those mountain infantry still advancing on foot. Kübler's officers stopped their staff cars by the side of the road, climbed out and spurred their men on eastwards. Lemberg, on to Lemberg. The name was hammered into every man. A motorcyclist driving too close to a truck ahead of him failed to see a pothole and was catapulted into the air. A few minutes later, his head bandaged, the motorcyclist was back with the column. In Kaltwasser, half a dozen miles from the heart of Lemberg, the motorised mountain troops overtook two buses crammed with Polish soldiers. The Poles, still bearing arms, stared in bewilderment as the *Jäger* hurried past.[8]

By the early afternoon of Tuesday, 12 September, the foremost *Gebirgsjäger* were engaged with Polish troops on the southwestern outskirts of Lemberg. As the motorised column pushed up the main road from Grodek, sharpshooters on rooftops began to snipe at the trucks. Polish artillery straddled the road while machine-guns strafed it. The *Sturmfahrt* ground to a halt. *Oberjäger* Franz Buchner's truck stopped abruptly near the city's west station as the motorised column came under rifle fire. The *Jäger* jumped out of the wagons and found cover in a ditch. Buchner took a swig from his canteen, then led his squad across the tracks and platforms until the men reached a row of houses. Polish bullets hissed past their heads as enemy shells began crashing around the station. On a broad meadow beyond the sidings, howitzers of 79th *Gebirgs* Artillery Regiment were already drawn up; the guns' barrels glowed as they fired round upon round into the city centre. Franz Buchner and his men continued into Lemberg until they reached a crossroad strafed by enemy machine-guns. The *Jäger* dashed across the road, diving into a ditch on the opposite side of the road for cover. 'Suddenly we encounter war in its cruellest form,' Buchner recalled. 'We are seized by shock because we land on and next to a long line of dead Polish soldiers. There's no time to think about how they had all died.' In an instant, the *Jäger* leapt out of the ditch anxious 'to get away from this place of misery'. They ran through alleys, through gardens, jumped over fences, 'far too rashly,' Buchner admitted. A straggler caught up with the squad. '*Herr Gruppenführer*, there's a group of Polish soldiers in a house!' The mountain men retraced their steps, found the house, fired into it and hurled hand grenades inside. Twenty-two men in brown uniforms, their hands raised, staggered out of the building. Buchner ordered the Poles to smash their guns on the doorstep then sent them to the rear escorted by a couple of riflemen. As night fell on Lemberg, Buchner led his men into a bakery. After a hot autumn day and hours of skirmishing his men were hungry and thirsty. As half his squad guarded the premises, the rest grabbed fresh bread, washed down with milk brought in a pail by the baker's boys. 'I've never liked milk much, but today it tastes wonderful,' the *Oberjäger* recalled. A messenger arrived: Buchner was to pull his men back to high ground near Lemberg's radio towers. He let his squad finish their meal then ordered each man to grab at least one slice of bread; there was no certainty when they might eat again.[9]

In western Lemberg, elements of 99th *Gebirgsjäger* Regiment moved through a cemetery. The men had already forced the Poles from a ridge of high ground; now they had one more peak to seize before the day was out. They would get no further than the graveyard. 'Polish bullets whistle around the gravestones, ricochets whizz around, but there's no sight of the brown steel helmets,' one *Gefreiter* Dussmann wrote. The company commander was killed, the squad leader wounded. Heavy machine-gun fire gave the mountain troops cover, but the Poles struck in the flank. 'A bullet rips the hand off a comrade next to me,' the *Gefreiter* recalled. He bandaged the wounded man, who immediately rejoined the battle. Neither rifle fire nor machine-guns could dislodge the Polish troops. The mountain men called up mortars. 'They land in the ranks of the attackers three or four times,' the *Gefreiter* observed. 'Their precise fire finally forces them to turn around.'

Night descended on Lemberg 'casting friend and foe into darkness', Dussmann recalled. 'In the twilight the crosses and gravestones seem eerie.' Dussmann's company had orders to hold the cemetery until nightfall, then fall back. As the last rays of light disappeared below the horizon, the guns opened up and the *Gebirgsjäger* fell back from the cemetery and re-grouped far to the west. 'Far on the horizon we see the bright glow of fire,' wrote Dussmann, 'the outlines of huge domed buildings stand out distinctly.' Lemberg was aflame.[10]

As in Warsaw, so in Lemberg: a few German soldiers could not take a city by *coup de main*. Suddenly Ludwig Kübler's position was precarious. His division was eighty miles ahead of the rest of XVIII *Gebirgskorps*, far in the enemy's rear. In front of 1st *Gebirgs* the Poles were reinforcing all the time. Ludwig Kübler had no idea how strong the enemy before him was.[11]

On the cusp of 12–13 September the men of 16th Company, 99th *Gebirgsjäger* Regiment, reached Lemberg's airfield, barely two miles from the city centre. The men settled down in the abandoned officers' quarters. There was no darkness this night. The sky had a bloody tint from the fires in the heart of the Galician capital. It was a restless night, too, thanks to sporadic rifle fire. Towards 4am the first 'morning greeting' was sent roaring towards the Polish positions as the *Gebirgs* artillery opened fire. The Poles responded in kind. Dawn that Wednesday was misty, murky, a veil of fog shrouded Lemberg and its environs. Around 7am, 16th Company moved out and was soon in the suburbs of the Galician capital. The traces of the previous day's fighting were obvious. 'We see so many things,' one *Oberjäger* wrote. 'Motor vehicles with their wheels in the air, dead horses lie in the street or in ditches. Pools of blood have turned the pavement red. Electricity wires are wrecked; many poles lie on the ground, their wires torn. A dead *Jäger* lies in a tangle of barbed wire.'[12]

Ludwig Kübler set up his command post in a villa in Konduktorska Street, a couple of miles southwest of the city centre. At dawn on the thirteenth, beneath the shade of some fruit trees on a lawn behind the villa, 1st *Gebirgs* Division's commander held court. With sweeps of his hand across a map of the city, he outlined his plans for the day's fighting to his regimental and battalion commanders. It was vital, Kübler explained, to seize the heights of Zboiska to the north of Lemberg to block the arrival of any Polish reinforcements, while the scattered troops in the city itself would re-group, probe, attack. The officers sat around motionless, their eyes fixed on their general. Five *Gebirgs* artillery batteries pounded away constantly as the *Generalmajor* concluded his briefing; 'Gentlemen, I'm done!' Kübler declared, then wished his commanders all the best. The shells from Kübler's field guns whistled and fizzed low over the villa as they headed towards the heart of Lemberg. Polish guns responded in kind; the shells landing a short distance behind the garden. 'That will cost Lemberg dearly,' Kübler snarled. 'If we don't establish our command post in Lemberg town hall today, then we'll do it tomorrow.'[13]

By mid-morning, a makeshift force of *Gebirgsjäger* led by a ruthless *Oberst*, Ferdinand Schörner – *das eiserne Ferdinand*, the iron Ferdinand – was sweeping through the suburbs of Lemberg, determined to seize the heights at Zboiska. They clambered through the goods yard of the city's western railway station, where twenty-five trains sat idly, unable to move. They stormed up a hill they dubbed the *Steinberg* (stone mountain) on the northwestern edge of Lemberg from where they had a commanding view of the land. They dashed down the hill and headed for Zboiska, but under the mid-day sun, the *Jäger* were wilting, sapped by the heat and the fact that they had not eaten since the previous day. Schörner was eager to give the shaken Polish troops no time to recover, but recover they did. Polish snipers hidden in trees surrounding Lemberg's Jewish cemetery began to pick off the exhausted *Jäger*. Ludwig Kübler grew impatient. Over a freshly-laid telephone line he stressed the importance of the Zboiska heights, then wished Ferdinand Schörner luck. And luck it was which ensured the heights fell into German hands. The *Jäger* came across a Viennese living in Lemberg who revealed there was a short cut to the heights which was not marked on the mountain men's maps. As night descended, the *Jäger* took the high ground, catching two astonished Polish officers unawares, and fell upon a bivouac; a few Poles were killed, most fled leaving behind vehicles loaded with food which the German troops eagerly seized. Within an hour, the Poles struck back with a series of well-led counter-attacks; on occasions they got within hand grenade range before they were driven off. But it was obvious that the village of Zboiska could not be held. The *Jäger* pulled back to the high ground to the southwest and dug in.[14]

In the western suburb, the *Gebirgsjäger* renewed their thrust. The September sun had burned away the mist veiling the city. 'There's not even a small cloud in the sky, the sun blazes down relentlessly,' one *Oberjäger* wrote. 'Our steel helmets become so hot that we can barely touch them any more.' The mountain men forced their way through the residential streets, over the railway line, through a small copse, then up a hill which dominated the ground west of Lemberg. The enemy fled towards the city's principal cemetery, leaving behind his dead. 'A Pole crouches by a gun,' the *Oberjäger* recalled. 'His lower jaw is half ripped away, blood trickling from his mouth.' The men stormed up the hill, hauling field guns with them. From the top Lemberg lay stretched out before them. Panting, their faces covered in dust, they looked across the city. There, the ruins of railway station. And down below, bitter fighting, still a long way from the city centre. Ludwig Kübler would not be moving his command post today.[15]

Far to the west, the gunners of 79th *Gebirgs* Artillery Regiment were marching relentlessly. They had rarely averaged fewer than twenty-five miles a day, but 13 September placed supreme demands on them. The regiment was expected to reach Grodek Jagiellonski, fifteen miles southwest of Lemberg, by nightfall – a march of forty miles – and have their guns in position by dawn on the fourteenth. The men watched as the *Jäger* were loaded on to trucks with their rifles, mortars, machine-guns and hurried in the direction of Lemberg. The artillerymen continued on foot, horses hauling their field guns. 'It's an inexorable advance,' one gunner wrote. 'Man and beast use their last ounce of energy.' The sun burned mercilessly, the *Jäger* racing past in their cars and trucks threw up clouds of dust surrounding the marching artillerymen. 'Pharynges and throats are hoarse,' the gunner recorded in his diary. 'Teeth grind away on the fine dusty sand. Eyes are red and burn. We can often no longer recognise the man in front of us.' The road to Grodek was strewn with the detritus of the Polish Army. 'The road has been torn up, wrecked by the bombs of our airmen. Dead Polish soldiers and horses lie on both sides besides limbers and carts, and a vast number of helmets, gas masks and ammunition cases.'[16]

After eight days on the march, *Gefreiter* Gebhard Mayer and his comrades were exhausted. Two hundred and fifty miles on foot already, thought Mayer. As the men of 2nd Company, 100th *Gebirgsjäger* Regiment, wearily marched through Sambor, a *Leutnant* suddenly fired the men up. 'The company's going into action.' The *Jäger* halted in a field, enjoyed food, and waited for several trucks to carry them the fifty or so miles to Lemberg. That afternoon the wagons trundled into the city's suburbs, where they immediately drew fire from the defenders. The *Jäger* dismounted and prepared to fight their way through to Kübler's command post and throw the Poles back to the high ground near Lemberg's transmitter. It was not to be. By dusk, Mayer and his comrades found themselves huddling in a ditch, expecting the Poles to attempt to dislodge them. 'There's no quiet all night long,' Mayer wrote. 'There's the repeated shrill sound of a Polish machine-gun or pistol – in the darkness it's particularly unpleasant.' The Poles knew the ground, the *Gebirgsjäger* did not. All through the night they fired wildly, but they did not attack.[17]

In the southwestern suburbs of Lemberg, war correspondent Leo Leixner sat around with numerous soldiers. It was an ominous night. 'The evening sky is a searing sea of flames,' Leixner observed. In the distance a thunderstorm flickered, giving the horizon a violet-red glimmer. The *Jäger* talked, thought about home and began humming a tune – *On the Heights at Grodek* – a wistful lament their fathers had taught them. 'One song captures the experiences of two generations,' thought Leixner.[18]

The exhausted gunners of 79th *Gebirgs* Artillery Regiment wearily marched into Grodek after nightfall. The town was deserted. No light shone from the windows, the streets, houses and pavements were shrouded in a ghostly darkness. After marching nearly 250 miles – forty miles that Wednesday alone – the gunners could barely focus their eyes any more. Their knees ached. 'Is it any wonder?' one artilleryman asked himself. Perhaps the men might sleep now? 'It was a vain hope,' the gunner lamented. Their commander ordered the guns into position on a railway embankment beyond a canal to the west of Grodek, 'ready to fire by dawn'. The gunners hauled two batteries through wet grass in complete darkness. 'Our mood is serious, our exhaustion overwhelming,' the artilleryman wrote. 'A lot of work and little sleep for our tired bones.' With the first strains of light, the guns were in position. Exhausted, the artillerymen fell into hastily-dug foxholes.[19]

Two days into the struggle for Lemberg the *Jäger* of 1st *Gebirgs* Division were still strung out across Galicia, from the western suburbs of Lemberg and the heights of Zboiska and Holosko to the north, and as far west as Sambor, forty miles from the Galician capital. Reinforcements were on their way: 2nd *Gebirgs* Division was on the march from Przemysl; 57th Infantry Division was ordered to race through the San valley and up the Sambor road. But the mountain men's position in Lemberg remained precarious – just how precarious *Leutnant* Herbert Hodurek realised as his motorised column raced along the road from Sambor. 'There in the distance, where the cannon thunder and where every moment there are bright flashes of lightning, that's where Lemberg must be, it seems that everything there is on fire,' he recalled. 'We cannot make out anything precisely – but the sky there at the front is red, blood red.' The *Sturmfahrt* had simply by-passed Polish troops in the Galician countryside. Now these scattered soldiers took aim at Hodurek's column. They struck in the dead of a starless night. 'Suddenly there's furious rifle and machine-gun fire,' the *Leutnant* wrote. 'Flames shoot up, there's flashing and crashing around us. Windscreens shatter, the wood and metal on the vehicles clatter and bang as the shots strike them.' Hodurek looked across at his driver; he had slumped backwards, his head leaning to one side, his hands still rigidly fixed to the steering wheel. 'I am paralysed by fear or, more accurately, surprise,' he recalled. 'I don't feel fear or anxiety at this moment – for the time being I'm incapable of such feelings.'[20]

Two names dominate accounts of the bitter struggle for Lemberg during the third week of September 1939: Zboiska and Grodek. At each town Polish troops tried to bludgeon their way through to the Galician capital repeatedly over four bitter days. At each town, they were bloodily repulsed repeatedly over four bitter days. On the hills of Zboiska, the Poles committed motorised infantry and light tanks. The tanks' guns began to target the *Jäger*'s individual foxholes before drawing fire themselves from German heavy mortars; at least one was knocked out. The Polish tanks turned about and withdrew out of range, choosing to spray the high ground with machine-gun fire. It went on like this until dusk on the fourteenth when the fighting died down. The road to Zboiska remained in German hands.[21]

At dawn the next day, 15 September, the Poles attacked again, this time falling upon the command post of I Battalion, 99th *Gebirgsjäger* Regiment. *Hauptmann* Josef Fleischmann and his men were washing, making coffee, some were still resting in the straw. Suddenly Polish cries of 'hurrah' penetrated the morning fog as a lieutenant led his men at the command post. He fell almost instantly and with his death, his men panicked and fled. It was over in a matter of minutes. 'Were it not for the dead Poles lying around then it would have all seemed to us like a short dream,' one of Fleischmann's staff observed.[22]

Twenty or so miles to the southwest, Polish soldiers took advantage of that same dawn mist to drive the *Gebirgsjäger* out of Grodek and force their way into Lemberg. They came over the meadow in front of the railway embankment where gunners and *Jäger* were dug in. The barrels of the *Gebirgs* artillery roared. 'The effect of the fire on the plain is devastating,' *Unteroffizier* Karl Doppelmayr observed in his diary. 'The Poles don't know which way to turn.' The *Jäger*'s machine-guns now opened fire. The attackers were cut down in swaths. 'Through our binoculars we can see dead and wounded lying around everywhere,' wrote Doppelmayr. In just one place did the Poles close within rifle range. They were driven back. More Polish troops began to swarm forward, emerging from a small copse south of the village of Bratkowice, a couple of miles west of Grodek. Again the artillery raged. 'The first shot tears apart a Pole who has just left the forest with a direct hit,' a mesmerised gunner wrote. Shells began to crash in the wood. Trees snapped. Smoke began to rise. And again the Polish assault faltered. The fighting was particularly brutal in the village of Hartfeld, just north of Grodek. Gunners fought alongside *Jäger* in their foxholes in hand-to-hand combat; rifles were fired at point-blank range and when that failed to stop the Poles, the mountain men brandished their rifle butts. The last-ditch stand worked; Hartfeld was held.[23]

It was dark before Karl Doppelmayr felt it was safe to move again. He grabbed four men and crept out into the valley to destroy several barns. The fires, he reasoned, would light up the landscape, preventing the Poles from attacking unseen. Some Polish troops had taken refuge in the outhouses during that morning's failed, bloody attempt to storm the railway embankment. Under cover of darkness they tried to slip away, but were captured by Doppelmayr's small party. 'The Poles are filled with terrible fear,' he observed. 'They seem to believe that they'll all be shot dead.' There was other booty on the battlefield: a couple of machine-guns and a field gun. The *Unteroffizier* and his men rounded it up, then set fire to the barns. 'The valley floor is lit all night long by the huge blaze,' Doppelmayr recorded. 'It means we can spend the rest of the night in peace.'[24]

The following afternoon, the Poles struck near the village of Dobrostany, five miles north of Grodek, surprising a column of motorised mountain infantry. The *Jäger* jumped out, hurriedly offloaded their machine-guns, mortars and light field guns, and set them up in a field beside the road. In minutes mortars were landing in a wood where the Poles were hiding, the rapid tack-tack-tack of the machine-guns accompanied this hellish concert. On the open ground, the *Jäger* were exposed. They moved to a potato field and began to dig in. The men hauled tent covers over them as darkness set in to shield them from the cool of night, then they settled down in their burrows and waited for dawn. But dawn did not come. 'As if a thousand throats are screaming,' one *Jäger* recalled, Polish cries of 'hurrah' pierced the night. In halting German the attackers called out: 'German soldiers, give yourselves up! Offensive!' Polish machine-guns barked. 'There's crashing on all sides, on all sides bitter fighting,' the soldier wrote. Dobrostany went up in flames sending thick clouds of smoke billowing across the potato field. Towards 2am the Polish pressure slackened. After suffering heavy losses, the Poles fell back.[25]

These nights at Grodek were the worst. Red, white and green flares sporadically bathed the landscape in a ghostly light. There were screams, cracks of rifle fire, grenades exploding. Fires in Hartfeld gave the night sky 'a suitably atmospheric and tragic ambience,' one artilleryman observed. *Oberfeldwebel* Gottlieb Wilm and his comrades in 179th Infantry Regiment marched into a village south of Grodek after dark on the sixteenth. In the distance was the dull rumble of artillery around Lemberg, the muzzle flashes lit up the landscape for a second. 'Far to the northeast we can now see the crimson glow of flames,' recalled Wilm. 'Lemberg is on fire!' It was, Wilm remembered, 'a terribly beautiful scene. Around us is the deepest night; before us is a bright, fiery red. Rain-laden clouds with the finest kaleidoscope of colours drift in the dark night-time sky.' Around midnight the men marched past a field, littered with German dead 'their faces to the ground, hands stretched in front of them, still clinging desperately to their guns'.[26]

Such scenes terrified some *Jäger* but inspired others. *Gefreiter* Hanns Pfeuffer captured both emotions in poetic form:

Streams of blood must run over the earth,
The ground trembles, the world shakes;
Where over decomposing, shot-up heaps
The last men run, hounded by fear
Fire mercilessly strikes the field.

There's drumming and drumming, rumbling and crashing!
The enemy has now got to know us!
For we have provoked this hell,
In which the victor of every battle –
Death – reaps his grim harvest.[27]

Death could only reap its grim harvest for so long. After four days of almost relentless fighting, *Jäger* Ernst Schulz awoke to 'an almost oppressive calm' on Sunday, 17 September. Schulz was not a typical mountain infantryman. He hailed not from the Alps but Frauenborn in the heart of Thuringia. Nor was the twenty-two-year-old a born warrior; he was a gardener by trade. Schulz and his comrades had spent the night on the heights at Zboiska, waiting for dawn, waiting for relief. There was the promise of food and rest. But then an artillery shell crashing into the sandy soil shattered the Sunday morning tranquillity. 'Shot followed shot,' recalled Schulz. 'Murderous shelling plastered the hollow.' The men grabbed their spades and thrust them into the sand, hastily digging shallow foxholes to shield themselves from shrapnel. All morning and all afternoon Polish shells rained down. 'They know this undulating terrain inside out, every foxhole,' Schulz lamented; the land was a Polish Army exercise area.[28]

Nearby, the Poles swarmed through a cornfield, despite German mortar fire straddling it. There was unease in the Polish cries drifting across the battlefield. The *Jäger* spied an opportunity. 'We must charge them,' a non-commissioned officer urged. The mountain troops fixed bayonets, reloaded their rifles, had their grenades ready. Then they stormed forward yelling 'hurrah', running, shooting, roaring. The Poles lay down in the cornfield and picked off the oncoming Germans. But they could not stop them. The *Jäger* smashed their way into the Polish lines with rifle butts and bayonets. The surprise German attack unnerved the Poles. 'The front ranks throw their guns away, fall down screaming, raise their arms and suddenly run away in chaotic flight,' one *Jäger* wrote. As the Poles fled, the German soldiers shot them in the back.[29]

Salvation for the beleaguered *Gebirgsjäger* came from the west and north. The first elements of VII Corps began to arrive on the seventeenth. In woodland near Janow, a dozen miles northwest of Lemberg, the *Landsers* of 7th Infantry Division ran headlong into *Polish 38th Division*, a unit formed almost entirely of ethnic Poles, not the Ukrainians the corps had encountered for the most part to date. The fighting among the trees and undergrowth would earn Janow a dubious sobriquet: the forest of death. 'What transpired here was the purest, most refined form of Polish spirit,' the corps' chronicler recorded. He continued:

The forest as a refuge and escape, the forest as a trap and ambush, the forest of darkness and thicket, as guardian angel and defender, the upturned tree trunks as our enemies, which creep around, move around, leap out, which are the front and back, in a word the forest is the ally of the defenders.

Late in the afternoon of the seventeenth, German infantry began moving through the forest. The *Landsers* quickly regretted advancing. 'The thicket, the trees, the bushes, all have been turned into our enemies,' VII Corps' diarist observed. 'It's as if the bushes themselves could fire – a horrible entanglement of machine-gun nests and shrubbery.' As dusk began to descend, the weight of German artillery began to tell. The Poles fell back, leaving behind 'the detritus of battle – overturned and destroyed vehicles, smashed and blown-up guns, their barrels burst and sticking out helplessly, burning strongholds, huge trees split, burning ammunition units. Among the casualties, mountains of dead horses.' German guns, the observer recorded, had 'reaped a terrible harvest among their crowded masses.' And then it dawned on the attackers: they were not grappling with the *38th Division* alone; they were fighting three enemy divisions.[30]

A few miles down the road from Janow, the men of 3rd Company, 99th *Gebirgsjäger* Regiment, were losing their battle against Polish superiority. So fierce was the enemy's fire that *Leutnant* Schwender and his comrades could barely lift their heads above their foxholes. Only a 2cm flak gun, directed not against Polish aircraft but Polish soldiers, offered any relief. But then an electrifying message arrived: panzers were on their way; they would strike at 3pm. The *Jäger* were overjoyed. But 3pm came and went and no German armour. Two hours later there was the clanking of caterpillar tracks and the first tanks of 2nd Panzer Division arrived. 'There was a wonderful sight as the battle ended in the twilight,' Schwender observed. 'Everywhere panzers were breaking through, their tracers tearing through the darkness like phosphorescent ribbons. After an hour the Poles final resistance was broken.'[31]

Ernst Schulz was still in his makeshift foxhole as night fell on the seventeenth. It was raining steadily now. The dull drone of motor engines was just about audible above the patter of the rain. Panzers, thought Schulz. Relief, thought Schulz. The long-awaited armour of 2nd Panzer Division had obviously arrived. But it had not. The rumble of the engines faded. The panzers did not come that night.[32]

Night at Janow brought its peculiar fears. 'This was not the darkness of silence and sleep,' VII Corps' chronicler noted, 'it was the darkness of terror.' The night was shattered by sporadic gunfire, the cries of sentries, the twitching and rustling of bushes. Daylight brought hope. Daylight brought relief.

As the icy night turned into the first half-light, the shadow world of the living parted with the world of the dead; as stiff limbs were warmly shaken, they saw in the thicket the first clearing glimmering: the eastern edge of the forest had been reached. We had passed through the quagmire of terror.

Polish 38th Division and the *ad hoc* units helping it had been beaten; the remnants struggled on to the southeast, seeking sanctuary in Lemberg.[33]

The rumble which had so raised the hopes of Ernst Schulz and his comrades after dark on the seventeenth returned at dawn the following day. This time the noise grew ever louder. The outline of these steel monsters was unmistakable. 'Finally they're here!' Schulz celebrated. The *Jäger* and panzer crews fraternised briefly. And then the mountain troops formed up behind the armour and began to attack the Poles who had spent the past five days trying to force them from Zboiska.[34]

A couple of miles west of Ernst Schulz's position, 7th Company, 99th *Gebirgsjäger* Regiment, were exhausted after seven days dug in on the high ground on the edge of Holosko. Lack of sleep was compounded by lack of food. And still the enemy came on. 'The Poles howl like wolves,' one officer recalled. They seized a machine-gun bunker, stormed a battalion command post. The company's machine-guns fired so many rounds the barrels glowed. 'The corpses must be piling up on the enemy's side,' the officer convinced himself. A few Poles smashed their way into the command post, but their attack was spent. They were taken prisoner. It seemed to be the Poles' last hurrah on the heights above Lemberg.[35]

The arrival of the panzers filled 3rd Company, 99th *Gebirgsjäger* Regiment, with renewed vigour. At dawn on the eighteenth, the men struck west in the dense mist, and entered the village of Domazyr, just outside Rzesna-Ruska. Twenty-five Poles fell into the company's hands almost immediately. The tally grew. The *Jäger* smashed in the doors of houses and cellars yelling: '*Polski raus!*' – Poles get out. Shaking, the startled Polish troops emerged. As the morning mist thinned, the company ran into a Polish colonel and a handful of cavalry. The colonel offered to surrender – and offered to surrender the rest of his regiment, twenty-two officers and 149 men.[36]

Southwest of Lemberg, too, Polish resistance was faltering. In these bitter final hours the struggle raged along roads, along the banks of streams, in woods and copses. The result was always the same. Death, destruction, desolation. War correspondent Leo Leixner drove along the road from Grodek to Janow. 'A field kitchen has been knocked into a ditch by a shell,' he wrote. 'Abandoned buses stand by the road, Polish caps and sacks lie around in vast quantities.' And yet off the road, in the rolling Galician countryside, life continued its course as if there was no war raging. 'The farmer drags his plough across the field to prepare to sow his grain for the winter,' the correspondent observed. 'Cattle graze in the meadows and maids raise water buckets from wells. A wonderful land appears before us; its fertility is so blatantly contrasted by the poverty of its people.'[37]

Grodek and the hills of Zboiska and Holosko were immortalised in the *Gebirgsjägers*' prose and poetry, but it was the struggle for Lemberg itself which made the gravest demand for sacrifices. 99th *Gebirgsjäger* Regiment alone lost nine men every day in the Galician capital – eighty-three soldiers in all by the ninth day of the battle, Wednesday, 20 September.

As the *Jäger* now pressed into Lemberg once more, they began to realise the sacrifices the city had demanded of their comrades. 'The closer we got to the edge of the city, the greater the signs of recent fighting became,' a young adjutant recalled. Houses were shot-up, trucks burned out, makeshift barriers had been pushed aside. The rotting carcasses of horses lined the roads into the city, lying in pools of their own blood, some still harnessed to their limbers. There were dead soldiers too, torn apart by German shells, as they moved along the road in formation. The smell was overpowering. *Leutnant* Hubert Hodurek and a comrade reached a college building close to the city centre and climbed on to its roof. 'Lemberg left a ghostly impression,' he recalled. 'There was no-one in the streets.' In one road a tram sat in the middle of the tracks where it had been abandoned by its driver and passengers. Lemberg, Hodurek concluded, was a ghost town.[38]

On the hills of Holosko, a German officer watched as Polish soldiers began to emerge from the forest, white cloths tied to sticks; one unit even surrendered using women's underwear. The wood echoed with the sporadic sound of pistol fire; soldiers were evidently revolting against their officers who rejected any thought of surrender. A few Polish batteries continued to send shells crashing into the forest – like Janow the wood was branded 'forest of the dead' by the *Jäger* – where the dead of a week's battle still lay. It was, one officer recalled, 'a scene of horror'.[39]

Near Grodek, the batteries of 79th *Gebirgs* Artillery Regiment were limbered and began to move east towards Lemberg – 'a sea of houses' in the distance. The guns were drawn up in a forest to the southwest of the city. As 20 September ended, the artillerymen contemplated their fate. 'Each man is lost in his own thoughts,' one gunner observed. 'What will the coming hours and days bring? The Poles will defend the city stubbornly. The assault will cost us sacrifices, many sacrifices.' The final orders were issued. At dawn on the twenty-first the batteries would bark and the *Jäger* would storm Lemberg.[40]

But they did not. The telephone in Ludwig Kübler's command post rang. It was the operations officer of XVIII *Gebirgs* Corps. His instructions were explicit: 'On the orders of the Führer, limit yourselves to purely defensive actions before Lemberg. Hold your positions. The Russians already enjoy complete freedom of action in Lemberg.' Kübler was stunned. His men were stunned. Lemberg was to fall to the Red Army – for three days now at war with Poland. 'Should 1st *Gebirgsjäger* Division, which had laid its claim to Lemberg in blood, be denied certain ultimate victory?' he railed. 'We could simply not believe it.' Kübler's men shared his bitterness. 'Lemberg to the Russians!' one *Leutnant* fumed. 'That's a bitter blow for us. We've held our own for seven days. And now, when the city of Lemberg lies before us like a ripe fruit, we are to begin the withdrawal.'[41]

Russian riders galloped into Malechow, just beyond Zboiska, riding past the *Jäger* occupying the village, waving as they went. A Soviet lieutenant climbed down off his horse and greeted the senior German officer with a hearty handshake and 200 cigarettes. '*Germanski und Bolshewiki zusammen stark,*' he proclaimed in broken German. *Together Germans and Bolsheviks strong.* 'He couldn't speak any more German,' one *Hauptmann* recalled, 'but his sentiments were clear.'[42]

Near Winniki, southeast of Lemberg, regimental adjutant *Hauptmann* Josef Remold could make out the silhouettes of medium tanks. Obviously the last reserves thrown into the battle for the Galician capital by the Poles, he thought. The regiment's anti-tank guns were aimed at the oncoming armour, extremely difficult given their speed and low outline. What hits were scored simply bounced off the angled armour plating. And as the tanks drew closer, the guns ceased fire; the red Soviet star could clearly be made out on the armour's hull.[43]

And in Lemberg itself, *Oberstleutnant* Max-Josef Pemsel, Kübler's chief-of-staff, shook hands with a General Ivanov; the Soviet officer was surrounded by Communist Party officials, including a disapproving commissar. Ivanov, however, was 'on good form'. The two men discussed the surrender of the city and the German withdrawal. 'We see the finest Russian tanks,' wrote Pemsel, 'and poorly-fed but disciplined troops and armed red mobs pouring from cellars.' This encounter with the Red Army proved eye-opening for battalion commander *Oberstleutnant* Mathias Kräutler. Kräutler knew the Russian soldier. He had fought against him a generation earlier. 'No more the simple, generally good-natured men, who were cheerful despite their poverty and with whom you could easily talk,' he recalled. 'Here before us stood well-armed, brutally-disciplined and led soldiers.'[44]

As his division prepared to fall back from the city, Ludwig Kübler rallied his men one last time. The general had a new nickname – *Der Bluthund von Lemberg*, the bloodhound of Lemberg. And his men? His men had earned distinction too. '*Das Edelweiss ist der Schrecken des Feindes geworden!*' Kübler declared in a stirring order of the day. The edelweiss has become the scourge of the enemy. 'We'll never forget this evening, standing among a half burned-out, shot-up Polish village, our feet burning, our stomachs growling, our faces filthy, covered in sweat,' one artilleryman enthused as Kübler's message was read out.[45]

In the grounds of a Greek Catholic church on a hill above the village of Jasniska, half a dozen miles northwest of Lemberg, the companies of 131st Infantry Regiment formed an open square in silence. Villagers crowded around, the women sobbing and wailing. Briefly, *Oberst* Franz Beyer addressed his men. They had lost fifty-eight comrades in the fighting around Lemberg, all but eight of them were being committed to the earth here. 'For the last time the companies present arms and the officers salute their fallen comrades, hands fixed to their steel helmets,' one infantryman recalled. 'Then one name after the other is called out and a dull roll of drums responds.' The band struck up the soldiers' hymn, *Ich hatt' einen Kameraden*, followed by the regimental march, *Erlherzog Carl*, before the regiment dispersed.[46]

The *Gebirgsjäger* too paid their respects. In the cemetery at Rzesna-Ruska, the mountain infantrymen of 12th Company, 99th *Gebirgsjäger* Regiment, gathered around a few simple wooden crosses on freshly-dug graves covered with flowers. In the light of the morning sun, the *Jäger* paused for brief reflection before leaving Galicia. In one grave a man killed by a shell, in another a soldier felled as he stormed a house, a hand grenade clasped in his hand, and then the freshest grave of all, a common grave, four machine-gunners laid side-by-side. 'They marched with each other, fought alongside each other in the front line, died with each other, and now rest side-by-side, still united but in death.'[47]

And then the men of the mountains turned west, for home, through the land which had cost them so much blood. Each step they took through Galicia reminded them of the sacrifices made. 'The road was terrible,' the chronicler of a battery in 79th *Gebirgs* Artillery Regiment wrote. He continued:

Shell craters, bits of equipment lying around and upturned carts, burned-out houses, abandoned guns, cadavers of horses which pollute the air, graves for dead Poles, but also graves for a fallen comrade decorated with a simple cross and steel helmet, lined our route of withdrawal and were testimony to the bitter fighting which took place here.[48]

As 100th *Gebirgsjäger* Regiment marched west through the San valley, *Oberjäger* Franz Buchner and his comrades were disheartened. 'Have our sacrifices all been for nothing?' Buchner asked himself. Buchner's company commander summoned him and unburdened himself of the thoughts tormenting him. 'He will never be able to understand the surrender of Lemberg to the Russians,' the *Oberjäger* observed. 'In the not-too-distant future we had to conquer Lemberg for a second time – and on this occasion we had to seize it back from the Russian Army.'[49]

Notes

1. *Oberjäger* Hans Peinitsch, 'Zwei Tage aus den polnischen Feldzug (aus meinem Tagebuch)' in BA-MA RH53-18/149 and *Jäger* Bernardi Alois, 'Aus dem Polenkrieg einer motorisierten Kolonne' in BA-MA RH53-18/18.
2. Buchner, 'Kampfziel Lemberg', p. 15, Kaltenegger, *Ludwig Kübler*, pp. 14, 18 and Kopp, Roland, 'Die Wehrmacht feiert: Kommandeurs Reden zu Hitlers 50 Geburtstag', *Militärgeschichtliche Zeitschrift*, Vol.62, 2003, pp. 522.
3. Kaltenegger, *Ludwig Kübler*, p. 24.
4. Kaltenegger, *Die Deutsche Gebirgstruppe 1935–1945*, p. 111, Leixner, p. 49 and *Der Polenfeldzug im Tagebuch eines Gebirgsartilleristen*, pp. 36–7.
5. *Leutnant* Schuhmann, 'Geschichtlicher Verlauf des Feldzuges beim III/99' in *Das Gebirgsjäger Regiment 99 im polnischen Feldzug*, p. 163.
6. *Der Polenfeldzug im Tagebuch eines Gebirgsartilleristen*, pp. 29–30.
7. *Leutnant* Schuhmann, 'Geschichtlicher Verlauf des Feldzuges beim III/99' in *Das Gebirgsjäger Regiment 99 im polnischen Feldzug*, p. 163, *Der Polenfeldzug im Tagebuch eines Gebirgsartilleristen*, p. 39 and Buchner, 'Kampfziel Lemberg', p. 49.
8. Combat Report by *Gebirgsjäger* Regiment 98 in BA-MA RH28-1/255 and *Das Gebirgsjäger Regiment 99 im polnischen Feldzug*, pp. 120–1.
9. *Das Gebirgsjäger Regiment 99 im polnischen Feldzug*, pp. 120–1 and *Kameraden unterm Edelweiss*, pp. 18–23.
10. *Gefreiter* Dussmann, 'Am Rande Lembergs', in *Das Gebirgsjäger Regiment 99 im polnischen Feldzug*, pp. 99–100.
11. Divisionsbericht über den Feldzug in Polen, p. 16 in BA-MA RH28-1/256 and *Das Gebirgsjäger Regiment 99 im polnischen Feldzug*, pp. 120–1.
12. *Oberjäger* Münzenmay, 'Kampf um Lemberg', in *Das Gebirgsjäger Regiment 99 im polnischen Feldzug*, pp. 57–8.
13. Leixner, p. 58 and Combat Report by *Gebirgsjäger* Regiment 98 in BA-MA RH28-1/255.

14. Combat Report by *Gebirgsjäger* Regiment 98 in BA-MA RH28-1/255.
15. *Oberjäger* Münzenmay, 'Kampf um Lemberg', in *Das Gebirgsjäger Regiment 99 im polnischen Feldzug*, pp. 57–9.
16. *Der Polenfeldzug im Tagebuch eines Gebirgsartilleristen*, p. 43.
17. *Kameraden unterm Edelweiss*, pp. 11–13.
18. Leixner, p. 66.
19. *Der Polenfeldzug im Tagebuch eines Gebirgsartilleristen*, pp. 46, 49.
20. Hodurek, pp. 14–15.
21. 14/9/39. Combat Report by Gebirgsjäger Regiment 98. BA-MA RH28-1/255 Gefechtsberichte über den Einsatz der 1 *Gebirgsjäger* Division in Polen.
22. Anon, 'Unser Bataillonsstab, einmal anders gesehen!' in *Das Gebirgsjäger Regiment 99 im polnischen Feldzug*, pp. 83–4.
23. Manz, p. 69 and *Der Polenfeldzug im Tagebuch eines Gebirgsartilleristen*, pp. 53–55.
24. Manz, p. 84.
25. Siebte Armeekorps, *Wir zogen gegen Polen*, pp. 118–19.
26. *Der Polenfeldzug im Tagebuch eines Gebirgsartilleristen*, pp. 54–55 and *Wir Marschierten Gegen Polen*, p. 55.
27. *Ströme von Blut muss der Boden laufen/Es zittert die Erde, es wankt die Welt / Wo über zersetzt, zerschossene Haufen / In jagender Angst die Letzten laufen / Schlägt unbarmherzig das Feuer ins Feld. Es trommelt und trommelt und dröhnt und kracht! / Der Feind uns jetzt kennenlernte! / Denn wir haben diese Hölle entfacht / In der der Sieger aus aller Schlacht / der Tod – hält grausige Ernte* in Manz, p. 67.
28. Jäger Ernst Schulz, 'Ein Tag vor Lemberg', in BA-MA RH53-18/149.
29. Siebte Armeekorps, *Wir zogen gegen Polen*, pp. 122–3.
30. Ibid, pp. 89–92.
31. *Leutnant* Schwender, 'Die 3 Kompanie bei Rzesna-Ruska' in *Das Gebirgsjäger Regiment 99 im polnischen Feldzug*, p. 104.
32. Jäger Ernst Schulz, 'Ein Tag vor Lemberg', in BA-MA RH53-18/149.
33. Siebte Armeekorps, *Wir zogen gegen Polen*, pp. 89–92.
34. *Jäger* Ernst Schulz, 'Ein Tag vor Lemberg', in BA-MA RH53-18/149.
35. Siebte Armeekorps, *Wir zogen gegen Polen*, pp. 130–1.
36. *Leutnant* Schwender, 'Die 3 Kompanie bei Rzesna-Ruska', in *Das Gebirgsjäger Regiment 99 im polnischen Feldzug*, pp. 104–5.
37. Leixner, p. 79.
38. *Leutnant* Dörr, 'Als Ordonnanz Offizier bei der Division, in BA-MA RH53-18/145 and Hodurek, p. 24.
39. Siebte Armeekorps, *Wir zogen gegen Polen*, pp. 130–1.
40. *Der Polenfeldzug im Tagebuch eines Gebirgsartilleristen*, pp. 78–9.
41. Divisionsbericht über den Feldzug in Polen, p. 47 in BA-MA RH28-1/256 and *Leutnant* Schuhmann, 'Geschichtlicher Verlauf des Feldzuges beim III/99' in *Das Gebirgsjäger Regiment 99 im polnischen Feldzug*, p. 167.
42. *Hauptmann* Wehnert, 'Bericht über den Einsatz der 2 Kompanie vor Lemberg' in *Das Gebirgsjäger Regiment 99 im polnischen Feldzug*, p. 98.
43. Kaltenegger, Roland, *Die Deutsche Gebirgstruppe 1935–1945*, p. 116.
44. Kaltenegger, *Die Stammdivision der deutschen Gebirgstruppe*, p. 105 and Kaltenegger, Roland, *Die Deutsche Gebirgstruppe 1935–1945*, p. 119.

45. *Der Polenfeldzug im Tagebuch eines Gebirgsartilleristen*, p. 82.

46. Schimak, Lamprecht, and Dettmer, *Die 44 Infanterie Division: Tagebuch der Hoch und Deutschmeister*, pp. 39–40.

47. *Oberjäger* Wahl, 'Abschied von Rzesna-Ruska', in *Das Gebirgsjäger Regiment 99 im polnischen Feldzug*, pp. 199–200.

48. KTB 5 Batterie/Gebirgs-Artillerie-Regiment 79 22/9/39. Cited in Kaltenegger, *Gebirgsartillerie auf allen Kriegsschauplätzen*, p. 78.

49. *Kameraden unterm Edelweiss: Kriegsgeschichte der 2 Kompanie, Gebirgsjäger Regiment 100*, p. 26.

CHAPTER NINE

Putting Death to the Test

Just what is war? A compilation of sacrifices and exhaustion, of thirst and occasionally hunger, of heat and cold.

– WILHELM PRÜLLER

THE blue-blooded Oskar Wilhelm Karl Hans Kuno von Preussen, Prince of Prussia, was an idealist, a dreamer. This campaign in Poland was a 20th-Century crusade. Von Preussen marched to the tune of cathedral music 'carried from afar' in the cities of the Reich. The twenty-four-year-old wrote home poetically:

Before us the endless, shapeless expanse of the steppe is spread out; it seems to glow threateningly in the east. There's smoke in the sky. All there is to do is advance to the distant lines, behind which our fate pushes heavy and dull. We will not escape it.

We carry the blood of two millennia of shining, towering history with us, and only a quiet radiance remained from the wreaths and ribbons, which bound it.

This was Oskar von Preussen's *Feuertaufe* – baptism of fire. He would not survive it. As he stormed the Widawka Heights south of Lodz with 51st Infantry Regiment on the afternoon of 5 September, he was mortally-wounded by Polish machine-gun fire.[1]

The feelings of Oskar von Preussen were typical of the men of 1939. They were convinced of the justness of their cause, convinced of the greatness of their *Volk*, convinced of the greatness of their Führer. Their lives found purpose, a greater meaning, in the scrub and woods of the Corridor, on the slopes of the Carpathians, on the lanes of Galicia. 'I leave my youthful days behind me,' *Leutnant* Bruno Steinbach wrote in his diary as he began the march on Lemberg with 100th *Gebirgsjäger* Regiment. 'A greater life lies before me. All cares and wishes are behind me.' Bruno Steinbach did not expect to return from this adventure in Poland, but that did not trouble him. 'My life was restless,' the officer wrote. 'That unease inside has now gone. Now a wonderful life lies ahead of me. It's wonderful to enter an age without end, eternity. I have one request: that with all my heart my death becomes my last and greatest deed.'[2] Bruno Steinbach survived the Polish campaign; he died two years later in the Russian steppe.

Men like Bruno Steinbach gave Mauritz von Wiktorin hope – and confidence. He had already experienced the exhilaration of war – as well as all its horrors –

a generation before as a junior officer in the Austrian Army. And now he would lead men into war once more, only this time his responsibilities were even greater – and so were his doubts. 'I now had to pass my trial by fire as a commander,' he recalled. 'I asked myself that anxious question: would the young men be up to the task?' After more than a year in command of 20th Motorised Infantry Division, Mauritz von Wiktorin was convinced they would be.[3]

Gebirgsjäger Helmut Loges was still searching for life's greater meaning. 'There was something of the daring curiosity of youth which wanted to put Death to the test,' he recalled. But war, so far, had been a disappointment for Loges. Three miles inside Polish territory on the road to Lemberg and nothing. Loges was still waiting for his baptism 'by lead and steel'. The mountain infantry's boots and the hoofs of their mules clattered on the Polish road snaking through the edge of the Carpathians. And then, from nowhere, a whistling noise. The *Jäger* hurried off the road, hauling their mules into a ditch. *So this is our baptism of fire*, thought Loges. The only casualty was a mule, struck in the mouth. It screamed with pain. As the mountain men prepared to move off they artillery opened fire. White puffs of cloud began to rise above the forests which lined the mountain road. The march resumed. A few more miles and the men passed through the village of Krempna, thirty-five miles southeast of Neu Sandez, at the foot of a hill where Polish troops were dug in. With darkness falling, the Polish 'concert' began, raining shells and bullets down on Krempna.

It turns into an extraordinarily bright night. The Poles have doused a wooden bridge in petrol and set it ablaze. Huge flames light up the valley, the small lime houses and mountainsides in an instant. A terrible but magnificent mise-en-scène for our baptism of fire. The comfortable rattle of Polish machine-guns mingles with the bright, lively *trrr trrr* of our machine guns, the gargling of the shells sailing over our heads, impacting with a flash, and the crackle and crashing of burning bridge timbers to become a sinister night-time concert.[4]

Justus Ehrhardt's first impressions of war were almost identical. Erhardt, a lowly *Schütze* (rifleman) arrived with 309th Infantry Regiment in the border town of Schneidemühl in the dying days of August. Schneidemühl, the *Landser* observed, was a hive of activity. 'From one hour to the next, the air is filled with the sound of marching columns, the clattering and crashing of countless vehicles and the hum of scores of engines.' And then came the order: march.

We looked out for the enemy, to the left, to the right and above us: we were in enemy territory. The first burning house smoulders to the right of the road. A thick wire entanglement beyond it. Bunkers, block houses, wooden barriers cleared away. Is the road mined? Onwards, ever onwards. German farmers on the road. Flowers, open arms, the joyous eyes of men and women. Marvellous, admirable delight. And the first happy children.

Wheels roll. The infantry marches. Guns slung on. Machine-guns free. Artillery overtakes us. We nod our heads as a greeting. The steel barrels are darkly threatening. We pass villages, here and there a swastika flag flies from the window. The first abandoned houses. Cattle cry helplessly in the stables, chickens flap about.

Motorised units clatter along the road. Every type of vehicle. The infantry marches. On the left, on the right, ever onwards. In front is the enemy…

There's roaring and rumbling: bombers accompanied by fighters. We look at each other and nod: They wouldn't have it any other way. Far in the distance the first impacts explode. March onwards. We march by day and night. By day the sun beats down. Clouds of dust are whipped up. Every road is filled with troops. There's rattling and rumbling, the ground shakes. The wheels on the guns grind. Cries, orders, the neighing of horses. Snorting and puffing, messengers on horseback gallop past. Motorcycles clatter along under clouds of dust. Men on the march.

The campaign was several days old before Ehrhardt and his men heard the 'clattering and crashing' of battle. 'Haystacks, farmhouses, German villages go up in flames,' the infantryman wrote. He continued.

Polish artillery fires at our road. We take up position. The battle intensifies. Shells come in, howling and hissing above us. They're the harmless ones, it's the others that you only hear when they're upon you. We have to halt and wait for hours, then we're off again. We've losses. The first graves have to be dug.[5]

The sight of the first dead was a sobering experience for every *Landser*. The campaign in Poland was a day old when panzer grenadier Bruno Fichte's half-track rolled over the border. Nervous and apprehensive, as a non-commissioned officer Fichte nevertheless had to inspire confidence in the men under him. Shortly after dawn on the third, the twenty-four-year-old found himself steeling his men in the face of an imminent Polish attack. Alongside him was his twenty-six-year-old comrade and friend Ernst Lenz 'a fine chap,' Fichte recalled. 'He dreamed of just once having a young girl. Nothing obsessed him more – he'd never had one,' the *Unteroffizier* recalled. He never would. 'I heard a crack, something hit my face and then trickled down it. After a while we withdrew and I dragged my friend – I only knew he had been hit. And then I saw that his head was split open, and what had hit me and stuck to my face and uniform was his brain.'[6]

Gefreiter Otto Mühlbacher stared helplessly at a comrade who had lost both his legs to a road mine near Jablunka. Words failed him. He was too choked with emotion. The wounded *Gebirgsjäger* panted. 'Suddenly everything in him gives in,' wrote Mühlbacher. 'For the first time in my life I have seen a person die.' Mühlbacher's *Leutnant* rounded up his company. The men put down their playing cards and grabbed their rifles and steel helmets for a simple funeral service on the edge of Jablunka. 'Never had we been stirred to the depths of our soul and never had presenting arms had such power as it did before the open graves into which the spruce coffins containing our comrades were lowered,' the *Gefreiter* recalled. The strains of a rather hoarse rendition of the *Guten Kameraden* echoed around the Jablunka Pass. 'We felt a lump in our throats and our eyes burned,' wrote Mühlbacher. 'Afterwards, no man wanted to look at the other. No-one wanted his weakness to be noticed.'[7]

Death, to Berliner Hans P, showed what 'war truly meant' – and showed a man for what he was. The theology student's motorised infantry platoon had been waiting to cross the Brahe north of Bromberg when a ferocious hail of Polish mortar fire began to fall on the cutting they were resting in. The men made a dash for safety, but not everyone had escaped the Polish trap; one vehicle suffered a direct hit, killing two men instantly, fatally wounding another and injuring a good half a dozen others. 'For the first time death had touched our company and – apparently indiscriminately – had snatched three comrades from us,' Hans wrote that evening. War had shown the strong men in the student's company to be cowards, and those who had never come to the fore until now to be men of courage, true warriors. 'All that is fake, all masks, all that is merely for show vanished,' wrote Hans. 'Each man stood there before all our eyes as he truly was.'[8]

And there were Polish dead. Entering the village of Ostrow Mazowiecka, fifty miles northeast of Warsaw on the main Warsaw-Bialystok highway, Fritz Fillies found the fresh traces of battle amongst the 'shot-up houses. Dead Polish soldiers lay in the doorways, or half hung out of opened windows. There was still blood visible. War had permitted no time for burial.' The soldiers marched on over the cobbled streets, past the bodies of Poles who had clearly bled to death.[9] War reporter Kurt Frowein came across a fatally-wounded Polish soldier, 'a small bloody heap of human misery, his legs drawn up to his chest in agony, his face a pale green colour.' The Pole cried out for water. Frowein unbuttoned the man's olive green tunic, now stained red by blood, and a medic handed a canteen. 'For the last time, a painful smile crossed his face as he uttered the word "thank you" in German,' Frowein recalled. The soldier died shortly afterwards; he was buried where he fell, a simple wooden cross covered by a Polish helmet marking the spot.

Kurt Frowein was moved by the plight of this Pole. He had 'died like a true soldier. He has defended the position which he occupied as ordered to the last. His cartridge pouches were empty, and in the magazine of his carbine there were just two bullets when he was fatally shot.' The Polish soldier inspired begrudging admiration and respect in many *Landsers*, disdain and disgust in others. 'The Polish troops fight well only sporadically,' one *Gefreiter* in 2nd Motorised Division wrote home. 'Their equipment is miserable. The relatively small losses we have suffered is purely down to our first-class equipment, better equipment and superior leadership, as well as the excellence of the German *Landser*.' To some Germans the enemy did not even look like soldiers. 'Their uniform – you really can't call it that – was so shabby that you would have been ashamed to run around in it as a soldier,' one non-commissioned officer observed. 'When you bear such a soldierly image in mind, then it's not so surprising that the Poles skedaddle in the face of our advance after a bit of resistance.' Erich Beck of 2nd *Leichte* Division was more magnanimous: 'We admired our opponent for their national pride and commitment. They demanded our respect.' They did, for the sight of olive-green troops swarming towards the German lines was both heroic and horrifying. 'Before any attack the Poles give three cheers – each one a long drawn out cry that sounds like animals baying for blood,' a soldier in XVI Corps wrote in a letter. 'Although they are absolutely suicidal in the face of our fast-firing machine guns I must admit that to stand and watch as those long lines of infantry come storming forward is quite unnerving.' But, as one General commented, 'all the dash and bravery could not compensate for the lack of modern arms and serious tactical training'.[10]

There was little dash evident aboard Hitler's special train. Life on the *Sonderzug* was monotonous. The Führer was not an early riser. He would emerge from his carriage around 9am each day and wander into the command wagon, set up by his military staff to follow the campaign's progress. The wagon was dominated by a large table with a map spread out on it; the Wehrmacht's Chief-of-Staff, Wilhelm Keitel, sat at one end, liaison officer Nikolaus von Vormann at the other next to a telephone, while Hitler's chief of operations Alfred Jodl stood over the table, explaining the situation based on the latest reports to hand. Mid-morning, a staff officer would enter with the draft of the daily military communiqué – which Jodl would always re-write to be as terse as possible. And then the 'chief' would 'drive off with his men', leaving his personal staff behind in the *Sonderzug* with little or nothing to do. 'The heat is simply terrible,' secretary Christa Schroeder complained. 'The sun beats down on the carriages all day long and there's nothing we can do about it. I am soaked to the skin.' The 'chief', meanwhile, was in his element. To prevent a repetition of the scenes in the first days of the campaign when Party bigwigs unceremoniously jostled for position in the motorcade, three Junkers 52 transport aircraft flew the Führer and his immediate entourage on the first stage of their journey, whereupon they would be met by their cars. Then the Mercedes raced down the Polish lanes, Hitler standing up 'exactly as he does in Germany' as he saluted the columns of soldiers. Huge crowds in *feldgrau* gathered around the car whenever it stopped. 'You can be proud to have taken part in a campaign the likes of which military history has never seen,' he told the men. It was a strangely emotional experience for the Führer. 'We shall not see their likes again,' he muttered watching his army cross the River San.

At dusk, the entourage would return for the evening briefing and situation conference; Hitler's military staff had busied themselves throughout the day collating reports and updating the situation maps. The Führer always listened closely, he never dictated his ideas or interfered in the operations – that would come in later years. After a brief supper, Hitler would return to the command wagon for the final reports of the day, before sinking into a chair and subjecting his audience to insufferable monologues until the small hours of the morning. Few men dared to interrupt him, except to agree with his thoughts.[11]

In April 1940, Tobis – one of the Reich's two principal film producers – unveiled a new documentary in German cinemas. *Feuertaufe*, 'the film of our Luftwaffe's action in Poland', vied for the ordinary German's Reichsmarks alongside more trivial fare such as the tedious melodrama *Mutterliebe*, *Mother's Love*, and the pro-Irish, anti-British thriller *Der Fuchs von Glenarvon*, *The Fox of*

Glenarvon. But *Feuertaufe* was not trivial fare. It was 'a document for present and future generations of the contribution to the history of Greater Germany's struggle for freedom,' a ninety-minute paean to the Reich and its Luftwaffe. The onerous tones of Herbert Gernot and Gerhard Jeschke provided the narration accompanied by the stirring orchestral sweep of Norbert Schultze, set to panoramas of the clouds over a Germany at peace pierced sporadically by the sun's rays, and the ruins of Warsaw, blackened and burned-out buildings, rail lines wrecked, parks cratered. *Feuertaufe*, its makers proclaimed, was 'real and simple, hard and pitiless – like war itself'.

Hard and pitiless indeed. Worshippers in Janow Lubelski, a small market town thirty-five miles south of Lublin, learned just how pitiless shortly before mid-day on 8 September. Father Czestaw Dmochowski was half-way through mass when the drone of aircraft engines drowned out his words. 'Surely they will not bomb an undefended town – there are only civilians here,' he reasoned. But the sound of the engines grew ever louder, then the first bombs fell. The worshippers fled from the church, including Father Dmochowski. 'The sight is indescribable,' he wrote. 'In the market square there are many dead, killed by the bombs. People groaning can be heard, mixed with the bleating of animals.' Janow Lubelski's ordeal lasted on and off for more than four hours. When it was all over, the priest surveyed the scene. 'All around are dead, burning houses, chimneys stand out impassively.'[12]

The following afternoon it was the turn of the fortress city of Brest-Litovsk. Maria Pasierbiriska was walking with her daughter when she spied a black bird circling far above the city. By Polish standards, Brest was well prepared to cope with air attacks. There were shelters and trenches for its citizens to take refuge in and its anti-aircraft guns still barked fiercely. Now those guns barked and the people of Brest dashed for the shelters. Maria Pasierbiriska was too slow. The first bombs were falling before she could carry her daughter into a trench. 'Suddenly the earth begins to shake down below, we are hit by a blast of hot air and enveloped in a deadly sweat,' she recalled. 'I press my daughter to me to die as close to her as possible – if we die, then together.' Her daughter protested, convinced the bombing was punishment for some childish misdemeanour. Ten times the bombers circled overhead. 'The enemy sows destruction,' Pasierbiriski recorded in her diary. 'Death has a rich harvest.' The heart of Brest was ravaged by the raid, but particularly harrowing was the sight of a trench in Mickiewicz Street which had taken a direct hit. 'The force of the explosion had been so terrible that the corpse of one of the women was literally blown to pieces,' one eyewitness recalled. 'Rags of clothing and flesh had been projected on to the balcony of a house several metres away.'[13]

Thirty or so miles north of Brest, a French reservist officer was fleeing Warsaw with his family, hoping to reach the apparent sanctuary of Lemberg. His train meandered through the Bug valley until it pulled into the small town of Czeremcha, an insignificant place, save for a small rail junction south of the town. The Luftwaffe had already visited at least once. The tracks in the station were torn up. Telegraph and telephone wires hung limply from broken poles. In a copse just outside Czeremcha the train ground to a halt. Railway workers threw themselves under the carriages. And then the train was rocked by a succession of explosions, twenty in all. Acrid, sickly smoke filled the carriages. Eight hundred men, women and children jumped out and scrambled under the train to join the railway workers. A humming noise filled the sky. Nine more German bombers approached. Some of the passengers made a run for the apparent safety of the trees. The wood offered no protection. Bombs shattered tree trunks, hurled stones on the forest floor through the air. Some Poles huddled together. A dog howled continuously. And in the middle of the wood, a woman began reciting the *de Profundis*. The sound of aircraft engines faded, the bombers turned to dots on the horizon. But then the aircraft turned around. More bombs fell. Finally the bombers passed. The passengers wearily returned to the train, miraculously undamaged. The French officer asked a railway official about the fate of the dead. 'There are no victims,' the railwayman told him. 'All is well. There are only some persons who have not re-joined the train.'[14]

Wherever Poles moved, civilians and soldiers, by road or rail, the Luftwaffe seemed to find them. Railway lines were 'synonymous with danger and death,' recalled Edward Sewanski, who fled the border town of Ostrow Wielopolski, fifty miles north of Breslau, at the first sound of battle. His weary march to Lodz was accompanied by a seemingly constant soundtrack: the drone of aircraft engines, the roar of bombers, the cannon of fighters thundering as they strafed the roads. Enemy pilots would often fly so low they simply tossed grenades out of their cockpits on the columns of misery below. War correspondent Carl Cranz joined an He111 bomber crew on a search for Polish troops retreating north and northwest of Lodz. They found them trudging along the main road from Leczyca eastwards towards Lowicz and Skierniewice, and ultimately Warsaw. The *Kette* (a flight of three aircraft) of medium bombers descended from almost 9,000 feet to barely 3,000 as they made their attack. Cranz's Heinkel jerked slightly, and the bombs began to tumble earthwards.

> A procession of bombs falls precisely on the target – right in the heart of the column, on and around the road. With a bright flash, flames shoot up from the impacts. Like huge mushrooms, the black clouds well up, roll across the land and are dispersed by the wind.
>
> Bomb after bomb falls. Bursts of fire rattle from the machine-guns. Like an imperious, fleeting comet, the sparkling bursts of tracer strike the scattering columns of lorries and horse-drawn wagons, the cavalrymen and marching troops below.

Lying down in the Heinkel's bulbous glass nose, a tall *Oberleutnant* aimed his machine gun at the Polish troops below. Cranz watched as a burst from the gun struck the fuel tank of a vehicle and a huge black cloud of smoke billowed over the column.[15]

Such scenes troubled aircrew initially. One *Leutnant* sent to bomb a station in Posen on the second day of war watched in horror as half of his sixteen bombs tumbled not on to the railway lines and platforms, but landed among neighbouring houses. He quickly steeled himself. 'On the third day I did not care a hoot, and on the fourth I was enjoying it,' he recalled. 'It was our before-breakfast amusement to chase single soldiers over the fields with machine-gun fire and to leave them lying there with a few bullets in the back.' Such sentiments were hardly surprising, given the instructions the men of Luftflotte 1 received from their commanding officer, *General der Flieger* Albert Kesselring. 'You have to kill any feelings,' he reportedly told them. 'An enemy of Germany is no human. There are no so-called "civilian targets" for the Luftwaffe, there are no feelings. The enemy has to be exterminated, erased from the face of the planet. Resistance has to be broken.'[16]

Despite Albert Kesselring's exhortations, it was impossible for the German soldier to kill all his feelings. The roads of Poland filled with women, children, old men fleeing the advancing Wehrmacht. *Gefreiter* Wilhelm Grossmann of 309th Infantry Regiment watched 'an endless column of misery' passing them: 'miserable *panje* wagons, heavy farmer's carts, carriages, carts, pedestrians, cyclists, cattle driven along. Miserable, worried figures wrapped in rags, sad, serious faces, lips pursed together, tears in their eyes, curious looks from children.' Tired horses strained at the reins as they struggled to haul carts piled high with a bizarre assortment of possessions – 'sacks with grain, flour, a broken bicycle, a crate with geese and chickens, beds, saucepans, toys, dirty clothes.' Grossmann's 309th comrade Kurt Schmoll marched past 'refugees on foot with their last cow on a tether or crammed together on fragile carts pulled by emaciated horses. Horses without masters trot alongside the road and run along with the German columns.' Justus Ehrhardt searched a deserted farmhouse in the Corridor. He found goats, half-starved, tied to a bedpost, startled cows trampling around, pigs grunting in the courtyards. A doll sat limply on a windowsill. A colleague was strangely touched by the sight of the doll. He picked it up and sat it up straight so that it could stare down the lane to the farm with its big round black eyes and see its owner returning. Even hardened warriors such as 3rd Panzer Division's commander Leo Geyr von Schweppenburg were touched by the Poles' plight. He watched them flee first eastwards in the face of Germans then, as September progressed, westwards in the face of the Russians. The roads were clogged with Polish civilians and soldiers; the latter marched into the arms of the Germans, preferring German to Russian captivity. 'The misery was grim,' Geyr recalled. 'The scenes on this journey were unforgettable. The most moving thing for me was the sight of a mother who lay with her child by the roadside, abandoned and alone. Faith without hope.'[17]

Twenty-nine-year-old Edward Serwanski had heeded the call to flee, looking for sanctuary in Lodz. 'The glow of flames from the fires in the direction of Lodz and Warsaw pointed the way,' the Pole recalled. Night just made the sight of evacuation more unreal. 'A human anthill wandered around – carts, horses, cattle, luggage and bundles dominated the scene,' Serwanski wrote. 'The cries and screams of animals, the shouts of people, the crying and screaming of children were all mixed up in the clouds of dust and sand.'

Having crossed the River Warthe, the forlorn column of evacuees approached Lodz. Far from offering sanctuary, Lodz itself was now being evacuated. From a vantage point overlooking the city and its environs, Edward Serwanski and a friend struggled to comprehend the scenes played out in front of them.

A terrible panic seized people. They fled blindly. People crossed ditches and later went across country through fields. The cries of animals, screams and calls tore through the air. We heard the sobbing of despair. Chaos and confusion, mixed with a mad urgency, dominated. Soon the roads and fields were littered with cases, bundles, various pieces of luggage which people had pointlessly taken from their homes. Most threw everything away when they couldn't follow the others.

The ever-growing column of misery struggled eastwards, eventually reaching the Vistula south of Warsaw. For mile-upon-mile the fields on the approaches to the river were strewn with abandoned carts, crammed with personal goods. Horses and cattle wandered around, masterless. Left by the roadside were bundles, chests, clothes, household goods, anything which would impede the crossing of the river was cast away.

Edward Serwanski tried to get some sleep under a tree. The cry: 'The Germans are coming' startled him. At the Vistula's edge, civilians jostled with dispirited Polish soldiers from shattered units, then struck out into the river. Overhead the Luftwaffe appeared. The cannons rattled and the bombs hurled up huge spouts of water. 'Men, civilians as well as soldiers, pressed into the water like a flock of sheep,' Serwanski remembered. The cries of the wounded, drowning and dying mingled with the bellows of animals and the thunder of bombs exploding, the scream of the Stukas and the hoarse rattle of their machine-guns.[18]

Such woeful treks invariably only led Poles back to their homes in the end. 'Be grateful that you are living in peace and order at home, you cannot imagine the terror which war brought to the people here,' *Feldwebel* Wilm Hosenfeld wrote to his wife. Hosenfeld was a schoolteacher, a veteran of the Great War, a former SA stormtrooper, and now a reservist called to the colours. It was his duty to serve. Yet the reality of war in the East troubled him. Every day he watched refugees, small children, women, girls, old men, file through the streets of Pabianice, a small town ten miles southwest of Lodz. 'Often they return home to their village and find their apartments turned to ashes.'[19]

The routes of retreat were littered with the detritus of a people on the move and a beaten army. Fritz Filles found

limbered Polish machine-guns without ammunition – the drivers had apparently made off with the horses. Sacks of pressed hay, wonderful for our hungry horses, haversacks with thick white rusks, flasks with coffee. Despite the cool morning which made hands cold and noses red, the coffee was still lukewarm. And then gasmasks, rucksacks, a wallet with illegible postcards and cheap, sleazy pictures of a nightclub dancer. These scenes of wild flight by the Poles went on for kilometres.[20]

American journalist John Raleigh was driven along the road from Lodz to Warsaw, a road strewn with burned-out tanks or staff cars, the odd arm or leg sticking out from the wreckage. The living fared little better, Raleigh observed. 'The faces of the people were terrible masks,' he wrote. 'Their stares, as they watched Nazi motorcycle runners and field police, reflected the despair they felt.'[21] Kurt Schmoll found the lanes of the Corridor lined with nothing but 'shot-up batteries, the cadavers of horses, dead people, bits of equipment.'

And in the towns and villages, nothing but destruction. There was barely a settlement unscarred by war. 'In the East all we can see are heaps of rubble, chimneys the sole reminders of Polish crofts,' Schmoll wrote gleefully. In towns, 'many homes are just smouldering heaps of rubble,' Justus Ehrhardt recalled. Walls collapsed into the streets, downed telephone and telegraph lines lay across the roads. When an attack by 311th Infantry Regiment ground to a halt in Stare Zalubicze, on the right bank of the Western Bug north of Warsaw, *Feldwebel* Hubert Hundreiser's platoon leader ordered his men to set the village on fire. 'Small puffs of smoke immediately began to rise, turning into bright flames in a flash, forcing the enemy to abandon his position,' Hundreiser recalled. 'The fire died out surprisingly quickly. All that was left standing of the wooden cottages were the stoves and the brick chimneys. They towered above the smouldering ruins like charred fists pointing the finger of blame.' Hundreiser felt no pity. The Poles had murdered ethnic Germans, he reasoned. This was their punishment.[22]

Such was 'war over Poland', infantryman Kurt Schmoll coldly observed. 'The sky no longer darkens. The blood-red glow of fire.' Wherever the German soldier marched, the flames of war were his constant companion. Accounts of the 1939 campaign are peppered with references to a sky tinged blood red, to the heavens glowing, to the horizon flashing like lightning by night as the muzzles of the German artillery fired. It was a scene which mesmerised many a *Landser*. 'The attack in the evening was a strange, beautiful sight in war,' one artillery battery with 1st *Leichte* Division recorded as it crossed the Warthe. 'Tracer flies across the river, again and again, shells leaving the barrels of the panzers flash brightly. The houses immediately burn like bright signals, the shimmer of the flames are reflected in the river. The smoke and haze of battle hangs over everything.' To infantryman Werner Flack, this campaign seemed to be a great drama played out against a fiery backdrop. As night fell in Upper Silesia, he was mesmerised by the death waltz of Gostyn, a small village southwest of Katowice.

Eerie ruins rise up from the ground and the ruins smoulder; the smoke is blacker than night; it licks with ravenous greed and bright flames, crackles and pops, hisses and stews. Sparks fly up into the grey sky; beams moan, groan, ache in the heat and collapse and a swarm of sparks rise up like a living soul. The horror peers out of houses which line the road through broken and smashed windows, while the flames of neighbouring fires play their game of sparks against panes which have remained intact. We don't want to believe our eyes. We never saw such a scene. Or had we only dreamed of such scenes in war? It's almost too much for today! We look and stare; we listen for the confusing sounds of burning barns and houses and think for a second: the harvest is in. But where there was grain is now a black pile which flames leap from, and white smoke rises like poisonous steam. And close to the flickering house there's a black figure lying on the half-burned floor amid the smoke and soot of the smouldering fire: a bundle of singed clothes perhaps? And yet it lies there so stretched out, strangely alive yet rigid.

As the campaign progressed, Flack's bloodlust and exuberance were tempered by the sights of battle. The scars of war became ever more apparent: scraps of uniform and bloodstained bandages lying in ditches, discarded cooking dishes, caps, steel helmets, a spade with a bullet hole, a canteen, a wrecked field gun, the trunks of trees spilt down the middle by shells. 'Our eyes move wearily from scene to scene and the further we march, words become less frequent,' Flack wrote. In the tops of unharmed trees, the birds sang. 'It is a tragic contrast,' the soldier observed. 'The birdsong doesn't capture the face of this world. The reality is bloody traces of the battle which has passed.'[23]

Such 'bloody traces of battle' could be found at every road junction, at every crossroads. On the way to Brest-Litovsk, a *Soldat* of 76th Infantry Regiment marched through the village of Ciechanowiec. The streets were still littered with the cadavers of horses, the bodies of men and all manner of equipment from Polish field batteries surprised the night before. 'We all pass the place where last night's palaver occurred,' the soldier wrote, staring at the disfigured corpses. 'Some men may have thought that they too could have faced the same fate.' Bruno Fichte came upon a similar sight – 'a real massacre'. In the late summer heat, the acrid, awful smell of bodies putrefying drifted across the Polish landscape. 'Human dismemberment was a daily occurrence,' Bruno Fichte remembered. His first sight of the dead was a Polish farmer, lying in a field, his stomach burst open. 'His intestines were hanging out and a dog was eating them, pulling him backwards, his hind legs digging into the ground.' *Schütze* Justus Ehrhardt marched through one small Polish town with every wall pockmarked by bullets, walls collapsed, ruins smouldering. The corpses of Polish soldiers were strewn everywhere. A black-and-white speckled cow wandered along next to the marching infantry. There was an almighty crash. The men dived for cover. Their horses reared up. And pieces of cow began falling from the heavens; the poor creature had wandered on to a mine.[24]

Such sights de-humanised some men. 'We were once stopped by a herd of cows and had to wait,' Fichte recalled. A *Gefreiter*, a former butcher, stepped forward. 'He took his gun and shot a cow dead. For nothing.' Fichte himself found it impossible not to be affected by his experiences in Poland. He did his best to suppress such memories 'otherwise no-one would have had any chance of survival. Feelings became less vivid over the years but in the end, the human never entirely vanishes. Something was always still there.'[25]

Fateful episodes of life and death were commonplace. Clearing out the Bzura pocket SS *Leibstandarte* platoon commander Hubert Meyer found himself caught up in hand-to-hand fighting with a Polish soldier among foxholes on the edge of the Kampinos forest. 'Another popped up behind me from the bushes along the bank – I had overlooked him,' Meyer recalled. His messenger, one *Sturmmann* Spiekhofen, shot the Pole dead instantly. 'We were exhausted, physically and emotionally. Each man lay down and slept where he had been standing,' Meyer continued. 'One non-commissioned officer reported Spiekhofen's deed to me. I could only shake his hand.' Meyer, who would go on to command an SS panzer division in the autumn of 1944, paused briefly for reflection. 'Life is all-in-all, yet it hangs by one silken thread,' he mused. 'One can lose it at any moment, as if it were nothing.'[26] At nightfall on 16 September, Wilhelm Prüller's 4th *Leichte* Division was subjected to ferocious Polish fire near the town of Zamosc, southwest of Lublin. 'The bullets just whistled!' the infantryman wrote in his diary.

> It's a curious feeling to hear the bullets above you and next to you, without ever knowing if they'll get you. When you hear them, you drop flat on the ground – at least during the first shots. Or take mortar or artillery fire. You hear them coming a long way off. And never a clue where they'll land.[27]

Panzer commander Willi Reibig bandaged the terribly-burned hands of a comrade. His vehicle had been driving down a forest lane near Mokra when it was struck by a Polish anti-tank shell. Signal flares on the tank exploded, quickly followed by a fuel canister. Shrapnel embedded itself in the commander's chest, while the burning fuel poured through the driver's slit, burning the driver's hands and face. 'In a flash everything was on fire,' the panzer commander recalled. He tried to open the turret hatch, but it was too hot. His burned driver tried to help him. 'I don't know how we got out of the panzer, or who got out first,' he told Reibig. As the two men hurriedly clambered out of the turret, the commander was struck by a blow on the back of his head and left shoulder, which knocked him off the blazing panzer but also knocked him out. 'Believe me, nothing is worse than lying wounded somewhere and you cannot move and there's no-one nearby to help you,' the officer told Reibig.[28]

Death, or the fear of it, preyed on the mind of every man. One soldier in 29th Infantry Division was convinced a 'lucky star' protected him. 'How very grateful we must be to the Almighty for protecting Germany from all manner of misery which I now see every day,' he wrote home. 'What my eyes will see – shells, mist, gas, smoke, noise, flames, air pressure,' wondered *Leutnant* Bruno Steinbach. 'The effects against non-living things are dreadful. What will happen to the man who is exposed to such things?' The only hope, Wilhelm Prüller reasoned, was to trust in God, one way or another. 'There's nothing to do but cross your fingers. If God pleases, I'll come home wounded, or healthy and untouched, or... not at all. We shall see.'[29]

The mental strains of battle were matched by the physical demands. As their forebears had done sweeping through France and Belgium in the summer of 1914, so the *Landser* of 1939 found the incessant marching exhausting. Poland's roads added to the infantrymen's misery. Most were dirt or dust tracks. The boots of the man in front, the hoofs of horses, the wheels of passing carts and trucks kicked up huge clouds of dust. For many *Landsers* the heat and the state of Poland's roads proved as great an obstacle as Polish resistance. The roads, one soldier driving towards Warsaw wrote home, were 'little more than dirt tracks with a hardened surface. Half an hour driving in such conditions and our faces are covered by a mask of red dust'. That dust, VII Corps complained as it marched through southern Poland, was the worst hardship the soldiers had to endure. 'It covers men, animals, vehicles, as if it wants to camouflage them against being sighted by aircraft, superfluous camouflage; for already the enemy has abandoned mastery of the sky to German airmen. Breathing becomes tormenting. Each man is a dusty spectre.' It was, one soldier observed, 'as if each man whipped up so much dust as a motor car normally did.' Water quenched the men's thirst, but not as well as a beer – 'even if it is only Polish Pivo'. Beer was a useful antidote to the September heat and Polish dust. The men of 45th Infantry Division marched into the town of Brzesko, between Krakow and Tarnow, and found a large brewery still intact. The *Landsers* had avoided Polish wells on their march east, convinced they were poisoned. Fifty thousand litres of beer from the brewery satiated their thirst. 'The supply,' recalled divisional chaplain Rudolf Gschöpf, 'lasted at least a couple of days.'[30]

When the infantry stopped, they slept for five minutes, ten, perhaps even thirty. They drifted into sleep almost immediately. The rifles slipped from their hands. Even the horses hung their heads. Sleep came wherever: on walls, in vehicles, by the roadside, standing, even on the move. 'I often find that I've slept on the march,' one *Gebirgs* artilleryman wrote in his diary. 'We link arms. One man leads, the other can then at least close his eyes.' This was war, wrote Heinz Borwin Venzky, and the soldier slept on hay or straw, on the pavement or in a field. 'The soldier sleeps despite the most incredible crashing, despite the most stale air and the coolest night.' And then the cry: 'Onwards!' The soldiers struggled to get up, then continued on their way. Medics treated men with footsores and blisters. But there was no let-up for those hobbling *Landsers*; they were expected to march at the double to catch up with their comrades. The lucky ones were given a lift in a car or truck.

By night, the dust did not seem to be as bad. But the coarse gravel on the Polish roads still hurt the feet, especially for the men with blisters – and that was most of them. It was often past midnight before the infantry reached their objective. The field kitchen was often waiting for them. The evening meal was hurriedly handed out – and eaten, washed down by black coffee. And then the men grabbed bundles of straw, tossed it down under the stars and fell down upon it. 'Soon all of us have gone to bed,' wrote Austrian *Gefreiter* Jakob Wildhaber. 'Each man thinks: *Thank God that today's behind us*. After several minutes they sleep the sleep of the just.'[31]

Gefreiter Hanns Pfeuffer turned to verse to capture the exertions demanded by the march on Lemberg:

And onward we go, the never-ending footsteps
The endless road of war.
Thirst torments us, sweat runs,
Even in the dark of night the road is so hot
The steep road of victory.
Feet bleed, eyes are red,

We lead our tired horses
Sleep is overpowering, the road endless,
Here through the ford, the bridge is blown up,
Only forward, march, march.

And onward we go, the never-ending footsteps,
We pursue and hunt the enemy!
Our boots rip, the soles are torn,
Thus we have hounded him through his land
And then we clobber him on the head![32]

But such exertions and such fitful sleep took their toll. How many days have we been on the march? Justus Ehrhardt asked himself. He looked at his comrades in 309th Infantry Regiment with admiration. 'They swallow dust, sleep standing up and marching, respond to enemy fire, roll up enemy positions, force the enemy to withdraw. At night they fall into straw somewhere, or a ditch besides their battle wagons.' There was no time to wash, no time to shave. 'We're unrecognisable in the mirror, brown, sunburned, dirty,' Ehrhardt wrote. 'And haven't the faces of our comrades become sharper and harder?' By 17 September, Wilhelm Prüller had had enough. 'I'm so sleepy I don't think I can stand it,' he wrote to his wife. 'It's already very hard to stand upright during the day, the last three weeks have been so incredibly exhausting.'[33]

The 'blitzkrieg' in Poland demanded about as much as man and beast could take. 45th Infantry Division marched 250 miles through southern Poland in thirteen days – nearly twenty miles each day. *Oberjäger* Hans May and his fellow mountain infantrymen covered 375 miles on foot in eighteen days – twenty-one miles daily – through the foothills of Slovakia and Galicia. The days were hot, the nights cool or cold. The men set off at or before dawn, and continued until or beyond midnight. The field kitchen usually could not keep pace with the advance, and what water there was by the roadside was filthy. And yet the further the *Gebirgsjäger* marched, the more buoyant was their mood. 'We knew that each kilometre we marched meant that the Poles had to go back too,' wrote May.[34]

In central and southern Poland, the echoes of 1914 and 1915 were everywhere. Crossing the Vistula west of Lublin, soldiers in 93rd Infantry Regiment stumbled across a German cemetery from the Great War. Time had taken its toll of the graveyard. The *Landsers* set about tidying the graves of 216 forebears killed in the summer of 1915, then erected a fresh cross with a brief inscription: *Unseren Kameraden* – our comrades. Reminders of sacrifices a generation before were particularly noticeable to those marching through Galicia. 'It was a strange stroke of Fate that the second great war which our generation had to experience began in a land which had been a theatre of war in the first,' battalion commander *Oberstleutnant* Mathias Kräutler observed. He continued:

Once again soldiers marched from the Austrian mountains, far from their homes, down the dusty roads of Galicia, they fought for bridges and fords on the Dunajec and San, again there was the strange-sounding name of

Przemysl which the Kaiser's warriors had made easier on the ear thanks to the popular soldiers' song about Fortress Przemysl, and once again, just as it had done twenty-five years ago, everything revolved around Lemberg.[35]

Everything revolved around Lemberg, but it was Przemysl, a fortress city on the San, which dominated the thoughts of many men marching east in 1939. The Russians had invested the fortress during the winter of 1914–15. When Przemysl finally fell, 120,000 Austrian soldiers marched into captivity. But the Russians did not enjoy their prize for long; German soldiers drove them out of the city in the summer of 1915. 'A bloody dump, this Przemysl!' one soldier in VII Corps told his comrades, recounting how his grandfather and father had stormed the citadel, and now he was following in their footsteps. 'It's a family tradition for us. Each generation is in Przemysl once.' There were other, more ominous stories. 'A reservist broke the silence with words that touched us deeply. My father fell here on the San. I don't know where, perhaps here,' one junior officer recalled. 'It became very clear to all of us that this was sacred ground, sacred because it had already drank the blood of a generation before us.'[36]

Lothar Rendulic belonged to that earlier generation. Twenty-five years earlier, the bespectacled *Leutnant* had arrived at a railway station in the heart of Moravia to entrain with his Austrian comrades in 99th Infantry Regiment. The young officer appeared more student than warrior, but the exterior belied a cold, ruthless infantryman. Yet the icy Rendulic was roused by the mood of his men whose excitement soon bubbled over into widespread cheering. Civilians rushed up to the train as it struggled through the lush Moravian terrain. Many bore baskets crammed with bread, cakes, butter, sausage, eggs and fruit for the soldiers. Workers in the fields briefly stopped gathering the harvest to wave at the passing soldiers. Late into the hot summer's night, the songs of soldiers drifted across the land. The train eventually ground to a halt and the infantrymen stepped out, formed up, and began their march to the east. The regiment crossed the San at Jaroslau, a dozen miles north of Przemysl, and marched into Galicia, a land of Poles and, for the most part, Ruthenians – Slavs from White Russia and the western Ukraine. The *Leutnant* was unimpressed by the 'small, low houses built mostly of wood and covered with straw'. Storks nested in the roofs, flattened clay served as the floor of homes. 'The quarters were the most primitive I had ever seen,' Rendulic recalled. 'Vermin, and bugs and fleas especially, were rife.' Inhabitants shared their homes with their animals, cooked on open fires, opening the door to get rid of the smoke. 'People led a life far from any culture and civilization.'

Twenty-five years later, *Oberst* Lothar Rendulic stood on the west bank of the San once more. Still bespectacled, but now with a short, neatly trimmed moustache, Rendulic was Chief-of-Staff of an infantry corps. A dedicated Nazi – he had joined the Party six years before the Reich had swallowed Austria – the officer rested in the small Galician village of Wola Buchowska. A quarter of a century before, the young Rendulic had been severely wounded here. Now he sought the exact spot. 'The place had not changed; the Galician villages seemed to be stuck in time,' he recalled. He followed the course of a stream, but dense undergrowth thwarted his progress. 'Nature,' Lothar Rendulic observed, 'does not rest.'[37]

Nature did not stop, but life in Galicia seemingly had. 'It was the same Galicia which our young soldiers knew from their fathers' stories,' wrote Mathias Kräutler. 'Nothing had changed in this land, the same misery in the cottages, the same poverty in the filthy villages, the run-down small towns, the same bottomless roads, the terrible paths, the depressing forests, the rocky gorges, the inaccessible mountains. All along the route of advance were military cemeteries, lonely soldiers' graves.'[38]

And now there were fresh German cemeteries in Galicia. 'We remember our dead,' wrote one *Jäger* Hermann as he mulled over the death of 116 of his 99th *Gebirgsjäger* Regiment comrades in nine days of fighting for Lemberg. He continued his eulogy:

No-one thought that he would have to die, the sacred belief in his *Volk* burned in his heart.

Far from home, on hallowed foreign soil, soaked in the blood of our fathers who fell in the Great War, you died for your *Volk*. We remember you, our dead comrades. Mourning with pride, we lower our flags over your distant graves. The flowers on your graves will fade but as long as a single German breathes, you will not be forgotten. The homeland mourns you, dead comrades, but your soul lives on among us; for you died for us, therefore all our gratitude belongs to you.

The homeland, Germany, greets you, and over your graves a new world rises.[39]

The propaganda books of 1939 and 1940 are filled with such hymns to the fallen, invariably accompanied by photographs of simple wooden crosses standing over earthen mounds covered perhaps by flowers or a steel helmet. The literature, the prose and poetry of the men of 1939 possesses none of the bitterness, none of the cries against the futility of war. These are clarion calls to war. Artilleryman *Gefreiter* Wolfgang Löffler wrote:

The war is delighted
That many young German oaks
Stand on their graves,
Building blocks for the German Reich.[40]

Would he become one of those building blocks, Wilhelm Prüller wondered. Or would he see his wife Henny and daughter Lore again? Thoughts of home, of his wife and child, dominated his diary. He spent his first wedding anniversary, 3 September, marching on Krakow. 'How can we celebrate it?' he pondered. 'I, in the woods, ready to attack. You, thinking of me, not knowing where I am. Sad, isn't it? But there's nothing to do about it, is there? It's just war! Just what is war? A compilation of sacrifices and exhaustion, of thirst and occasionally hunger, of heat and cold. I hope it's finished soon.'[41] And each night in Poland as he scribbled his diary entry, Wilhelm Prüller closed it with the same words: 'Today I'm still alive, and so are you and Lore. All of us!'

Notes

1. Bähr and Bähr, pp. 13–14.
2. 'Aus den Briefen und Aufzeichnungen Bruno Steinbachs', *Die Gebirgstruppe*, Heft Nr.2–4, 1957, pp. 284–5.
3. Asmus, *Die 20.Inf.Div.(mot) Chronik und Geschichte*, Band 2, p. 17.
4. Kaltenegger, Roland, *Die Stammdivision der deutschen Gebirgstruppe: Weg un Kampf der 1 Gebirgs-Division 1935–1945*, pp. 96–7.
5. Hoffmann, Oberleutnant Dr. (ed), *Infanterie Regiment 309 marschiert an den Feind*, pp. 6–9.
6. Schüddekopf, *Krieg: Erzählungen aus dem Schweigen*, pp. 30–31.
7. *Gefreiter* Otto Mühlbacher, 'Wie ich Polen erlebte', in BA-MA RH53-18/149.
8. Hammer, I und Neiden, Suzanne zu, *Sehr selten habe ich geweint*, Schweizer Verlag, Zurich, 1993, pp. 22–3.
9. Fillies, pp. 145–6.
10. Based on Piekalkiewicz, *Polenfeldzug: Hitler und Stalin zerschlagen die Polnische Republik*, p. 79, *Gefreiter* W.K, 2 Kompanie/Infanterie Nachrichten Abteilung 2, 2 Infanterie Division (Mot), 10/9/39, in Buchbender, p. 40, *Unteroffizer* K.A, Third Army, 8/9/39, in Buchbender, p. 39, Luck, p. 29, Lucas, *Kampfgruppe*, p. 13 and Mellenthin, p. 4.
11. Life in the *Sonderzug* is based on Vormann, pp. 79–81, 87–9, TB Rosenberg, 29/9/39 in Rosenberg, pp. 98–100 and Schroeder's letter of 11/9/39 in *Er war mein Chef*, pp. 98–9.
12. Böhler, *Grösste Härte*, p. 74.
13. Böhler, *Grösste Härte*, p. 64 and Polish Black Book, p. 62.
14. Polish Black Book, pp. 35–6.
15. Anon, *Wach auf, es ist Krieg! Wie Polen und Deutsche den 1 September 1939 erlebten*, p. 87 and Grabler, pp. 95–8.
16. CSDIC SRA No.75, 30/4/40 in NA WO 208/4117 and Krzysztof, *Luftflotte 4*, pp. 44–5.
17. Based on Hoffmann, Oberleutnant Dr. (ed), *Infanterie Regiment 309 marschiert an den Feind*, pp. 73–4, Kurt Schmoll, 'Die Kriegsfackel loht über polnische Land' in *Infanterie Regiment 309 marschiert an den Feind*, pp. 31–3, Ehrhardt, pp. 20–21 and Leo Freiherr Geyr von Schweppenburg, 'Einsatz der 3 Panzer Division in Polenfeldzug' in BA-MA RH27-3/243.
18. Anon, *Wach auf, es ist Krieg! Wie Polen und Deutsche den 1 September 1939 erlebten*, pp. 86–8.
19. Brief, 27/9/39 in Hosenfeld, p. 254.
20. Fillies, pp. 145–6.
21. Raleigh, p. 182.
22. Kurt Schmoll, 'Die Kriegsfackel loht über polnische Land' in *Infanterie Regiment 309 marschiert an den Feind*, pp. 31–3, Ehrhardt, pp. 20–22 and Hundreiser, pp. 19–22.
23. Kurt Schmoll, 'Die Kriegsfackel loht über polnische Land' in *Infanterie Regiment 309 marschiert an den Feind*, pp. 31–3, Paul, *Brennpunkte*, p. 31 and Flack, pp. 33–4, 64.
24. Asmus, *Die 20.Inf.Div.(mot) Chronik und Geschichte*, Band 2, p. 56, Schüddekopf, Carl, *Krieg: Erzählungen aus dem Schweigen*, pp. 30–2 and Ehrhardt, p. 63.
25. Schüddekopf, *Krieg: Erzählungen aus dem Schweigen*, pp. 30–2.

26. Lehmann, *Leibstandarte*, i, p. 117.

27. KTB Prüller, 16/9/39.

28. Reibig, pp. 18–19.

29. Brief, 21/9/39, Angehöriger des Jägerbataillons an daheim in Lemelsen, and Schmidt, *29 Division, 29 Infanterie Division (mot.), 29 Panzergrenadier Division*, p. 36, 'Aus den Briefen und Aufzeichnungen Bruno Steinbachs', *Die Gebirgstruppe*, Heft Nr.2–4, 1957, pp. 284–5 and KTB Prüller, 16/9/39.

30. Lucas, *Kampfgruppe*, p. 13, Siebte Armeekorps, *Wir zogen gegen Polen*, pp. 77–8 and Gschöpf, p. 80. Lack of clean drinking water was a constant bugbear of the German soldier in Poland. Storming Polish bunkers on the River Narew, north of Warsaw, was particularly exhausting in the heat, Willy Wagemann of 45th Infantry Regiment recalled. A *Gefreiter* and a priest volunteered to carry pails to a fountain in the grounds of a shot-up farm – under enemy fire. 'Our thirst,' wrote Wagemann, 'was greater than our respect for the enemy.' As the pair came back with pails and canteens half-filled with water, Polish guns opened fire. The men jumped for cover. 'Our chaplain landed in a latrine,' Wagemann remembered. 'He stood up to his hips in shit, his hands holding the canteens high up. Despite cleaning himself thoroughly, he smelled until the end of the campaign.' See Allmayer-Beck, *Die Geschichte der 21 (ostpr/westpr) Infanterie Division* pp. 539–40.

31. The description of the strains of marching is based on *Gefreiter* Jakob Wildhaber, 'Endlose Strassen', in Manz, *Alpenkorps in Polen*, pp. 31–2, *Der Polenfeldzug im Tagebuch eines Gebirgsartilleristen*, pp. 18, 23 and Venzky, p. 41.

32. *Und weiter geht es im ewigen Tritt / Die endlose Strasse des Krieges./ Es quält der Durst, es rinnt der Schweiss, / Noch im Dunkel der Nacht ist die Strasse so heiss, / Die steile Strasse des Sieges. Es bluten die Füsse, die Augen sind rot, / Die müden Pferde wir führen / Der Schlaf übermannt und endlos der Weg, / Hier durch die Furt, gesprengt ist der Steg, / Nur vorwärts, marschieren, marschieren ./ Und weiter geht es im ewigen Tritt, / Den Feind wir verfolgen und jagen! / Das Schuhwerk zerrissen, die Sohlen zerfetzt, / So haben wir ihn durch sein Land gehetzt / Und ihn dann aufs Haupt geschlagen!* From Hanns Pfeuffer, 'Marschieren' in *Der Polenfeldzug im Tagebuch eines Gebirgsartilleristen*, p. 28.

33. Hoffmann, *Infanterie Regiment 309 marschiert an den Feind*, pp. 6–9 and KTB Prüller, 17/9/39.

34. *Oberjäger* Hans May, 'Von den Marschleitungen der Gebirgsjäger in Galizien', in Manz, *Alpenkorps in Polen*, p. 30.

35. Kaltenegger, Roland, *Die Deutsche Gebirgstruppe 1935–1945*, p. 117.

36. Siebte Armeekorps, *Wir zogen gegen Polen*, pp. 82–3 and Rossino, p. 202.

37. Rendulic, pp. 48–50, 226–8.

38. Kaltenegger, Roland, *Die Deutsche Gebirgstruppe 1935–1945*, p. 117.

39. *Jäger* Hermann, 'Wir gedenken unserer Toten' in *Das Gebirgsjäger Regiment 99 im polnischen Feldzug*, p. 233.

40. *Es hat der Krieg gefällt / manch junge deutsche Eiche / auf ihren Gräbern aber steht, / Baustein zum Deutschen Reiche.* From *Gefreiter* Wolfgang Löffler, 'Artillerieunterstützung angefordert,' in BA-MA RH53-18/17.

41. KTB Prüller, 3/9/39.

CHAPTER TEN

Shoot Them to the Last Pole

Only the generations who follow us will understand the importance of this age.
But we all want to stand up to history, full of pride, having done our duty.

– GEFREITER, 292nd INFANTRY DIVISION

And we have seen – and experienced – tragic scenes:
German soldiers burning, torching, plundering, without giving it a second
thought...

– OBERSTLEUTNANT HEINRICH VON NORDHEIM

IT WAS precisely mid-day on the third day of September when the *Landsers* of 42nd Infantry Regiment marched into the centre of Czestochowa on the main road to Warsaw. The men were in an excellent mood, convinced the city, one of the most holy shrines in the Christian world, home to the icon of Black Madonna in the hilltop monastery of Jasna Gora which dominated Czestochowa, was pacified – so convinced, in fact, that they removed their bullets from their rifles. Shops and businesses were closed. Inhabitants offered no resistance, remaining out of sight. The regiment established itself in the town hall and settled in for the day.

The men of the 42nd were still in Czestochowa – Tschenstochau to the Germans – twenty-four hours later, their rifles now loaded. Some were waiting in the playground of a technical school for the field kitchen to hand out lunch. Around the corner their comrades were guarding the arrival of a column of 300–400 prisoners, civilians, partisans, slowly moving along Strazacka Street. Suddenly gunfire raked the column. The soldiers hit the ground, their prisoners scattered. Almost simultaneously wild shooting echoed around the technical school courtyard. The *Landsers* ran for cover, their company commander screaming: 'Shoot, shoot, shoot!' It was all over in a matter of minutes. No-one knew who fired the first shots. Perhaps it was Polish soldiers. Perhaps it was Polish civilians. Perhaps it was German soldiers accidentally discharging their weapons. But now there were eight dead *Landsers* and fourteen wounded comrades.

Battalion commander *Oberstleutnant* Kurt Uebe responded immediately, ordering his men to search the houses of Czestochowa. *Alles heraus*! Everybody out! they screamed. Some Poles refused to leave. They were shot on the spot. The rest – men, women, children, Poles and Jews – were led through the streets into the city centre, to Magnacki Square. By late afternoon some 10,000 inhabitants had been rounded up. The women and children were sent home. The men were searched. Any man possessing a razor blade or knife was hauled away to an air raid trench and shot. Some were led away to the city's prison, others were ordered to return to their houses, and others still were led towards a church where they were shot at by machine-guns and pistols. Kurt Uebe counted 99 dead by the day's end; later investigations suggested as many as 227 civilians were shot on that bloody Monday by German soldiers. But the *Landsers* who had searched the apartments and houses of Czestochowa found no guns, no evidence of cityfolk shooting at them.[1]

Just three days earlier, the regiment had marched into Poland clutching a proclamation from their Commander-in-Chief, Walter von Brauchitsch. 'The Wehrmacht does not regard the population as its enemy,' the general declared. 'All international laws will be adhered to.'[2] Brauchitsch's words would quickly be shown to be worthless.

For days Fritz Fillies and his comrades had observed life in the village of Wasily Zigny, twenty or so miles northeast of Mlawa, through their binoculars. From afar it had appeared wretched. Now, as they marched through it on the morning of 1 September, Wasily Zigny seemed even more wretched. 'This was not merely poverty, this was also not simply misery,' the junior officer observed. 'Here there was not merely a boundary between nations, rather it seemed that here that what we understood as life in Europe ended.' Would it be the same across Poland, Fillies and his men asked themselves. If it was 'then Europe ended here and Asia began.'[3]

To men like Fritz Fillies, the reality of Poland merely confirmed all the prejudices, all the stereotypes, all the images of a land without order, a people lacking culture. 'When you see such people, your mind boggles that something like this is still possible in the 20th Century,' one soldier told his wife. Civilisation ended on the German-Polish border. 'These people are not one level of civilisation, but many levels of civilisation, behind the Germans,' wrote artilleryman Emil Falckenthal. 'Two thousand years ago our ancestors lived better – and above all more cleanly.' One *Landser* in Tenth Army agreed. 'The conditions we met were as primitive as one imagines them to be in darkest Africa – but these people here are Europeans.'[4]

Two words crop up repeatedly in German soldiers' descriptions of life in Poland: *Dreck* and *Schmutz* – muck and filth. A reservist *Hauptmann* with 179th Infantry Regiment was billeted in the village of Jasionka, east of Neu Sandez, as his company marched through Galicia. Here thrived not civilisation, but *polnische Wirtschaft* – chaos. The single-storey thatched cottages of Jasionka were 'extremely primitive'. The floor consisted of clay, beds were covered with straw, the smell from the adjacent stable filled the rooms. Diet comprised potatoes, herbs, beans, milk and dairy produce and, twice a year, meat, while pails drew dirty water from a nearby well. There were no newspapers, no books except prayer books, no radios. Villagers moved around in 'little more than torn rags'. Children suffered rickets, did not wash, did not comb their hair, and ran around barefoot. *Unteroffizier* Hermann Ritter von Ingram of 309th Infantry Regiment marched past 'dilapidated cottages, their thatched roofs rotting, falling down'. Pigs, goats, chickens and ducks wandered in and out of the run-down homes, while 'greasy, ragged figures pressed their unwashed faces against the small dirty window panes to look at the parade of German soldiers from the safety of their stinking holes'. Farmhouses and mansions were no better kept, von Ingram recalled. Courtyards and paths were covered with 'a sewage-ridden morass'; inside floors were filthy, piles of washing up filled the sink, greasy cooking pots were littered around in the kitchen. 'Never have I believed more clearly that here two entirely different cultures lived side by side – two cultures which would never unite.'[5]

To the invader, no-one encapsulated all the filth, all the dirt, all the misery of Poland better than the country's Jewish population. This was, pioneer Herbert Otto wrote, 'land of the Jews, in which whoever travels will be visited by lice, a land that any pioneer will remember, stating: "Ah, Poland, it reeks."' The *Soldat* used every pejorative imaginable to describe the Jews of Poland: *Bestien* (beasts), *teuflisch* (devilish), *schmierig und dreckig*, (greasy and dirty), *widerlichster* (most repulsive), *Schweine* (pigs) as years of anti-Semitic propaganda, years of hatred fanned by Jew-baiting rags such as *Der Stürmer*, boiled over. To some, the Jewish populace merely lived up to all the stereotypes. Raciaz, fifty miles northwest of Warsaw, was 'a true nest of Jews', *Hauptmann* Heinrich Dombrowski wrote. 'We've probably never seen so many Jews all in one go! You couldn't call this colony of dirty huts a proper town. It would be unthinkable for civilised people to be able to live in these filthy huts! Many harsh but typical words fly at the inhabitants from the marching column; they stare silently at the troops.' Krasnik, twenty-five miles southwest of Lublin, was 'a large town of Jews, far from welcoming. All over there was a smell of cess.' In Bircza, near Przemysl, the *Landser* 'could see these beasts living in human form. With their beards and kaftans, their devilish expressions they made an awful impression upon us. Anyone who was not yet a radical enemy of the Jews should have been here.' Touring the Jewish quarter of Krakow was akin to 'entering a foreign world,' wrote war correspondent Leo Leixner. 'Here, like a procession of the phantoms of world history with their stuttering, restless gait are all the evil spirits of Shylock in their stained kaftans, sometimes a fox-red rabbi's beard lights up and from his eyes glows an ominous greed which perhaps at this moment is eclipsed by the flicker of unrestrained fear.' To one *Landser*, the Jews of a small town near Lublin, did not simply live up to the stereotypes presented in *Der Stürmer*, they surpassed them. Three out of four inhabitants were Jewish – 'proper Jews that is, bearded and dirty. The whole population is infected – utterly filthy. You cannot imagine what we see here. And this civilised people wanted to conquer Berlin! We make sure that we don't come into contact with the inhabitants at all.' In Siedlce, fifty miles east of Warsaw, one *Gefreiter* observed that the town's 30,000 Jews 'lie around like pigs in the street, most fitting for the "chosen people".' Now a new 'chosen people' had come to this land. 'Wherever we stand for our Greater German nation we are proud to be able to help the Führer. Only the generations who follow us will understand the importance of this age. But we all want to stand up to history, full of pride, having done our duty.'[6]

Some Jews welcomed the invader. Perhaps it was opportunism, perhaps it was genuine enthusiasm. '*Chail Chitler,*' they cried at the advancing troops. In Zambrow, on the main road from Warsaw to Bialystok, the inhabitants 'did not particularly like the Polish Government' and greeted the East and West Prussians of 21st Infantry Division. 'The Jews immediately began to deal with German soldiers and declared that they would very much welcome German rule.'[7] Such opinions would quickly evaporate.

Convinced the Pole was backward, filthy, subhuman, the *Landser* was told by his superiors that the inhabitants of this land were also *fanatisch* (fanatical), *verhetzt* (whipped up), *hinterhältig* (devious), *innerlich feindlich* (inwardly hostile). He would poison wells, destroy food supplies. He was capable of acts of sabotage behind the line, he would wage a partisan war against German soldiers, against German installations, vehicles, railway lines.[8] And so, despite Walther von Brauchitsch's very public appeal, the German soldier *did* regard the Pole as his enemy. 'The German soldier must never forget that when not dealing with members of the German *Volk* he is faced by a civilian population which may seem friendly outwardly but which is inwardly hostile,' he instructed every German soldier invading Poland. Any Pole who damaged – or even tried to damage – the property of ethnic Germans would be executed. Any act of sabotage would be punishable by death. So too any attack against a German soldier, official or *Volksdeutsche*. All weapons had to be surrendered immediately. Anyone who failed to comply would face 'the harshest punishment' – normally up to fifteen years in prison. Alcohol was banned. A curfew would be enforced 'from dusk until dawn'.[9]

One word in particular haunted the German Army: *Freischärler* – sharpshooter or *franc-tireur*. The civilian taking up arms to battle the invader. In 1914 Germany's image around the world had been harmed irreparably by its acts of revenge against the people of Belgium, 'the German atrocities' – hostages seized, buildings razed, monuments destroyed, prisoners executed.[10] A generation later, the German soldier had learned nothing from his experiences in Belgium. 'See in every Polish citizen a fanatical enemy who will fight against you with every means possible,' one battalion commander warned his men on the eve of war. XVI Corps' commander Erich Hoepner told his leaders to tackle the '*franc-tireur* war using the most severe measures'. Someone scribbled across the general's order: *No mercy.* 'Any Polish civilian who carries a weapon will use it against German soldiers,' *Generalleutnant* Diether von Böhm-Bezing told the men of his 252nd Infantry Division. 'No German soldier should hesitate to use his weapon. He should shoot first.'[11]

It was a threat more imagined than real. But threats imagined could provoke very real retaliation, as the inhabitants of the small town of Zloczew, a dozen miles north of Wielun, found. By the third day of war, Zloczew was overflowing with refugees as German soldiers on bicycles and motorcycles – elements of 95th Infantry Regiment and the SS *Leibstandarte Adolf Hitler* – rode in. Officers set up a temporary headquarters. Despite the occupation, eighteen-year-old Janina Modrzewska, remembered 3 September as a day when 'peace ruled'. But as darkness fell, the peace in Zloczew was shattered as the troops began to raze the town. At least 100 refugees were staying in the house sheltering Janina. As the orgy of violence began, she jumped from a window into the garden and hid among blackcurrant bushes. From there she watched the soldiers shoot one refugee after the next. 'Among the wounded was a young girl who had been shot from behind – her innards were hanging out of her stomach.' Janina picked up a small child, no older than eighteen months old, crawling over the body of a dead woman. As she did 'a German soldier smashed its skull with a rifle butt'. A woman the teenager knew, Jozefa Btachowska, was screaming; she had been shot in the hand. A German soldier put her out her misery, pushing her with all his strength into a blazing house. Btachowska was burned alive. 'German soldiers shot not only at those fleeing, but at anyone that they saw on the lane, street or in the courtyards,' Janina remembered. By the time the shooting eventually ceased, some 200 people had been killed. Some of the corpses were tossed into the burning houses, others were buried. Four out of every five homes in Zloczew were destroyed by the flames. The fires raged for days. There was no motive for the destruction of Zloczew, nor would anyone ever be brought to trial for the atrocity.[12]

Zloczew was not a singular act. Setting a town or village ablaze was a typical method of retaliation, as the engineers of 10th Pioneer Battalion demonstrated when they were shot at advancing through the town of Wyszanow, two dozen miles south of Kalisz. 'Flames engulf the houses,' one *Feldwebel* wrote gleefully. 'Their restless, ghostly tongues are the sole indictment of the *franc-tireurs* and snipers of Wyszanow.' There was, the non-commissioned officer declared, only one punishment fitting for such 'guerrillas': death. 'Well then, we have buried each one of them – of course in an un-Christian fashion – in his own crematorium!' Half a dozen miles to the east, the village of Ostrowek was already aflame. 'You could hardly imagine more spectacular fireworks,' an officer from 10th Artillery Regiment wrote. Barns and thatched cottages leading down to a small river, the Struga Weglewska, burned, set on fire by hand grenades 'to smoke out the last hiding place'. As the regiment and its horse-drawn artillery galloped across the river they were bathed 'in a bright glow' from the flames. 'On the other side of the ford there's acrid smoke and scorching heat,' wrote the officer. 'Farms are spread out for kilometres. All are ablaze. Everywhere the crackle of fires and ruins collapsing.' Down the road in Komorniki, *franc-tireurs* had reportedly shot at the artillerymen. Every inhabitant of the village was rounded up and forced to sit in a field, watched over by German soldiers. 'They stare at their burning cottages,' wrote an artilleryman. 'The wind carries the fire from thatch to thatch.' The flames, the gunner observed, 'flicker in all four directions and show that German troops have met resistance in many villages.' On the road to Warsaw, 31st Artillery Regiment passed through the village of Opatow, northwest of Czestochowa, 'more or less destroyed by fire' after advancing infantry reported being 'shot at from the houses by civilians and attacked'. But not just Opatow burned, artillery commander *Oberstleutnant* Heinrich von Nordheim recalled, 'farms everywhere were ablaze, set on fire by someone – the reason is incomprehensible – who presumably "thought nothing more about it".'

Von Nordheim and his men rested in the village of Lobodno, ten miles from Czestochowa, where their slumber was interrupted by the sound of gunfire. Two soldiers from a medical company strolled through the centre of the village having just shot dead two civilians approaching them – again, the horrified von Nordheim observed, 'thinking nothing more about it'.[13]

What Heinrich von Nordheim witnessed that Sunday afternoon in September 1939 was not unusual. In Zloczew, in Czestochowa, in Lobodno and a hundred other towns and villages across Poland, the German soldier exacted revenge without remorse – and invariably without trying his victims. 'As we're in enemy territory I trust no-one!' one *Soldat* wrote home. 'The pistol should talk before I believe someone – we've got enough ammunition.' The pistol did talk. Daily. The mounted infantry of 11th Cavalry Rifle Regiment were convinced civilians had prepared an ambush for them as they rode near the Carpathian village of Skomielna Biala, south of Krakow. By the time one 'partisan' was delivered to the *Leutnant* in charge of one cavalry squadron, there was 'no longer any life in the fellow – he was merely a bundle in the form of man. On a tree, fate overtakes him.' A short time later a second Pole joined him, swinging from the same tree. Clearing out the Bzura pocket, 41st Infantry Regiment fell upon the village of Pludwiny, a dozen miles northeast of Lodz. 'Polish civilians and soldiers are dragged out everywhere,' one *Unteroffizier* in 41st Infantry Regiment wrote. 'When the action is over, the entire village is set on fire. No-one is left alive, even all the dogs are shot.' Nor was the German soldier averse to using Polish hostages as human shields. When 102nd Infantry Regiment attacked the town of Blaszki, near Kalisz, its advance was halted in a cemetery by fire from the church. The *Major* leading the assault grabbed a Polish farmer from a crowd watching the fighting. The officer held the Pole 'by the scruff of the neck, the farmer in one hand, a pistol in the other' and moved gingerly through the churchyard. Shaking, with a pistol in his back, the farmer cried out in Polish: 'Do not shoot. Whoever is in there should come out.'[14]

No-one felt the German soldier's wrath more than Poland's Jews. Their homes and businesses were plundered; a transport unit arriving in Kielce was told it could take what it wanted from Jewish shops. 'I didn't see anything wrong in taking things,' one soldier recalled. 'Our *Unteroffizier* said that everything belonged to the company.' In Radom, jewellers and clothes shops were raided, banks robbed, Jewish girls raped. *Gebirgsjäger* entering the Galician town of Sambor during the march on Lemberg were billeted in a school which 'had to be cleaned'. The soldiers quickly found 'people of Israel in their kaftans and round, little black hats', handed them brooms and buckets, and ordered them 'to make the schoolhouse spotlessly clean. You can imagine what was going through their pale faces.' In the Galician town of Krosno, fifty miles east of Neu Sandez, a *Gebirgsjäger* thrust a broom into the hand of a Jew so that he could sweep rubbish from the market place. 'The Jew whimpers and begs, as if he's being led like a lamb to the slaughter,' a *Leutnant* laughed. 'Evidently for the first time in his life, the Jew is doing a proper day's work.' More Jews arrived, crammed into a car, brooms in hand. They were ordered to clean up the barracks in the town's airfield. But before they began their work, the soldiers decided to have some fun, ordering the Jews to pose for a photograph. 'Was what we were watching just an act, or were their tears an expression of fear of the *"furor Teutonicus"*?' the same *Leutnant* wondered. The *Gebirgsjäger* laughed. A Jewish woman howled hysterically until she was led away to a military policeman.[15]

Plunder, pillage, rape, arson, beatings, public humiliation. Summary executions were a logical progression. Pioneers entering Pinczow, twenty-five miles south of Kielce, found the town still smouldering after comrades in VII Corps had set it ablaze. And in Pinczow's market square 'laid out in their black kaftans, lie the corpses of Jews shot dead. House walls are spattered with blood.' An elderly Jew was brought screaming before 3rd Panzer Division's commander Leo Geyr von Schweppenburg; two panzer grenadiers claimed the pensioners had shot at them from a window in Wlodawa on the Bug. Geyr was sceptical. 'He didn't look the type.' The General ordered a court-martial, which quickly acquitted the Jew. 'During the night, he was shot dead – allegedly trying to escape,' wrote Geyr. The General ordered further courts-martial into the shooting, but the perpetrators were never punished. It was also usual practice to use Jews as hostages, as the doctor of 101st Infantry Regiment observed in the town of Solec, on the Vistula southeast of Radom. Around thirty Jews were locked in a church cellar. One was shot trying to escape, the rest were kept at bay using hand grenades. 'There had to be calm,' noted the surgeon, 'one way or another.' The local commandant ordered the cellar set on fire and bricked up. He managed to prevent the flames spreading to neighbouring buildings – and was hailed 'as the fire chief of Solec'.[16] The Jews of Konskie, forty or fifty of them, were also rounded up. On Tuesday, 12 September, a Luftwaffe reconnaissance unit moved into the town, southeast of Lodz. At least four men, including an officer, were killed while seizing Konskie. That afternoon their bodies were laid out in a churchyard to await burial. A rumour ran through Konskie: the corpses had been mutilated. Soldiers and men from the *Reichsarbeitsdienst*, the Labour Service, began searching nearby homes and arrested the first Jews they found. They thrust shovels into the Jews' hands – and when the shovels ran out, they ordered the men to dig with their bare hands. As the Jews dug a mass grave, the soldiers beat them with rifle butts and bits of broken fence. And when the Jews collapsed to the ground, the troops thrust boots into their faces. Konskie's commandant, a police *Major*, tried to maintain order. The Jews, he declared, were 'guilty of all the misfortune which had befallen the world', but this was not the way to avenge the death of four comrades and he ordered the fifty prisoners to return to their homes. But the mob was unwilling to allow the Jews to leave, as documentary filmmaker Leni Riefenstahl recalled. The soldiers lashed out at the prisoners with their boots. 'Did you not hear what the officer said? Do you want to be German soldiers?' Riefenstahl screamed at the troops. 'Put a sock in it – away with you woman,' one yelled. 'Shoot this woman,' cried another, who turned his rifle on the filmmaker. A horrified Riefenstahl was led away from the scene by her staff. As of yet none of Konskie's Jews had died. But at that moment a staff car pulled into the square with a reservist officer, *Leutnant* Bruno Kleinmichel, at the wheel. When Kleinmichel saw the seething crowd, he fired two warning shots into the air. It provoked a massacre. The troops opened fire at the fleeing Jews; twenty-two were killed.[17]

Atrocities in September 1939 were not solely the domain of the invader, however, as panzer grenadier Bruno Fichte realised as he awoke on Tuesday, 5 September, to find the bodies of his comrades swinging from trees, their stomachs slashed; Polish shock troops had attacked the unit's messengers during the night while they slept. 'You could understand their anger,' Fichte remembered, 'but this was the most senseless thing they could have done, for with it began our hatred.' Wilhelm Prüller came across the mutilated body of a motorcyclist, killed as he tried to repair his vehicle, and seven soldiers who had been set upon by the inhabitants of a village; they gouged out the men's eyes and castrated them. 'These are the only "deeds" the Poles have to boast of,' Prüller fumed. 'Cowards, cowards, they are. You can hardly get them to fight a decent fight. But they are very good at murdering.' In the Corridor, Polish cavalry fell upon a German medical company. The men wore white armed bands marked with the Red Cross; their vehicles were similarly marked. The cavalry attacked anyway, shooting the drivers, tossing the wounded off their stretchers. 'Unarmed, utterly defenceless, they fell victim to the Polish lust for murder,' the *Völkischer Beobachter* screamed. Not all fell victim. Eight medics managed to struggle to Krone to raise the alarm. Such acts were, at times, endorsed by Polish Army officers, even encouraged by them. 'When we march into Berlin, we will kill all the German pigs and only allow as many people that can fit under a pear tree to live,' a captain in *59th Infantry Regiment* told his men on the eve of war. 'So, men, if you see a German on the way, you know what you have to do.'[18]

Most of the Poles' anger was directed not at the invader but at the 'enemy' already in their midst: the ethnic Germans, as thirty-year-old Otto Bäcker discovered. From his farm in the village of Gross Lunau (today Wielkie Lunawy) Bäcker had watched German bombers roar over the Vistula valley at dusk on the first day of war. Swaths of black cloud rolled across the clear sky to the north from the direction of Graudenz, half a dozen miles to the northeast. Deep down the farmer and his young family were delighted. Since the beginning of June the Bäckers had become increasingly concerned by the tension in the Corridor between Poles and the German minority: *Volksdeutsche* had been arrested, imprisoned, abused, their homes and businesses burned down. Now Otto Bäcker could see 'the day of our liberation dawning, but before this liberation there would be war, blood and death'. Daybreak on 2 September brought terror and panic to the streets of Gross Lunau. Endless columns of Poles filed through the town, fear etched into their faces, heading south. A Polish policeman thumped on the Bäckers' door and ordered the entire household to report to the police station. There the family was ordered to join other ethnic Germans on a march towards the historic town of Thorn. The police officers guarding the column drove the civilians on relentlessly. When the procession of misery halted briefly, several *Volksdeutsche* made for a well. The guards forced them back with their rifle butts. The Germans protested, pleaded for water. A policeman filled his canteen with water then wandered back as the civilians stretched out their hands. The guard, *Volksdeutsche* Erhard Wittek recalled, 'turned the bottle upside down and, with its contents pouring on to the ground, walked up and down, the water gurgled out and ran into the sand'.

In Thorn, a furious crowd lined the streets, barracking the *Volksdeutsche* – 'A bullet is too good for Hitler's dogs' – hurling stones at them, jumping into the road and bashing at least one man on the head with rock until blood flowed. Police and Polish soldiers spurred the column on, over the Vistula, through the town of Aleksandrow Kujawski, then on towards Wloclawek. It wasn't the endless, pointless marching. It wasn't the senseless beatings, the insults, the uncertainty, the threat of death. It was the lack of water which tortured the prisoners most. 'The Polish guards could easily have allowed the exhausted people to drink at wells, brooks or lakes along the way,' Otto Bäcker observed. 'For the Poles, it was a source of great amusement, however, to deliberately torment the Germans with thirst.' As the march continued, the guards became increasingly nervous – and increasingly brutal. As the moon appeared over the Vistula valley on the night of 4–5 September, at least one captive decided to make a break for freedom, dashing through willow bushes and across potato fields. The guards took aim. The prisoner threw up his arms and sank to the ground, hit by at least one bullet. The shooting provoked panic. The column scattered. The ethnic Germans began to run. The guards raised their rifles again. Otto Bäcker threw himself to the ground. Other *Volksdeutsche* kneeled in the road, their hands in the air. 'Shoot on the orders of the captain,' one soldier yelled. Volleys of fire pierced the night. 'My kneeling comrades fall down moaning and crying,' Bäcker recalled. He was struck in the ankle, probably by a ricochet. But the farmer realised he was one of the fortunate ones. 'Looking around me it looks terrible. Everywhere badly injured comrades are rolling in their own blood, which forms in small dark puddles on the road.' A column of senior Polish military and civilian officials in limousines pulled up, inquired about what had happened, then ordered the road cleared. The bodies of the living and dying were 'dragged like dead cattle by the arms and legs to the roadside'. A short time afterwards, Polish infantry on bicycles arrived. Some rode over the bodies of the *Volksdeutsche*, others climbed off their bikes and pounded the wounded with their rifle butts. One soldier spied Otto Bäcker's watch. 'Why does this dog still need a watch?' he said to a comrade and ripped it off the farmer's arm. In doing so, he realised Otto Bäcker still had a pulse. 'This pig is still alive.' Bäcker felt a blow to his head. 'I get a strange feeling, one thousand stars dance before my eyes, and my head feels as if it is going to explode,' the farmer wrote. 'I still have just enough presence of mind to roll into the ditch. Then night immediately envelops me. The blow was too much, even for my thick skull.'

Otto Bäcker and some 3,000 fellow *Volksdeutsche* were eventually freed by German troops five days later in Lowicz as Polish troops unleashed their offensive on the Bzura. It would be another dozen days before he returned to his farmhouse – 'once again a piece of the German Reich'. But the ordeal haunted him:

A dream enveloped my thoughts
Of an endless forced march
Along roads, lined by a thousand graves,
And with us, there marched Death.[19]

Thousands of ethnic Germans were arrested, rounded up, force-marched from the border regions and sent eastwards in the first days of September. Paul Wiesner from Wollstein – today Wolsztyn – and 120 fellow *Volksdeutsche* were packed into horse-drawn carts and led to Poznan, three dozen miles away. They reached the historic city on the morning of Sunday, 3 September. The populace were out in force to greet the Germans, showering the carts with stones, bricks, mud. 'They were so angry that they jumped on to our carts and beat us bloodily with clubs,' recalled Wiesner. After two days living on the floor of a school without receiving any food, the column was moved on foot, passing through Kostrzyn, a dozen miles east of Poznan. 'There the mob again bloodily attacked several people,' Paul Wiesner later testified to German investigators. 'Four women in our group were stripped down to their underwear.' To farmer's wife Emilie Feiertag, there was no doubt that 'the actions of the Polish soldiers were planned – they had lists in their hands naming the *Volksdeutsche* families and all their members.' When she wandered around the town of Samara in the wake of the Polish troops, she found the corpses of a couple in a field; the man's intestines were hanging out; his wife was missing one eye and her brain was smeared on the ground. In a nearby wood there was an open grave where a young married couple had been tossed, their cadavers bent to fit into the hole. 'Everywhere around our village and the neighbouring village we found murdered *Volksdeutsche*.' Some ethnic Germans found themselves thrust into the Polish Army. The Germans were unwilling to serve. Their fellow Polish soldiers viewed them with mistrust. Thirty ethnic Germans served in Paweł Pawliczak's company. Rumours abounded that the men were spies. Five were shot on the spot. As the company retreated towards Warsaw, order began to break down. Paranoia worsened. The men decided that 'whoever is German is a spy and doesn't deserve to live.' They lined the *Volksdeutsche* up and shot them, one by one. None begged for mercy. They awaited their execution with tears streaming down their faces.[20]

But no Polish act fuelled German propaganda or enraged the ordinary *Landser* more than the pogrom against the *Volksdeutsche* minority in the city of Bydgoszcz. Mass in Bydgoszcz – Bromberg to the Germans – had been particularly well attended on the first Sunday in September. The day had dawned with clear blue skies and the autumn sun beating down on a city famed for its granaries and mills which lined the waterfront on the Brahe. There had been a handful of air-raid warnings, but no attacks yet by the feared German Air Force. As the city's Polish inhabitants poured out of the churches, they mingled with the retreating soldiers of *9th* and *27th Infantry Divisions*, streaming east having been defeated in the battle of the Corridor. The carts and wagons of the defeated troops filled the streets, knocking down street lamps, flattening water hydrants. Someone cried: 'The Germans are coming.' The worshippers panicked. Shots were fired.

The crowd became even more alarmed. Another cry: 'Get them, kill the *szwaby* – Hun – the pigs, the spies, they have shot at us!' echoed around the streets of Bydgoszcz. What followed was the *Polowanie na Niemców* – the hunt of the Germans – as soldiers and civilians raged through the streets seeking revenge. The soldiers entered the houses of *Volksdeutsche* first. They stole money and valuables. Then the mob entered. They smashed everything, beat the occupants, shot them, smashed in faces beyond recognition while the victim's family watched. Johanna Giese and her family were ordered out of their cellar. Her son-in-law went first. He was shot four times. Giese's nineteen-year-old son Reinhard tried to escape. He jumped over a fence and ran for his life. The mob caught him and shot him in the chest. Reinhard's mother carried her son-in-law into a bedroom and laid him down on a chaise long before fleeing the city. When she returned two days later she found his body under the kitchen table, his head cracked open, his brain on the floor. The kitchen walls were smeared with blood and bits of brain.

The violence spilled from the city centre into the suburbs. Polish soldiers stormed the home of nineteen-year-old Vera Gannot and hauled her family out of the garden shed where they were hiding. 'Down with the German swine!' the soldiers cried and began to batter her father Willy with rifle butts. He fell to the ground, where he was bayoneted before being shot six times. The mob left, only to return shortly afterwards armed with clubs and sticks, beating the surviving Gannots before withdrawing once more. The mob did not subside for long. They returned once again to 125 Thorner Strasse. This time Vera Gannot tried to flee through the waters of the Brahe, only to be dragged out of the river by between ten and fifteen Poles and carried back to her house. There she was stripped, pinned on the ground and raped while her mother was held at gunpoint in another room. When the Poles finally left, the nineteen-year-old barely recognised her home. The pillagers had taken money, handbags, watches, jewellery, dishes, even the washing, and chopped up the Gannots' furniture with hatchets.[21]

And the violence spilled beyond Bydgoszcz into the surrounding villages, especially along the road to Inowroclaw – Hohensalza to Germans – a road 'sown with the cadavers of hundreds of horses' piled in the ditches and adjacent fields. And alongside the heaps of dead horses 'mounds of murdered Germans piled up'.[22]

Late on Sunday afternoon, a Polish battalion commander tried to curb the excesses. 'Gentlemen, there is no evidence at all to establish *franc-tireur* activities on the part of the Germans,' he told his men. 'Get this idea out of your heads.'[23] But the mob could not be halted. The plundering, the murdering, the looting, the arson continued. The red-brick Lutheran church in Schwedenhöhe was raided then set ablaze. 'Only the ruins of the outside walls remained,' one worshipper lamented. 'The church was entirely plundered.' The tower still stood and on it the hands of the clock were fixed at the moment the fires raged: 5.45.

Attacks on ethnic Germans continued throughout the night and into Monday. That morning seven soldiers and a Polish neighbour appeared at Josef Lassa's front door. The Pole's fist smashed Lassa in the face. He turned to the troops.

'This one's a Hitler. You can shoot him right now.' Lassa's wife protested. 'Shut your mouth, you're all coming now,' her neighbour told her. The family was marched down the road accompanied by scores of incandescent Poles. 'Another Hitler lives there,' they told the soldiers, 'you can take him with you right now.' Sixty-five-year-old Bruno Belitzer was forced out of his house and told to face a wall with his hands raised alongside Josef Lassa. The road was littered with dead *Volksdeutsche*. 'Live well, Josef,' Belitzer told his neighbour. 'I must die now. I die for my Fatherland.' A soldier yelled: 'What did you say, you pig?' and shot Bruno Belitzer before smashing his face in with his rifle.

It would be early on Tuesday morning, 5 September, before the *Landsers* of 122nd Infantry Regiment tentatively entered the northern outskirts of Bydgoszcz. Polish troops had pulled out of the city the previous afternoon, leaving the militia to defend it. The advancing German troops were in no mood for clemency. They had already dealt with armed civilians in villages on the road to Bydgoszcz. Now in the city it ran into 'fanatics' and 'the most evil type of urban proletariat. There's a lot of bitterness in the companies concerning these cunning fighting methods,' the regimental diarist wrote. 'Whoever offers resistance is shot dead.'[24] By the day's end after twenty years, Bydgoszcz was Bromberg once more. The city's German minority limply saluted their liberators. 'We cannot be happy about your arrival because our grief is too great,' one *Volksdeutsche* woman told the *Landsers*. 'All our husbands are dead.'

The entry of German soldiers prompted many *Volksdeutsche* to return to the city. A 'column of misery of the living' shuffled along the road from Inowroclaw hauling carts, pushing prams or bicycles with sacks swinging on the handlebars. 'Mothers with sweat dripping off their faces, with exhausted cheeks, depressed and apathetic, summon their last strength to push their prams,' one German journalist wrote. 'In these prams lie not only the crying child, but also sacks, piles and bundles of possessions – precisely what hands could grab during the eviction from houses and farms – piled upon it.'

The city's German-language newspaper, *Deutsche Rundschau*, reappeared on 9 September. 'Nothing is as yet known about the fate of a terribly-long list of compatriots,' it lamented. Four days later, death notices began to fill its pages, with thick black borders and German crosses:

Max Sauerland (sixty-eight) Father
Karl Sauerland (nineteen) Brother
Erna Sauerland (thirty-six) Sister

They died in their firm belief in Germany.

Gustav Dreger (seventy-six)
Ferdinand Dreger (seventy-four)

Our father was murdered by gangs of Polish soldiers/marauders on 4 September in the forest. He died in happy expectation, in love with the Führer, *Volk* and country.[25]

The notices continued to appear well into October. No fewer than 300 *Volksdeutsche* – and perhaps as many as 1,000 – died in Bromberg in 1939.

Goebbels' propaganda machine quickly gave it a name: *Bromberger Blutsonntag* – Bromberg's bloody Sunday. 'The shadows of death have hung over Bromberg these past few days,' the *Völkischer Beobachter* declared. 'In every road and garden lie the most bestially-mutilated bodies of murdered *Volksdeutsche*.' Readers were spared no detail: the corpses of men, women, children covered in blood, faces smashed in or sliced up, shallow graves filled with mutilated bodies. 'There's nothing to compare these outrages to,' the newspaper concluded. 'No examples.'[26] The people of Czestochowa, Zloczew and countless other Polish towns and city would probably disagree.

In all, an estimated 5,500 ethnic Germans died at the hands of Poles and the Polish authorities, some before but most during the 'campaign of eighteen days'. There never was a systematic 'terror campaign', as Goebbels and his propaganda apparatus had claimed in the final months of peace. But now the Reich had real atrocities to trumpet to the world. German newspapers talked of *Mordgier* (lust for murder), *grauenvolle Untaten* (terrible outrages), *Greuelpropaganda* (horror stories). But the butcher's bill was not high enough, not even for Joseph Goebbels. The 'official' death toll of *Volksdeutsche* in Poland, the Propaganda Ministry instructed, was 58,000 – more than ten times the true figure.[27]

Accompanying hundreds of *Volksdeutsche* on their marches of misery across Poland were captured German soldiers. *Leutnant* Udo von Ritgen, an adjutant in 3rd Infantry Regiment, was captured near Graudenz in the first days of the war, and taken to Thorn for interrogation, where he was stripped of all possessions, even his epaulettes. He was left only his uniform and dog tags, dog tags which his interrogator told him 'would soon fulfil their purpose'. Ritgen protested at his treatment. 'Germany is not at war with Poland because there was no declaration of war,' the former Austrian Army officer questioning him sneered. 'You are to be treated therefore merely as robbers, murderers and marauders, not as soldiers.'

With German troops closing in on Thorn, the *Leutnant* and other German prisoners and *Volksdeutsche* were marched along the Vistula to Wloclawek, thirty miles away. During the night of 3–4 September the column came across the bodies of upwards of 100 ethnic Germans by the roadside, some shot dead, most battered to death by rifle butts. Ritgen's column continued, hounded by the soldiers guarding it who branded the prisoners 'Hitler's dogs, Hitler's murderers.' Ritgen was struck on the head by a bar wielded by a Polish soldier. A Luftwaffe officer was knocked to the ground by punches from a Pole incensed by German bombing raids. When the prisoners entered Wloclawek, they were barracked by the town's inhabitants who told them they would face the same fate as the murdered *Volksdeutsche*. Verbal abuse turned to physical abuse as the townsfolk grabbed rocks and pieces of wood and hurled them at the German captives. A Pole lunged out of the crowd and thrust a knife into the back of a *Gefreiter*. A German civilian was shot in the head as he stumbled through the streets. The column's guards were powerless to intervene. The senior officer simply told the prisoners 'we should be happy that we had not all been slaughtered'.

By 12 September the unfortunate column of prisoners had reached the town of Kutno, thirty miles to the south. There they were joined by more than 550 men of 30th Infantry Division, captured by the Poles during their offensive on the Bzura, forced into a single room – and not allowed to leave, even to relieve themselves. Udo von Ritgen complained. 'Shit in your pants, you dog,' the guard told him. Ritgen protested again. A Polish captain explained that 'everything was connected with revenge – German aircraft had dropped poisoned chocolate and sweets and women and children had died.' The *Leutnant's* misery ended six days later when German troops captured Ilow as they overran the Bzura pocket.[28]

Another regimental adjutant captured by the Poles was marched into a field with upwards of sixty comrades, where the prisoners were formed into two lines. The guards opened fire. 'I can assure you that I have never hit the ground more quickly in all my life than on that evening,' the *Oberleutnant* from Vienna wrote to a friend. The guards checked each body – but evidently not thoroughly for nine men, including the junior officer, 'crawled out from the piles of dead unharmed'.[29]

Understandably, the German warrior feared falling into the hands of his foe. Luftwaffe aircrew were particularly harshly treated in retaliation for their raids on Polish towns and villages, often shot on the spot by their captors. A tearful seventeen-year-old infantryman from Bavaria pleaded to a Polish Colonel not to gouge out his eyes. The Officer was horrified. Captured Germans were 'treated honourably'; maltreatment of prisoners was 'out of the question'.[30]

The fate of Polish prisoners of war was even more bitter, more bloody. Like their foe, they feared captivity. 'A large number of the Poles don't dare to surrender because their officers tell them that they'll be shot by us, tortured etc,' *Soldat* Wilhelm Prüller noted in his diary. It was, of course, 'pure rubbish,' Prüller continued. 'Nothing happens to them.' One of the better camps for captured Poles was run by Great War veteran *Feldwebel* Wilm Hosenfeld. At the end of September, Hosenfeld was ordered to take command of an abandoned factory in the 'ugly' industrial town of Pabianice, near Lodz. The works had been hurriedly turned into a makeshift transit camp for Polish troops captured on the Bzura. The red-brick building, its courtyards piled with rubbish, its workshops filled with rusting machinery, was now home to some 2,000 soldiers. They slept on a thin covering of straw cast over the stone workshop floor. Their captors had set up three boilers in an old storeroom to provide hot water and warm food – much needed now that the sun of early September had been replaced by rain and cold. 'These poor Polish prisoners, encircled for days by the iron ring of German troops, have to lie around in the dirt and cold, they are starving and weary; all they wish for is to be able to "crash out" and sleep. ' Each night fresh columns of Poles arrived for processing – 'emaciated figures emerging from the darkness, shuffling along, in green-brown dirty tunics, their faces are weary and grey, sullen and indifferent to their fate'. Most of the prisoners were anonymous – 'the same faces, the same distress, the same fear, the same muted devotion, the same deepest misery' – but a few stood out: one with his arm in a bandage, one hobbling along on a crutch. 'No-one speaks – they silently wander through the night,' Hosenfeld observed. 'We only hear the weary noise of a thousand feet, trudging slowly over the hard pavement.' The reservist was moved by his foe's plight. 'They lack any life, are apathetic, indifferent. By the slightest good fortune they have escaped the hell of war. The eyes of every man are still filled with the horror and misery of death.'[31]

Other prison camps were less organised, less ordered, less structured – with fatal consequences. Some 4,000 men from *18th Infantry Division* were kept in a field at Zambrow, seventy miles northeast of Warsaw, guarded by armoured cars with machine-guns in the corners. Captured horses were kept in a neighbouring paddock, but on the night of 11 September the animals broke free and stampeded across the field. The prisoners panicked. The guns on the armoured cars opened fire, only stopping ten minutes later when German troops became caught in the crossfire. In those ten minutes, around 200 Polish soldiers were killed and another wounded. Officially, the Poles had been killed during a breakout attempt. In Szczucin, by the banks of the Vistula, the village school was turned into a processing camp for Polish prisoners. There on 12 September, while being interrogated, a Polish officer grabbed the gun of a German non-commissioned officer, killed him, then turned the gun on himself. German soldiers responded immediately. Brutally. Hand grenades were thrown into the schoolhouse, then shots were fired inside, before the building was set ablaze. As it burned, the few survivors tried to flee. All were shot dead. The next day, local Jews were ordered to bury the dead – some forty Polish prisoners and thirty refugees. And when they had dug the mass grave, the Jews too were shot and tossed into the same pit before a thin layer of earth was thrown over them.[32]

Such excesses and atrocities were possible, in part, because of the mentality of the men ordered to watch over their former foe. Guard duty, a *Gefreiter* in 179th Infantry Regiment guarding Polish prisoners southwest of Lemberg wrote, 'was proof of our domination'. He saw only 'decayed, brutal faces, some with hate-filled eyes and glances distorted by rage'. The men longed 'to beat these cultureless beasts to a pulp' – the Poles had, after all, 'maltreated many Germans in a bestial manner'. But the guards did not retaliate, claimed the soldier; the captives were 'treated more than fairly'. It was harder for other soldiers to show restraint. 'These inhuman Poles who fall into our hands, these Poles who bestially murder prisoners of war, who bayonet the wounded, should they be used for even the lowest work?' *Gebirgsjäger* Franz Ortner asked himself. 'No! It is ten times better to shoot them, shoot them to the last Pole, or to put it better, to the last bullet.'[33]

There were at least sixty documented incidents of German soldiers executing captured Polish soldiers, individual or *en masse*. The most blatant, most brutal act occurred in broad daylight on the afternoon of Saturday, 9 September, on the edge of Ciepielow, twenty miles southeast of Radom. For an hour the Poles of *74th Infantry Regiment* offered bitter resistance in the woods around the town, before some 300 soldiers surrendered to 15th Motorised Infantry Regiment. An hour after the battle, regimental commander *Oberstleutnant* Walter Wessel, strutted down a road where fourteen of his men had died. A monocle fixed firmly in his eye, he surveyed the dead, including a popular *Hauptmann*, Lewinski. Wessel was furious. 'Pure cheek to want to stop us,' he raged, declaring the

300 captured Poles were not soldiers but partisans – even though each man wore a uniform. Wessel ordered the prisoners to remove their jackets, then they were marched off down the road single-file. 'Five minutes later I hear a dozen German machine-pistols bark,' one *Landser* wrote in his diary. 'I hurry in that direction and see the 300 Polish prisoners lying in the ditch, shot.'[34]

Rolling towards Brest-Litovsk, Wolfgang Fischer's pioneer unit was held up for a quarter of an hour by a skirmish. A Polish soldier finally dropped his weapon and walked down the road, his hands raised, accompanied by four *Landsers* and a *Gefreiter*, his pistol cocked. Fischer's *Feldwebel* asked what was going on. 'That's one of those damned snipers,' the *Gefreiter* replied. 'The pigs hid in the trees in the avenue and allowed the first vehicles through. Then they shot at the commander's vehicle. Our adjutant is dead. This pig here will be bumped off.' The 'pig', Wolfgang Fischer remembered, 'looked very human'. The twenty-year-old was not the only German soldier uneasy with the methods used by his comrades in Poland. Commanders were horrified by the indiscipline, the raping, pillaging, the murders. 'We have seen – and experienced – tragic scenes,' *Oberstleutnant* Heinrich von Nordheim, commander of a detachment in 31st Artillery Regiment told his officers. 'German soldiers burning, torching, plundering, without giving it a second thought – mature men, who are not in the slightest bit aware that what they are doing contravenes laws and conventions and offends the honour of the German soldier.' Nordheim pleaded to his men's better nature. 'We are in enemy territory and see the consequences of war! What would we think and say and how would we act if the enemy faced us, our relatives and our property in our own land?' Daily the list of excesses and atrocities reported to Fourteenth Army's commander General Wilhelm List grew longer – 'looting, requisitioning of goods which are not needed for day-to-day living, arbitrary executions, abuse of defenceless people, rape and murder, burning down of synagogues, drunkenness'. List promised no mercy to the offenders. 'I will most severely punish all those who harm the reputation of the German soldier and the standing of the German Reich.' The Army's Commander-in-Chief, Walther von Brauchitsch, also weighed in. Too many men had 'acted like farm hands' in Poland. All this drunkenness, all this raping, robbery, abuse was down to weak officers, the General declared. Such officers were 'parasites who do not belong in our ranks'. But Walther von Brauchitsch also realised that many in the Officer Corps were distinctly ill at ease with the murders and atrocities occurring daily in Poland. There were too many rumours, too much gossip, too many reports reaching the headquarters of the General Staff. Walther von Brauchitsch turned a blind eye to them – and ordered his men to do the same. 'Avoid all gossip and spreading of rumours,' he instructed. 'Any criticism of measures by the State leadership must cease.'[35]

The rumours, the gossip, the criticism would not stop. Nor too would the murders. Poland's misery at the hands of the Nazis was only just beginning.

Notes

1. Böhler, *Auftakt zum Vernichtungskrieg*, pp. 100–6 and Böhler, *Grösste Härte*, pp. 106–9.
2. Appeal to the Polish population, 1/9/39 in Krausnick, *Hitlers Einsatzgruppen*, p. 56.

3. Fillies, p. 35.
4. Böhler, *Auftakt zum Vernichtungskrieg*, p. 199, Falckenthal, p. 40 and Lucas, *Kampfgruppe*, p. 13.
5. *Hauptmann* d.R. Körner, 'Polnische Kultur', in *Wir Marschierten Gegen Polen*, pp. 47–9 and *Unteroffizier* Hermann Ritter von Ingram, 'Marschunterkünfte', in Hoffmann, Oberleutnant Dr. (ed), *Infanterie Regiment 309 marschiert an den Feind*, pp. 48–9.
6. Attutides to Jews based on Rossino, 'Destructive Impulses: German Soldiers and the Conquest of Poland,' *Holocaust and Genocide Studies*, vol.11, No.3, p. 355, *Hauptmann* Heinrich Dombrowski, *Mit der 6 Kompanie die Schöpffer Regiments (IR400) von Elbing bis Warschau: Tagebuch eines Kompanieführers aus dem Polenfeldzuge* in BA-MA RH37/3094, Böhler, *Auftakt zum Vernichtungskrieg,,* p. 47, *Gefreiter* G (7/111 *Gebirgsartillerie* Regiment), 'Erinnerung an den Polenfeldzug', BA-MA RH53-18/17, Leixner, pp. 37–8, Brief *Gefreiter* H.K., 527th Infantry Regiment, 12/8/40 and Brief *Gefreiter* W.W., 507th Infantry Regiment, 25/8/40 in Manoschek, pp15–16.
7. Böhler, *Auftakt zum Vernichtungskrieg*, p. 46 and *Major* Hannes Wolff, *Kommandeur Nachrichten Abteilung* 21, 'Unsere Nachrichten-Abteilung im Polenfeldzug,' p. 15 in 'Tapfer und Treue: Erlebnisberichte, Aufzeichnungen aus den Kriegsjahren, 21 ostpr-westpr Infanterie Division', BA-MA RH26-21/223.
8. See, for example, Eighth Army's warning of 1 September. 'In Poland a secret organisation has been formed – *Tajna organizacja konspiracyna* – which in the event of an invasion by German troops will organise terrorist acts behind the front. We are dealing with carefully-selected, specially trained, armed and with explosive supplied Poles – mostly coming from Pomerelia; their task can be assumed to be harassing the troops by throwing bombs at marching columns, quarters, vehicles, railway property, transports etc. The report also talks of the possibility of such terrorists using bacteriological warfare and committing sabotage against military camps.' AOK 8Ic/AO Nr.622/39, 1/9/39 in KTB 17 Infanterie Division, Polenzeldug, Anlagen, BA-MA RH 26-17/77.
9. Merkblatt für das Verhalten des deutschen Soldaten im besetzten Gebiete in Polen, c.1/9/39 in BA-MA RH20-8/169 Tagesbefehle, Reden, Aufrufe AOK 8 Polenfeldzug and Brauchitsch's instructions, c.1/9/39 in BA-MA RH20-8/169 Tagesbefehle, Reden, Aufrufe AOK 8 Polenfeldzug.
10. The *franc-tireurs* of Belgium were invariably a phantom, as *Major* Christian von Harbou recalled a quarter of a century later: 'After a few hours every civilian was treated as an enemy. Whoever shot from a house was regarded as a *franc-tireur*, even if he was a Belgian soldier. Enormous nervousness on our side; and then Germans shot at Germans.' Horne, John and Kramer, Alan, *German Atrocities 1914: A History of Denial*, p. 405.
11. Rossino, pp. 125, 204 and Hürter, p. 177.
12. Böhler, *Grösste Härte*, p. 42.
13. *Feldwebel* Simmel, Company Truppführer 3.(mot)/Pi.10, 'Brückenschlag und Häuserkampf im Ostrowek, in BA-MA RH12-5/339, Böhler, *Auftakt zum Vernichtungskrieg*, p. 123, and Dienstunterricht des Kommandeurs der III Abteilung Artillerie Regiments 31 nach dem Einsatz der Abteilung in Polen, Okecie, vor Warschau, October 12th 1939 in BA-MA RH41/1177.
14. Böhler, *Auftakt zum Vernichtungskrieg*, pp. 125, 199, Lt Walter L, 'Die 2 Schwadron des Kav-SR 11 im Kampfe gegen Polen', 3/9/39 in BA-MA RH53-18/148 and KTB Lt Hans

W, "Mit der IR102 im Polenfeldzug", 4/9/39 in BA-MA Msg1/1631. Cited in Böhler, *Auftakt zum Vernichtungskrieg*, p. 74.

15. Böhler, *Auftakt zum Vernichtungskrieg*, pp. 192, 198 and Lt Franz P, 4 Gebirgsfahrkolonne, 'Erinnerungen an Polen', in BA-MA RH53-18/17.

16. Böhler, *Auftakt zum Vernichtungskrieg*, p. 112, Leo Geyr von Schweppenburg, 'Einsatz der 3 Panzer Division in Polenfeldzug' in BA-MA RH27-3/243 and Rgt Arzt des IR101, 12/9/39 in BA-MA, MSg1/541, cited in Böhler, p. 195.

17. Bruno Kleinmichel was stripped of his rank and sentenced to two years in prison for 'conduct unbecoming an officer'. The massacre at Konskie is based on Böhler, *Auftakt zum Vernichtungskrieg*, pp. 195–6 and Böhler, *Grösste Härte*, pp. 121–2.

18. Schüddekopf, *Krieg: Erzählungen aus dem Schweigen*, p. 31, KTB Prüller, 12/9/39, *Völkischer Beobachter*, 6/9/39 and Lindenblatt and Bäcker, *Bromberger Blutsonntag*, p. 92.

19. *Über die Seele kommt dann ein Träumen / von dem endlosen Marsch durch die Not / auf den Strassen, die Tausende Gräber säumen, / und mit uns, da zog der Tod*. Lindenblatt and Bäcker, *Bromberger Blutsonntag*, Arndt, Kiel, 2001, pp. 133, 140–220.

20. Lindenblatt and Bäcker, *Bromberger Blutsonntag*, p. 133, *Tod Sprach Polnisch*, pp. 71, 99.

21. *Tod Sprach Polnisch*, pp. 57–8.

22. *Tod Sprach Polnisch*, pp. 102–5.

23. De Zayas, p. 138.

24. KTB 122 Infanterie Regiment, 5/9/39, in BA-MA RH37/6360.

25. *Deutsche Rundschau*, 9/9/39, 13/9/39, 19/9/39.

26. *Völkischer Beobachter*, 9/9/39.

27. De Zayas, p. xvi.

28. Allmayer-Beck, *Die Geschichte der 21 (ostpr/westpr) Infanterie Division*, pp. 541–4.

29. Letter from Vienna, 20/9/39. Author's papers.

30. AOK Abt Ic/AO Nr.434/39g in KTB AOK14 Anlagen, 24/9/39, BA-MA RH20-14/77.

31. KTB Prüller, 19/9/39 and Hosenfeld, Brief c.30/9/39 in Hosenfeld, pp. 258–62.

32. Böhler, *Auftakt zum Vernichtungskrieg*, pp. 174–6.

33. *Gefreiter* Müller (5 Kompanie), 'In Rudki am 16 September', in *Wir Marschierten Gegen Polen*, pp. 44–5 and Rossino, p. 203.

34. Böhler, *Auftakt zum Vernichtungskrieg*, p. 172.

35. Fischer, *Ohne die Gnade der späten Geburt*, p. 44, Dienstunterricht des Kommandeurs der III Abteilung Artillerie Regiments 31 nach dem Einsatz der Abteilung in Polen, Okecie, vor Warschau, 12/10/39 in BA-MA RH41-1177, KTB AOK14 Anlagen, 18/9/39 and Tagesbefehl AOK14, 19/9/39 in BA-MA RH20-14/77, OKH Nr. 5354/39 PA(2) Gr.I/Ia in Groscurth, pp. 386–7.

CHAPTER ELEVEN

A Boiling Kettle of Fire and Blood

Warsaw has earned the admiration and reverence of free nations all over the world and its spirit was, is and will ever be the symbol of the spirit of the Polish nation.
– GENERAL JULIUSZ ROMMEL

We may only hope for one thing: No German city should suffer this fate.
– GENERALMAJOR HANS FELBER

IN THE small town of Borowa-Gora, fifteen miles north of Warsaw by the banks of the Western Bug, ten-year-old Janina listened to the rumble of guns coming from the south. 'The sun filtered through red and yellow acers as if reflecting the blood and fire from the Polish battlefields,' the schoolgirl recorded in her diary. By night, the sky was 'stained with smoke and flame'. Janina's parents were dejected. 'Warsaw's on its last legs,' her father told her. 'It's only a matter of days.' The youngster looked for answers to her country's plight. Why, oh why, are the Nazis winning the war? she asked her diary.[1]

Winning the war? Twenty-two days after German troops swarmed across the Polish border, the Reich's leaders believed they had *won* the war. The announcer on the *Reichsrundfunk*, the state radio, read a curt communiqué from the Headquarters of the Supreme Command. 'The campaign in Poland is over,' he began. 'Only a tiny remnant is now fighting a hopeless battle in Warsaw.'[2] The stage was set for the last act of the terrible drama.

For four centuries, Warsaw had been the intermittent capital through its nation's troubled history. It was used to being invested and fought over, by Prussians, by Swedes, by Russians. The last seemingly invincible force, the Red Army, had been smashed at the gates of the city by Polish military prowess just nineteen years previously. The spirit of 1920 would save the capital once more. 'I am certain that you will stand up to the German onslaught with utter determination and that the barbaric grabbing hand will not reach the walls of our capital,' Juliusz Rommel, commander of the grandly-titled *Army of Warsaw*, told his men. 'Your strength will thwart this hand and break it.' Behind the bushy moustache and fixed expression was a proven leader, a national hero after his cavalry actions against the Soviets a generation before. But such brilliance seemed to desert Juliusz Rommel in September 1939. Events at the front quickly overwhelmed him, he left his troops behind and arrived in Warsaw, in circumstances never satisfactorily explained, to take charge of the newly-formed *Army of Warsaw*. His supreme commander, Edward Smigly-Rydz, gave Rommel explicit instructions: hold Warsaw 'as long as there is sufficient ammunition and food'. The Polish Army had to buy time. 'We must fight so that we may survive as long as possible. There is not another way out,' the Marshal warned him. 'The war will soon be decided on the Western Front, and I firmly believe that it will end victoriously.'[3]

In the fortnight since the abortive attempt to seize the city by panzers, the Polish capital had not been spared the horrors of war – but neither had it been subjected to the full force of the Wehrmacht. The Luftwaffe had busied itself dropping leaflets over Warsaw urging the citizens to capitulate:

Inhabitants of the City of Warsaw!
   You are surrounded on all sides. Offering further resistance is senseless. Whoever is encountered bearing weapons will be shot. For every German soldier killed in Warsaw, twenty of you will be shot dead.
   If the city offers resistance, then it will be destroyed by our artillery and aircraft.
Send responsible citizens to our Army so that they can surrender the city and protect you from destruction.

The pleas fell on deaf ears. Most Poles never picked up the fliers, convinced the paper carried poison.[4]

Nor did Warsaw accept more traditional calls to surrender. Mid-morning on 16 September, a staff car bearing the white flag and escorted by two panzers rolled across the Polish lines. A *Major* insisted upon seeing the Commandant of Warsaw to present the German demand for the city's unconditional surrender. 'Warsaw's situation is hopeless,' the letter he bore read. 'Refusing the German offer of surrender merely means unnecessary bloodshed from which the population cannot be spared as Warsaw will be treated as a fortress.' The officer got no further than a regimental command post in the suburb of Praga. A telephone call was put through to Rommel and his staff. The General shook his head. He would not meet the *parlementaire*. He would not consider Warsaw's surrender. The Germans, Rommel's staff realised, 'wanted to shift responsibility for the destruction of the city to the leaders of Warsaw's defence, if they didn't accept this humanitarian gesture by the cultured Germans.'

And so it proved. The official German communiqué on the sixteenth proclaimed 'that the ruling Polish caste was willing to sacrifice the entire population of Warsaw, without batting an eyelid, for the sake of its selfish goals out of pride and blindness'.[5]

Ignoring German propaganda and pleas to surrender, Warsaw's inhabitants were roused by their own leaders' words. 'The ruins will disappear,' the city's president, Stefan Starzynski declared. 'We will reconstruct them. Poland has been destroyed more than once. We will create monuments worthy of the nation. Revenge will be bitter.' Army propagandist Colonel Waclaw Lipinski urged Warsaw's populace to ignore German claims that the war in Poland was almost at an end. 'We have the will to fight and we will continue to do so. We must remember the words engraved on the hearts and spirits of every Pole: to be beaten in battle but not to surrender is victory.' *New York Times* correspondent Jerzy Szapiro, who somehow reached the capital on 11 September after a tortuous journey from the east, found civilians patrolling the streets bearing arms, their only uniform armbands. The Poniatowski Bridge still spanned the Vistula, despite frequent air attacks. And the spirit of the populace remained firm. 'We must get revenge for Nazi barbarism,' one Varsovian told Szapiro. 'Our spirits are still good. We have enough food to last for weeks.' Daily the country's leaders pleaded to the Allies to come to their aid, to strike into the heart of Germany, to bomb Berlin. Juliusz Rommel turned such pleas into reality; the Allies were attacking on the Western Front, he insisted. The enemy's best units were being sent to the Franco-German frontier. 'As a result he no longer enjoys the upper hand over us in Poland,' he told his men.

> He merely expects our courage to have vanished and that we will stop resisting. But each battle in which we thwart him, each blow which we ward off, each day the fighting persists speeds up his downfall. We must therefore endure and fight until the victorious conclusion.[6]

And so Warsaw's inhabitants, Army Group North's commander Fedor von Bock recorded furiously, were 'left in the dark' about their nation's true predicament. They were, however, 'told of the great successes by the English and French as well as the lie that the Germans are killing all prisoners'.[7]

Not that the population would be allowed to leave even if the Poles requested. The Germans ruled that there would be no evacuation of Warsaw. Staying in the capital, the civilians would use up food supplies and hasten the city's fall. The only people to leave Warsaw were 1,000 or so foreign nationals and a smattering of diplomats. In the rain of 22 September, two columns of empty troop trucks rolled through Nasielek, a town twenty-five miles north of the Polish capital on the main road to Brest-Litovsk. There was an uneasy hour-long cease-fire along a six-mile stretch of the front, only partially observed. The wagons stopped in the suburb of Praga, where the evacuees loaded their luggage and climbed aboard to a soundtrack of machine gun and mortar fire. On the road back the column passed field kitchens, ammunition trains and artillery heading for the front line, crossed temporary bridges over the Bug and Narew and finally came to a stop outside the railway station in Nasielek shortly before dawn on the twenty-third. 'Here to everyone's surprise, food stands have been set up,' *Obersturmführer* Walter Harzer, a company commander in the SS *Deutschland* Regiment, wrote in his diary. 'There is everything which the heart desires! Ham rolls, coffee, schnapps, smoked food. In the end, even we soldiers stuff our faces on this food at the expense of the Foreign Ministry.' The diplomats and foreign nationals got on to the waiting trains and headed for Berlin. It was the last humane act in the Battle for Warsaw.[8]

At dawn on the seventeenth, the guns drawn up around Warsaw belched steel and death once more. Heavy shells landed in the city at the rate of forty an hour. The Royal Palace, part of the *sejm* – home of the Polish parliament – the philharmonic orchestra's concert hall, all were set ablaze. 'People fell in great numbers in the streets,' one resident recalled. 'Tens of houses were burning, falling down or turning into rubble. Thousands of people were trapped under the debris of collapsed churches during Sunday services.'

As artillery and air raids softened up Warsaw, small task groups – *Kampfgruppen* – probed its defences. A company of engineers, bolstered by a smattering of infantry, half a dozen panzers and a couple of anti-tank guns, began clearing out the town of Falencia, ten miles southeast of the Polish capital. Searching the outskirts of the town house by house, they found plenty of evidence that the enemy had simply melted away, discarding his soldier's uniform in favour of civilian clothes, leaving his gun behind. As the company moved deeper into Falencia, 'a funeral cortege' of civilians wearily followed the German troops 'probably because they believed that now they would be safe and would finally get something to eat,' one junior officer observed. What Polish soldiers were found quickly raised their hands. In all, 800 men were rounded up by the time Falencia had been cleared out. They were guarded by just five pioneers because, as one of the German soldiers observed, 'none of them thought about fighting any longer.'[9]

On the east bank of the Vistula, the men of 12th Artillery Regiment began moving into the suburb of Praga from the northeast. Machine gun fire from hedges lining a railway embankment strafed the men as they edged forward. The closer the reconnaissance troops got to the houses of Praga, the stiffer the resistance became. '*Herr Generaloberst*, it's already 9.30,' a young *Leutnant* said. 'It's time we turned around.' The general agreed. At fifty-nine, *Generaloberst* Werner Freiherr von Fritsch had been in the Army forty-one years and one day. This was *his* Army. Just eighteen months earlier he had been its Commander-in-Chief, until trumped-up charges of homosexuality prompted Hitler to dismiss him. Now Fritsch was merely the honorary colonel of an artillery regiment, accompanying his men on a patrol. Crawling and crouching, Fritsch fell back with the troops under sporadic machine-gun and rifle fire. As the men sought a ditch for cover, the General collapsed, struck in the left thigh by a bullet. The young *Leutnant* loosened Fritsch's jacket and trousers. 'Leave me,' the General insisted, then passed out. Within seconds he was dead; the bullet had severed an artery. A shot passed through the *Leutnant*'s trousers; a stretcher-bearer was killed instantly by a bullet to the head. Eventually the *Generaloberst*'s body was carried to a small church, where his comrades held a brief memorial service. Alfred Jodl, Hitler's senior military adviser, began the Führer's evening briefing solemnly. 'Today one of the finest soldiers that the German Army has ever known died, *Generaloberst* Freiherr von Fritsch.' Hitler nodded insincerely. '*Ja*, if only I had stopped him joining his regiment!' The Führer did little more than acknowledge the general's death in a curt communiqué, then ordered a state funeral for Fritsch – which he did not attend.[10]

As Werner von Fritsch lay mortally wounded in a ditch in a Warsaw suburb, schoolteacher and politician Adam Czerniakow hurried to the meeting house of the city's Jewish Citizens' Committee. The committee had set up a makeshift hospital, overseen burials in the Jewish cemetery, tried in vain to appeal to fellow

Jews across the globe to come to their aid and struggled to organise food supplies. Today, Friday, 22 September, was the holiest day in the Jewish calendar – *Yom Kippur* – the Day of Atonement. 'Atonement indeed,' Czerniakow succinctly observed in his diary.

By the beginning of the fourth week of September 1939, life for the inhabitants of Warsaw as they knew it was breaking down. Bread was at a premium; snake-like queues developed in front of the handful of bakeries still operating. There was no longer any meat. Inhabitants resorted to eating horses – there were enough dead animals in the city's streets. Warsaw's newspapers encouraged its people to eat the animals, to use their bones as stock for soup. The constant bombing, the shelling, the German leaflets urging them to surrender gnawed at the Varsovians' morale. 'We realised that there was no hope for us, that nobody was coming to our rescue,' hospital secretary Marta Korwin recalled. Rumours abounded. The Western Front was ablaze. Aid was flooding in from across the British Empire. British soldiers had landed near Danzig; their arrival in Warsaw was imminent. The water mains were smashed so fires raged unchecked, while people huddled around the few water fountains now working. Paranoia was rampant; an elderly music teacher with a Germanic surname was bound, gagged and stuffed in the cellar of her apartment. Her crime: sending 'coded messages' to the German bombers through her piano playing. Some soldiers deserted, some Varsovians resorted to plunder, all were subjected to flying courts-martial. Traitors, saboteurs and spies were executed following summary trials. Scores of inhabitants saw the writing on the wall. They streamed out of the city towards the German lines hoping for salvation – and food. But the German troops did not let them pass. 'Send them back,' Johannes Blaskowitz instructed his men. 'Don't let them through.'[11]

Time for Warsaw was running out. The Gods were against it. Late in the afternoon of the twenty-third dark yellow and black clouds began to form over the beleaguered city, accompanied by a hideous growling which almost drowned out the noise of bombs and shells falling. 'It seemed as if some infernal powers were waging a battle,' Marta Korwin remembered. Everyone expected rain, but instead hailstones 'as big as chestnuts' bombarded Warsaw, so many that the streets turned white. This was not how September should be, the hospital secretary mused. 'September is always beautiful in Poland – the air is soft, the sky is pale blue and the clouds, if any, are small, white and friendly. Everything in September seems to be resting and peaceful.' After dusk that same day, pianist Wladyslaw Szpilman took a break from composing to wander through the streets of his city. Now dark blood-red clouds of smoke hung over the city. The smoke and flames gave the streets of the capital, still littered with the 'poisoned' German leaflets, a ruddy hue. 'Two bodies lay under a street lamp at the crossroads, one with arms spread wide, the other curled up as if to sleep,' the pianist observed. 'Outside the door of our building lay the corpse of a woman with her head and one arm blown off. Her blood flowed into the gutter in a long, dark stream.' Szpilman watched a horse-drawn cab slowly make its way through the ruined city as if it was a typical evening. First there was a whistling noise, then a roar, then a blinding white flash. When the musician opened his eyes again, the cab had disintegrated. 'Splintered wood, the remains of wheels and shafts, bits of upholstery and the shattered bodies of the driver and horse lay by the walls of the buildings.' Wladyslaw Szpilman continued on his way home.[12]

The 22, 23 and 24 September were terrible days for the citizens of Warsaw. On the Sunday, German gunners concentrated their fire on the city centre. The polytechnic, the Seventeenth-century Krasinski Palace – built for one of the city's greatest mayors – the administrative headquarters of the Polish Army were all set ablaze. Of greater importance to the defence of the city was the loss of electricity – the power station was finally knocked out – water and food as the warehouses went up in flames. Before the power faded for good, Stefan Starzynski made a final appeal to his fellow Varsovians.

I wanted Warsaw to be great. I believed Warsaw would be great. I and my staff members drew up plans, made sketches of a great Warsaw of the future. And Warsaw is great. It happened more quickly than we expected. Not in fifty years, not in 100, but today I see a great Warsaw.

As I speak to you now, through the windows I see, enveloped by clouds of smoke, reddened by flames, a wonderful, indestructible, great, fighting Warsaw in all its glory.

And although ruins lie where fine orphanages should stand, even though where there should be parks there are barricades covered with corpses, even though our libraries are engulfed by flames, even though hospitals burn, then not in fifty years, nor 100 years, but today Warsaw, which is defending Poland's honour, is at the peak of its greatness and glory.

Yet for all the greatness and glory, Warsaw was doomed. Stefan Starzynski knew it, and told his cityfolk. 'It's too late for help,' he warned. 'Before it arrives there will be only rubble here, a land razed, strewn with corpses.' The only hope was that the justice of God would prevail. 'What we are waiting for is revenge,' he declared. 'A day will come when Berlin will be set afire, when German women and children will die just as ours are dying.'[13]

As the bombardment of shells and bombs pelted Warsaw, the steel ring drawn around the city by Eighth Army tightened. The mission troubled the Army's Chief-of-Staff, Hans Felber. On the one hand, Warsaw was a 'nest of evil Polacks'. On the other, he feared for the fate of the capital's civilians. From an observation post he saw dense columns of smoke rising above Warsaw and shot-up houses burning fiercely. 'You have to feel truly sorry for the poor civilian populace,' he confided in his diary. Felber steeled himself. War was war. 'We have to smash the last remnants of the Polish Army – whatever it costs. War cannot be waged too gently.'[14]

A thin layer of cloud hung 6,000ft above Warsaw initially as Monday, 25 September, dawned and an artillery barrage began a day-long symphony of death and destruction. 'The mortars spoke incessantly, one battery after another, showering a hot rain of metal over Poland's capital, bursting in windows and tearing out window frames and doors,' one eyewitness wrote. 'The earth quivered and our eardrums seemed about to split. Looking to Warsaw we saw columns of smoke soaring languidly, as if from mighty cigars. In all directions, long smoky tongues of fire spurted up every second. In the heavens the clouds were as red as blood.' After two hours, the guns fell silent and the cloud dispersed as the first of 400 bombers approached the Polish capital 'methodically, in waves'. From his Ju87 Carl Cranz observed thirty-four Stukas hurtle down towards the city below 'like meteors', every sinew of the aircraft 'straining to breaking point', the 'trumpets of Jericho' screeching 'a terrifying steel howl'. And then, almost instantaneously, the flash of fire on the ground, followed by puffs of smoke. Tramlines buckled and the roads leading to four bridges over the Vistula smashed. As he pulled up, Cranz noticed 'the red glow of fire from the flames flicker across the city'. A German war correspondent watched as 'countless German aircraft dive down on the abandoned city from the cloudy sky like ghostly shadows. Fires flare up, fanned into bright conflagrations by the morning breeze. Black clouds of smoke drift over the fluttering signs of fire. Roofs fly up in the air, houses collapse in on themselves.'[15]

After a matter of minutes, the cloud of smoke over the city was so great it was impossible to bomb accurately. Polish colonel Tadeusz Tomaszewski watched as the fire defence officer struggled to cope with news of fresh fires pouring into his command post. 'He recorded each report of a fire with a small red flag on a large road map,' Tomaszewski recalled. 'By 10am, this map was covered with red; the small red flags had run out. The fire officer stopped work, he was powerless in the face of the elements, the lack of water and appliances.' So eager was the Luftwaffe to test the theories of air power that more than two dozen Ju52 transporters were pressed into service as makeshift bombers. One in six bombs dropped was an incendiary; the cargo holds of the Junkers were crammed with incendiaries. Over Warsaw, crew members tossed the bombs out of the door using potato shovels. Carried by a strong easterly wind, the incendiaries drifted away from the heart of the capital and landed to the northwest of the city – in some cases among German lines.[16]

The vast majority of bombs fell upon the centre of the city. The flames engulfed the Holy Spirit Hospital, the Pavilions of Jesus children's hospital, museums, theatres, churches, tenement blocks; communications with the troops in the front lines were severed. At the peak of the conflagration, 200 fires raged simultaneously. With water supplies severed, the flames swept through Warsaw unchecked. 'City life is totally paralysed,' the diarist of the city's civil defence organisation recorded. 'For the first time no newspaper has appeared today.' And yet, the people of Warsaw showed 'great initiative, energy and devotion'. With no water to douse the fires, Warsaw's inhabitants tossed sand on the flames or pulled down buildings with axes to halt the flames. Weary figures moved between the flames and ruins. 'Men of goodwill are burying the dead where they find them – in a garden, or a square or the courtyard of houses,' one eyewitness observed. 'Famished people cut off pieces of flesh as soon as a horse falls, leaving only the skeleton.' Wladyslaw Szpilman never left his apartment block. He spent the entire day with ten neighbours huddled in a toilet, listening to the 'thunder of guns' and 'boom of nose-diving aircraft', breathing air 'heavy with smoke and the dust of crumbling bricks and plaster'. Thirteen-year-old Janina Bauman hunkered in the basement in Ulica Granicza (Border Street) alongside her neighbours and any refugee who now called the tenement block their home. The people tossed mattresses or bedding on the filthy floor. Some tried to read by the dim light of candles, some talked, some joked nervously. The air was stuffy, dusty. No hot food, no water. At any moment, neighbours and strangers expected to be buried alive in the wake of a direct hit. Near misses caused the walls of the basement to shudder and shake. 'Time stopped,' Janina recalled. 'Life seemed to be coming to an end. We could only pray to be swallowed up by the inferno quickly and painlessly.' The lure of what was going on proved too strong for the schoolgirl. With a friend she struggled through the herd and dark passages up to the remains of a shop. 'An immense wall of flame stood in front of the shop's broken window,' the youngster wrote. 'The other side of the street was on fire.'[17]

The approaches to Warsaw were guarded by more than half a dozen obsolete, ill-equipped and in some cases disused fortifications which dated from the days of Russian rule. Most of these red-brick fortress still had garrisons – and still posed a threat to the besiegers. Before there could be any thought of taking Warsaw, the forts had to be neutralised.

As the bombers approached the Polish capital that Monday morning, pioneers and assault troops began moving stealthily through the city's outskirts. They moved in small groups, three or four strong, hiding in gardens, using hedges, shell craters, piles of rubble as cover. The advance proved infuriating. Each time pioneer Georg Pickel reached a row of houses he believed the Poles were defending, the enemy had fallen back to another row or an apartment block. Just to make sure, he tossed a grenade into each home, then searched every room. The picture was always the same. The enemy had gone. 'The Poles had taken to fleeing – they were too cowardly to fight man against man,' he grumbled. They shot at the stormtroops from cellars or rooftops, each time falling back before the pioneers could engage them. Other raids proved more rewarding. Pioneers attached to 20th Infantry Regiment were roused from their foxholes at 4.30am. The men rolled up the canvas which served as their beds, stuffed it in their belts and grabbed their rifles. A young *Leutnant* was charged with reconnoitring Fort Mokotow, four miles south of the city centre, ahead of the main assault. The men crept forwards with machine guns, wire-cutters, smoke and hand grenades, explosive charges, wire cutters and a flamethrower. The residents of Mokotow could be seen running away as they caught sight of the advancing Germans in the first rays of dawn. The streets of Mokotow were lined with fruit trees 'with very fine apples and plums hanging down,' *Unteroffizer* Xaver Kotheder recalled, 'but none of us had the time to stick one in our pockets'. After hand-to-hand fighting with around twenty Polish soldiers in houses on the edge of the fort, the stormtroops charged up the earthwork ramparts, tossing hand grenades into casemates as they went. The young *Leutnant* climbed down into the central courtyard. A solitary Polish soldier strolled across the quadrangle, a hand towel slung over his arm. So shocked was he when he found the German officer before him, he was unable to speak. The rest of the fort's garrison, more than 280 men and four women, were still asleep, the courtyard haphazardly filled with weapons and kit. All fell into the hands of the young *Leutnant*.[18]

A stone's throw from the fort, shock troops of 41st Infantry Regiment began making their way forward into the suburb of Mokotow itself under the umbrella of German howitzers. They were making good progress. Adolf Hitler could see so. The Führer was visiting his men investing Warsaw ahead of the final onslaught against the Polish capital. He had an excellent vantage point – the tower of a race course which dominated the skyline, rising more than 160ft. From up there, the view was magnificent, mesmerising, moving. 'Huge fires smouldered in the city; the rising smoke continually darkened the heavens,' wrote Conrad von Cochenhausen, the commander of 10th Infantry Division, accompanying the Führer on his visit to the front. 'German aircraft continued their journeys above the clouds of smoke; one pushed through the layer of smoke in a dive and the loud crash of the heavy 50kg bombs mingled with the continuous roar of shells landing, fired in from all sides by German artillery.' It was, Cochenhausen thought, an unforgettable moment and one which left Hitler deeply moved. Before departing, the Führer buttonholed Johannes Blaskowitz. Warsaw must fall by 2 October. Eighth Army's commander assured him it would.[19]

Adolf Hitler left as the attack by the men of 41st Infantry began to falter. Barricades had been thrown across the streets using upturned trams. The Poles had dug trenches in the gardens of homes. They had mined the streets. They shot from every window, from cellars, from rooftops. Cadets from Warsaw's military academy provided the backbone of the defence. Despite the support of pioneers with flamethrowers, grenades and demolition charges, despite a handful of panzers and field guns, the *Landsers* of 41st Infantry Regiment had advanced just two blocks by dusk.[20]

It was a taste of what the German soldier could expect when the main assault was launched.

Above Warsaw, war correspondent Peter Supf watched as a huge bluish black cloud began to grow – 'a cloud of doom, a shadow of damnation, eclipsing the light of the sun, whose rays hesitantly shine past the dark edges,' he wrote. 'German aircraft continually approach it and if they disappear in its dark void. It becomes so dark that the crew have to switch on their onboard lights, and the smell of fire pierces the gaps in the cockpit windows.'[21]

All day, Polish flak fired doggedly. As evening set in, 'the muzzle fire of guns' flashed amid the pall of smoke, but to no avail; just three German aircraft were lost during the 25 September attacks on Warsaw. With the sun disappearing, 'all over Warsaw there was the red glow of fire, visible far and wide'. Peter Supf revelled in the city's dance of death. 'Huge jets of flame shoot up and for a few terrible seconds light up the clouds of smoke hanging over the city,' he wrote. 'Poland is going down in a sea of flames.' Eighth Army's Chief-of-Staff Hans Felber was more magnanimous. Watching the bombardment from an observation post to the southwest of Warsaw, the General thought to himself: I hope that this does not happen to our German cities. 'This side of the war is most horrible,' he continued in his diary. 'The fateful destruction of cities, their culture and their children. The civilians are to be pitied.'[22]

Darkness offered Warsaw respite. Colonel Tadeusz Tomaszewski left his command post. He was appalled by what greeted him:

From an angle, the merging of the flames gave the impression that all Warsaw, including Praga, was aflame, as if everything was a single sea of fire and smoke. People emerged from cellars, foxholes and hastily-dug ditches. Some wandered around in silent despondency looking for shelter, others ran to smother the fire, to prevent it spreading. Thousands of corpses were spread across the entire city, barely covered with soil. The cadavers of horses, awful skeletons, blocked the roads, beginning to decompose.[23]

To the defenders of Warsaw, there was little doubt that the raid of 25 September had been a *nur Terrorangriff* – pure terror attack. The bombardment had been directed not at the troops in the front line but at the city and its inhabitants. Life for the soldiers was hard 'but still bearable', Tomaszewski wrote. 'They could still fight, carry out counter-attacks, defend themselves, hold out.' The question as this terrible Monday drew to a close was not whether the defenders of Warsaw could endure, but whether they could allow the civilians' agony to continue. To Tadeusz Tomaszewski 'the issue was as clear as day, or more precisely, as dark as night'; Warsaw should surrender.[24]

In the meeting house of Warsaw's Methodist community at the corner of Zbawiciela Square, civilian leaders gathered to discuss the capital's fate. The men were depressed. They knew the city would fall, yet no-one dared to say so aloud. Having decided nothing, a delegation of the city's fathers visited Juliusz Rommel's command post. 'All of them speak of the terror of the present day,' the General wrote. 'None of them wants to utter the word "surrender", but I know precisely why they have come – for help, for advice.' Juliusz Rommel had given his word that his nation's capital would be held to the last round. The delegation agreed. Warsaw would fight on.[25]

That night the inhabitants of Warsaw took shelter in cellars, in basements, in the vaults of major buildings and churches. 'The noise of collapsing masonry echoes under the vaults,' wrote one resident. 'Every minute may be the last of our lives. There is only one little lamp whose flame flickers before the altar.' A shell smashed through a second-floor window in Marta Korwin's hospital and exploded under the bed of a wounded Polish lieutenant. His body parts were plastered around the room, 'on the wall, on the ceiling,' Korwin observed. In Warsaw's central hospital, nurse Jadwiga Sosnkowska worked by candlelight as surgeons hacked off the legs and arms of bomb victims. An elderly couple who had lost an eye each, a pregnant woman with her intestines blown out, tossed into a common grave. 'As human wreckage was laid on the table, the surgeon vainly endeavoured to save the lives that were slipping through his hands,' she recalled. The sight of one casualty in particular, a sixteen-year-old girl, affected Sosnkowska particularly. 'Both her legs up to the knees were a mass of bleeding pulp, in which it was impossible to distinguish bone from flesh. Both had to be amputated above the knee.' The girl died shortly afterwards 'like a flower plucked by a merciless hand'.[26] All night long casualties streamed into the hospital. They waited in the corridors; the wards were full.

For three hours that night the German guns fell silent. The Führer had ordered it. But this was no act of humanity. Hitler wanted to spare Russian diplomats fleeing the stricken city. Varsovians took advantage of the lull to hurry to the banks of the Vistula to fill their pails. Jadwiga Sosnkowska took a break from her blood-soaked operating theatre to survey the city she loved. 'Warsaw was burning, our hospital was in flames, the windows were smashed, the doors blown in, and there was neither light nor water nor food,' she wrote.[27]

Warsaw's reprieve lasted until 8am on Tuesday, 26 September. The sky was shrouded by cloud and a light autumn mist which mingled with the swaths of smoke rising from the countless fires to thwart the penetrating rays of the sun. From Eighth Army's command post the sight of the Polish capital hidden by huge columns of smoke seemed 'chillingly beautiful' to Hans Felber. 'We may only hope for one thing,' he confided to his diary. 'No German city should suffer this fate.'[28] And then the guns barked once more as the artillery unleashed its barrage, prelude to the final assault on Warsaw. 'High above our heads there was a howling and roaring, every second heavy German shells hurtled from dozens of tubes towards the enemy – all hell must have been let loose in his positions,' company commander Fritz Fillies recorded. Fillies and his men had spent seven days outside Praga investing the Polish capital. It was a dreary existence in a dreary land in front of a dreary suburb of a dreary capital. 'Every day was the same,' wrote Fillies. 'Grey skies above us, brown clouds over the city. Damp in the fire positions, on the fields and meadows to the edge of the cobbled streets.' Infrequent but sudden Polish raids against the German lines and sporadic shelling were all Fillies' company saw of the enemy, except for the nightly stream of deserters. 'Each one said the same thing,' he remembered. 'They had had enough.' Now the last act had begun: an end to Fillies' dreary existence. He watched, transfixed, as German guns pulverised the Polish lines:

> Amidst the great swath of smoke and earth flying up over there it was barely possible to still be able to make out the flashes of individual shells landing. The waltz of death danced around the enemy's ground, thunderous and booming, forwards and backwards, backwards and forwards, left and right; it wasn't possible that a single strip of land had been spared under such fire. The enemy responded to our fire less and less.[29]

The barrage lifted thirty minutes later, only to move inside Warsaw, trapping the Polish troops in the foremost lines between a rain of steel to their rear and storming German soldiers in front of them. Barbed-wire cutters and assault troops with flamethrowers led the way, entering a city hidden by a 'great pall of smoke and dust' as the Luftwaffe swarmed overhead 'like hornets, raining death and destruction'.[30] Pioneers swept into Fort Dabrowski, one of the relics of Russian rule which defended the southern approaches. The stormtroops sprayed the bunkers with jets from flamethrowers. The Poles emerged, hideously burned, their faces blackened by smoke. Two hundred defenders gave themselves up.

Fritz Fillies watched a huge brown-black cloud of smoke begin to tower over the city. 'It hung there for hours, barely changing. Warsaw's power station had been destroyed, we soon learned.' It was too much for many Polish soldiers, who raised the white flag or crossed the lines to desert. They were, Fillies saw, 'emotionally shattered'. He continued: 'They were tired, very tired. For too long there had been too little sleep, for them and for us. But we found it easy to bear, especially as we were confident that there would be a successful conclusion for us in front of Warsaw.' These fresh prisoners presented a dejected, demoralised picture. 'Each one said the same thing: "We should finish it, we don't care, we can't take it any longer",' Fillies recalled. But the company commander's experiences were not typical. There were still more than 58,000 men defending the Polish capital as the final battle for Warsaw began. Everything suggested they would defend their capital stubbornly. Discipline remained firm. Officers inspired the men 'to resist to the end, summoning truly great examples of courage', Hans Felber observed. There was also the darker side of enemy resistance, the Eighth Army Chief-of-Staff heard; there were instances of Polish soldiers surrendering, then tossing grenades hidden in their clenched fists. 'Of course, there wasn't much left of them,' the staff officer wrote. 'But this also cost us senseless blood.' And there were the Varsovians to contend with. Most, like the soldiers defending the city, were determined to hold Warsaw to the last man.[31]

And so it proved. Resistance almost everywhere was determined, as pioneer *Unteroffizier* Richard Bremer found as he entered the suburb of Mokotow, moving past terraced houses pockmarked by bullets from the previous day's fighting. Black-out tape had failed to stop the street lamps shattering. Slit trenches had been dug in the parks where signs still stood among the tree stumps and charred branches: *Nie dreptac trawnikow* – do not trespass on the grass. Trams had been slung across the streets, their windows smashed, their struts warped, and mines laid in the road. With bullets whistling above their heads and shells crashing down, the pioneers lay in the street and prodded for mines with long rods. 'Every advantage rests with our dug-in enemy, every disadvantage is suffered by the attacker in the open,' he complained. The Bavarians of 20th Infantry Regiment reported that the Poles fought 'with courage born of desperation'; each house had been turned into a small fortress, each street took hours to clear out. Even when the infantrymen advanced, certain they had 'smoked out' the defenders, they found themselves shot at from houses in their rear.[32]

That evening as Maximilian von Weichs pored over reports of the day's fighting, XIII Corps' Commander became disheartened. His men had fought bravely, but barely anywhere had they reached their objectives. The Poles had shown themselves to be highly adept at street fighting. German losses as a result were grievous. And come the morning, his men would have to do it all again. 'It was hardly an encouraging prospect,' Weichs conceded. At the front, one of Weichs' men watched night envelop Warsaw. 'The sky over the silhouette of the city is blood-red,' he recorded in his diary. 'Will the garrison finally realise the madness of this resistance and lay down its arms?'[33]

'The thundering of the guns never stopped,' a young Jewish girl recorded in his diary that evening. 'Hundreds of bombers darkened the sky.' Warsaw was no longer fighting back, she observed. The anti-aircraft guns had ceased firing. The bombs tumbled down relentlessly, reducing once fine tenement blocks into mountains of rubble. 'The city was a boiling kettle of fire and blood.'[34]

It could not go on like this, but Warsaw's leaders seemed to believe more in the power of words than deeds. As fighting raged in the suburbs of their city, they met in the vaults of a bank. The capital's president, Stefan Starzynski, urged continued resistance. He brushed aside objections that the city would be flattened in doing so. 'We will build such a beautiful city a third time,' he told his colleagues icily.

The generals were more sober. The city was without water, without food – every warehouse had been razed to the ground by fire. The spectre of disease hung over the city. Juliusz Rommel told the politicians he was satisfied that he, his men and the city had fulfilled their grave responsibility. 'Continuing to resist would merely lead to carnage for both the Army and the populace,' he concluded. It was time to bring the curtain down on the final act of the terrible drama.[35]

In Rommel's headquarters, the printing presses were hastily put into action. Without electricity, without newspapers, single sheets of paper were the sole means of communicating with more than one million civilians. In defeat, Juliusz Rommel was unbowed. 'On a level playing field, the Polish soldier is not inferior to the enemy, in fact he is far superior,' he told his men. His decision to call off the struggle had been taken solely 'to end the suffering of the inhabitants of Warsaw'. The General addressed the civilian populace in a similar vein. 'The fate of the war is changing,' he declared:

> The population of the capital has set a heroic example of perseverance, resolve and boundless willingness to sacrifice. With its brave defence, Warsaw has earned the admiration and reverence of free nations all over the world, and its spirit was, is and will forever be the symbol of the spirit of the Polish nation, because by sacrificing itself, it fought for the honour and independence of Poland.[36]

And yet for all this defiance, for all this browbeating, Juliusz Rommel kept his composure and kept his dignity. He expected no less from his countrymen. 'I call upon the population of Warsaw to accept the entry of German forces quietly, calmly and honourably.'[37]

Long before Juliusz Rommel's appeal was distributed among the soldiers and civilians, Tadeusz Kutrzeba left the command post in the Postal Savings Bank in the heart of Warsaw on a wretched journey to conduct surrender negotiations. This war had spared Kutrzeba nothing. He had lost the battle on the Bzura. Now he was forced to discuss his capital's surrender. Mid-morning on the twenty-seventh he reached a school building in the small town of Sulejowek, a dozen miles east of the capital, home to *Generalleutnant* Walter Petzel, commander of I Corps. As Petzel read out the terms of surrender, Kutrzeba bit his lip, hiding the pain which gnawed at his soul, before signing the document. It was too much for the Colonel who accompanied him; the staff officer broke down in tears and ran out of the schoolroom. Petzel offered the forlorn General his hand. 'The fortunes of war favoured our side more,' he told him. 'We were adversaries, but we are not personal enemies.' The two Polish officers then climbed into a staff car and were driven back across the Vistula, never uttering a word. Shortly after mid-day they arrived at Eighth Army's headquarters in the suburb of Okecie. A barrage of flashes from cameras greeted Kutrzeba as he stepped out of the vehicle. The ensuing discussions with Blaskowitz's staff were conducted in private, however. Given the solemnity of the hour, the talks were relatively cordial. The Germans offered soup and bread and inquired about the fate of the Polish capital. 'Warsaw is no longer recognisable,' Kutrzeba lamented.

It was still light as the General and his comrade wearily returned to their headquarters five miles to the northeast. 'There were scores of people in the streets, breathing fresh air, seeking water, or merely there out of curiosity,' Kutrzeba observed. 'I got the impression that the moral state of the city would worsen severely if these impoverished and worn-out people were driven back into the cellars or if the fighting flared up again. For a brief moment, they understood reality: that life is beautiful, even if fighting is a necessity.'[38]

'The victory is ours!' a jubilant Hans Felber recorded in his diary. 'Our greatest triumph is what we have spared in blood! The war is over. These have been extremely anxious weeks for us, but given the outcome we would gladly have borne it all.' The capture of the Polish capital, wrote Felber, was the *Schlussbukett* – the bouquet at the final curtain.[39]

In the corridor of her hospital, Jadwiga Sosnkowska counted the cost of Warsaw's futile defiance of the Wehrmacht. She walked past 'long rows of more than a hundred yards of mutilated bodies of soldiers, women and children'. There was still a pall of smoke refusing to leave the heavens above the forlorn city. Slowly, the clouds thinned and light was gradually cast upon Warsaw. 'It was then that I saw the most terrible sight – a river of blood literally flowing down the corridor, washing the bodies of the dead, dying and still living martyrs,' the nurse wrote.

Janina Bauman stepped out into a 'dead town, ruined and burnt to the ground'. Buildings smouldered, the pavements and streets were littered with deep craters. Emaciated figures moved among the rubble, hunting for food. They found the cadaver of a horse lying in the bottom of a crater. Jumping down into the hole wielding knives, they began to hack away at the dead creature, then they fought over the scraps.

It would be two more days before pianist Wladyslaw Szpilman dared to leave the toilet which had become his sanctuary. He wished he hadn't. 'Decaying bodies were piled up in the streets. The people, starving from the siege, fell on the bodies of horses lying around.' The musician walked past a collapsed building where the bodies of two of his sister's friends were entombed. 'You had to hold a handkerchief to your nose – the nauseating stink of eight rotting bodies seeped through the blocked-up cellar windows, through nooks and crannies, infecting the air.' Szpilman returned home deeply downcast. 'The city no longer existed.'[40]

The Bavarians of 20th Infantry Regiment were still fighting in the suburb of Mokotow when news came through of the cease-fire. It took until dusk before the chatter of machine guns and sounds of battle finally faded as word reached Polish and German soldiers alike. The men of the 20th commandeered wrecked homes, fixed wooden boards to the windows, raided the pantries and settled in for the night.

The following afternoon the regiment marched into the remains of Fort Mokotow, four miles from the centre of Warsaw. For the first time in days the autumn sun penetrated the smoke and cloud which had obliterated the skies above the Polish capital. Its rays gave the red-brick walls of the fort a golden hue. In the inner and outer courtyards lay fresh graves, their borders decorated with the last flowers of the summer – bright daisies and dahlias. Simple wooden crosses, with names hastily engraved, stood at the head of each resting place and on the earthen mound, a steel helmet.

The infantrymen lined up in the wide, open main courtyard in the shadow of the imposing red ramparts. The regimental band struck up for the first time since the Bavarians had crossed the Polish border. The guard presented arms as their commander, *Oberst* August Schmidt, entered the courtyard and inspected his men, his hand firmly fixed to his helmet. At the end he stood before them and spoke.

> There is no better place for this ceremony than this fort before the gates of Warsaw, whose conquest has cost so much blood. The regiment has played a vital role in the Polish capital's capitulation to the German Army. Many of the finest gave their lives for us, for Germany, for the Führer. All those who lay scattered on Poland's meadows the regiment salutes today, salutes them with the song of the good comrade: *Einen Bessern findst Du nicht* (You will not find anyone better).

Schmidt removed his helmet. His men did likewise. 'We shall now pray.' As they did the huge courtyard was bathed in the golden rays of the autumn sun.[41]

After nightfall on the last day of September, the garrison of Warsaw vacated the city it had defended, shuffling wearily along the main highway to Poznan in its earth-brown uniforms. A column of German armoured troops moved up the road to meet the surrendering army, entering the ruins of the capital's suburbs in the process. The moon at times disappeared behind thick clouds of smoke drifting from the Polish capital to the west; two days after the city had surrendered, the fires burning there continued to give a dark-red tint to the night sky. In the ruins of a brickworks, men, women and children huddled around a fire, as a dog next to a smashed wooden fence whimpered and a child's cries pierced the night. The flash of headlight beams ahead signalled the approach of the Poles. A staff officer climbed out of his car, saluted stiffly, reported the surrender of his division, then returned to his car. His men came on foot, four abreast, dejected, dishevelled, tired, hungry, cigarettes limply hanging out of the corner of their mouths. The expressions on their faces were blank, except for the occasional sullen smile. Many asked about their loved ones, calling out the names of their home towns – towns now ravaged and, in instances, erased by war. 'Columns of trucks, horse-drawn carts and field kitchens roll past,' a *Propaganda Kompanie* reporter observed as he watched the garrison of

Warsaw march into captivity. 'Sitting down are broken, shattered, exhausted men. Yet more infantry and artillery without guns, without arms. This beaten column shuffles along the road for kilometres. There are thousands to come yet. German panzers guard the column of the captured Polish Army.'[42]

The last Polish soldier to leave his capital was Juliusz Rommel; he and his staff were led to the command post of Eighth Army. There, at 5pm on the first day of October, in the courtyard of an abandoned factory, the commander of the *Army of Warsaw* formally surrendered the city. Johannes Blaskowitz treated his prisoner with dignity. '*Herr* Commander-in-Chief, you left the fortress as the last man. In doing so you carried out your difficult duty as a military leader of his people.' Juliusz Rommel's voice trembled slightly, but he was unrepentant. He had surrendered the city *only* to save its civilian population. His men could have held out much longer. As he was escorted to a staff car, waiting to take him to a prison camp at Hohenstein near Dresden, the Polish general turned to Blaskowitz: 'The fate of soldiers is changeable.'[43]

German soldiers had already moved in to collect their prize before Juliusz Rommel had even left Warsaw. The entry was low key. No martial music, no marching songs. 'As long as the beaten Polish army passed us, the march past took place in silence,' a German war correspondent wrote magnanimously. 'Only when the last Polish troops had crossed the demarcation line did German military tunes strike up for the first time.'[44]

The men of 10th Infantry Division were overawed by what they found as they marched into Warsaw on a gloriously sunny Sunday morning, 1 October. There wasn't a single house untouched by the fighting, not a single pane of glass unbroken in a window, Conrad von Cochenhausen, the division's commander observed. Fires raged – there was no water to extinguish them. There was no electricity, no gas, no heating, no food. The sewers had collapsed; drinking water mixed with human waste. Long queues developed around the few water fountains still working. Weapons lay scattered around the city, dumped in a disorderly fashion in public places, sometimes in the Vistula, by the Polish troops as they pulled out. And then there were the people, two million of them, living in the cellars, 'most half-starved and thirsty; distraught and crushed', a few sheepishly emerging from their hiding places, the pain and misery of the past four weeks etched on their faces. 'Everywhere we saw fresh graves in squares, everywhere we came across funeral processions,' Cochenhausen recalled.[45] The mood of his men was solemn. One 10th Infantry *Soldat* found Warsaw 'the saddest city in Europe'. He continued in a letter home to his family:

The population is starving terribly and has no shelter. Misery with all its terrible frightfulness is worse nowhere than here in this badly-haunted heap of rubble. Our bombers and artillery have been too thorough. Beside famine there is a great danger of epidemic. Ten thousand civilians still lie under the ruins. No water, no light. We often share our meagre supplies, because the misery of the women and children tugs at our hearts. The whole city is without food. No house has any windowpanes. Those which are not bombed out, are badly damaged. That is this grey, awful city.[46]

Jewish teacher Chaim Kaplan was surprised by how healthy the conquerors appeared. 'Until now I had been certain that they were starving and we were well fed,' he wrote in his diary. 'Now, I see the exact opposite. We are hungry and they give us free bread.' The entering German soldiers made a powerful impression on the teacher. 'You almost began to believe that this was indeed a people fit to rule the world by virtue of power and strength.' The conquerors would quickly destroy Chaim Kaplan's initial impressions.

Notes

1. Phillips, pp. 59–64.
2. OKW Communiqué, 23/9/39.
3. Drescher, pp. 191–2, 335.
4. Drescher, p. 724, Elble, p. 176 and KTB Bock, 23/9/39.
5. Drescher, pp. 413–14, 417, 420.
6. *Polish Black Book*, p. 74, *New York Times*, 17/9/39 and Appeal by Rommel, 22/9/39 in Drescher, pp. 568–9.
7. KTB Bock, 23/9/39 Johannes von Blaskowitz was equally scathing. 'What shocked even the most hardened soldier was how a misguided population, completely ignorant of the effect of modern weapons, could contribute to the destruction of their own capital,' he wrote. Giziowski, p. 140.
8. Drescher, pp. 469, 472.
9. Liere, *Pioniere im Kampf: Erlbenisberichte aus dem Polenfeldzug 1939*, pp. 58–9.
10. *Fritschprozess*, p. 146 and Drescher, pp. 656–7. Werner von Fritsch was buried four days later at the Invalidenfriedhof, the great cemetery founded by Frederick the Great in the heart of Berlin and the last resting place of Scharnhorst, Seeckt, Schlieffen and other doyens of German military history. In his funeral oration, Walther von Brauchitsch proclaimed the *Generaloberst* as 'one of the best the Prussian Army has known. A man who since his earliest days as a *Leutnant* dedicated his life in solemn, ceaseless devotion to service, service to his *Volk* and Fatherland, service to the Army… The *Generaloberst* has returned home to the great army. He will live for eternity in us and in our deeds if they correspond to his demands.' Hitler was furious at Brauchitsch for his fulsome praise of Fritsch. His Wehrmacht adjutant Rudolf Schmundt seethed: 'Brauchitsch regards Fritsch as the creator of the new army. The Führer is grossly offended, because *he* is the creator of the new German Army.' See *Fritschprozess*, p. 147, *Völkischer Beobachter*, 27/9/39 and Vormann, p. 156.
11. Czerniakow, p. 76, Korwin-Rhodes, pp. 136–7, Szpilman, p. 37 and KTB AOK8 23/9/39 in BA-BA RH20-8/11.
12. Korwin-Rhodes, pp. 40–1, 152–3 and Szpilman, pp. 39–40.
13. Drescher, p. 603 and author's papers.
14. KTB Felber, 23/9/39 and 24/9/39 in BA-MA RH20-8/1.
15. Bethell, *The War Hitler Won*, p. 139, Drescher, p. 606, Grabler, pp. 239–40, Supf, p. 91.
16. Drescher, pp. 604–5, 730.
17. Drescher, p. 607, *Polish Black Book*, p. 84, Szpilman, p. 40 and Bauman, pp. 24–5.
18. *Gefreiter* Georg Pickel, 'A Raiding Party of 2/Pi.10 in House-to-House Fighting for Warsaw' in BA-MA RH12-5/339. See also BA-MA RH37/6385 and *Unteroffizier* Xaver Kotheder, 'Wie wir Fort Mokotow nahmen,' in *Mit dem XIII Armeekorps in Polen*, pp. 47–9.

19. 'Die 10 Division im polnischen Feldzug,' speech by von Cochenhausen in Regensburg, 31/10/39 in BA-MA RH26-10/544 and KTB AOK8, 25/9/39 in BA-MA RH20-8/11.

20. 'Die 10 Division im polnischen Feldzug,' speech by von Cochenhausen in Regensburg, 31/10/39 in BA-MA RH26-10/544 and Schmidt, *Die Geschichte der 10 Infanterie Division*, p. 51.

21. Supf, p. 92.

22. Drescher, p. 605, Supf, p. 93 and Giziowski, p. 142.

23. Drescher, p. 731.

24. Drescher, pp. 731–2.

25. Drescher, pp. 733–4.

26. *Polish Black Book*, pp. 85–6, Korwin-Rhodes, pp. 171–2 and Owen and Walters, *Voice of War*, p. 16.

27. KTB AOK8, 26/9/39 in BA-MA RH20-8/11, *Polish Black Book*, pp. 85–6 and Owen and Walters, *Voice of War*, p. 17.

28. KTB Felber, 26/9/39 in BA-MA RH20-8/1.

29. Fillies, p. 192.

30. Giziowski, p. 142.

31. Fillies, pp. 185–6, 192, 198–9, Drescher, pp. 570–1, KTB Felber, 25/9/39, in BA-MA RH20-8/1 and AOK8 Unterlagen für die Angriff auf Warschau, 23/9/39, in BA-MA RH20-8/282.

32. *Mit dem XIII Armeekorps in Polen*, pp. 51–3 and BA-MA RH37/6385.

33. Weichs, *Erinnerungen*, BA-MA N19/7, pp. 27–8 and *Mit dem XIII Armeekorps in Polen*, p. 56.

34. Dollinger, Hans (ed), *Kain, wo ist dein Bruder?*, p. 33.

35. Drescher, pp. 735–9 and Polish communiqué, 26/9/39, in author's papers.

36. Drescher, pp. 801, 803, 805.

37. Drescher, p. 805.

38. Drescher, pp767–73.

39. KTB Felber, 27/9/39 and 29/9/39 in BA-MA RH20-8/1.

40. Owen and Walters, *Voice of War*, p. 17, Bauman, pp. 26–7, and Szpilman, pp. 40–2.

41. BA-MA RH37/6385.

42. Kabisch, pp. 31–2. Hans Felber, Eighth Army's Chief-of-Staff, agreed. Touring a makeshift prison camp housing the Warsaw garrison, he noted: 'A beaten army is truly all that remains of the proud Polish Army.' See KTB Felber, 1/10/39 in BA-MA RH20-8/1. XIII Corps' commander von Weichs was rather more impressed by the garrison as it filed down the roads out of Warsaw. Their bearing and discipline was admirable. 'The Poles bore their grave fate with dignity' See Weichs' unpublished memoirs in BA-MA N19/7, p. 29.

43. BA-MA RH20-8/11, BA-MA RH20-8/169, and Weichs, *Erinnerungen*, in BA-MA N19/7, pp. 29–30. Also see *Mit dem XIII Armeekorps in Polen*, p. 54.

44. Urban, p. 228.

45. 'Die 10 Division im polnischen Feldzug,' speech by von Cochenhausen in Regensburg, 31/10/39 in BA-MA RH26-10/544. See also KTB Felber, 6/10/39 in BA-MA RH20-8/1 and BA-MA RH37/6385.

46. Soldat J.S., Staff, 10 Infanterie Division, 2/10/39. Buchbender, pp. 40–1.

47. Kaplan, p. 23.

CHAPTER TWELVE

A Chain of Tragedies

*The German is now lord in this country. Whoever is not
with us is against us – and anyone who is against us will be destroyed.*
– GAULEITER ARTHUR GREISER

*Our only hope is that the defeat of the Nazis will surely come.
We have only one doubt – whether we shall live to see that day.*
– CHAIM KAPLAN

THURSDAY 5 October dawned with clear blue skies over Warsaw. Bright red swastika banners swung gently from the lamp posts of Ujazdowski Avenue, once the heart of the Polish capital's diplomatic quarter and one of the few streets relatively unscathed by a month of battle. German soldiers in their *feldgrau* tunics and steel helmets stood to attention in front of the shells of buildings and heaps of rubble. Shortly before mid-day a motorcade rolled slowly through the streets, heavily protected by armoured cars, until it came to a halt near Ujazdowski Avenue. To a tumult of cheering and applause, Adolf Hitler, dressed in a long black leather coat and brown cap, stepped out of his Mercedes Benz G4. It was a perfect early autumn day. The mid-day sun streamed over the rooftops. Tenth Army commander Walther Reichenau strode up. 'Führer,' he declared brashly, 'I give you Warsaw.' The street was filled with the sound of fife and drum, trumpets and horns, the clatter of horses' hoofs, the rumbling of wheels and caterpillar tracks and the thud of gleaming jackboots on the concrete road surface. For the next two hours, Hitler stood on a tribune accompanied by his generals and watched 15,000 men, selected from six divisions which had invested Warsaw, march, ride and roll past his outstretched hand. Many men wore freshly-awarded Iron Crosses, some even wore two crosses. All were dressed in *feldgrau* which bore the exertions of the past month. 'Let whoever wants to come, come!' a *Propaganda Kompanie* reporter gushed after watching the parade. 'What can happen to Greater Germany? Her Army is marching here, more solid, more steely, more ready to strike a blow than ever!' The parade over, the Führer briefly toured Belvedere House, home of Marshal Pilsudski until his death in 1935; outside stood a German honour guard, one of the few magnanimous gestures in the Reich's occupation of the Polish capital. And then the Führer and his entourage drove back to the airfield, where a fine meal had been arranged by the field kitchen in one of the few hangars still standing. Before eating, Hitler addressed the foreign journalists following his visit. 'You've seen Warsaw for yourselves,' he told them. 'I can do the same to all Europe's cities if I want. I have enough ammunition.' And then he turned to eat. He spied a table covered with white cloths, filled with dishes and plates and decorated with flowers and immediately turned about and headed for his aircraft without saying a word.[1]

Back in the Reich Chancellery in Berlin that evening, the Führer penned a final order of the day to his troops in Poland:

Soldiers of the Wehrmacht in the East!

This day brings to an end a battle which is testimony to the best of German soldiering.

The German Volk proudly joins me in thanking you. Thanks to you, the nation once again looks to its armed forces and leadership with unshakeable faith.

We honour our fallen comrades who gave their lives, as did the two million dead of the World War, so that Germany might live.

I know that you are prepared for anything given your faith in Germany.[2]

Perhaps Adolf Hitler did not know it. Perhaps he did not care. But 'this day' did not bring an end to the battle in Poland. Not quite.

In the harbour of Danzig, the sailors of the *Schleswig-Holstein* had been kicking their heels for more than a week. After the fall of Gdynia, the aged battleship had been without gainful employment. The *SX* had now been joined in the Bay of Danzig by her sister, *Schlesien* – another veteran of the titanic clash of the castles of steel at Jutland more than two decades earlier. The warships' inactivity did not last long. On 25 September the sisters received fresh orders: bombard Hela.

For a fortnight, Polish sailors at the tip of the Hela peninsula – a spit of land twenty miles long and but a few hundred yards wide arching into the Bay of Danzig with a naval base at the eastern end – had been cut off from the rest of Poland. Cut off, yet still they refused to submit. In fact, they were doggedly holding on, spurred on by their leader and spiritual head of the modern Polish Navy, Vice Admiral Jozef Unrug. Unrug commanded more than 2,000 men, plus the remnants of the Gdynia garrison who had fled across the bay, several bunkers, gun emplacements, batteries and anti-aircraft guns.

It was the batteries which most concerned the 28cm guns of *Schleswig-Holstein* and *Schlesien*; the latter's crew were anxious to prove themselves for the first time in battle. 'Thank God that we'll finally get our turn,' the men in the forward main turret said. 'We will smoke out the Polacks' batteries!' As the Luftwaffe and German guns pounded Warsaw, so the stukas and the shells of the two battleships pummelled the fortifications of Hela. 'The 28cm barrels thunder at the same time as 15cm casemate guns open fire,' wrote naval correspondent Fritz Otto-Busch aboard *Schlesien*. 'In an instant, the ship is enveloped by a black-yellow cloud of smoke which the wind carries to the leeward. The shells crash down on Hela with dark coloured flashes and mushroom clouds shoot up from the ground.'

And on the peninsula, Busch observed the bright orange-yellow flashes of the Polish 152mm and 105mm guns. The enemy was firing back. Proof came seconds later as tall columns of water shot up around the *Schlesien*. The *SX* wasn't so fortunate. 'She is surrounded by the explosion of Polish shells while her turrets and casemates belch fire, death and smoke and her shells roar through the air towards the peninsula, howling and crashing,' wrote Busch. But as the smoke cleared and columns of water sank back to the abyss, it became clear that the enemy shells had enveloped *Schleswig-Holstein*, but not hit her. For its troubles, the Polish battery was silenced as the turrets of both ships directed their attention at it.[3]

Ashore, terrain and Polish determination conspired against the men of 207th Infantry Division as they tried to force their way to Hela through the sand and woods. 'There's whistling and hissing above us, thunder and crashing,' a *Soldat* in 207th Infantry Division wrote as he began the push along the peninsula. 'We splash through the water, our lungs wheezing, and then we lie down in the dunes, as wet as poodles but alive.' The attackers saw an olive-green helmet rise slightly above a parapet ahead of them. The *Landsers* took aim, fired three shots then stormed forwards. The Polish sailors fled, the Germans chasing them, shooting over the undulating sandy terrain, screaming 'Hurrah' at the top of their voices. At the peninsula's narrowest point, the sailors exploded countless torpedo warheads to turn the tip into an island. But such acts could not save Hela indefinitely. With supplies running out, Jozef Unrug signalled his willingness to surrender. Shortly before midnight on the first day of October, the garrison of Hela laid down their arms. The following day, Fritz Otto Busch joined a platoon of sailors from *Schleswig-Holstein* as they marched into the Polish base to collect their prize. 'Bombs and shells have ripped huge craters close to the barracks,' he observed. 'The dying cinders of fires, burned files and papers smoulder.' Polish marines with large canvas bags containing what possessions they had slung over their shoulders filed out of the base to be taken by boat to Gdynia. In the harbour at Hela, every warship and vessel was destroyed or damaged. The destroyer *Wicher* lay on its side; the minelayer *Gryf* sat on the harbour bed, its superstructure and masts sticking out of the water at an angle; the funnel and masts of the gunboat *General Haller* barely pierced the waves; the upturned hull of an unidentified vessel could be seen in the middle of the harbour; in shallow water near a jetty, the smashed remains of seaplanes. It was, wrote Busch, 'a picture of absolute destruction'. And on a floating crane, still undamaged and the tallest structure for miles around, a huge red naval battle ensign, the *Reichskriegflagge*, was unfurled.[4]

Another Polish fortress had already fallen by the time the German battle flag was raised over Hela. For nearly three centuries there had been some form of fortification in the swampy terrain where the Vistula was joined by the Bug and Narev rivers just eighteen miles northwest of the heart of Warsaw. It took Napoleon to turn the half-finished bastion of Modlin into a formidable fortress, a fortress which kept the Russians at bay for ten months in 1813. In their century-long rule the Russians bolstered Modlin's defences. So too did the Poles when independence came. Bunkers, anti-tank and anti-aircraft defences were all added. The latter proved particular deadly; no battery in Poland accounted for more German aircraft than the guns of Modlin. The Luftwaffe could not force Modlin to surrender. Only a ground assault would suffice.

By the final week of September 1939 five German divisions, including one panzer, had been drawn up around the ten forts which ringed the central citadel of Modlin. Driving along the road from Nasielsk, ten miles northeast of Modlin, panzer company commander *Hauptmann* Ernst Collin was drawn to a 'huge cloud of smoke on the horizon'. Collin left his vehicle in a small copse and moved on foot through a village. From behind a garden fence, the junior officer observed one of Modlin's outer forts and sketched the terrain. There would be no repeat of the massacre on the first day of the war, the officer thought. This time, 7th Panzer Regiment would not go into battle blind. German shells crashed down on Fort 1, barely 1,200 yards away. The Poles responded only sporadically, erratically. Now the Luftwaffe joined in the bombardment. 'We watch a Stuka attack on Modlin – a gripping drama,' wrote Collin. 'It must be the end of the world for the Poles.' It was not, for the barrage by Stuka and German guns resumed at dawn the following day as Adolf Strauss unleashed his II Corps at the northern semicircle of fortifications. The attackers subdued a couple of forts but captured none by nightfall; the Poles offered desperate resistance. The fearsome-looking Strauss with his piercing eyes now brought psychology into play. A major from the staff of the *Army of Warsaw* was led through the front line with instructions to inform the defenders of Modlin that the capital had fallen. He urged them to raise the white flags above the fortress at dawn the following day. But dawn of 28 September brought white flags only above the main citadel; the outlying forts continued to resist. The assault resumed; SS troops took one bulwark, panzers and infantry another. The defender of Modlin, Brigadier Wiktor Thommée, had seen enough. Shortly after mid-day on the twenty-eighth, Thommée sent a *parlementaire*, Leopold Cehak, through the German lines. Cehak was taken to a large country house in Jablonna, ten miles southeast of the fortress. Point by point, Adolf Strauss went through the terms of surrender – identical to those laid down to the defenders of Warsaw. Cehak nodded. He made only two requests: that the 3,000 wounded in the fortress receive medical aid and that the rest of the garrison be fed; German shelling had destroyed Modlin's stores. Adolf Strauss offered to do what he could. And so at 8am on Friday, 29 September, Wiktor Thommée walked out of Modlin to formally surrender the fortress with full military honours. More than one thousand officers and 17,784 men fell into German hands, plus nearly 6,000 horses, more than 350 machine guns, sixty-plus mortars, over 100 guns and five armoured cars; another 4,000 men had been captured in the outlying forts.[5]

The last act in the 'campaign of eighteen days' was played out not in a fortress, not in a great city, but in the woods and copses north of the small town of Kock in central Poland, a couple of dozen miles outside Lublin. And the last battle was fought not by an elite cavalry regiment or even Polish armour, but the remnants of fortress troops from Brest, cavalry brigades, infantry, reservists, militia, in fact anything the *Samodzielna Grupa Operacyjna Polesie* – Independent Operational Group Polesie – had managed to accumulate. After clashing with the Red Army east of Brest, General Franciszek Kleeberg had decided to march his group to the rescue of Warsaw. Kleeberg forced the Bug near Wlodowa, then struggled through the swampy terrain. It quickly became obvious there was no hope of saving the capital. The General came up with a fresh plan. His troops would raid the Army's principal arsenal near Deblin, a good fifty miles to the west on the banks of the Vistula, and then wage a guerrilla war against the occupiers. Kleeberg got no more than half way towards his objective when he ran into the armour and infantry of XIV Corps in the woods and undergrowth north of Kock. If the Germans expected to overrun a demoralised, exhausted enemy, they were bloodily mistaken. Panzer grenadier Bruno Fichte, a veteran of the battle for Warsaw, threw himself on to the swampy ground on the edge of Kock as Polish machine-gun fire raked the town's outskirts. An *Unteroffizier*, Fichte's former instructor, fell with a stomach wound just a few feet in front of him. 'I could touch the soles of his boots, but I could not help him,' Fichte recalled. The *Unteroffizier* screamed for two hours until the cries faded to a rattle. Then he died. Once night shrouded the battlefield, Bruno Fichte fell back. 'The dead remained down, and we dragged back those wounded we could,' he recalled. 'Under this fire no-one could look around for the others, many remained down.' The first day at Kock cost the attackers heavy casualties. The next evening, Fichte attacked again, this time with a handful of panzers and armoured cars against high ground around the town. And again the Poles stood firm. In the darkness, Bruno Fichte and a *Gefreiter* approached a copse – unaware that fires were raging behind them. Silhouetted against the flames, the two soldiers presented a perfect target. 'There was an explosion and I was thrown off my feet,' Fichte remembered. 'There was a burning sensation. I felt myself and suddenly realised that I had my intestines in my hand. A hit to the stomach.' Convinced he was dying, Bruno Fichte lay on his back and waited for the end to come. 'As I slipped from consciousness my final thought was: I would have gladly had a son.' For Bruno Fichte, the battle of Kock was over. For his comrades it would drag on for three more days. There were cavalry charges by Polish *ulans*. Their infantry fixed bayonets. Their howitzers and field guns fired into the German lines. They fought in the swamps, in the forests, in the villages, in the cemeteries around Kock. And in the end it came to naught. With food and ammunition running out, with his *ad hoc* force obviously surrounded, Franciszek Kleeberg ordered his men to lay down their arms. At 11am on Friday, 6 October, 1,225 officers and 15,600 marched westwards in perfect order into captivity. Kleeberg was the last to leave. He was led to the schoolhouse in the village of Serokomla, half a dozen miles northwest of Kock, where he formally surrendered. After thirty-six days, the 'campaign of eighteen days' was at an end.[6]

And so at Kock, Hela, Modlin, Warsaw and countless other towns and villages in the dying days of September and first week of October a vanquished army marched into captivity. 'On the roads thousands of Polish soldiers, their weapons surrendered, are going home,' Wilhelm Prüller noted. 'Poland has ceased to exist. Its beaten army moves in rows of thousands and thousands along the road.'[7] More than half a million Polish soldiers fell into German hands; at least another 100,000 were captured by the Red Army; and somewhere between 100,000 and 150,000 men escaped to Romania. Sixty-six thousand of their comrades were left on the battlefields of Poland. Poland's material losses were almost total: 3,200 field guns destroyed or captured, 16,500 machine guns and 1,700 mortars. For the Wehrmacht such a success was bought remarkably cheaply: 11,000 dead, 30,000 wounded and 3,400 missing. The losses were not evenly spread, however. 1st Light Division's thrust through southern Poland cost it fewer than 225 dead. The mountain infantry of 1st *Gebirgsjäger* Division suffered twice as many dead and nearly 1,000 wounded in the march on Lemberg. One in three of 24th Infantry Division's 390 fallen in Poland died on the Bzura. In the seven days of that same battle, 30th Infantry Division lost a third of its fighting strength – 1,800 front-line infantrymen. No armoured unit suffered heavier losses than 4th Panzer Division. It was in action for just twenty days – enough time, however, for 1,600 casualties to be inflicted upon it, nearly a third of them dead. Equipment losses were equally grave: a quarter of Panzer Mk Is and IIs were destroyed in Poland and, more worryingly, four out of ten Mk IIIs and one third of the new Mk IVs. The rest of the *Panzerwaffe* was worn out by the rapid victory, although its overall losses – 217 vehicles, mainly the obsolescent Mk Is and Mk IIs – were relatively slight. It would be at least November before the panzer divisions could roll into battle again.

Heinz Guderian was nevertheless delighted. His panzers 'had fully proved their value and the work which had gone into building them up had been well spent'. The old guard in the army were delighted too. Senior generals praised the *Panzermann* for his unflinching drive, frequently risking his life to force his men forward. But privately the panzer commander was sceptical of their praise. 'The efforts to undermine me can already be felt,' he wrote to his wife. Still, Heinz Guderian was undaunted – and unrepentant. 'I have found satisfaction. The facts speak for themselves.'[8]

Guderian's bluster tells only half the story of the war in Poland, however. 'Blitzkrieg' posed problems which Germany's military planners had not anticipated. The panzers smashed through Poland far more rapidly than expected. The result was that the armour frequently outran its supply lines. At times XIX Panzer Corps' spearheads were 200 miles ahead of the supply columns. The supply chain could not cope. Fuel, ammunition, spare parts – all failed to reach the front-line in time. By mid-September, the Corps was all but out of fuel. 'Major elements of each division are immobilised by lack of fuel,' Guderian complained. 'The fuel situation is a cause of great concern.' Fuel, or lack of it, was not the panzer's sole Achilles heel, however. Maulings at Mlawa and in the suburbs of Warsaw proved the tank was unsuitable for either assaulting fortified positions or street fighting. And although the panzers had smashed their way through the Polish Army in the first week of September 1939, it had been the infantry who had actually destroyed the enemy forces, mopping up in the armour's wake. 'It is only too easy for a stubborn enemy, such as we had on the Bzura, to hide and let the vehicles roll past,' 4th Panzer Division's commander Georg-Hans Reinhardt conceded. Nothing should impede the panzers' advance, Reinhardt wrote, but at least some should carry troops into battle 'if the battlefield is really to be taken and controlled'.[9]

The 'campaign of eighteen days' revealed other shortcomings. The light divisions lacked the firepower of their fully armoured counterparts; all were disbanded and turned into panzer divisions before the Wehrmacht struck west the following spring. The ordinary *Landser*, too, was not without his failings. 'Infantry is far below the standard of 1914,' Army Group North's commander Fedor von Bock complained. The ordinary infantryman marched well but lacked a thirst for battle. He relied too much on his officers to lead the way – and his officers had suffered heavy casualties accordingly. It was an opinion shared by the Wehrmacht's foe. 'The fighting value of the German infantryman was lower than the one I had seen in World War I,' wrote Captain Klemens Feliks, an intelligence officer in *33rd Infantry Division*. The *Landser*, Feliks observed, 'did not distinguish himself in the attack'; wherever there was opposition he halted. Instead, he relied almost entirely on the panzers to punch their way through. Without the panzers, the Pole wrote, 'they fight badly and have a habit of fleeing'.[10] Five years later the Germans would hurl the same criticism at the Allied soldier in Normandy...

To the world, of course, victory in Poland had been an unparalleled feat of arms, 'a great and unique victory,' Hitler told the Reichstag the day after his return from Warsaw. 'Germans soldiers have once again firmly fixed the laurel wreath, treacherously taken from them in 1918, to their heads.' Wherever the Pole was encountered, he was driven back or smashed. 'In fourteen days the German Army covered distances and occupied territory which twenty-five years ago took more than fourteen months.' It was a victory attributable not to good fortune but 'first-class training, finest leadership and fearless courage'. It was a victory attributable to the ordinary infantryman who had 'added a new page to his immortal and glorious history', to the 'men in black of our *Panzerwaffe*' who ignored superior enemy forces and attacked repeatedly, and, not least, it was a victory attributable to 'all our courageous airmen'.[11]

Those 'courageous airmen' had played, in the words of their vainglorious Commander-in-Chief 'a decisive role' in the Reich's victory. That victory cost it 285 aircraft destroyed, a similar number damaged, and fewer than 800 men killed. 'The German sword has struck like lightning,' Hermann Göring declared. 'Through your fearless action you have demonstrated that you are standard-bearers of traditional German soldierly spirit and, at the same time, of the spirit of National Socialist warriors overcoming all resistance.' From the very first day, as Edward Smigly-Rydz attested, the Luftwaffe had deprived the Polish Army of its eyes. But it did so very much more, as one Polish Colonel conceded. It smashed railway lines and roads, telephone and telegraph wires. It utterly disrupted the ability of Poland to mobilise her army, to move her army, to communicate with her army, to lead her army into battle. 'Orders and reports clashed,' the Colonel complained. 'If they arrived at all, then they arrived in the hands of the person supposed to be receiving them in the wrong order. The words were often totally distorted.' Such chaos and confusion had contributed decisively to Poland's downfall. 'The German Army would undoubtedly have achieved this end alone,' Luftwaffe General Staff officer Wilhelm Speidel concluded, 'but it's hard to say how long it would have taken.'[12]

To the ordinary soldier, the defeat of Poland merely affirmed the Reich's right – and the Reich's might. 'None of us who marched towards Warsaw had anything but the slightest doubt that we would be anything but victors from the very first day,' artillery commander *Oberstleutnant* Heinrich von Nordheim told his men at the end of the campaign. 'Anyone who has driven through Warsaw these past few days has probably never seen a more impressive picture of war. And fully aware of this picture, and remembering the burning villages along our route of advance, he may be thankful that the villages and towns of our homeland have been spared this desolation and destruction.'[13] That Germany had been spared such destruction was attributable, in most *Landsers'* eyes, solely to the genius of Hitler's leadership. 'It was Adolf Hitler who cancelled this shameful debt of Versailles for all of us, cancelled it in a way which at the beginning no-one believed possible,' Wilhelm Prüller recorded in his diary. 'He put the German people, in this war against Poland, to the strongest test they have undergone since the World War. And now 82,000,000 Germans have fallen in to report to the Führer: Adolf Hitler! Thy German people have withstood this test!'[14] Another soldier, a mountain infantryman with 137th *Gebirgsjäger* Regiment, turned to verse:

We soldiers are faithful to you, Führer!
Through you we are building a new East!
One word from you and we are ready,
To storm the West at any moment.
For you gave us the power of belief.
You have created a new Germany,
Which at any moment is strong enough,
To hit those who attack her honour![15]

Flushed with success, the *Landser* was home on German soil long before the guns fell silent in Poland in many cases. In the former border town of Schneidemühl the reception for soldiers returning was as warm as it had been for those heading east barely four weeks earlier. As the troops of 8th Machine-Gun Battalion trundled slowly through its streets, townsfolk tossed cigarettes, chocolate, fruit, newspapers and flowers into the vehicles. The welcome was the same in Deutsch-Krone. And then the battalion rolled into barracks. 'A bed and bath again at last, pleasures we've only dreamed about for a long time,' one gunner enthused.[16]

The armour of 5th Panzer Division ground to a halt an hour outside the Silesian town of Oppeln (today Opole in Poland). The field kitchen quickly handed out a meal – lentils, by now traditional fare for the panzer men. They wolfed down the food, hurriedly washed their dishes, then were on the move again. At mid-day on the first day of October, they rumbled through the heart of Oppeln. 'People packed together stand everywhere,' wrote *Oberleutnant* Heinz Borwin Venzky. 'Everyone is celebrating.' Countless Silesians stepped forward and fixed flowers to the slowly-moving panzers – so many the vehicles quickly resembled 'a garden on the move'. There were flowers too in the dour Ruhr city of Wuppertal. The streets were showered with them. The shops were closed. The pavements were filled with people as 1st Light Division returned home. The crowds were so dense they spilled into the roads leaving barely enough room for the panzers to pass. The girls of Wuppertal stretched their arms out to the passing soldiers. Children and women tossed flowers, sweets, apples and cigarettes into their vehicles. The scenes were identical in the industrial Hessian city of Kassel as 15th Infantry Regiment entered at the end of October. Again the people cheered, tossed flowers, presented the men with presents. The festivities merely stirred melancholy feelings in one *Feldwebel*. He watched as a middle-aged woman dressed in black wept in the street. 'Who knows if we too will be absent when the regiment next returns home?' he wondered. 'The war is still not over. Of course, we've scored a success, but we're still a long way from our goal.'[17]

Time and again, whenever trains or columns returning from Poland stopped in the towns and villages of the Reich, the populace responded. Wilhelm Prüller was 'treated royally' by nurses of the Red Cross who handed the men coffee, bread, butter, soup, more coffee, more bread and butter on the train to Vienna. He stared out of the window of the express training pulling through Silesia. It seemed every window in every house was decorated with the swastika flag 'the visible sign that the war with Poland has been brought to a victorious end'. Farm hands waved in the fields. Women presented flowers. Children handed out sweets. Girls rushed forward with bread, butter, cakes, tea, fruit, perhaps even a glass of wine. Sometimes the crowds sang. 'Every man knows why he marched into Poland and what he fought for,' one *Gebirgsjäger* enthused, 'for our beloved German home!' Other mountain infantry marched into Baden, just south of Vienna, under torchlight to the sound of fife and drum, with arms shouldered. 'We were surrounded by an indescribable tumult,' one *Gefreiter* recalled. 'Every resident of Baden wanted to see their warriors. The eyes of the young girls scan the column looking for "him". The shining eyes of the populace will be an unforgettable memory for us soldiers. We felt that the homeland stood alongside us.'[18]

It was the end of October before 57th Infantry Division was ordered west. 'Where precisely, no-one knows,' one *Soldat* wrote. 'Just to Germany – and that's enough. That is worth spending days on the road, crammed in a railway wagon among horses' hoofs, or on the banks and floor, in the corners and luggage racks of compartments.' Westwards, westwards the trains rattled. The men drew a cartoon on one of the carriages – a *Landser*'s rifle butt crashing down on the head of a Pole, while British premier Neville Chamberlain angrily, and impotently, shakes his fist. *Wir schlugen kräftig zu und siegten über die Polen*, the caption declared. (We bashed and beat the Poles). Westwards, ever westwards, for days on end through Galicia and southern Poland. 'One morning the landscape has a different appearance,' one infantryman observed. 'The thatched cottages, the neglected villages, the filthy gipsy children on the railway embankments have disappeared. Clean roads run through the land, white, cosy houses, farming villages, small towns, people in clean clothes who wave at us – we are in Germany again.'[19]

For the Poles, there were no celebrations. Theirs was a land of bleak desolation. The land beyond the Warthe turned into a watery desert as the rivers and streams, unchecked by the hand of man, now flooded. Reservist officer Udo von Alvensleben, a veteran of the trenches of Flanders and northern France a generation before, drove through Upper Silesia bound for Krakow. The roads were filled with refugees returning home, '*panje* carts loaded with families on beds and chests, women wrapped in blankets, children on their laps, men pushing carts forwards'. Alvensleben's bus rolled past burned-out wooden cottages, bomb craters, the ruins of railway stations. 'The history of Poland is a chain of tragedies of which the current one is the greatest,' the reservist noted. *Feldwebel* Wilm Hosenfeld, billeted in the provincial town of Pabianice, caught a tram into Lodz ten miles away. It stuttered past long queues outside the city's bakeries, past Lodz Cathedral where the eternal flame on the memorial to the Unknown Soldier burned once more. 'You only need to talk to people – each time you learn about their cruel experiences and fates,' he wrote home. 'A man from Warsaw sits next to me. He's looking for his children who should be in Kalisz.'[20]

Nowhere encapsulated Poland's plight, all the misery, all the desolation, all the privations better than Warsaw. There was barely a house, tenement block, factory or public building which did not bare the scars of war. Perhaps half the homes were still habitable, yet they had cardboard or boards nailed over the windows shattered by the bombing and shelling. 'Ruins were rising up, piles of stones and masonry, blocks of cement, mixed with twisted iron bars,' one foreign journalist observed. The Ministry of Finance, an impressive relic of the Kingdom of Poland from 1815, was now 'a pile of debris blackened by fire, all it consists of is a row of broken columns'. The Grand Theatre, ten years younger than the ministry, 'gutted by fire'. It was all too much. 'I wandered silently in ruins of blocked streets which only two months earlier were full of life and joy,' he recorded. 'I have seen the debris of the fine aristocratic palaces and the ruins of simple homes of the suburbs, I have visited the workmen's districts in the suburbs of Praga which are literally razed to the ground.'[21] American reporter John Raleigh saw that every fourth or fifth house had been flattened. He continued:

> Blocks of flats had their entire fronts sheared away, exposing the rooms – charred and filled with splintered furniture. We were told that hundreds had been entombed alive when the cellars in which they had sought safety crashed in and they were buried beneath the debris…

Dead horses littered any open space, their sides ripped open by shrapnel. Shreds of uniform hung off a wrecked field gun, here and there overturned trams, ripped up railway lines, cars, even furniture, all tossed into the roads to halt the Germans' progress. Two of Warsaw's principal streets were now 'nothing more than great mountains of bricks, mortar and rubbish'. Raleigh was appalled:

> Only the hand of a tremendous earthquake could have equalled the extent of the damage. More terrifying than this setting of destruction were the faces of the people. Some walked aimlessly about, their eyes streaming tears... Warsaw is a city of ghosts.[22]

Perhaps not entirely. Barely a fortnight after the city's fall, Jewish schoolteacher Chaim Kaplan found life in the capital returning to some form of normality. The shops were closed, the markets were still burned out, yet Warsaw bustled with activity as Varsovians traded in the streets.[23]

Life in the Polish capital was rather better for General Staff officer Hellmuth Stieff, billeted in the Hotel Europieski in Pilsudski Square. The Europieski had been damaged during the siege – entire wings were uninhabitable – but now, in mid-November, the lights worked, so too the central heating and hot water, the invader drank in the bars and cafes long after the Poles had been driven indoors by the curfew. Yet the thirty-eight-year-old *Major* was troubled by the contrast between the life of the occupier and the plight of the Varsovian. 'You cannot be happy for one moment if you stay in this city when you see roast goose in a splendid hotel dining room while at the same time women, who perhaps just three months ago looked magnificent, sell themselves for rye bread from our *Landsers* so they can make some form of living,' he wrote home. 'The majority of the millions who live in the city eke out a miserable existence somewhere and somehow. What's happening here is an indescribable tragedy. You do not feel like victors but like the guilty party! It is not just me who feels this way – the men who are billeted there feel the same.'[24]

Panzer commander Heinrich Eberbach watched Varsovians attempt to conduct daily business amid 'burned-out houses, streets and squares covered with ruins and rubble, deep craters'. Long queues stretched in front of shops – still not re-opened – and the few water fountains still functioning. Crowds gathered around the trucks of the Nazi welfare organisation, the *Nationalsozialistischen Volkswohlfahrt*, as its members handed out bread and food. Disarmed Polish soldiers wandered around the streets, while piled up in the middle of one square were guns, rifles, military kit, destroyed vehicles. The fire brigade and labour service cleared the barricades which four weeks earlier had thwarted Eberbach's attempt to seize Warsaw by *coup de main*. And yet despite this chaos, the *Oberstleutnant* watched as 'the privileged,' strolled down the main streets in their Sunday best 'occasionally greeting each other as if nothing has happened'. Heinrich Eberbach had seen enough of Warsaw. On a bright and cold early autumn night, he drove out of the city. 'Slowly we're beginning to trust the Polish landscape. There are stars here too. The chimneys of destroyed houses eerily tower into the black of night, and still we come across shot-up vehicles by the roadsides, shot-down aircraft, and occasionally also a destroyed tank. Already it is so long ago.'[25]

On All Souls' Day, five weeks after the fighting for the Polish capital had ended, one Warsaw resident moved through the city after nightfall. There was a spectral glow in the mist-shrouded streets from the faint light cast by the few working street lamps. Amid the gloom, candles flickered on the top of small piles of soil, heaped where once there had been paving stones. 'They were everywhere, in gardens, on squares, in the centre of flower beds, in the streets where the pavement had been torn up, along the footpaths,' the Pole noted. 'Pitiful graves, dug in haste, under the hail of bullets or shells, by nameless passers-by.' He followed a crowd silently moving through Warsaw's streets, carrying candles, paying its respects. 'The farther I proceeded on my pilgrimage, the more lights I discovered,' the Varsovian observed, 'tiny flickering lights, even among the debris of collapsed houses under whose ruins there lay the bodies of those who had to be denied their sepulchre.' One of Europe's great cities had become 'a vast graveyard, a field of death', and yet 'death candles symbolised the flame of remembrance – and of hope.'[26]

The Germans too held their ceremonies in Warsaw. Two days after parading his men for his Führer, Conrad von Cochenhausen gathered his division at dusk in Pilsudski Square, opposite Poland's memorial to the unknown soldier. So vast was the square that the 15,000 Bavarians of 10th Infantry Division filled only half of it. Drum rolls and orders echoed around the expanse. The charred and damaged buildings which ringed the square added to the darkness until 20th Infantry Regiment marched in under torchlight. The strains of the Bavarian Last Post drifted across the square before the division's Catholic priest, *Heeresoberpfarrer* Kuffner, led a service of remembrance. The soldiers to a man removed their helmets as the priest led them through prayer. And then Conrad von Cochenhausen addressed his division. 'Our loyal dead, now covered by Polish soil, have not died in vain,' he assured them. 'The historic German dream has been fulfilled, the gate to the East has been opened, a people without space has found space. Those who died for it has given meaning to his life.'[27]

The people without space had indeed found space – 72,500 square miles of Polish soil to be precise, home to more than twenty million people, not 700,000 of them ethnic Germans. Roughly half of that land, including Danzig and the Corridor, was swallowed up by the Reich in two new *Gau* – districts – Warthe and West Prussia. What was left – the regions of Lublin, Radom, Krakow and Warsaw and their eleven million inhabitants – was formed into a vassal state, the General Government, headed by one of Hitler's oldest friends, Hans Frank, a member of the Party since the movement's earliest days and a veteran of the failed 1923 *Putsch* to seize power. Frank was a rare breed among the Nazi hierarchy, a cultured, educated man, a trained lawyer. He was also a committed National Socialist –'down to the depths of my soul' – who viewed his mission in the East with almost religious fanaticism. 'We are God's tool for the destruction of evil forces on this earth,' he confided in his diary. 'We fight in God's name against the Jews and their Bolsheviks. God protect us.'[28]

Frank made the historic seat of the kings of Poland, Wawel Castle overlooking the Vistula in the heart of Krakow, his home. And his arrival in Krakow on 7 November was akin to a coronation. The streets of Krakow were bedecked with swastika flags, a brownshirt guard of honour bearing torches stood at the entrance to the castle, while the local *Volksdeutsche* militia, concentration camp guards and soldiers lined the brightly-lit quadrangle, and the sound of a quintet from the Silesian Philharmonic Orchestra filled the autumn night as the Governor General entered. The swastika, he promised his audience, would always fly above the castle and the *Hakenkreuzgeist*, the spirit of the swastika, would fill it rooms, halls and passageways.[29]

Hans Frank's instructions from his Führer were unequivocal – and brutal. The Polish people would become Germany's slaves, surviving by 'only the barest means', using rules and methods unheard of in the Reich. 'Shrewdness and ruthlessness in this ethnic struggle must spare us from having to go into battle once more because of this land,' Hitler told him. Frank was as good as his master's word. 'Poland should be treated like a colony where the Poles become the slaves of the Greater German Reich,' the Governor General told his staff. Poland would be stripped of machinery, of raw materials, of people, its schools, universities and colleges would be closed.[30] But the Nazis did not stop there. They sought to erase every vestige of *Polentum* – 'Polishness'. The Polish Arms were torn down in every town and village, monuments to Polish national heroes were toppled, singing the national anthem was banned – punishable by imprisonment, sometimes death. Entire towns and villages with Slavic-sounding titles received new Germanic ones. Any street names connected with Germany's defeat in 1918 were banished. So too streets named in honour of great anti-German Poles; suitable Germanic names, artists, writers, musicians were to be found in their place. And the main square in every town and city would be retitled: Adolf Hitler Platz. The Polish victory at Tannenberg over the Teutonic Knights in 1410 cast a particularly baleful shadow over Nazi ideology. Frank presented the banners captured by the Poles more than five centuries before to Albert Forster in a symbolic ceremony in Marienburg, once a Teutonic stronghold. The banners, Frank declared, were reminders of 'an unhappy hour in Germany's history'. Such an hour would never be repeated, the Governor General confidently predicted. 'The Poland of Versailles no longer exists and will never re-arise again.'[31]

Beyond the Bug and the San, the land was now Russian. The *Landser* fell back from Brest, from Lemberg, from scores of towns and villages and headed west. Wilhelm Prüller was dumbfounded. Briefly captured by Poles during the bitter clashes in the woods and forests around Tomaszow and liberated by the Russians, the Austrian pulled out of the town of Zamosc, southeast of Lublin. 'The Germans are leaving this area. I just don't understand that,' he recorded with frustration in his diary. 'What was the battle of Tomaszow for? It cost us numberless casualties – and now it's to be Russian territory.' Wherever the German Army withdrew, Polish soldiers emerged from the woods and copses and followed the *Landsers* westwards, away from the 'Red terror, yesterday's enemies'. They clogged the German routes of withdrawal with men, horses and carts – just as they had hindered the Wehrmacht's advance just days earlier. Wherever the men of 45th Infantry Division stopped to talk to the inhabitants of Galicia, the feelings were the same. 'We are not happy with the Germans, but we'd rather have them than the Russians,' one old man told Rudolf Gschöpf, 45th Infantry Division's chaplain. Near Rzeszów the retreating German infantry were approached by village fathers begging them to stay.[32] Such voices would soon fade.

Dawn had yet to cast its first rays upon the streets of the Baltic resort of Orlowo, a couple of miles south of the port of Gdynia. German police, masters of this town for less than a month, were already marching through Orlowo clutching rifles. On billboards and gable ends notices in Polish and German were hurriedly pasted:

> In the interest of public safety it has been arranged that the Polish population of Orlowo shall be evacuated. Each person may take with him such personal belongings as he can carry. Houses must be left open with keys in the doors. Those who resist will be immediately shot. Destruction of furniture and dwellings will be treated as sabotage.[33]

The inhabitants of Orlowo were given until 9am that morning, Thursday, 12 October, to leave their homes. Few saw the placards. Fewer still were ready to leave with minimal possessions. But all morning and into the afternoon, rifle butts battered against the doors of homes and apartments and the Poles were hauled out. Some were forced to march to a camp a couple of miles away, others were crammed into railway wagons. 'Anyone who saw this tragic possession will certainly never forget it,' a Polish engineer recalled. Children hung around their mother's neck. Anyone who stopped was beaten by a rifle butt and forced to move on. Those in the trains fared no better. With nothing to eat, nothing to drink and nowhere to relieve themselves, they spent three days crawling through the Polish countryside. 'Thus driven along, the people went with the dignity of Christian martyrs in Nero's time.' Within a month the Poles of Orlowo and Gdynia – now renamed Gotenhafen, harbour of the Goths – had been deported, some to the Reich as slave labour, most to the General Government.

Thus did a people without space find space – at the expense of the Pole. 'Never again will even a centimetre of ground which we have conquered belong to a Pole,' proclaimed Arthur Greiser, *Gauleiter* of the new Wartheland district which stretched from Posen to Lodz – now renamed Litzmannstadt in honour of Karl Litzmann, the Great War general who seized the city. In Thorn on the Vistula, the city's newspaper – *Thorner Freiheit* – predicted 'three to four million Germans' would be resettled in the Reich's 'eastern territories'. No more than 750,000 Germans took up the invitation to move to Poland, many of them *Volksdeutsche* scattered across the countries of eastern Europe. For any Pole who stood in the way of the settlers, who opposed the 'peace and order' imposed by the Nazis on this conquered land, retribution would be swift, brutal, arbitrary, indiscriminate. 'The German is now lord in this country,' Arthur Greiser declared. 'Whoever is not with us is against us – and anyone who is against us will be destroyed.'[34]

And so it proved. When the farm of a *Volksdeutsche* leader near Tuchel was burned down, police were sent into the nearby villages to round up ten Poles known for their *deutschfeindlichen Einstellung* (hostility towards Germans). They lined them up against the wall and shot them 'as revenge and as a deterrent'. The remaining villagers were ordered to rebuild the razed farm and make good the damage caused. A nationalist poster daubed on the walls of a Warsaw suburb – 'No German will spit in our faces or make Germans of our children' – prompted the arrest of eleven Varsovians; nine were executed, three of them Boy Scouts. The murder of two German soldiers by criminals in a restaurant in Wawer, on the southeastern edge of Warsaw, provoked a massacre of the local populace. Within two hours, police and soldiers were on the streets of the small town, hauling inhabitants out of their beds. A train carrying workers heading for the capital pulled into Wawer station and was halted, its passengers forced out, and ordered to muster with the rest of the hostages in a railway tunnel. Every few minutes a dozen or so Poles were led from the tunnel, ordered to kneel and shot. More than 100 Poles were executed; the remaining hostages were ordered to dig their graves. The restaurateur was hanged and buried. His corpse was quickly exhumed and hung once more, this time in public, as a warning to the people of Wawer. The Nazis settled old scores too. Poles who had committed 'anti-German' offences *before* the invasion were arrested, imprisoned, executed; sixty-year-old Michal Haremza was sentenced to death by a court in Bromberg for protesting against the Germans during the first days of September when the city was still in Polish hands. In West Prussia, *Volksdeutsche* were actively recruited by police leaders for a *Selbstschutz* (self defence) organisation which exacted swift and brutal retribution against any Poles who caused them displeasure – more than 4,000 in the first six weeks of the German occupation alone. Almost daily German newspapers in the east reported executions, hangings, and prison sentences meted out by 'special courts' to saboteurs, agitators, demonstrators. Hans Frank did not care. 'In Prague, for example, big red posters were put up, saying that today seven Czechs had been shot,' he told a correspondent of the *Völkischer Beobachter*. 'To that I say: If I wanted to put up posters for every seven Poles shot, then there would not be enough forests in Poland to produce the paper for such posters.'[35]

It was Poland's Jews who suffered the most. They were forced to bow to any German soldier they encountered. They were banned from trains, from parks and gardens. There were beatings and arbitrary attacks every day. In Lodz, home to the second largest Jewish community in Poland, Mary Berg watched 'uniformed Germans' set upon a Jewish man who had been lost deep in thought on a pavement. After ferociously beating him with truncheons, the attackers tried to bind the man's legs with rope and tied the rope to the back of a taxi and ordered it to drive down the street. 'The unfortunate man's face struck the sharp stones of the pavement,' a horrified Berg observed, 'dyeing them red with blood.' The taxi scurried off down the road. The SS drove in trucks through the streets of the provincial town of Turek, northwest of Lodz, their commander lashing out with a long whip at any Jews he saw. Eventually, the column stopped and forced several Jews to crawl through Turek to a synagogue, singing all the way – and whipped by the SS all the way. In the synagogue, the SS ordered the Jews of Turek to drop their trousers, and then whipped their victims some more. When one man soiled himself, the SS troops forced him to smear the muck in the face of a fellow Jew. Every element of Jewish life was destroyed. Synagogues were burned down in their hundreds – often while Jews were still inside worshipping. On the eve of the Jewish New Year, German police stormed the synagogues which bordered the main square in Mielec, in the Vistula valley east of Krakow, forced worshippers into a courtyard, doused them with paraffin and set them ablaze. The invader relished the chance to destroy the Talmudic Academy in Lublin. 'We threw the huge library out of the building and carried the books to the market place, where we set fire to them,' one soldier recalled. The bonfire lasted for twenty hours. The Jews of Lublin gathered in the square to watch the destruction, tears streaming down their faces. To silence the Jewish cries, the soldiers called upon a military band to blare out Germanic anthems across the square. Jewish schoolteacher Chaim Kaplan watched the Nazis enter the Warsaw's Tlomacka Library 'like true Vandals'. All the historic books and manuscripts were loaded on to trucks and carried away. 'This is a burning of the soul of Polish Jewry.' Every day Kaplan's diary, his 'scroll of agony', recorded fresh outrages, new restrictions on the liberty, on the rights, on the lives of the capital's Jewish population. 'Our only hope is that the defeat of the Nazis will surely come. We have only one doubt – whether we shall live to see that day.'[36]

The Jews and Poles were not the only ones powerless in the face of their Nazi overlords. The German Army observed all that happened in Poland with its arms folded. Since late October, the Wehrmacht had handed over administration of this land to the civilian authorities. The soldiers still stationed in Poland were ordered to concern themselves only with military assignments and duties. But many officers found it impossible to ignore the atrocities they witnessed daily. 'The wildest fantasies of horror stories are rot compared with the reality of organised gangs of murderers, robbers and plunderers who apparently act with the highest authorities turning a blind eye,' General Staff officer *Major* Hellmuth Stieff wrote indignantly. This was not revenge for the persecution of ethnic Germans before the war, this was the 'extermination of an entire race with women and children, possible only by a race of subhumans who no longer deserve the German name.' Stieff continued:

> *I am ashamed to be a German!* This minority, which besmirches the name of Germany by murder, plunder and arson, and will become the nemesis of the entire German people, if we do not put a stop to their handiwork. Such crimes must provoke the avenging nemesis. Otherwise this rabble will turn against the decent people one day in the same manner and terrorise our people with the same pathological rage.[37]

Johannes Blaskowitz shared Hellmuth Stieff's deep unease. Reports of excesses, atrocities, rapes, murders, ill treatment poured into the general's headquarters, the former hunting lodge of the Tsar at Spala, southeast of Lodz. Despite his abhorrence of the Nazi regime, despite Hitler's apparent displeasure at his handling of the battle on the Bzura, Blaskowitz had been named commander of *Oberost* – the Supreme Command in the East. To Blaskowitz, it seemed the Wehrmacht was being tarred by the actions of the SS and police – all the Polish people saw were men dressed in *feldgrau* killing people, seizing hostages, beating Jews. Brutality alone would not bring peace to Poland, the general warned. 'It is in the interests of both the Wehrmacht and civilian administration that there's a reasonable régime in Poland and that the populace is provided with the most basic means for living and working,' he complained to Berlin. Hitler was furious at the Army's protests. The Wehrmacht 'should not stick its nose into matters which it knew nothing about,' he fumed to his Army adjutant Gerhard Engel. 'You cannot fight a war using Salvation Army methods.'[38]

But the howls of protest did not fade. They grew louder. Rumours of 'outrages' in the East swept through the entire Officer Corps, even reaching its most senior field marshal, the ninety-one-year-old Great War commander August von Mackensen. 'I am afraid of the harmful impact on the spirit of the troops as well as a lowering of respect for our Army – in fact the entire nation,' he complained. It was a warning reiterated by Johannes Blaskowitz and his subordinates. The regime in Poland blackened 'the honour of the whole German nation,' warned XI Corps commander General Alexander Ulex. Blaskowitz was even blunter. In four months of Nazi rule in Poland, the General had seen relations between the Army, SS, police and Party disintegrate. Soldiers viewed the SS with a mixture of 'abhorrence and hatred' and were 'repelled and revolted' by their actions. Unless the excesses were curbed, the General warned Berlin, 'very shortly we will be faced with the rule of the thug. The idea that we can intimidate and subjugate the Polish people with terror will certainly prove to be wrong. This people's capacity for enduring suffering is too great for that.'[39]

Walter von Brauchitsch was all too aware of the growing rift between the Party and the Army. He invited the head of the SS Heinrich Himmler to address senior commanders so they could understand the policy in Poland 'from his side' and quash the 'unwelcome rumours' circulating in the Officer Corps. And so, on 13 March 1940, the generals gathered in the Rhineland city of Koblenz – first for a pep talk on the impending offensive in the West, then for a half-hour address from the *Reichsführer SS*. The bespectacled SS leader was not a great orator. Nor was he an honest one. In Poland he had to put down 'a very serious resistance movement'. And in putting down this movement, he stressed, 'only the truly guilty parties have been punished, never innocent people', adding 'I am doing nothing which the Führer is not aware of'. Heinrich Himmler's address was merely a sop to the generals. The SS, the police, the Party were the power in Poland, not the Wehrmacht. Hans Frank knew it. 'There is no authority here in the General Government which is higher in rank, influence and authority than the Governor General,' he told his staff. 'Even the Wehrmacht has no governmental or official functions of any kind here. It has no political power whatsoever.'[40]

In Warsaw, scaffolding now surrounded the statue of Prince Jozef Poniatowski atop his horse. A huge black billboard, its entire façade covered by an enormous Nazi eagle, obscured this hero of the Napoleonic wars. Five huge red swastika flags flew alongside the new gaudy monument in the capital's greatest square. Pilsudski Square no longer bore the name of the marshal. Like every principal square in every town in Nazi-occupied Poland, it was now Adolf Hitler Platz. Today, Sunday, 1 September 1940, was a public holiday across Poland in honour of the victory begun precisely twelve months before. Varsovians were not in the mood for celebrating. They crammed into the churches and sang their national anthem in secret, with tears running down their faces. Jewish schoolteacher Chaim Kaplan surveyed twelve months of Nazi rule. 'In this year of torments, Polish Jewry has been destroyed,' he wrote in his diary. All property had been confiscated, all means of income blocked, historic communities had been uprooted, cemeteries flattened, all human rights erased. 'This is an existence of dogs who lick the bones under their masters' feet.' But the ordinary Pole was suffering, too, Chaim Kaplan acknowledged. 'Poland is turned into a cemetery.'[41]

The ruins of September 1939 still stood. The streets of Warsaw had been cleared. The trams and trains ran. The markets and shop were filled with bustle, the restaurants filled with gossip and patrons, the borders of autumn flowers in the Saxon garden bloomed. But, as Udo von Alvensleben observed, 'behind the scenes there's terrible misery, artificially hidden'. Prices had rocketed. Beggars roamed the streets. Ragged figures lined up in front of one of 250 food kitchens established to feed Varsovians. Refugees and deportations had swelled the number of inhabitants by one third. And executions and arrests continued almost daily.[42]

The conqueror never failed to remind Varsovians of the defeat of their nation. The public holiday on 1 September was swiftly followed by an anniversary victory parade. In their large black limousines, the golden pheasants of the Nazi Party rolled past the starving Poles as a light drizzle fell on Warsaw. Swastika flags flew across the city as troops marched down the recently-renamed *Strasse des Sieges* – Street of Victory – and, with typical Nazi tactlessness, Luftwaffe squadrons rumbled overhead, a potent reminder of those black days twelve months before.

Varsovians responded, as they did to every brash and arrogant display by the invader, with an act of defiance. They gathered on the edge of Adolf Hitler Platz where the autumn light streamed through the colonnades and painted the tomb of the Unknown Soldier and large bronze plaque a soft blue. They were forbidden to congregate here. German soldiers were forbidden to salute the fallen warrior. Both sides ignored the ban. Today, a mountain of flowers towered above the grave. As darkness gripped the Polish capital, the tomb flickered in the glow of countless candles. 'This place is a Polish national monument,' observed Wilm Hosenfeld, now a *Leutnant* with an Army security unit in Warsaw, 'and burning hopes and powerless anger may awaken in the hearts of the Polish people when they step up to it.'[43]

Notes

1. The parade in Warsaw and Hitler's visit is based upon: Raleigh, pp. 193–7, 201, BBZ, 7/10/39, KTB *Hauptmann* Kretzschmar, 5/10/39 in BA-MA RH24-10/554, KTB AOK8, 5/10/39 in BA-MA RH20-8/11 and von Weich's memoirs in BA-MA N19/7, pp. 30–1. Hans Felber, Eighth Army's Chief-of-Staff, feared for the safety of Hitler throughout the brief visit. 'This city is in no way secure,' he confided in his diary. See KTB Felber, 6/10/39 in BA-MA RH20-8/1.
2. Tagesbefehl, 5/10/39. Author's papers.
3. Busch, pp. 53–55.
4. Russ, pp. 134–5 and Busch, pp. 56–8.
5. Straub, Walter, Oberst, *Das Panzer Regiment 7 und 21 und seine Tochterformationen im Zweiten Weltkrieg* and Drescher, pp. 866–68.
6. Schüddekopf, *Krieg: Erzählungen aus dem Schweigen*, pp. 33–34 and Hoffmann, *Die Magdeburger Division*, pp. 81–3.
7. KTB Prüller, 28/9/39.
8. Guderian, *Panzer Leader*, p. 82, letters from Kluge and Bock to Guderian in Bradley, *Generaloberst Heinz Guderian und die Entstehungsgeschichte des modernen Blitzkrieges*, pp. 220–1, and Guderian's letter to his wife, ibid, p. 221.

9. XIX Pz Corps, Quartiermeister Nr.061/329, 3/10/39 in Steiger, pp. 114, 124, KTB XIX Pz Corps, 14/9/39, 16/9/39, and Lehmann, *Leibstandarte*, i, pp. 121–2.

10. KTB Halder, 24/9/39 and KTB Bock, 8/9/39 and author's papers.

11. Reichstag speech, 6/10/39 in author's papers.

12. Göring's Tagebefehl, 27/9/39, in Supf, pp. 97–8; see also Buchner, *Der Polenfeldzug 1939*, p. 191 and Speidel, Part 3, p. 104.

13. Dienstunterricht des Kommandeurs der III Abteilung Artillerie Regiments 31 nach dem Einsatz der Abteilung in Polen, Okecie, vor Warschau, 12/10/39 in BA-MA RH41-1177.

14. KTB Prüller, 8/10/39.

15. *Wir Soldaten sind Dir Führer treu! / Wir schufen durch Dich den Osten neu! / Ein Wort von Dir, wir sind bereit, / Zu stürmen den Westen jederzeit. / Denn Du gabst uns die Glaubenskraft. / Du hast ein neues Deutschland geschafft, / Das stark genug zu jeder Zeit, / zu schlagen den, der an Deine Ehre greift!* From *Gefreiter* Tumpold, 10/GJR 137, 'Es geht um den Wald von Stronjowice' in BA-MA RH53-18/149. It wasn't just the *Landser* who was fulsome in his praise of Hitler. 4th Panzer Division's commander Georg-Hans Reinhardt was asked to the Reich Chancellery at the end of October to receive the Knight's Cross. After a simple meal of soup, *der lange Reinhardt* was invited to join Hitler in private 'to talk about our wartime experiences. We were repeatedly astonished how much precise information the Führer had about everything, and also that some of the Führer's wishes and concerns concur with ours. Only a genius – that's precisely what the Führer is – can possess such all-embracing knowledge.' See Hürter, p. 136.

16. BA-MA RH37/7535.

17. Venzky, pp. 62–3, Bericht 2/Nachrichtenabteilung 82 in Paul, *Brennpunkte*, p. 49, and Lemelsen, and Schmidt, *29 Division, 29 Infanterie Division (mot.), 29 Panzergrenadier Division*, pp. 40–1.

18. KTB Prüller, 8/10/39, Manz, *Alpenkorps in Polen*, pp. 153–4 and BA-MA RH53-18/152. Some of these receptions were heartfelt, but most were not. They were stage-managed events, the 'spontaneity' courtesy of instructions of local Party leaders. Not all their efforts succeeded, however. Nazi officials in the historic Rhineland city of Trier demanded the people celebrate the historic occupation of an enemy capital. Not a house, not a window should be lacking a swastika flag. Banners should be displayed in the streets, trams and buses should fly pennants, and shops should hang portraits of the Führer in their windows, the Party ordered. Few citizens responded.

19. Gehring, Egid (ed) *Abbeville: Erinnerungsbuch der Division Blümm*, p. 47.

20. TB Alvensleben, 9/10/39, 16/10/39 in Alvensleben, pp. 21–2, 32, and Brief, 19/10/39, in Hosenfeld, p. 271.

21. *Polish Black Book*, pp. 76–81.

22. Raleigh, pp. 192, 226–7.

23. Kaplan, p. 32.

24. Stieff Briefe, 21/11/39. Stieff, pp. 106–9.

25. Drescher, pp. 843–44.

26. *Polish Black Book*, pp. 101–2.

27. 'Die 10 Division im polnischen Feldzug,' speech by von Cochenhausen in Regensburg, 31/10/39. BA-MA RH26-10/544.

28. Schenk, *Hans Frank*, p. 138.

29. Schenk, *Hans Frank*, pp. 153–4.

30. Schenk, *Hans Frank*, pp. 144, 148.

31. Burleigh, p. 173, 174–6.

32. KTB Prüller, 28/9/39, and Gschöpf, p. 100, Kaltenegger, *Die Stammdivision der deutschen Gebirgstruppe*, p. 105 and Kaltenegger, *Die Deutsche Gebirgstruppe 1935–1945*, p. 116.

33. *German New Order in Poland*, p. 179.

34. *Ostdeutscher Beobachter*, 7/5/41, *Thorner Freiheit*, 30/3/40, Schenk, *Hans Frank*, p. 150 and *The German New Order in Poland*, p. 72.

35. *Weichsel Zeitung*, 25/10/39, Lukas, p. 35, *The German New Order in Poland*, pp. 47–8, Kershaw, ii, pp. 242–3 and *Völkischer Beobachter*, 12/2/40.

36. Gilbert, *Holocaust*, pp. 97, 101, Müller, *Das Heer und Hitler*, p. 438, *Forgotten Voices of the Holocaust*, p. 76, Kaplan, pp. 39, 55–56.

37. Stieff Briefe, 21/11/39. Stieff, pp. 106–9.

38. Blaskowitz memorandum, Oberost Ic/AO Nr.80/39, 27/11/39, in Groscurth, pp. 426–7 and KTB Engel, 15/10/39, 18/11/39.

39. Mackensen to Brauchitsch, 14/2/40. Müller, *Das Heer*, p. 675, Nazism, p. 939, and Blaskowitz memorandum, 6/2/40, in NO-3011.

40. Krausnick, *Hitler's Einsatzgruppen*, p. 87, Müller, 'Zu Vorgeschichte und Inhalt der Rede Himmlers vor der höhreren Generalität am 13/3/40 in Koblenz', VfZ, vol.18, 1970, p. 108 and Tagebuch Frank, 8/3/40, in NCA, iv, pp. 906–7.

41. Kaplan, pp. 172–3.

42. TB Alvensleben, 21/9/40 in Alvensleben, p. 141 and Briefe Meier-Welcker, 30/9/40 and 2/12/40, in Meier-Welcker, pp. 87, 88.

43. Meier-Welcker, Brief 6/10/40, in Meier-Welcker, p. 89, and Hosenfeld Brief 7/9/40 in Hosenfeld, pp. 382–3.

Epilogue: It Is God's Will For Us To Live

Terrible methods have been used here. We have acted as if we were the masters and would never leave.

— HAUPTMANN WILM HOSENFELD

IN A forest just off the main road between Warsaw and Brest-Litovsk chaplain Rudolf Gschöpf held his final service of this stifling Saturday. For the past few days the forty-one-year-old had been heavily in demand. His fellow Austrians felt uneasy. The shadow of great events hung over them. Gschöpf tried to ease the burden on comrades by holding short ceremonies in the numerous billets of the *Fünfundvierziger* – the 45s – scattered around the valley of the Bug.

Oberleutnant Hermann Witzemann gathered his platoon around him in a copse as the sun began to dip beyond the horizon far to the west. The last rays of sunshine pierced the pine trees which danced gently in the summer breeze. 'We stand on the eve of momentous events,' the junior officer wrote home. 'None of us knows whether he will survive what is to come.' For days Witzemann and his platoon had been tormented by questions and doubts, but not any more. 'One thing I know is that whatever happens is in God's hands,' the officer assured his loved ones. 'I am calm and confident, because I know that even amid war and destruction Jesus Christ is and remains my saviour. I would gladly die for my people and my German Fatherland, for you, my beloved, at home, for our children and for a better, honourable, fair future.'[1]

One hundred and fifty miles to the south, the thoughts of *Oberleutnant* Ital Gelzer drifted homewards. In a large tent surrounded by tall pines, the officer pored over a map littered with arrows, all pointing in the direction of Lemberg. Life was almost idyllic for Gelzer and his comrades in Galicia. After dark the men gathered around campfires. On occasions the twenty-seven-year-old from the university city of Freiburg would dig out his accordion and sing Swiss tunes. Such frivolity took Gelzer's mind off darker thoughts. He was, after all, a small cog in a gigantic wheel. If he could see the bigger picture, he told himself, perhaps he would be worried.[2]

Artilleryman Hubert Hegele had enjoyed a fine midsummer's day on an old Galician estate in the village of Grodzisko in the San valley between Rzeszow and Przemysl. There had been no duties for Hegele this Saturday. It was almost as if it was a holiday. Yet in the background there was something unsettling, something hanging over the men. There were rumours of a coup in Moscow and talk of marching through Russia, through the Ukraine, through the Caucasus, to Iraq to support the natives in their revolt against the British. *Something* was up. There was no hiding it. The engineers had carried out final inspections of the vehicles, the men had received numerous inoculations, church services had been held in the field, and now the men had been told to send what money they had back home to their loves. What money? thought Hegele. All his was devoured by card games. The Polish sand and dust on the road running past the *Jäger*'s camp was churned up repeatedly by the mountain boots of his 1st *Gebirgs* Division comrades, by the hoofs of mules and the wheels of their carts. They marched eastwards, towards the Russo-German border. No, there was no hiding it. 'Everything points to things happening again soon,' the Bavarian wrote in his diary.

It was now dark by the banks of the Bug. Rudolf Gschöpf wandered to the northern outskirts of the village of Terespol, a couple of miles west of the heart of Brest. The doctors and orderlies of 135th Infantry Regiment were furiously digging slit trenches around their forward first-aid post. It was now long after midnight. Saturday, 21 June, had become Sunday, 22 June 1941. The medics rested in a small cottage, where Gschöpf joined them, trying to ease the tension. The chaplain stared out of the window, across a flat field towards a railway bridge spanning the Bug. A train rattled westwards, carrying goods from the people of the Soviet Union for the people of the National Socialist Reich in accordance with the two nations' treaty signed less than two years before.

Alongside the cottage, engineers silently erected a huge rather primitive-looking scaffold to hold a rocket launcher. Once up, the weapon was loaded, ready to fire. Gschöpf looked eastwards towards the great fortress of Brest-Litovsk. The houses, the barracks, the bunkers, the casemates, all were silent. Nothing stirred. The waters of the Bug babbled gently. It was now gone 3am. The chaplain stepped outside on this warm midsummer night to catch some fresh air and await the impending dawn.

In Galicia, Hubert Hegele could just make out the black outlines of pioneers and *Jäger* – 'a platoon of ghosts' – moving forward silently towards the Russian frontier.

Now Hegele received orders to move to the front. He stuffed his peaked cap in his belt and donned his steel helmet, then began hauling a field gun without a noise first down a road, then across a meadow, carefully avoiding any divots or hollows which might cause the gasmasks, spades and rifles strapped to the gun to rattle. Now, perhaps 200 yards away, blurry, lay the border, a mass of black figures, pioneers, lying in the grass in front of it. And a bit further on, in a guard post, two Russian border guards stood watch, suspecting nothing.

The *Jäger* looked up. In a cloudless sky the stars flickered and blinked. It was a comforting sight, but gradually the blackness of the heavens began to fade, turning to the silvery grey of the first strains of dawn.

'In these final minutes they are no clear thoughts – they're not needed anyway,' wrote Hegele. 'With a brief prayer I ask our Lord to stand by me.'

He studied the faces of his comrades. Each one looked forwards, his face an ashen grey, his heart thumping. In front, movement. The pioneers began to clear a path through the barbed wire with their cutters.

The platoon commander raised his hand. The men stared at him. Two shots pierced the silence. The Russian border guards collapsed instantly.

It was 3.15am precisely. The banks of the Bug shuddered and shook. A hurricane raged above Rudolf Gschöpf's head the like of which he had never experienced before – nor would he experience again. Every gun in 45th Infantry Division's arsenal – nine light and three heavy batteries – opened fire at once. Rocket launchers flung smoke shells over the river into the fortress, 2,800 rounds in all in a matter of minutes. Sporadically two huge 60cm howitzers thundered, belching one huge shell every five minutes. Gschöpf stared across the Bug at the fortress. Huge black fountains of earth were kicked up as each shell came crashing down.

Hubert Hegele and his comrades hauled their 8cm field gun through the Russian wire and across a Galician meadow. 'A *Staffel* of bombers roars past – the droning of their motors provides the perfect overture for the battle,' the mountain man recorded in his diary. 'The first shells from our artillery howl over us.' The infantry swept forward, soon leaving the gunners behind. The first refugees, 'weeping women and children', wandered around aimlessly, their homes aflame, all manner of household items under their arms. *Jäger* escorted the first Russian prisoners, evidently Mongols – whose eyes 'flashed with the implacable hatred of a mortal enemy' – to the rear.

Gefreiter Hans Teuschler waited by the water's edge for the barrage to subside. It went on for three, four minutes, this 'terrible roaring, crashing, clattering and howling, as if hell was truly on earth'. At 3.19 the barrage moved forward 100 yards. The stormtroops and pioneers pushed their rubber boats into the Bug and struck for the opposite bank. There they climbed a steep embankment, stripped away a puny barbed-wire entanglement and moved through grass more than a yard high towards the heart of the citadel. The men ran a gauntlet of gates as they headed for the fortress' core; the Soviets set up machine-gun posts behind each one, and each one had to be knocked out by hand grenades. Light Soviet tanks rumbled into view until machine gun and small arms fire drove them away. The attackers paused in a courtyard near a large gateway to re-group and recuperate. It was an inviting target for the defenders of Brest, who began to pour fire into the rubble-strewn square. Hans Teuschler was not willing to die here. 'Who will volunteer to go with me?' he asked. Six men raised their hands. They ran across a canal bridge, past comrades locked in mortal combat with Russian anti-tank guns, past a casemate, past scores of tents, until through the smoke and dust they could make out an officer and two men stood on top of a gun position, waving furiously. Don't shoot, they urged, we are Germans. But then the trio vanished. They lay down around the casemate and began picking off the attackers at will, as if it was a rabbit hunt. A machine gunner at Teuschler's side told the *Gefreiter* to get down. The warning came too late. Hans Teuschler was struck in the chest. He slumped, grasped the gunner's hand, bade him farewell, and prepared to die, thinking of God and his home.

Hubert Hegele and his fellow *Gebirgs* artillerymen had hooked their gun to the back of a truck and now raced through the lanes of Galicia towards the town of Oleszyce, eighteen miles northeast of Jaroslaw. The road to Oleszyce was littered with the sights of war: houses burned, gable ends had collapsed, telephone and electricity wires hung limply, and dead *Jäger* and pioneers lay by the wayside. The gunners found respite from war in the grounds of a manor house on the edge of Oleszyce. 'Suddenly here the war is as good as over,' Hegele recorded in his diary. 'There's no shooting, no crashing, only a huge blazing barn next to us collapses.' The men sat on the barrel of a gun and munched sandwiches.

In 45th Infantry Division's command post, *Generalmajor* Fritz Schlieper reviewed the morning's fighting. It was impossible for his artillery to support the assault on Brest – friend and foe had locked horns in the ruins of the citadel. In the tangled mess of buildings, bushes, trees and rubble, it was impossible to distinguish any front line. Schlieper threw his reserves into the fray, for what it was worth. 'Where the Russians had been driven out or smoked out earlier, fresh forces appeared a short time afterwards from cellars, houses, canal drains and other hiding places,' the *Generalmajor* lamented. 'They shot with such marksmanship that losses piled up. ' Anything and everything was tried. The attackers grabbed a passing assault gun unit and ordered it to direct its barrels at the citadel. The 7.5cm shells barely dented the thick walls of the fortress.

When Hans Teuschler regained consciousness his eyes struggled to make sense of the chaos around him. A machine gunner, his chest burst open, groaned out of pain and thirst. 'Do you have something to drink, comrade?' he asked. Summoning what little strength he had, Teuschler handed the man his canteen. A few yards away another machine gunner lay slumped, lifeless. And across the battlefield there were the constant cries of wounded Germans. 'Medic, medic! God in Heaven, help me!' Teuschler struggled to turn himself over to be more comfortable. His *feldgrau* tunic and shirt were soaked with blood which poured from a small wound in his left collar bone. The *Gefreiter* pressed a bandage against the entry point and drifted in and out of consciousness.

Russian fire rudely disturbed Hubert Hegele's lunch. 'There's crashing and smashing from all sides,' he wrote. 'Behind every bush, from every treetop – and there are many of them – from every possible position, hot steel whistles towards us.' It was impossible to bring the 8cm gun to bear here. Only close-quarters weapons would suffice: the pistol, the bayonet, the hand grenade. Pioneers, *Jäger*, artillerymen, all tossed their grenades into the grounds of the estate. More grenades. Suddenly there was silence. 'Are the Reds done in already?' Hegele asked himself. 'Now we're storming a park,' his platoon commander told him. 'Ready! Go!' Ten men dashed through a gate and into the estate. The platoon leader fell instantly; reeling back from the blow of a bullet, he fell into the arms of the man running behind him, almost knocking him to the ground. The fight between Russian and German which ensued was brutal, hand-to-hand. The men brandished pistols, hand grenades and, as a last resort, the short spades they carried for digging trenches. The fighting at Oleszyce dragged on all Sunday afternoon. Each time the mountain troops thought they had subdued their foe, the fighting flared up again. As the day drew to a close, flamethrowers were called up and the estate was finally pacified.

There was nothing Rudolf Gschöpf could do for his comrades in the citadel, but he could accompany a reconnaissance unit on a thrust into the city itself. Brest was empty, save for a scared and intimidated civilian populace. Stormtroops forced their way into a barracks on the edge of the city. Again, the Russians had gone. The building had been cleared out. All that was left was a consignment of 150 new Zeiss binoculars, freshly embossed with the Soviet star.

In the citadel, Russian soldiers continued to offer resistance 'from the most unimaginable hiding places'. They shot at the invader from rubbish bins, from beneath piles of old clothes. Occasionally the Austrians succeeded in subduing a casemate or driving the Soviets from a house, but they couldn't take the citadel. Fritz Schlieper was forced to concede that the assault on Brest had failed. It had cost him twenty-one officers and 290 NCOs and men killed. There could be no repeat of Sunday, 22 June. Fortress Brest would be starved and pummelled into submission by siege warfare, shelling and bombing.

Like Fritz Schlieper, *Major* Hans Steets was taking stock of the day's events. Like 45th Infantry, 1st *Gebirgs* Division had suffered bitter losses – eighteen officers alone – in sixteen hours of constant fighting. Few prisoners had been taken. Who was not captured was dead on the battlefield, the operations officer convinced himself – and his masters. An entire Soviet division, the 97th Rifle, had been destroyed. As Sunday turned to Monday, Steets wrote the epitaph of the first day of the Russian campaign in the division's war diary. 'This first day of fighting was the hardest and bloodiest day of fighting the division has known.'

Hubert Hegele agreed. 'The first day of battle in the Russian campaign is over,' he wrote in his diary that night. 'It was hard, more than hard.' Will it continue like this here? he asked himself. 'Many of our comrades are already buried beneath the warm Polish soil.' Hegele tried to sleep. It was impossible. Too many things had passed that day, too many comrades had fallen. 'And now there's a solemn silence over the battlefield on the border,' he observed. 'In the cloudless night sky above us millions of stars glisten, on Earth the white flares of the Germans and the red of the Russians; they create the "magic of the night". And tomorrow?'

It was a terrible night for defender and attacker of Brest-Litovsk alike. The howitzers howled constantly. The shrill sound of rifle fire echoed around the walls of the fortress all night long. 'Never have I longed for the coming day as much,' *Gefreiter* Hans Teuschler recalled. He rifled through the backpack of a fallen comrade, finding cheese and bread which he carefully divided to last him four or five days. If he was to die, he told himself, at least he wouldn't die of hunger.

Hans Teuschler spent two nights in his foxhole, wounded, tired, scared. Finally, under the cover of darkness, he summoned the strength to struggle back through the ruins of Brest to a first-aid post. Many of his fellow *Fünfundvierziger* were not so fortunate: 482 men were killed in the assault on the Bug fortress, thirty-two of them officers – including *Oberleutnant* Hermann Witzemann. The last fort, the eastern one, fell on the morning of Sunday, 29 June, its defenders' will to resist shattered finally by a 3,800lb bomb which shook the entire city when it exploded. Women and children emerged from the ruins of the fort, followed by 400 soldiers. The commandant – a Russian major – and a Soviet commissar took their own lives.

For a week 1st *Gebirgs* Division battered its way across Galicia. This was no *Sturmfahrt*. It was a sluggish, methodical, costly advance on Lemberg; *Oberleutnant* Ital Gelzer was among its casualties. And then the unexpected. On the penultimate day of June, the Soviets pulled out of the Galician capital. A mountain reconnaissance unit tentatively marched into the city at dawn the following day. The inhabitants showered the *Gebirgsjäger* with flowers. At 4.20am on Monday, 30 June, the Reich's battle ensign was raised over the citadel in the city centre. Lemberg was finally in German hands. *Hauptmann* Josef Remold, now a battalion commander, returned to the battlefield of 1939. He sought the last resting places of fallen comrades. He looked in vain. 'The enemy's hate had flattened them to the ground.'[3]

With Brest still aflame and with Russian soldiers still holding out in the cellars and underground passageways, Rudolf Gschöpf entered the city to bury his division's dead. He found a cemetery in the grounds of a Russian Orthodox church in southern Brest, an ideal place for a common grave for the men of the 45th. The division spent another week in the fortress. The men collected their dead and carried them to the graveyard and carefully laid them to rest in the newly-designated *Heldenfriedhof* – heroes' cemetery. In their honour one of Brest's main streets was renamed *Straße der 45*, Road of the 45th.[4]

For the second time in two years German blood had been spilled in fighting for Lemberg and Brest. It would be spilled a third time as war's wheel of fortune turned once more.

As for the men of 1939, Fate looked favourably on some, but most faced death, suicide, execution, imprisonment, persecution, or starvation:

Major Henryk Sucharski, the defender of the Westerplatte, spent the rest of the war in prisoner-of-war camps and died in a military hospital in Italy barely a year after the end of the conflict. His men swore never to reveal the major's breakdown and so in post-war Poland, Sucharski became celebrated as a national hero, whose name was given to schools, streets and squares and whose body was eventually interred on the peninsula.

Tadeusz Kutrzeba and *Juliusz Rommel* spent the remainder of the war in German prison camps. Rommel returned to Poland upon liberation in 1945; he basked briefly in the limelight as a war hero, then retired from public life to concentrate on writing. Kutrzeba joined Polish exiles in London, wrote his memoirs and nurtured research of the 1939 campaign. He died in January 1947 before he could return to his native land.

Their leader *Edward Smigly-Rydz* escaped internment in Romania and eventually returned to Warsaw in disguise in late 1941 determined – at the age of fifty-five – to fight with the Polish resistance movement as an ordinary soldier; he died of a heart attack before he could do so.

Johannes Blaskowitz spent the remainder of the war out of favour with Adolf Hitler but rarely out of service, commanding all German forces in southern France by the time the Allies invaded in August 1944. He ended the war as the senior officer in the Netherlands, signing the instrument of surrender. Like many senior generals he faced charges at Nuremberg for war crimes, in his case against the Polish populace. He committed suicide – or perhaps was murdered – as he awaited trial in early 1948. *Hans Felber,* his chief-of-staff in Poland, commanded German corps in Russia and was later given command of an Army until he was dismissed in March 1945.

Heinz Guderian's star reached its zenith when his panzers brought France to her knees in May and June 1940. He then led his armour across Russia to within sight of the spires of the Kremlin but was dismissed in the winter of 1941 for disobeying Hitler's order not to retreat. After a period as the inspector of the Reich's armoured forces, he was appointed Chief of the General Staff in the wake of the July 1944 plot to kill the Führer. Guderian was dismissed for good the following spring after a particularly fiery argument with Hitler. He retired to write his bestselling memoirs, dying aged sixty-five in 1954.

Like Heinz Guderian, *Leo Geyr von Schweppenburg* would rise to become one of Germany's greatest proponents of armoured warfare. He clashed instantly with Erwin Rommel when sent west in 1944 to take charge of the panzers massed to defeat the impending Allied invasion, favouring holding the armour back to smash the invader *en masse* rather than concentrating them close to the coast as Rommel favoured. Rommel was proved right; within a month of the Normandy landings, Geyr was dismissed.

Ludwig Kübler, the 'bloodhound of Lemberg', earned another soubriquet before the war's end: *Adriashreck,* terror of the Adriatic. It was a fitting nickname. Sent to maintain order in Yugoslavia, he decided there was only one solution to suppress the partisan movement: 'terror against terror, an eye for an eye, a tooth for a tooth! In this struggle anything which brings success is right and necessary.' If innocent civilians were caught in the crossfire, the *General der Gebirgstruppe* reasoned, it was the partisans to blame, not the German Army. At the war's end, Kübler fell into the hands of the Yugoslav forces. He was force-marched to Belgrade where he was executed in the summer of 1947 for war crimes.[5]

Hans Frank also faced the hangman. Arraigned at Nuremberg on charges of crimes against humanity, the former Governor General was contrite and – unlike most of his fellow defendants – willing to take responsibility for the atrocities committed in his country's name. He told the tribunal's judges: 'A thousand years will pass and still Germany's guilt will not be erased.'

Johann Adolf Graf von Kielmansegg accompanied the armour of 1st Panzer Division as it rolled westwards to the Channel in the spring of 1940. He rolled eastwards to the gates of Moscow the following year. After the failed attempt on Hitler's life in 1944, the Gestapo held him prisoner for two months, then released him for lack of evidence. When the *Bundeswehr* was formed post-war, it looked to Kielmansegg to command an armoured division; he eventually rose to command NATO ground forces in central Europe, dying in 2006 aged ninety-nine.

Generals *von Rundstedt* and *von Bock* both became field marshals having led the German Army to victory in the West in May and June 1940. They led army groups into Russia the following summer with less success: Bock was dismissed with his men at the gates of Moscow in December 1941; von Rundstedt was sacked for arguing with Hitler over the fate of his troops at Rostov. Both men found further employment, however. Bock was again in command in the East, leading the German summer offensive in 1942 – until he earned his Führer's displeasure and was dismissed for good. He was killed in an Allied air attack in the dying days of the war. The remainder of von Rundstedt's war was spent in the West. His career finally came to an end in the spring of 1945 at the age of sixty-nine; he died eight years later.

The shadowy *Albrecht Herzner*, who had led the premature raid on the Jablunka Pass, received the Iron Cross, Second Class, for his actions in the Carpathians. Two years later he led Ukrainian 'volunteers', the *Nachtigall* – Nightingale – battalion into Lemberg to 'liberate' the Galician capital. Herzner died in September 1942 while recovering from a spinal injury he suffered in a car crash. He may, or may not, have been murdered.

Liaison officer *Nikolaus von Vormann* spent the rest of the war in a series of staff and front-line commands, serving with distinction on the Eastern Front. After the war he wrote an account of the Polish campaign, dying in 1959.

Gerhard Engel served as his Führer's Army adjutant until early 1943 when he was transferred to a front-line command, first at the head of a regiment, later in charge of an infantry division. Post-war he worked as an arms dealer.

The slavish *Wilhelm Keitel* was promoted to field marshal in the summer of 1940. He would lend his signature to numerous illegal orders which earned him the death penalty at Nuremberg, as did the sharper but no less complicit *Alfred Jodl*. Both men were hanged on the same day in October 1946.

Kurt von Briesen led his division into Paris the following June. In Russia he was given command of LII Corps. He died – characteristically – visiting his men in the front line when Soviet fighters strafed his staff car on the Dnieper.

Conrad von Cochenhausen, conqueror of Warsaw, was no Kurt von Briesen. When surrounded by Soviet troops at the gates of Moscow while commanding 134th Infantry Division at the end of 1941, Cochenhausen suffered a nervous breakdown and shot himself. His lifeless body was found by his men slumped in a staff car.

Ignacy Paderewski's *monument to Grunwald in Krakow*, intended 'to raise hearts with a visible symbol of the sacred past', was first hidden behind a wall of wooden planks, then razed by the Germans over the winter of 1939–40. The bronze statue of King Jagiello was melted down, save for his sceptre and sword which were hidden by Polish workers. Over four years in the mid-1970s, the statue was restored and rebuilt.

No such fate awaits the *Tannenberg memorial*. As the Red Army engulfed East Prussia, German troops hurriedly removed the coffins of Paul von Hindenburg and his wife and sent them west, as well as the standards of the German regiments which fought in the battle. Hitler was told that the invading Soviet soldiers found only 'a pile of rubble'. They did not. Only Hindenburg's tomb and the main tower were blown up by retreating German engineers. Bricks from the monument rebuilt the shattered villages of East Prussia – now under Polish rule – while the granite was swallowed up by Polish and Soviet war memorials.

Victory over Poland in 1939 gave *Albert Forster* the new title and new domain, *Gauleiter* of Danzig-West Prussia, which he had predicted before the war, and new responsibilities, chiefly to Germanise Polish lands, which he did, expelling several hundred thousand Poles so German settlers could move in. By the spring of 1945, gone was the brashness of the summer of 1939. There were 4,000 Red Army tanks bearing down on his city, he bleated to Hitler. The Führer assured his loyal *Gauleiter* that he would save Danzig and there was nothing more to worry about. But the *Gauleiter* did worry. He packed all his personal belongings, his furniture, his papers, and fled by boat across the Bay of Danzig first to the Hela peninsula and from there to Holstein in northern Germany. He was arrested by British soldiers and eventually turned over to the Poles, who found him guilty of crimes against humanity and hanged him in Warsaw in February 1952.[6]

The defenders of the *Polish Post Office* in Danzig were held in the city's Viktoria School for almost a month, paraded sporadically in front of Nazi Party leaders and journalists. 'Everywhere are characters you would not like to meet on your own in the dark,' the *Danziger Vorposten* sneered. 'You can already believe that each one of these civilian prisoners is capable of gouging the eyes out of wounded German soldiers, murdering *Volksdeutsche*, setting fire to homes and farms, raping women and girls and assaulting children.' Albert Forster toured the school with his entourage, observing roll call. 'Wait you pigs,' he laughed. 'You'll get your just desserts!'[7] Thirty-eight men were tried by a military court at the end of September for being partisans. Most were executed by an SS firing squad on the same day that Adolf Hitler reviewed his victorious soldiers in Warsaw. The post office building was rebuilt in the late 1940s. Today it continues to handle the city's mail, but it also houses a small museum dedicated to the men who defended it on 1 September, 1939.

The *Hela* peninsula, one of the last strongholds of Polish resistance in 1939, was held to the very end of the war by the Germans. Its final commander capitulated an hour before midnight on 8 May, 1945, declaring: 'The struggle is at an end.' Across the water, the city which gave the Bay of Danzig its name had already been in Soviet hands for six weeks. As Albert Forster fled the Hanseatic port in the dying days of March 1945, the men of 4th Panzer Division wearily pulled through Danzig, unable to defend it any longer. Amid the howling and crashing of shells, the crackling and spitting of fires, the thunderous din of houses collapsing, war reporter Robert Poensgen could see 'ruins, nothing but ruins, the city is lifeless and empty'. The bridges over the Mottlau and the tentacles of the Vistula which stretched to the Baltic burned. Danzigers stood in their doorways, sullen expressions frozen into their faces, unable to comprehend the soldiers were abandoning them. But abandon them they did.[8] Today life in the city thrives once more, but it is Poles who inhabit the port – now renamed Gdansk.

Warsaw suffered an even more bitter fate. After nearly five years of brutal Nazi rule, its people rose up against their oppressors with the liberating Red Army at the gates. Only the Soviets did not enter the Polish capital in the summer of 1944 – it would be January before the first 'Ivan' marched into Warsaw. And so, the rebellion was crushed mercilessly by the Germans, as *Wilm Hosenfeld* witnessed. Hosenfeld had spent the majority of the war in rear-area duties in Poland and in its capital especially. The former schoolteacher had been an enthusiastic Nazi, a member of the SA pre-war, but he grew to despise the regime and all it stood for, especially its treatment of the Jews. The Warsaw uprising in the summer of 1944 was as close as the *Hauptmann* got to the 'terror of this war'. It shook him deeply. 'We must close our eyes and hearts,' he wrote home to his family. 'The people are destroyed without pity. Now I understand the meaning of war.' To his diary on 11 August he confided the following:

> It's clear to me that we have written off Warsaw – and with it Poland – and the war as well. We are abandoning a place which we have held for five years, a place we strengthened and proclaimed to the world as a forfeit of war. Terrible methods have been used here. We have acted as if we were the masters and would never leave.
>
> Now, when we have to accept that everything is lost, we are destroying all our work, destroying everything which our civilian administration – which believed it had a great cultural mission here – was so proud of and which it wanted to prove to the world was needed. Such is the bankruptcy of our policy in the East. With the destruction of Warsaw we are erecting the monument to this policy.[9]

When the uprising ended in October, the Nazis tried to ensure the city and its people would never rise again, systematically dynamiting, burning, and demolishing what was left of the Polish capital on the west bank of the Vistula.

The fates of *Wilm Hosenfeld* and Jewish pianist *Wladyslaw Szpilman* converged in the ruins of Warsaw in the dying days of 1944. Szpilman had spent the war first performing in the capital's Jewish ghetto, later working in a forced labour battalion, and finally in hiding, eventually in the attic of a partially dilapidated town house. As the year ebbed away, the building was occupied by German staff officers charged with defending Warsaw, including Hosenfeld. The two men met as the desperate pianist searched a kitchen for food. Rather than report the Jew's presence, the German officer provided food – bread and jam – an eiderdown, even a greatcoat to keep the Polish winter at bay. The two uneasy friends shook hands for the last time on 12 December. 'If you and I have survived this inferno for over five years,' Hosenfeld assured the musician, 'it's obviously God's will for us to live.'[10]

Warsaw fell to the Red Army six weeks later. It was, as one woman working for the Polish underground observed moving through the smitten city, 'a wilderness'. She was surrounded by 'terrible sights such as I'd never seen before' and the pervading smell of dust, smoke and decomposing corpses. 'It seemed as if the world had fallen apart,' she recalled.[11]

Scrambling around among those ruins was Wladyslaw Szpilman, wearing the overcoat Wilm Hosenfeld had given him – a coat which almost cost him his life as Soviet troops opened fire on him initially. He barely recognised the city he had grown up in. 'There was not a single intact building as far as the eye could see,' he remembered. There were, however, mountains of rubble, a tangled mess of telegraph and telephone wires, ripped-up tram lines, and skeletons lying next to rusting rifles.

Wilm Hosenfeld fell into Soviet hands as the Eastern Front crumbled. The pianist tried to track him down, but did not know his saviour's name and failed. Hosenfeld died in Russian captivity in 1952 having endured years of torture.

Wladyslaw Szpilman resumed his music career as one of Poland's greatest concert pianists. And he performed in a school – originally built as homes for German officers in Warsaw by Jewish forced labour – to youngsters who never knew the misery men had endured to put up their schoolrooms. 'I pray,' he wrote, 'they may never learn what such fear and suffering are.'[12]

Notes

1. Briefe, 21/6/41. In Bähr and Bähr, pp. 34–5.
2. Briefe, 13/6/41 and 19/6/41 in Bähr and Bähr, pp. 39–41.
3. Kaltenegger, Roland, *Die Deutsche Gebirgstruppe 1935–1945*, p. 116.
4. The fighting at Brest is based on Gschöpf, pp. 204–226.
5. Kaltenegger, *Ludwig Kübler*, pp. 283–84, 300–1.
6. I am indebted to Michael Miller for providing details of Forster's later life.
7. Schenk, *Post von Danzig*, p. 82.
8. Paul, *Der Endkampf um Deutschland*, pp. 230, 232.
9. Hosenfeld, pp. 824, 827–8.
10. Szpilman, pp. 175–81.
11. Davies, *Rising 44*, p. 492.
12. Szpilman, p. 189.

Advance in Poland

And always the sand which devours our feet,
The cheerful marching songs resound,
And always the expanse which numbly envelops us,
And always the distance turned red!

The miserable villages which treat us with hostility,
The cottages lurking by the roadside,
Death blocks our path with festering horses,
Acrid smoke emerges from collapsing walls.

And always the wind, which sings so softly to us,
From birches and thin pines!
And yet how strangely this song lingers in our souls!
Just march so that we don't hear it!

March, comrades, the road is still long,
We do not want to ask how far.
One day, victory will flourish in us, one day we will be spared
The sand and the days of silence.

– Hauptmann *Max Matheis*[1]

Note

1. *Und immer der Sand, der den Tritt uns verschlingt / das munternde Marschlied ertötet / und immer die Weite, die stumm uns umringt / und immer die Fernen gerötet! / Die elenden Dörfer, sie feinden uns an / die Hütten am Wegrande lauern / der Tod sperrt mit stinkenden Pferden die Bahn / stösst Glutrauch aus fallenden Mauern. / Und immer der Wind, der so leise uns singt / aus Birken und hageren Föhren! / Wie fremd doch dies Lied in der Seele uns schwingt! / Marschiert nur, damit wir es nicht hören! / Marschiert Kameraden, der Weg ist noch weit, / wir wollen die Ferne nicht fragen. / Einst blüht uns der Sieg, einst sind wir befrei / vom Sand und den schweigsamen Tagen.* Hauptmann Max Matheis, 'Vormarsch in Polen', *Mit dem XIII Armeekorps in Polen*, p. 1.

Appendix

Heer	Waffen SS	Kriegsmarine	British Army
Generalfeldmarschall	Reichsführer-SS	Grossadmiral	Field Marshal
Generaloberst	SS Oberstgruppenführer	Generaladmiral	General
General	SS Obergruppenführer	Admiral	Lieutenant General
Generalleutnant	SS Gruppenführer	Konteradmiral	Major General
Generalmajor	SS Brigadeführer	Vizeadmiral	Brigadier
Oberst	SS Standartenführer	Kapitän zur See	Colonel
	SS Oberführer		
Oberstleutnant	SS Obersturmbannführer	Fregattankapitän	Lieutenant Colonel
Major	SS Sturmbannführer	Korvettenkapitän	Major
Hauptmann	SS Hauptsturmführer	Kapitänleutnant	Captain
Oberleutnant	SS Obersturmführer	Oberleutnant zur See	Lieutenant
Leutnant	SS Untersturmführer	Leutnant zur See	2nd Lieutenant
		Stabsoberfeldwebel	
Stabsfeldwebel	SS Sturmsharführer		Sergeant Major
Hauptfeldwebel	SS Stabsscharführer	Oberfeldwebel	
Oberfeldwebel	SS Hauprscharführer	Stabsfeldwebel	
Feldwebel	SS Oberscharführer	Feldwebel	Colour Sergeant
Unterfeldwebel	SS Scharführer	Obermaat	Sergeant
Unteroffizier	SS Unterscharführer	Maat	
Stabsgefreiter		Matrosenhauptgefreiter	
Obergefreiter	SS Rottenführer	Matrosenobergefreiter	Corporal
Gefreiter	SS Sturmmann	Matrosengefreiter	Lance Corporal
Oberschütz/Oberjäger	SS Oberschutz		
Schütze/Jäger/Grenadier	SS Schütze	Matrose	Private

Maps

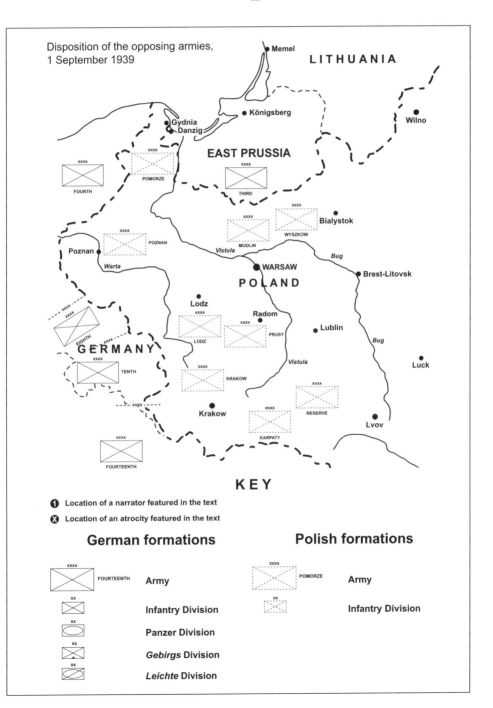

Disposition of the opposing armies,
1 September 1939

LITHUANIA

Memel

Königsberg

Wilno

Gydnia
Danzig

EAST PRUSSIA

POMORZE

FOURTH

THIRD

Bialystok

MODLIN

WYSZKOW

Vistula

Bug

Poznan

POZNAN

Warta

WARSAW

Brest-Litovsk

POLAND

Lodz

Radom

Lublin

LODZ

PRUSY

Bug

EIGHTH

GERMANY

Vistula

Luck

TENTH

KRAKOW

RESERVE

Krakow

KARPATY

Lvov

FOURTEENTH

KEY

1 Location of a narrator featured in the text

X Location of an atrocity featured in the text

German formations

FOURTEENTH   Army

Infantry Division

Panzer Division

Gebirgs Division

Leichte Division

Polish formations

POMORZE   Army

Infantry Division

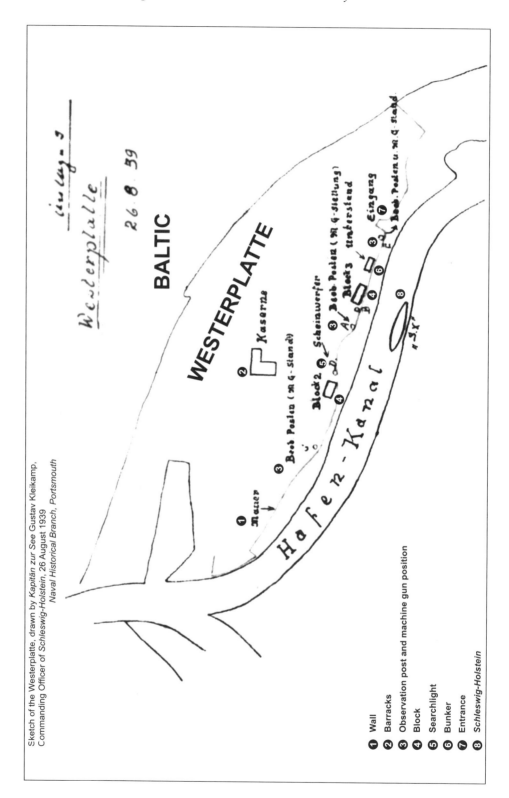

Sketch of the Westerplatte, drawn by *Kapitän zur See* Gustav Kleikamp,
Commanding Officer of *Schleswig-Holstein*, 26 August 1939
Naval Historical Branch, Portsmouth

1. Wall
2. Barracks
3. Observation post and machine gun position
4. Block
5. Searchlight
6. Bunker
7. Entrance
8. Schleswig-Holstein

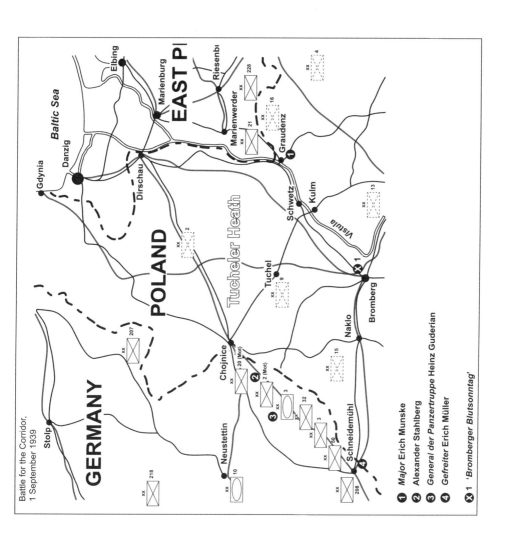

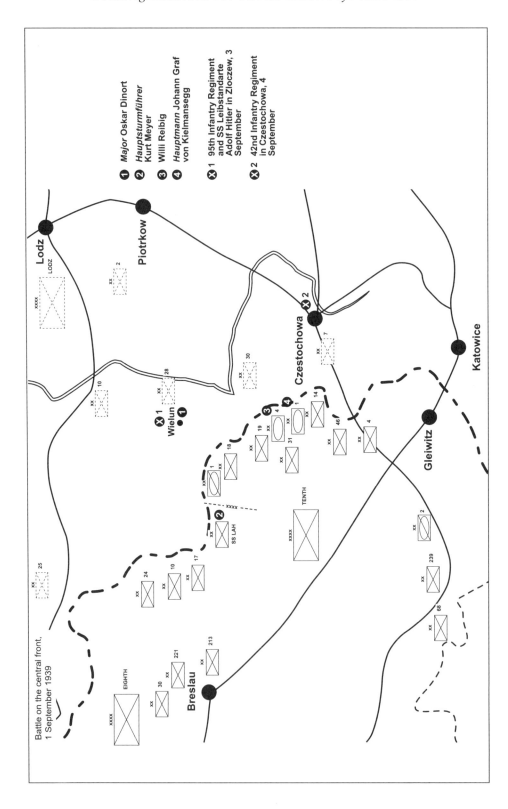

Battle on the central front, 1 September 1939

1. Major Oskar Dinort
2. Hauptsturmführer Kurt Meyer
3. Willi Reibig
4. Hauptmann Johann Graf von Kielmansegg

X 1. 95th Infantry Regiment and SS Leibstandarte Adolf Hitler in Zloczew, 3 September

X 2. 42nd Infantry Regiment in Czestochowa, 4 September

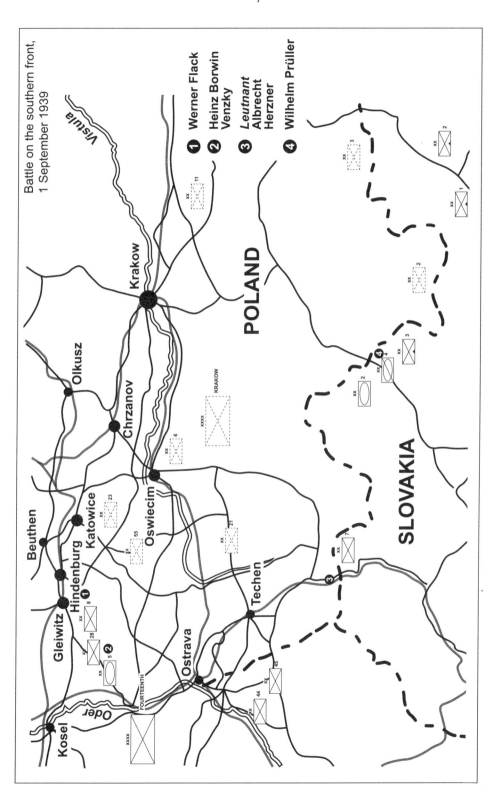

Battle on the southern front,
1 September 1939

1 Werner Flack

2 Heinz Borwin
   Venzky

3 *Leutnant
   Albrecht
   Herzner*

4 Wilhelm Prüller

297

Battle of the Corridor,
4 September 1939

① *Generalleutnant* Leo Geyr von Schweppenburg

② Emil Falckenthal

③ *General der Panzertruppe* Heinz Guderian

❌1 'Bromberger Blutsonntag'

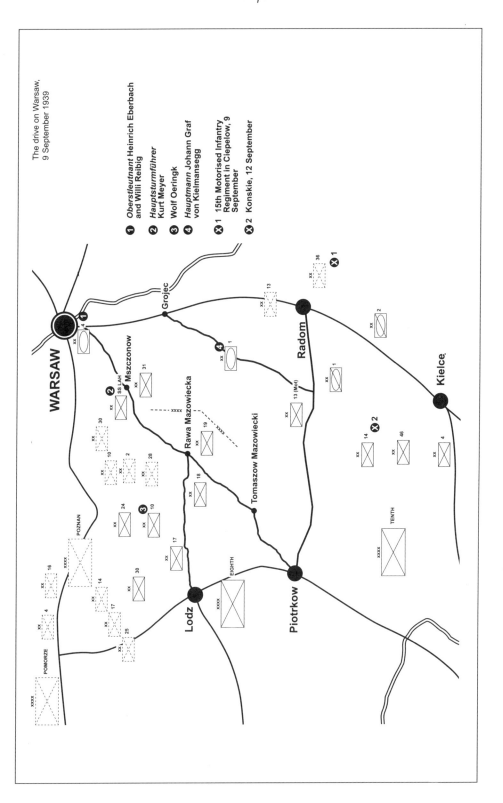

The drive on Warsaw,
9 September 1939

❶ *Oberstleutnant* Heinrich Eberbach
and Willi Reibig

❷ *Hauptsturmführer*
Kurt Meyer

❸ Wolf Oeringk

❹ *Hauptmann* Johann Graf
von Kielmansegg

✕1 15th Motorised Infantry
Regiment in Ciepelow, 9
September

✕2 Konskie, 12 September

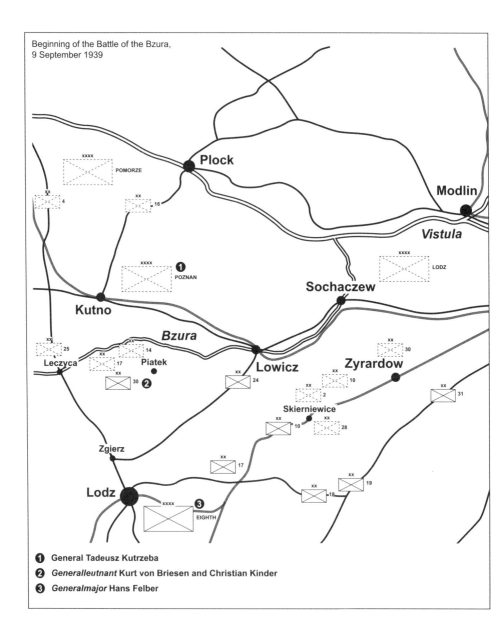

Beginning of the Battle of the Bzura,
9 September 1939

❶ General Tadeusz Kutrzeba
❷ *Generalleutnant* Kurt von Briesen and Christian Kinder
❸ *Generalmajor* Hans Felber

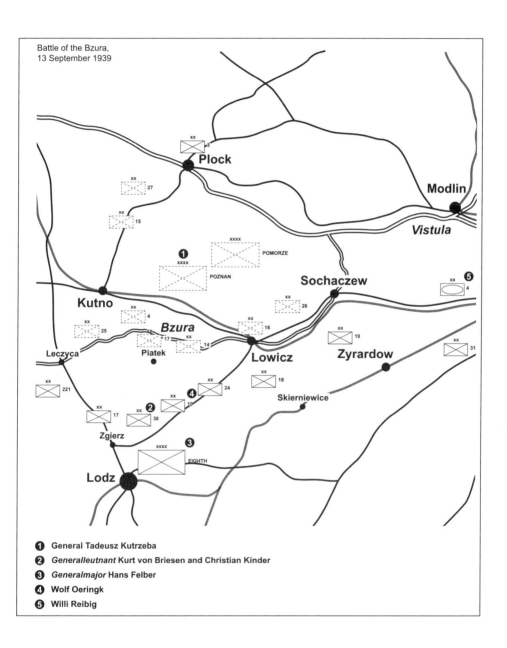

Battle of the Bzura,
13 September 1939

1 General Tadeusz Kutrzeba
2 *Generalleutnant* Kurt von Briesen and Christian Kinder
3 *Generalmajor* Hans Felber
4 Wolf Oeringk
5 Willi Reibig

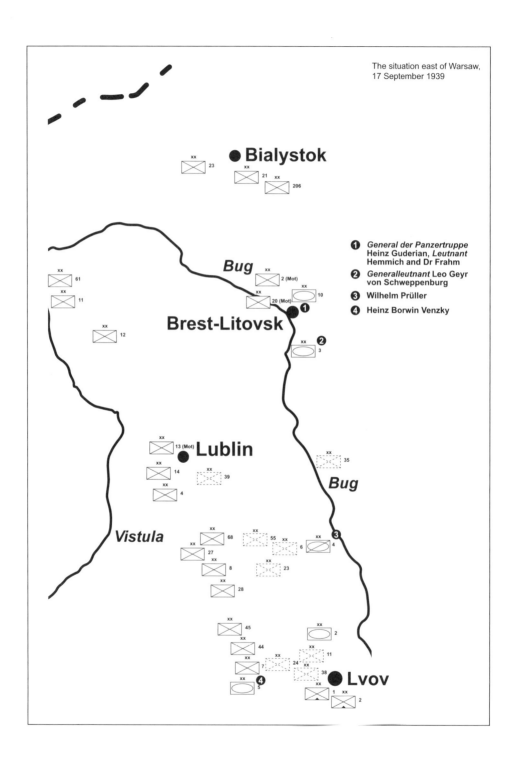

Maps

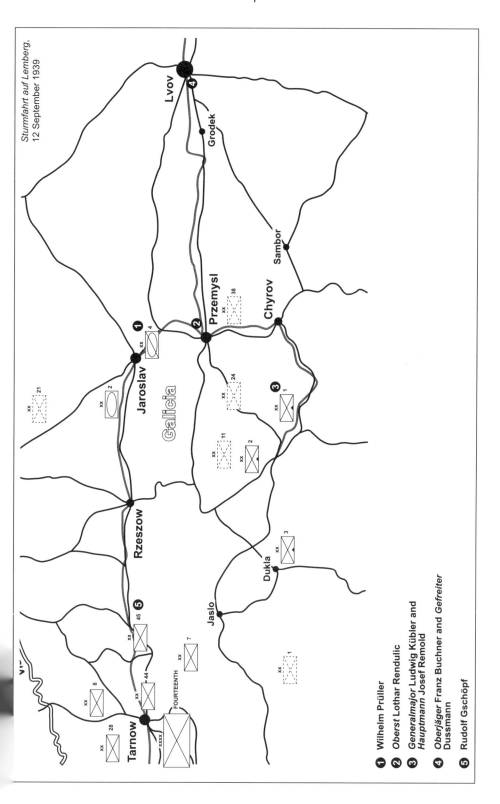

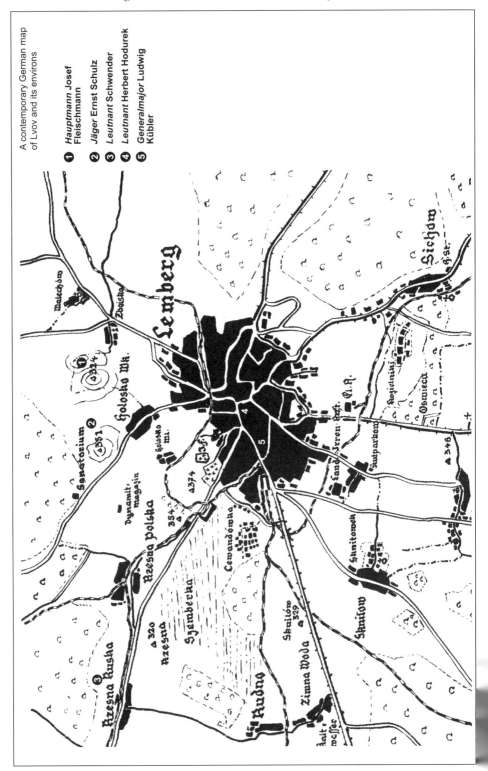

A contemporary German map of Lvov and its environs

1 *Hauptmann Josef Fleischmann*
2 *Jäger Ernst Schulz*
3 *Leutnant Schwender*
4 *Leutnant Herbert Hodurek*
5 *Generalmajor Ludwig Kübler*

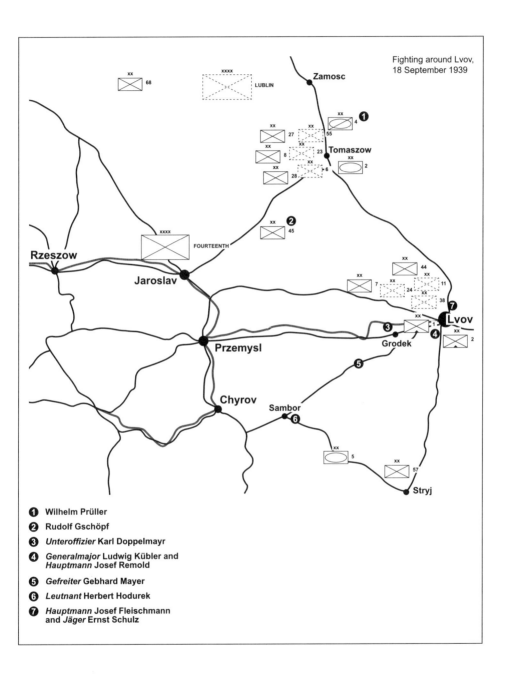

Fighting around Lvov,
18 September 1939

❶ Wilhelm Prüller

❷ Rudolf Gschöpf

❸ *Unteroffizier* Karl Doppelmayr

❹ *Generalmajor* Ludwig Kübler and
Hauptmann Josef Remold

❺ *Gefreiter* Gebhard Mayer

❻ *Leutnant* Herbert Hodurek

❼ *Hauptmann* Josef Fleischmann
and *Jäger* Ernst Schulz

Bibliography

Unpublished Sources

Bundesarchiv Militararchiv, Freiburg im Breisgau
N	**Personal papers**
N19/7	Memoirs of Field Marshal von Weichs
N671/4	Tagebuch Wolfram von Richthofen, Polenfeldzug
RH12/5	**Files of the Inspectorate of Pioneers**
RH12/5/240	Der Sturm auf Zitadelle von Brest-Litowsk 1939
RH12/5/339	Pioniere in Polenfeldzug
RH20/8	**Files of Eighth Army**
RH20/8/1	Tagebuch Hans Felber, Polenfeldzug
RH20/8/2	Armeebefehle AOK 8, 1/9/39–12/10/39
RH20/8/11	KTB AOK 8, Polenfeldzug
RH20/8/40	'seit heute wird zurückgeschossen…' AOK 8 in Polen
RH20/8/46	Die Armee Blaskowitz in Polenfeldzug
RH20/8/169	Rede, Tagesbefehle, Flugblatter AOK 8 in Polen
RH20/8/282	Unterlagen für die Angriff auf Warschau
RH20/14	**Files of Fourteenth Army**
RH20/14/2	KTB AOK 14, Polen
RH20/14/77	AOK 14, Anlangen zum KTB, Polen
RH24/10	**Files of X Corps**
RH24/10/554	Tagebuch von Hauptmann Kretzschmar, X Armeekorps Stab
RH26	**Files of Infantry Divisions**
RH26/10/476	Papers of 10th Infantry Division
RH26/10/544	'Die 10 Division im polnischen Feldzug'
RH26/17/77	Papers of 17th Infantry Division
RH26/20/143	20th (Motorised) Infantry Division in the Polish Campaign
RH26/21/223	'Tapfer und Treue: Erlebnisberichte der 21 Infanterie Divison'
RH26/45/154	Tagebuch Dr Leo Losert, Brest-Litovsk
RH27	**Files of Panzer Divisions**
RH27/3/243	3rd Panzer Division in Poland
RH27/4/197	4th Panzer Division in Poland
RH27/5/2	Anlage zum KTB 5th Panzer Division
RH28	**Files of Gebirgs Divisions**
RH28/1/255	'Gefechtsberichte über den Einsatz der 1 Geb Div in Polen'
RH28/1/256	'Divisionsbericht über den Feldzug in Polen'
RH29	**Files of Calvary Divisions**

| RH29/1/259 | Bericht über Einsatz der 1 Kav.Bde im polnischen Feldzug |

RH37 — **Files of the Inspectorate of Infantry Divisions**

RH37/3094 — 'Mit der 6 Kompanie die Schöpffer Regiments (IR400)'

RH37/4975 — 'Tagebuchnotizen als Beitrag zur Geschichte des IR 68'

RH37/5025 — 'Infanterie Regiment 67 in Polenfeldzug'

RH37/6385 — 'Der 20 (Regensburger) Infanterie Regiment in Polenfeldzug'

RH37/7535 — 'MG Btl 8 in Polenfeldzug'

RH53 — **Files of Wehrkreiskommandos**

RH53/18/17 — Wehrkreiskommando XVIII Feldzug in Polen 1939

RH53/18/18 — Gebirgsjäger Regimentern 98 und 136, Infanterie Regiment 199 ('List') in Polen

RH53/18/144 — Aufmarsch, Durchmarsch durch die Slowakei

RH53/18/145 — Erlebnisberichte, Polenfeldzug

RH53/18/149 — Erlebnisberichte, Polenfeldzug

RH53/18/152 — Erlebnisberichte, Polenfeldzug

RH53/18/155 — Reports of Polish prisoners in German camps

Naval Historical Branch, Portsmouth

NHB 713 — KTB *Schleswig-Holstein* 24 August 1939–16 March 1940

NHB 714 — KTB *Schleswig-Holstein*, Anlagen

Published Sources

Newspapers

Der Adler

Die Kriegsmarine

Völkischer Beobachter, Berliner Ausgabe

Die Wehrmacht

Films

Feuertaufe (1940)

Books

Primary Sources

Alvensleben, Udo von, *Lauter Abschiede: Tagebuch im Kriege*, Ullstein, Frankfurt am Main, 1979

Bähr, Walter and Bähr, Hans (eds), *Kriegsbriefe Gefallener Studenten 1939–1945*, Rainer Wunderlich Verlag, Tübingen, 1952

Bauman, Janina, *Winter in the Morning: Young Girl's Life in the Warsaw Ghetto and Beyond, 1939–45*, Virago, London, 1991

Baumgart, Winfried, 'Zur Ansprache Hitlers vor den Führern der Wehrmacht am 22 August 1939', *Vierteljahrshefte für Zeitgeschichte*, Band 16, 1968

Below, Nicolaus von, *At Hitler's Side*, Greenhill, London, 2001

Boehm, Hermann, 'Zur Ansprache Hitlers vor den Führern der Wehrmacht am 22 August 1939', *Vierteljahrshefte für Zeitgeschichte*, Band 19, 1971

Broszat, Martin et al (eds), *Bayern in der NS-Zeit: Soziale Lage und politische Verhalten der Bevölkerung im Spiegel vertraulicher Berichte*, Oldenbourg Verlag, Munich, 1977

Buchbender, Ortwin und Sterz, Reinhold, *Das andere Gesicht des Krieges: Deutsche Feldpostbriefe 1939–1945*, Verlag CH Beck, München, 1982

Burckhardt, Carl, *Meine Danziger Mission 1937–1939*, Fretz & Wasmuth, Munich, 1960

Burdick, Charles and Jacobsen, Hans-Adolf (eds), *The Halder War Diary 1939–1942*, Greenhill, London, 1988

Ciano, Count Galeazzo, *Ciano's Diary 1939–1943*, Heinemann, London, 1947

Ciano's Diplomatic Papers, Odhams, London, 1948

Czerniakow, Adam, *The Warsaw Diary of Adam Czerniakow: Prelude to Doom*, Stein & Day, New York, 1979

Documents on German Foreign Policy, Series C and D, HMSO, London, 1949–1983

Dollinger, Hans (ed), *Kain, wo ist dein Bruder?*, Fischer, Frankfurt am Main, 1987

Eichelbaum, H (ed), *Schlag auf Schlag: Die deutsche Luftwaffe in Polen*, Bücherei des Wehrmacht-Presse-Verlagen, Berlin, 1939

Ehrhardt, Justus, *Vormarsch im September: Infanterie im Polenfeldzug*, Ensslin & Laiblin, Reutlingen, n.d.

Engel, Gerhard, *Heeresadjutant bei Hitler 1938–1943. Aufzeichnungen des Majors Engel*, DVA, Stuttgart, 1974

Fillies, Fritz, *Meine Kompanie in Polen*, Deutscher Verlag, Berlin, 1940

Fischer, Wolfgang, *Ohne die Gnade der späten Geburt: Antwort an meinen Sohn*, Herbig, Munich, 1990

Flack, Werner, *Wir marschieren für das Reich: Deutsche Jugend im Kampferlebnis des polnischen Feldzuges*, Stalling Verlag, Oldenburg, 1940

The French Yellow Book, Hutchinson, London, 1940

Galland, Adolf, *The First and The Last*, Methuen & Co, London, 1955

Das Gebirgsjäger Regiment 99 im polnischen Feldzug, Bonner Universität Buchdruckerei, Bonn, 1939

Gehring, Egid (ed) *Abbeville: Erinnerungsbuch der Division Blümm*, Zentralverlag der NSDAP, Munich, 1941

Generalstab des Heeres, *Kampferlebnis aus dem Feldzug in Polen 1939*, Mittler & Sohn, Berlin, 1940

Gerbet, Klaus (ed), *Generalfeldmarschall Fedor von Bock: The War Diary 1939–1945*, Schiffer, Atglen, 1996

Goebbels, Joseph, *Die Tagebücher von Joseph Goebbels*, fifteen volumes, K G Saur, Munich, 1993–1996

Grabler, Josef, *Mit Bomben und MGs über Polen*, Bertelsmann, Berlin, 1940

Gschöpf, Rudolf, *Mein Weg mit der 45 Infanterie Division*, Buchdienst Südtirol, Nuremberg, 2002

Guderian, Heinz, *Achtung! Panzer!*, Arms and Armour, London, 1992

Guderian, Heinz (ed), *Mit den Panzern in Ost und West: Erlebnisberichte von Mitkämpfern aus den Feldzügen in Polen und Frankreich 1939/40*, Volk und Reich Verlag, Berlin, 1942

Guderian, Heinz, *Panzer Leader*, Michael Joseph, London, 1952

Hammer, I and Neiden, Suzanne zu, *Sehr selten habe ich geweint*, Schweizer Verlag, Zurich, 1993

Henderson, Sir Nevile, *Failure of a Mission*, Hodder & Stoughton, London, 1940

Heusinger, Adolf, *Befehl in Widerstreit*, Wunderlich Verlag, Tübingen, 1950

Hindenburg, Paul von, *Out of My Life*, Cassell, London, 1920

Hodurek, Herbert, *Ein kleines Edelweiß, Österreichischer Milizverlag*, Salzburg, 1997

Hoffmann, *Oberleutnant* Dr. (ed), *Infanterie Regiment 309 marschiert an den Feind*, Herbert Stubenrauch Verlagsbuchhandlung, Berlin, 1940

Hosenfeld, Wilm, *Ich versuche jeden zu retten: Das Leben eines deutschen Offiziers in Briefen und Tagebüchern*, Deutsche Verlags-Anstalt, Munich, 2004

Hundrieser, Hubert, *Grünes Herz in Feldgrau: Kriegstagebuch eines ostpreussischen Fortsmanns*, Arndt, Kiel, 2000

Kabisch, Ernst, *Deutscher Siegeszug in Polen*, Union Deutsche Verlagsgesellschaft, Stuttgart, 1940

Kameraden unterm Edelweiss: Kriegsgeschichte der 2 Kompanie, Gebirgsjäger Regiment 100, Buchdienst Südtirol, Nuremberg, 1998

Kaplan, Chaim A, *Scroll of Agony*, Hamish Hamilton, London, 1966

Keitel, Wilhelm, *The Memoirs of Field Marshal Keitel*, William Kimber, London, 1965

Kesselring, Alfred, (ed) *Unsere Flieger über Polen: Vier Frontoffiziere berichten*, Im Deutschen Verlag, Berlin, 1939

Kielmannsegg, Johannes Graf von, *Panzer zwischen Warschau und Atlantik*, Die Wehrmacht, 1941

Kinder, Christian, *Männer der Nordmark an der Bzura: Aus den Gefechtshandlungen einer Infanteriedivision in Polen*, Mittler & Sohn, Berlin, 1941

Kleist, Peter, *The European Tragedy*, Times Press, Isle of Man, 1965

Knappe, Siegfried, *Soldat*, Dell, New York, 1993

Korwin-Rhodes, Marta, *The Mask of Warriors: The Siege of Warsaw September 1939*, Libra, New York, 1964

Helmut Krausnick (Hrsg.), *Helmuth Groscurth: Tagebücher eines Abwehroffiziers 1938–1940*. DVA Stuttgart 1970

Kubizek, August, *The Young Hitler I Knew*, Greenhill, London, 2006

Leixner, Leo, *Von Lemberg bis Bordeaux: Fronterlebnisse eines Kriegsberichters*, Franz Eher Verlag, Munich, 1941

Liere, Oberstleutnant, *Pioniere im Kampf: Erlbenisberichte aus dem Polenfeldzug 1939*, Wilhelm Limpert Verlag, Berlin, 1942

Lipski, Józef, *Diplomat in Berlin, 1933–1939: Papers and Memoirs of Józef Lipski*, Columbia University Press, New York, 1968

Lubbeck, William, *At Leningrad's Gates*, Pen & Sword, Barnsley, 2007

Luck, Hans von, *Panzer Commander*, Dell, New York, 1991

Manoschek, Walter (ed), *Es gibt nur eines für das Judentum: Vernichtung: Das Judenbild in deutschen Soldatenbriefen 1939–1944*, Hamburger Edition, Hamburg, 1995

Manstein, Erich von, *Lost Victories*, Greenhill, London, 1987

Manz, Major, (ed), *Alpenkorps in Polen: Im Auftrage des Generalkommando XIII AK*, NS-Gauverlag, Innsbruck, 1940

Martienssen, Anthony (ed), *Führer Conferences on Naval Affairs 1939–1945*, Greenhill, London, 1990

Mellenthin, F W von, *Panzer Battles*, Ballantine, New York, 1984

Meier-Welcker, Hans, *Aufzeichnungen eines Generalstabsoffizier 1939–1942*, Rombach, Freiburg, 1982

Meyer, Kurt, *Grenadiere*, Schild Verlag, Munich, 1978

Mit dem XIII Armeekorps in Polen, Bayerland Verlag, München, 1940

Nazi Conspiracy and Aggression, United States Government Printing Office, Washington DC, 1946

Oberkommando der Wehrmacht (ed), *Der Sieg in Polen*, Verlag Wilhelm Andermann, Berlin, 1939

Oeringk, Wolf, *Ziel Warschau: Nach den Aufzeichnungen eines Infanteristen*, Verlag von Anton & Co, Leipzig, 1940

Phillips, Janine, *My Secret Diary*, Shepheard Walwyn, London, 1982

Der Polenfeldzug im Tagebuch eines Gebirgsartilleristen, NS Gauverlag, Innsbruck, 1940

Pruller, Wilhelm, *Diary of a German Soldier*, Faber, London, 1963

Raleigh, John, *Behind the Nazi Front*, Harrap, London, 1941

Reibig, Willi, *Schwarze Husaren: Panzer in Polen*, Mittler, Berlin, 1941

Rendulic, Lothar, *Soldat in Stürzenden Reichen*, Damm Verlag, Munich, 1967

Rosenberg, Alfred und Hans-Günther (ed), *Das politische Tagebuch Alfred Rosenbergs aus den Jahren 1934/35 und 1939/40*, dtv, Munich, 1964

Schmidt, Paul, *Hitler's Interpreter*, Heinemann, London, 1951

Schroeder, Christa, *Er war mein Chef*, Herbig. Munich, 1985

Shirer, William, *Berlin Diary*, Alfred Knopf, New York, 1941

Shtemenko, S M, *The Soviet General Staff at War*, Progress, Moscow, 1985

Siebte Armeekorps, *Wir zogen gegen Polen*, Berlin, 1940

Speer, Albert, *Inside the Third Reich*, Sphere, London, 1971

Stahlberg, Alexander, *Bounden Duty*, Brassey's, London, 1990

Steinbach, Bruno, 'Aus den Briefen und Aufzeichnungen Bruno Steinbachs', in *Die Gebirgstruppe*, Heft Nr.2–4, 1957

Stieff, Hellmuth, *Briefe*, Siedler Verlag, Berlin, 1991

Supf, Peter, *Luftwaffe schlägt zu! Der Luftkrieg in Polen*, im Deutschen Verlag, Berlin, 1939

Thaer, Albrecht von, *Generalstabsdienst an der Front und in der OHL: Aus Briefen und Tagebuchaufzeichnungen 1915–1919*, Vandenhoeck und Rupprecht, Göttingen, 1958

Trevor-Roper, Hugh (ed), *Hitler's Table Talk, Oxford University Press*, Oxford, 1988

Trevor-Roper, Hugh (ed), *Hitler's War Directives*, Pan, London, 1966

Treue W, (ed), 'Rede Hitlers vor dem deutschen Presse, 10 November 1938' *Vierteljahrshefte für Zeitgeschichte*, Band 6, 1958, pp. 175–91

Szpilman, Wladyslaw, *The Pianist*, Phoenix, London, 2002

Venzky, Heinz Borwin, *Schwadron Marsch*, Gerhard Stalling Verlag, Oldenburg, 1941

Vogel, Rudolf, *Grenzerjunge im Blitzkrieg*, Union Deutsche Verlagsgesellschaft, Stuttgart, 1940

Vogelsang, Thilo (ed), 'Neue Dokumentation zur Geschichte der Reichswehr 1930–1933', *Vierteljahrshefte für Zeitgeschichte*, Band 2, Heft 4, 1954, pp. 397–436

Vormann, Nikolaus von, *So begann der Zweite Weltkrieg*, Druffel Verlag, Leoni am Starnberger See, 1988

Wach auf, es ist Krieg! Wie Polen und Deutsche den 1 September 1939 erlebten, Verlag Deutsch-Polnische Geseellschaft der Bundesrepublik Deutschland, Bielefeld, 1989

Wagner, Elisabeth (ed), *Der Generalquartiermeister: Briefe und Tagebuchaufzeichnungen des Generalquartiermeisters des Heeres*, Günter Olzog Verlag, Munich, 1963

Weizsäcker, Ernst von, *Die Weizsäcker Papiere 1933–1950*, Propyläen Verlag, Frankfurt, 1974

Westphal, Siegfried, *The German Army in the West*, Cassell, London, 1951

Wir Marschierten Gegen Polen: Ein Erinnerungsbuch an den polnischen Feldzug vom Infanterie Regiment 179, E Mühlthalers Buch und Kunstdruckerei, Munich, 1940

Secondary Sources

Adamthwaite, Anthony, *The Making of the Second World War*, Allen & Unwin, London, 1997

Allmayer-Beck, Christoph Freihher von, *Die Geschichte der 21 (ostpr/westpr) Infanterie Division*, Schild Verlag, , 1990

Anon, *Der Tod sprach polnisch: Dokumente polnischer Grausamkeiten an Deutschen 1919–1949*, Arndt, Kiel, 1999

Asmus, Dietwart, *Die 20.Inf.Div.(mot) Chronik und Geschichte*, Band 2, Selbstverlag, Hamburg, n.d

Bartov, Omer, *Hitler's Army*, Oxford University Press, Oxford, 1991

Baumont, Maurice, *The Fall of the Kaiser*, Allen and Unwin, London, 1931

Bekker, Cajus, *The Luftwaffe War Diaries*, Macdonald, London, 1967

Besymenski, Lev, *Stalin und Hitler: Pokerspiel der Diktatoren*, Aufbau Verlag, Berlin, 2002

Bethell, Nicholas, *The War Hitler Won*, Futura, London, 1976

Blandford, Edmund, *Target England: Flying with the Luftwaffe in World War II*, Airlife, Shrewsbury, 1997

Böhler, Jochen, *Auftakt zum Vernichtungskrieg: Die Wehrmacht in Polen 1939*, Fischer, Frankfurt am Main, 2006

Böhler, Jochen (ed), *Grösste Härte: Verbrechen der Wehrmacht in Polen, September-Oktober 1939*, Deutsche Historische Institut Warschau, Warsaw, 2005

Bradley, Dermot, *Generaloberst Heinz Guderian und die Entstehungsgeschichte des modernen Blitzkrieges*, Biblio Verlag, Osnabrück, 1978

Bradley, Dermot, *Walter Wenck: General der Panzertruppe*, Osnabrück, 1982

Breithaupt, Hans, *Die Geschichte der 30 Infanterie-Division, 1939–1945*, Hans-Henning Podzun, Bad Nauheim, 1955

Breloer, Heinrich (ed), *Mein Tagebuch: Geschichten vom Überleben 1939–1947*, Verlagsgesellschaft Schulfernsehen, Cologne, 1984

Bücheler, Heinrich, *Hoepner: ein deutsches Soldatenschicksal des 20 Jahrhunderts*, Mittler, Herford, 1980

Buchner, Alex, *Der Polenfeldzug 1939*, Druffel Verlag, Leoni am Starnberger See, 1989

Buchner, Alex, 'Kampfziel Lemberg', *Der Landser*, Nr.2257

Burleigh, Michael, *Germany Turns Eastwards*, Pan, London, 2002

Busch, Fritz-Otto, *Unsere Kriegsmarine im polnischen Feldzug*, Franz Schneider Verlag, Berlin, 1940

Carsten, F L, *The Reichswehr and Politics 1918–1933*, University of California Press, Berkeley, 1973

Citino, Robert, *The Evolution of Blitzkrieg Tactics: Germany Defends Itself Against Poland, 1918–33*, Greenwood, Westport, 1987

Corum, James S, 'Inflated by Air: Common Perceptions of Civilian Casualties from Bombing', Unpublished paper, Maxwell Air Force Base, Alabama, April 1998

Davies, Norman, *Rising '44*, Pan, London, 2004

Davies, Norman, *White Eagle, Red Star*, Pimlico, London, 2003

Dirks, Carl, and Janssen, Karl-Heinz, *Der Krieg der Generäle: Hitler als Werkzeug der Wehrmacht*, Ullstein, Munich, 2001

Domarus, Max, *Hitler: Speeches and Proclamations 1939–1940*, I B Tauris, London, 1997

Drescher, Herbert, *Warschau und Modlin im Polenfeldzug 1939: Berichte und Dokumente*, Selbstverlag, Pforzheim, 1991

Elble, Rolf, *Die Schlacht an der Bzura im September 1939 aus deutscher und polnischer Seite*, Verlag Rombach, Freiburg, 1975

Evans, Richard, *The Third Reich in Power*, Allen Lane, London, 2005

Frieser, Karl-Heinz, *The Blitzkrieg Legend*, Naval Institute Press, Annapolis, 2005

Fritz, Stephen G, *Frontsoldaten*, University Press of Kentucky, Lexington, 1995

Geschichte der 3 Panzer Division 1935–1945, Verlag der Buchhandlung Günter Richter, Berlin 1967

Gilbert, Martin, *The Holocaust*, Harper Collins, London, 1989

Giziowski, Richard, *The Enigma of General Blaskowitz*, Leo Cooper, London, 1997

Golczewski, Frank, *Das Deutschlandbild der Polen 1918–1939*, Droste, Düsseldorf, 1974

Hake, Friedrich von, *Das Waren Wir! Das Erlebten Wir! Der Schicksalsweg der 13. Panzer-Division*, Nebel Verlag, Eggolsheim, n.d

Hamann, Brigitte, *Winifred Wagner: A Life at the Heart of Hitler's Bayreuth*, Granta, London, 2006

Hamburg Institute for Social Research, *The German Army and Genocide: Crimes Against War Prisoners, Jews and Other Civilians 1939–1944*, The New Press, New York, 1999

Hartmann, Christian and Slutsch, Sergei, 'Franz Halder und die Kriegsvorbereitungen im Frühjahr 1939. Eine Ansprache des Generalstabschefs des Heeres,' *Vierteljahrshefte für Zeitgeschichte*, Band 45, 1997

Hegner, H S, *Die Reichskanzlei 1933–1945: Anfang und Ende des Dritten Reiches*, Frankfurter Bücher, Frankfurt am Main, 1959

Hinze, R, *19 Infanterie und Panzer Division*, Podzun-Pallas Verlag, Friedberg, n.d.

Hoffmann, Dieter, *Die Magdeburger Division: Zur Geschichte der 13 Infanterie und 13 Panzer Division 1935–1945*, Max Schlutius, Magdeburg, 1999

Hoffmann, Peter, *Stauffenberg: A Family History*, Cambridge University Press, Cambridge, 1995

Hooton, E R, *Phoenix Triumphant: The Rise and Rise of the Luftwaffe*, Arms and Armour, London, 1994

Horne, John and Kramer, Alan, *German Atrocities 1914: A History of Denial*, Yale University Press, New Haven, 2001

Hürtner, Johannes, 'Es herrschen Sitten und Gebräuche, geanuso wie im 30-jährigen Krieg: Das erste Jahr des deutschen-sowjetischen Krieges in Dokumenten des Generals Heinrici,' *Vierteljahrshefte für Zeitgeschichte*, Band 48, 2000

Hürter, Johannes, *Hitlers Heerführer: Die Deutschen Oberbefehlshaber im Krieg gegen die Sowjetunion 1941–1942*, Oldenbourg Verlag, Munich, 2006

Irving, David, *Goebbels*, Focal Point, London, 1996

Irving, David, *Göring*, Grafton, London, 1991

Irving, David, *Hitler's War*, Hodder and Stoughton, London, 1977

Irving, David, *The Rise and Fall of the Luftwaffe: The Life of Field Marshal Erhard Milch*, Futura, London, 1976

Irving, David, *The War Path*, Macmillan, London, 1978

Jentz, Thomas, *Panzer Truppen*, Volume 1, Schiffer, Atglen, 1996

Kaltenegger, Roland, *Die Deutsche Gebirgstruppe 1935–1945*, Bechtermünz Verlag, Augsburg, 2000

Kaltenegger, Roland, *Die Stammdivision der deutschen Gebirgstruppe: Weg un Kampf der 1 Gebirgs-Division 1935–1945*, Leopold Stocker Verlag, Graz, 1981

Kaltenegger, Roland, *Gebirgsartillerie auf allen Kriegsschauplätzen*, Schild Verlag, München, 1998

Kaltenegger, Roland, *Ludwig Kübler: General der Gebirgstruppe*, Motorbuch Verlag, Stuttgart, 1998

Kershaw, Ian, *Hitler 1936–1945: Nemesis*, Allen Lane, London, 2000

Kershaw, Ian, *The Hitler Myth*, Oxford University Press, Oxford, 1987

Kielmannsegg, Johannes Graf von, *Der Fritschprozess 1938*, Hoffmann & Campe, Hamburg, 1949

Kopp, Roland, 'Die Wehrmacht feiert: Kommandeurs Reden zu Hitlers 50 Geburtstag', *Militärgeschichtliche Zeitschrift*, Band 62, 2003

Krausnick, Helmut, *Hitlers Einsatzgruppen. Die Truppe des Weltanschauungskrieges 1938–1942*, Fischer, Frankfurt am Main 1993.

Kroener, Bernhard, *Der starke Mann im Heimatkriegsgebiet: Generaloberst Friedrich Fromm*, Ferdinand Schöningh, Paderborn, 2005

Krzysztof, Janowicz, *Luftflotte 4*, Kagero, Lublin, 2003

Kursietis, Andris, *The Wehrmacht at War*, Aspket, Netherlands, 1999

Kwasny, Achim, *Panzer-Regiment 6 im Polenfeldzug 1939*, Deutsches Wehrkundearchiv, Lage, 2003

Latzel, Klaus, *Deutsche Soldaten – nationalsozialistischer Krieg?* Ferdinand Schöningh, Paderborn, 1998

Lehmann, Rudolf, *The Leibstandarte*, Volume 1, J J Fedorowicz, Winnipeg, 1987

Lemelsen, Joachim and Schmidt, Julius, *29 Division, 29 Infanterie Division (mot.), 29 Panzergrenadier Division*, Podzun-Pallas-Verlag, Bad Nauheim 1960

Lindenblatt, Bernhard and Bäcker, Otto, *Bromberger Blutsonntag: Todesmärsche, Tage des Hasses, Polnische Greueltaten*, Arndt, Kiel, 2001

Lucas, James, *Kampfgruppe*, Cassell, London, 1993

Lukas, Richard, *The Forgotten Holocaust: The Poles Under German Occupation*, Hippocrene, New York, 2001

Macksey, Kenneth, *Guderian: Panzer Leader*, Greenhill, London, 1997

Maier, Klaus, *Germany and the Second World War*, Volume 2, Oxford University Press, Oxford, 1991

Maier, Klaus, *Guernica 26/4/37: Die deutsche Intervention in Spanien und der 'Fall Guernica'*, Rombach Verlag, Freiburg, 1975

Messerschmidt, Manfred, *Die Wehrmacht im NS-Staat*, R V Decker Verlag, Hamburg, 1969

Michaelis, Rolf, *SS Heimwehr Danzig*, Shelf, Bradford, 1996

Moynahan, Brian, *The Claws of the Bear*, Hutchinson, London, 1989

Müller, Klaus-Jürgen, *Das Heer und Hitler*, Deutsche Verlagsanstalt, 1969

Müller, Rolf-Dieter and Volkmann, Hans-Erich (eds), *Die Wehrmacht: Mythos und Realität*, Oldenbourg Verlag, Munich, 1999

Mulligan, Timothy, *Lone Wolf: The Life and Death of U-boat ace Werner Henke*, Praeger, Westport, 1993

Murray, Williamson, *Luftwaffe: Strategy for Defeat 1933–45*, Grafton, London, 1988

Neumann, Joachim, *Die 4 Panzer Division 1938–1943: Bericht und Betrachtung zu zwei Blitzfeldzügen und zwei Jahren Krieg in Russland*, Selbstverlag, Bonn, 1985

Noakes, Jeremy (ed), *Nazism 1919–1945, Volume Three: Foreign Policy, War and Racial Extermination – A Documentary Reader*, University of Exeter Press, Exeter, 1995

Nowak, Karl, *Versailles*, Payson & Clarke, New York, 1929

O'Neill, Robert, *The German Army and the Nazi Party*, Corgi, London, 1968

Oven, Wilfred von, *Hitler und der Spanische Bürgerkrieg*, Grabert, Tübingen, 1978

Owen, James and Walters, Guy, *The Voice of War: The Second World War Told By Those Who Fought It*, Viking, London, 2004

Padfield, Peter, *Dönitz: The Last Führer*, 2nd edition, Cassell, London, 2001

Paul, Wolfgang, *Brennpunkte: Die Geschichte der 6 Panzerdivision (1 leichte) 1937–1945*, Biblio Verlag, Osnabrück, 1984

Paul, Wolfgang, *Der Endkampf um Deutschland*, Wilhelm Heyne Verlag, Munich, 1978

Paul, Wolfgang, *Das Potsdamer Infanterie Regiment 9 1918–1945*, Biblio Verlag, Osnabrück, 1984

Pfundtner, Hans, *Tannenberg: Deutsches Schicksal, Deutsche Aufgabe*, Gerhard Stelling Verlag, Berlin, 1939

Piekalkiewicz, Janusz, *Polenfeldzug: Hitler und Stalin zerschlagen die Polnische Republik*, Gustav Lübbe Verlag, Bergisch Gladbach, 1982

Polish Ministry of Information, *The German Invasion of Poland. The Polish Black Book*, Hutchinson, London, 1941

Polish Ministry of Information, *The German New Order in Poland*, Hutchinson & Son, London, 1942

Rathke, *Hauptmann* A, *Ewige Infanterie*, Verlag für Vaterländische Literatur, Berlin, c.1942

Read, Anthony and Fisher, David, *The Deadly Embrace*, Michael Joseph, London, 1988

Riekhoff, Harald von, *German-Polish Relations 1918–1933*, Johns Hopkins Press, Baltimore, 1971

Roos, Hans, *A History of Modern Poland*, Eyre & Spottiswoode, London, 1966

Rossino, Alexander B, 'Destructive Impulses: German Soldiers and the Conquest of Poland,' *Holocaust and Genocide Studies*, vol.11, No.3, 1997

Rossino, Alexander B, *Hitler Strikes Poland: Blitzkrieg, Ideology and Atrocity*, University Press of Kansas, 2003

Ruhnau, Rüdiger, *Die Freie Stadt Danzig 1919–1939*, Kurt Vowinckel Verlag, Berg am See, 1979

Runzheimer, Jürgen, 'Der Überfall auf den Sender Gleiwitz im Jahre 1939', *Vierteljahrshefte für Zeitgeschichte*, Band 10, No.4, 1962

Runzheimer, Jürgen, 'Die Grenzzwischenfälle am Abend vor dem deutschen Angriff auf Polen', in Graml Hermann and Benz, Wolfgang (eds), *Sommer 1939*, Stuttgart, 1979

Russ, William, *Case White: The German Army in the Polish Campaign*, Nafziger Collection, West Chester, 2006

Schenk, Dieter, *Hans Frank: Hitlers Kronjurist und Generalgouverneur*, S Fischer Verlag, Frankfurt am Main, 2006

Schenk, Dieter, *Hitlers Mann in Danzig: Gauleiter Forster und die NS-Verbrechen in Danzig-Westpreussen*, Dietz, Bonn, 2000

Schenk, Dieter, *Die Post von Danzig: Geschichte eines deutschen Justizmords*, Rowohlt, Hamburg, 1995

Schimak, Anton, Lamprecht, Karl and Dettmer, Friedrich, *Die 44 Infanterie Division: Tagebuch der Hoch und Deutschmeister*, Verlag Austria Press, Vienna, 1969

Schindler, Herbert, *Mosty und Dirschau 1939: Zwei Handstreiche der Wehrmacht vor Beginn des Polenfeldzuges*, Verlag Rombach, Freiburg, 1971

Schmidt, August, *Die Geschichte der 10 Infanterie Division*, Nebel Verlag, Eggolsheim, n.d

Schüddekopf, Carl, *Krieg: Erzählungen aus dem Schweigen*, Rowohlt, 1997

Schüddekopf, Otto Ernst, *Heer und Republik, Quellen zur Politik der Reichswehrführung 1918–1933*, Norddeutsche Verlagsanstalt, 1955

Seaton, Albert, *The German Army*, Sphere, London, 1982

Slutsch, Sergei, 'Der Eintritt der Sowjetunion in den Zweiten Weltkrieg', *Vierteljahrshefte für Zeitgeschichte*, Band 48, 2000

Smith, Lyn, *Forgotten Voices of the Holocaust*, Ebury, London, 2006

Speidel, Wilhelm, *The Luftwaffe in the Polish Campaign of 1939*, unpublished US Air Force study in the author's papers

Spiess, Alfred and Lichtenstein, Heiner, *Unternehmen Tannenberg*, Moewig, Munich, 1982

Steiger, Rudolf, *Armour Tactics in the Second World War: Panzer Army Campaigns of 1939–41 in German War Diaries*, Berg, Oxford, 1992

Stjernfelt, Bertil and Böhme, Klaus-Richard, *Westerplatte 1939*, Verlag Rombach, Freiburg im Breisgau, 1979

Straub, Walter, Oberst, *Das Panzer Regiment 7 und 21 und seine Tochterformationen im Zweiten Weltkrieg*, Selbstverlag, n.d

Strauss, Franz Josef, *Die Geschichte der 2 (Wiener) Panzer Division*, Nebel Verlag, Eggolsheim, n.d

Strohmeyer, Curt, *Stukas, Erlebnis eines Fliegerkorps*, Die Heimbücherei, Berlin, n.d.

Suchcitz, Andrzej, 'Poland's Defence Preparations in 1939', in Stachura, Peter (ed), *Poland Between the Wars 1918–1939*, Palgrave, London, 1998

Suchenwirth, Richard, *Command and Leadership in the German Air Force*, unpublished US Air Force study in the author's papers

Taylor, Telford, *Munich: The Price of Peace*, Doubleday, New York, 1979

Teske, Hermann (ed), *General Ernst Köstring: Der militärische Mittler zwischen dem Deutschen Reich und der Sowjetunion 1921–1940*, Mittler & Sohn, Frankfurt am Main, 1965

Tettau, Hans von, and Versock, Kurt, *Die Geschichte der 24 Infanterie Division*, Nebel Verlag, Eggolsheim, n.d

Tietz, Jürgen, *Das Tannenberg-Nationaldenkmal*, Verlag Bauwesen, Berlin, 1999

Toland, John, *Adolf Hitler*, Ballantine, New York, 1977

Tooze, Adam, *The Wages of Destruction: The Making and Breaking of the Nazi Economy*, Allen Lane, London, 2006

Turnbull, Elizabeth and Suchcitz, Andrzej (eds), *Edward Roland Sword: The Diary and Despatches of a Military Attaché in Warsaw, 1938–1939*, Polish Cultural Foundation, London, 2001

Uhl, Matthias, and Eberle, Henrik, *The Hitler Book: The Secret Report by His Two Closest Aides*, John Murray, London, 2006

Urban, Thomas, *Von Krakau bis Danzig: Eine Reise durch die deutsch-polnische Geschichte*, CH Beck Verlag, Munich, 2000

Volkmann, Major E O, *Revolution über Deutschland*, Gerhard Stalling, Oldenburg, 1930

Volkogonov, Dmitri, *Stalin: Triumph and Tragedy*, Grove, London, 1991

Watt, Donald Cameron, *How War Came*, Mandarin, London, 1991

Watt, Richard, *Bitter Glory: Poland and its Fate 1918–1939*, Hippocrene, New York, 1998

Wegner, Bernd (ed), *From Peace to War: Germany, Soviet Russia and the World 1939–1941*, Berghahn, Oxford, 1997

Welch, David, *Propaganda and the German Cinema 1933–1945*, I B Taurus, London, 2001

Westwood, David, *German Infantryman 1933–1940*, Osprey, Oxford, 2002

Wheeler-Bennett, John W, *Hindenburg: The Wooden Titan*, Macmillan, London, 1936

Wheeler-Bennett, John W, *The Nemesis of Power: The German Army in Politics 1918–1945*, Macmillan, London, 1967

Zaloga, Steven, *Poland 1939: The Birth of Blitzkrieg*, Osprey, Oxford, 2002

Zaloga, Steven and Madej, Victor, *The Polish Campaign 1939*, Hippocrene, New York, 1985

Zamoyski, Adam, *The Forgotten Few*, John Murray, London, 1995

Zayas, Alfred de, *The Wehrmacht War Crimes Bureau*, University of Nebraska Press, 1989

Index